Collecting Music in the

ARAN ISLANDS

Collecting Music in the
ARAN ISLANDS

A Century of History and Practice

DEIRDRE NÍ CHONGHAILE

THE UNIVERSITY OF WISCONSIN PRESS

Publication of this book is supported by the National University of Ireland and the
Oxford University Press *Music & Letters* Trust.

The University of Wisconsin Press
728 State Street, Suite 443
Madison, Wisconsin 53706
uwpress.wisc.edu

Gray's Inn House, 127 Clerkenwell Road
London EC1R 5DB, United Kingdom
eurospanbookstore.com

Printed in the United States of America
This book may be available in a digital edition.

Library of Congress Cataloging-in-Publication Data
Names: Ní Chonghaile, Deirdre, author.
Title: Collecting music in the Aran Islands : a century of history and practice /
Deirdre Ní Chonghaile.
Description: Madison, Wisconsin : The University of Wisconsin Press, [2021] |
Includes bibliographical references and index.
Identifiers: LCCN 2020044313 | ISBN 9780299332402 (hardcover)
Subjects: LCSH: Ethnomusicology—Ireland—Aran Islands—History. | Sound
recordings—Collectors and collecting—Ireland—Aran Islands. | Folk
music—Ireland—Aran Islands—History and criticism.
Classification: LCC ML3654.7.A73 N53 2021 | DDC 780.9417/48—dc23
LC record available at https://lccn.loc.gov/2020044313

Cover image excerpted from a sequential visual artwork that forms part of a
multidisciplinary project titled *Carrying the Songs*, curated by Alannah Robins and generated
by multiple artists between March and September 2020. Creators of the image include Árainn
artists Seán Ó Flaithearta, Fionnuala Hernon, and Cyril O'Flaherty,
as well as Aoife Casby, Andrea Rossi, Lelia Ní Chathmhaoil, Maeve Curtis, and
Noelle Gallagher. See https://interfaceinagh.com/carrying-the-songs/.

ISBN 9780299332440 (paperback)

Dedicated to my parents,
MÁIRTÍN and MÁIRE,
and to my grandmother
MAIRÉAD

Contents

Illustrations

Acknowledgments

In remembrance of those collaborators who, sadly, have not lived to see this book published: Heinrich Becker (1907–2001), Petairín a' Bheagach Ó Maoláin (1910–2003), Bridgie Uí Dhonnchadha (1916–2003), John Beag Johnny Ó Dioráin (1925–2004), Pádraig Mhurchadha de Bhailís (1927–2005), Dara Pheaits Mhicil Bán Ó Conghaile (1924–2005), Peter Kennedy (1922–2006), Tom Mhaidhle Seoighe (1958–2007), Tom Munnelly (1944–2007), Stiofán Ó Conghaile (1936–2008), Seán Roantree (1947–2008), Ciarán Ó Con Cheanainn (1981–2009), Nell Quinn (1913–2009), Máirín Uí Choncheanainn (1944–2009), Tom Bheairtlín Bhaba Ó hIarnáin (1923–2009), Vailín Bheairtlín Aindí Ó Maoláin (1935–2010), Maeve Dan Uí Fhlaithearta (1938–2010), Mícheál Bhaba Pheige Ó Miolláin (1935–2010), George Pickow (1922–2010) and Jean Ritchie (1922–2015), Muiris Ó Rócháin (1944–2011), Seán Ó Conghaoile (1940–2011), Éamon de Buitléar (1930–2013), Paddy Quinn (1935–2014), Patsy Bhid Bhile Ó Tuathail (1938–2015), Canon Pádraig Ó Fiannachta (1927–2016), Paddy Mullen (1946–2016), Josie Sheáin Jeaic Mac Donncha (1943–2017), Alan Jabbour (1942–2017), Fiachra Mac Gabhann (1971–2018), Nicola Gordon Bowe (1948–2018), Máiria Pheaitín Terry Nic Dhonncha (1926–2019), Liam Mac Con Iomaire (1937–2019), Dara Mullen (1926–2019), Breandán Ó Madagáin (1932–2020), and Mairéad and Tim Robinson (1935–2020).

This book was written with the support of the National Endowment for the Humanities Keough Fellowship at the Keough-Naughton Institute for Irish Studies at the University of Notre Dame; the Alan Lomax Fellowship in Folklife Studies at the John W. Kluge Center at the Library of Congress; the National University of Ireland (NUI) Fellowship in Irish/Celtic Studies held at the

Moore Institute for Research in the Humanities and Social Studies at NUI Galway; and a brief but vital writer's residency at Áras Éanna, Inis Oírr, the Aran Islands. Publication of this book is supported by the National University of Ireland and the Oxford University Press *Music & Letters* Trust. My digital catalog of the recordings Sidney Robertson Cowell made in Ireland was created with the support of a Moore Institute Visiting Fellowship at NUI Galway; I am grateful to the Irish Traditional Music Archive for making the catalog available online.

My thanks to the University of Wisconsin Press for selecting this book for a first-time authors' workshop at the American Folklore Society annual meeting in Bloomington, Indiana, in 2011, and for their unstinting support, positivity, and professionalism throughout the project; to James P. Leary, Gage Averill, and Jack Santino for comments on early drafts; and to the readers of the completed book manuscript for their generosity.

I am grateful to Alannah Robins and her fellow artists for generously agreeing to have an excerpt from their beautiful sequential visual artwork *Carrying the Songs* featured on the book's cover. The full list of artists is available at https://interfaceinagh.com/carrying-the-songs/.

Mo bhuíochas le RTÉ Raidió na Gaeltachta for commissioning *Bailiúchán Bhairbre*, my producer Máirtín Jaimsie Ó Flaithbheartaigh, and my aunt Kathleen, who first suggested a radio series devoted to her sister's recordings; the experience of researching and presenting the series laid the foundations of chapter 4.

Buíochas ó chroí le Dáibhí Ó Cróinín for alerting me to Sidney Robertson Cowell and her work in Ireland and, later, to the Eugene O'Curry song manuscripts he uncovered in Leipzig, interventions that formed the basis of over half of this book, including chapters 1 and 3 and appendix 1. His support, generosity, and guidance throughout were equally crucial.

Assistance over the past twenty years and more has come from a wide variety of sources, some of which I will have forgotten to name here; I hope such unintended omissions will be forgiven.

In Árainn, my thanks to Treasa Ní Mhiolláin, Tomás and Dara Bhaba Pheige Uí Mhiolláin, Mary Conneely, Fergus Ó Conghaile, Sheelagh Conneely, Kathleen Póil, Mícheál Mhaidhcilín Ó Conghaile, Mary Quinn, Locko Cullen, Delia Bheairtle Sheáin Uí Chonghaile, Máirtín Ó Concheanainn, Johnny Joyce, Steve Kilmartin, Áine Pheaits Bheairtlín Ní Fhlaithearta, Bairbre Uí Chonaill, Pat

Joe Jack Ó Flaithearta, Caitríona Ní Bhuachalla, Maggie Pheaits Bheairtlín Seoighe, Rónán and Sinéad Mhic Giolla Pháraic, Ath. Connla Ó Dúláinne, Ath. Ciarán de Bláca, Ath. Máirtín Ó Conaire, Nóirín Gill, Joe Antaine Ó Briain, Pádraig Ó Tuairisc, Enda Mullen, Mícheál Tom Burke Ó Conghaile, Anna Tom Burke Ní Chonghaile, Elizabeth Zollinger, Pádraig Gillan, Pádraig Ó Cadhain, Antaine Powell, Mairéad Ní Eithir, Mary Ratcliffe, Kathleen Aindí Uí Dhioráin, Gráinne Jennings Uí Chonghaile (1945–2015), Michael Gill, Michael Joyce, Mairéad Uí Fhlaithearta, Maggie Dainín Uí Fhlaithearta, Fiona Dan Uí Dhioráin, Eddie Beatty, Máirín Uí Fhlaithearta, Úna Ní Fhlaithearta, Ruairí Ó hEithir, Bertie, Treasa, and Noel Seoighe; the Ó Goill family, Ronan, Fionnghuala, Éamon, Oisín and Cóil; the Ó hIarnáin family, Beairtle, Marian, Oisín, Conal, and Órnaith; the Ó Maoilchiaráin family, Martin, Bridie, Pádraig, Éamon, Seán, and Máirtín; and the Roantree family, Seán, Jackie, Oisín, and Megan.

In Inis Meáin, my thanks to Dara Beag Ó Fáthartaigh, Máirín Mhéiní Uí Chonghaile, Mairéad Conneely, Ruairí Roger Ó Concheanainn, Máire Pháidín Uí Mhaoilchiaráin, Peadar Sheán Shiúnac Mhac Conaola, Órla Breathnach, Treasa Ní Fhátharta, Áine and Tarlach de Blácam, Pádraig Dara Beag Ó Fátharta, Mairéad Ní Fhátharta, Geraldine McElroy Faherty, and Ciarán Ó Ceallaigh.

In Inis Oírr, my thanks to Jimmy Ó Catháin, Seóna Ní Chonghaile, Máire Ní Dhomhnaill Uí Uallacháin, Pádraig, Máirtín and Peadar Ó Domhnaill, Dara Ó Conaola, Lasairfhíona Ní Chonaola, MacDara Ó Conaola, Mícheál Ó hAlmhain, Áine Uí Almhain, Pádraig, Peadar and Mairéad Póil, Mícheál and Catherine Uí Chatháin, Ruairí Sheáin Ó Conghaile, Alissa Zimman, Bríd Folan, Val Ballance, Pól Breathnach, Bríd Seán Sailí Uí Chonghaile, Paddy Crowe and crew, and Barra de Bhaldraithe and Mairéad Ní Ghallchóir, Áras Éanna.

In Conamara, I am grateful to Meaití Jó Shéamuis Ó Fátharta, Róisín Nic Dhonncha, Bríd Uí Mhadaoin, John Bhaba Jeaic Ó Conghaile, Pat Maguire, Gearóid Breathnach, Margaret Breathnach, Johnny Mháirtín Learaí Mac Donnchadha, Máire-Áine Nic Dhonnchadha, Bob Quinn, Toner Quinn, Mícheál Ó Catháin, Peadar Ó Ceannabháin, Saileog Ní Cheannabháin, Seán Crean, Ciarán Ó Fátharta, Caitríona Ní Oibicín (d. 2013), Máire Ní Neachtain, Michelle Ní Chróinín, Majella Ní Chríocháin, Cóilín Ó Ceallaigh, Síle Denvir, Michael Gibbons, Dara Cannon, Tomás Mac Con Iomaire, Máirín Ní Mhaoileoin, Seán Ó hÉanaí, Máirtín Davy Ó Coisdealbha, Jackie Geary, Loretta Ní Ghabháin, Sr. Regina de Búrca (d. 1999), Mícheál Ó Conghaile and Deirdre Ní Thuathail, Cló Iar-Chonnacht, and Mairéad in Leabharlann na Ceathrún Rua.

Elsewhere in the west of Ireland, I am grateful to Olof Gill, Rory McCabe, Cora Keating, Clare Island; Kieran Concannon, Inishbofin; Harry Hughes, Vince Hearns, Mairéad Uí Choncheanainn, Gearóid Denvir, Louis de Paor, John Moulden, Méabh Ní Fhuartháin, Nessa Cronin, Verena Commins, Dara Ó Cualáin, Michael Lydon, Pauline Nic Chonaonaigh, Ríóna Ní Fhrighil, Lesa Ní Mhunghaile, Liam Ó hAisibéil, Eilís Ní Dhúill, Tim Collins, Máire-Bríd Uí Mhainnín, Úna Ní Chiosáin, Patsy Nic Fhlannchadha, Seán Mac Íomhair, Tom Kenny, Muireann Ní Chíobháin, Alf Mac Lochlainn (1926–2018), Kathleen Loughnane, Caitríona Hastings, Rose Ní Dhubhda, Méadhbh Nic an Airchinnigh, Ciaran McDonough, Marie-Louise Coolahan, Ailbhe Nic Giolla Chomhaill, and Máirín Seoighe.

In the south of Ireland, my thanks to Seán Ó Morónaigh, Liam Ó Dochartaigh, Feargal Mac Amhlaoibh, Muireann Nic Amhlaoibh, Mícheál de Mórdha, Dáithí de Mórdha, Edna Uí Chinnéide, Aoife Granville, Audrey O'Carroll, Breandán Feiritéar, Billy Mag Fhloinn; Nicky McAuliffe of Cordal and Máire Ní Fhlannagáin of Tralee, Co. Kerry; Proinsias Ó Drisceoil, Ógie Ó Céilleachair, Ann Mulqueen, Ciarán Ó Gealbháin, Jimmy O'Brien-Moran, Rachel Ní Riada, Eoiní Maidhcí Ó Súilleabháin, Peadar Ó Riada, Séamus Ó Súilleabháin, Sheila Beecher, Tomás Ó Canainn, Melanie Marshall, Chris Morris, Pádraigín Riggs, Seán Ó Duinnshléibhe, Seán Ua Súilleabháin, Liam P. and Tomás Ó Murchú, Síle Ní Mhurchú, Pádraig Ó Macháin, Sorcha Nic Lochlainn, Roibeárd Ó hÚrdail, Claire Ní Mhuirthile, Seán Ó Laoi, Neil Buttimer, Graham Ellis, Eilís Ní Shúilleabháin, Máire Ní Chéilleachair, Peter Murray, Mel Mercier, Carmel Daly, Kelly Boyle, Gillian Cotter, Anna Maria Dore, Aibhlín Dillane, Valentina Ottaviani, Ruth Stanley, Tríona Ní Shíocháin, Patrick Egan, Crónán Ó Doibhlin; and Tony Perrott, Audio-Visual Department, University College Cork.

In the east of Ireland, I am grateful to Attracta Halpin, NUI; Steve Coleman, Adrian Scahill, Barra Boydell, Lorraine Byrne Bodley, Brian Ó Catháin, Éamon Ó Ciosáin, and Estelle Murphy, Maynooth University; Regina Uí Chollatáin, Meidhbhín Ní Úrdail, Ríonach uí Ógáin, Anna Bale, Bairbre Ní Fhloinn, Críostóir Mac Cárthaigh, Séamus Ó Catháin, Jonny Dillon, Eimear Ní Cheallaigh, Angela Bourke, Tiber Falzett, Michelle Agar, Patricia Kelly, Harry White, and Thérèse Smith, University College Dublin; Ian Lee, Proinsias Ó Conluain, Ciarán Mac Mathúna (1925–2009), Harry Bradshaw, Pat Butler, Barbara Durack, and Peter Browne, RTÉ; Eoghan Neff, Danny Diamond, Grace Toland, Nicholas Carolan, Liam O'Connor, Maeve Gebruers, and Treasa Harkin, Irish

Traditional Music Archive; Gráinne Mac Lochlainn, Jenny Doyle, Honora Faul, Tom Desmond, Gerry Long, and Joanne Carroll, National Library of Ireland; Marie Bourke and Niamh MacNally, National Gallery of Ireland; Bernadette Cunningham, Petra Schnabel, and Antoinette Prout, Royal Irish Academy; Sunniva O'Flynn and Emma Keogh, Irish Film Institute; Stephen McCarron, Máirín Nic Eoin, Anne Burke, Liam Mac Cóil, Fintan Valley, Theo Dorgan, Paula Meehan, Ríona Nic Congáil, Ruth Lysaght, Máire Ó Baoill, Seamus Heaney (1939–2013), Sinéad Nic Dhonncha, Brian Ó Dálaigh, Matthew Hébert, Antaine Ó Faracháin, Ciarán Ó Coigligh, Pádraig Ó Ciardha, Mick O'Connor, Frank Harte (1933–2005), Ruairí Ó hUiginn, Colleen Dube, Christiaan Corlett, Cathal Goan, Claire Cunningham, Conor Kennedy, and Jimmy Kelly (1942–2018); Máirín, Niamh, and Rónán Kelly.

In the north of Ireland, my thanks to Ronan Doherty, Aisling Ní Churraighín, Anthony McCann, Pádraigín Ní Uallacháin, Liz Doherty, Edel McLaughlin, Jimmy McBride, Mícheál Ó Geallabháin, Thomas Johnson, Conor Caldwell; and Owen McFadden, BBC Northern Ireland.

In England, I am grateful to Frank Shovlin, Finola Ryan, Delphine Mordey, Ruth Chan, Hélène La Rue (1951–2007), Aisha Sowky, Simon Keegan-Phipps, Martina Thomson, Katy Salvidge, Ann Mann, John S. O'Neill, Simon Ross and Thomas Fairfax, Colette and Tim Hayward, Tom Western, Ron Stradling, Giles Bergel; Malcolm Taylor, Cecil Sharp House; Antony Gordon and Janet Topp-Fargion, British Library; Julie Snelling, BBC Written Archives; and Olwen Terris, British Film Institute.

In Scotland, mòran taing to Calum MacGillEain, Fiona Dalgetty, Emily Edwards, Dòmhnall Uilleam Stiùbhairt, Lori Watson, David Kilpatrick, Dick Gaughan, Dòmhnall Angaidh Mac Illinnein, Kieran Halpin, Cathlin Macaulay, Hugh Cheape, Fiona Black, and Maighread Stiùbhairt.

Throughout Europe, my thanks to Susanne Ziegler, Berliner Phonogramm-Archiv; Ralph Roger Glöckler; Christoph Mackert and Thomas Thibault Döring, Universitaetsbibliothek Leipzig, Germany; Fenella Bazin and Cinzia Curtis in the Isle of Man; Mícheál Briody and Lily Neill in Helsinki; Ole Munch-Pedersen and Alina Järvelä in Copenhagen; Angun Sønnesyn Olsen and Ellen Røyrvik in Bergen; Séamas Ó Direáin in A Coruña; Guy Livingston and Camille Moreddu in Paris; and Sandra Meyer in Vienna.

In Canada, I am grateful to Mike Kennedy, Burt Feintuch, Heather Sparling, Stephanie Conn, Ann Saddlemyer, Cleo Paskal; Anita Best in Newfoundland;

Laurie Brinklow, Institute of Island Studies, University of Prince Edward Island; and Gearóid Ó hAllmhuráin, Cecilia McDonnell and Tiarnán Ó hAllmhuráin, Montréal.

In the United States, I am grateful to Karen Jabbour, Chloe Veltman, Maureen Loughran, Delphine Schrank, John Morrissey, Henry Glassie, Julie Henigan, Scott Spencer, Elaine Ní Bhraonáin, George Boziwick, Myron Bretholz, Bob Waltz, Richard Carlin, Jo Radner, Gary Galván, Don McCormick, Kevin Donleavy, Carl Rahkonen, John Wolford, Peter Stone, Tes Slominski, Paul Keating, Nicholas Wolf, Jim and Maria Concannon, Carol Concannon, Barra Ó Donnabháin (1941–2003), David and Rosaleen Gregory, John C. Messenger (1920–2010), Jack Coogan, James S. Rogers, James S. Donnelly, Jr., Judith Cohen, Lauren Weintraub Stoebel, Matthew Allen, Tadhg Ó Fátharta, Veerendra P. Lele, James L. Foy, Siobhan Duran, Jeff Titon; Sara Velez, New York Public Library; Lauren Weiss Bricker, California State Polytechnic University, Pomona; George Stoney (1916–2012), New York University; Donald Hill, Oneonta University; Seamus Connolly and Beth Sweeney, Boston College; Marilyn Graf, Archivist of Traditional Music, Indiana University; Jean Whipple, Ohio State University; Neti Vaan, Devin Flanigan Blankenship, Bairbre Ní Chiardha, Sheila Leary; and Diarmuid Ó Giolláin, Mary O'Callaghan, Declan Kiberd, Chris Fox, Aedín Ní Bhróithe-Clements, and Ian Kuijt, University of Notre Dame.

Special Thanks

At NUI Galway, I am especially grateful to Daniel Carey, Martha Shaughnessy, David Kelly and their colleagues at the Moore Institute; Tadhg Ó hIfearnáin and his colleagues in Roinn na Gaeilge; and the team at the James Hardiman Library including Kieran Hoare, Marie Boran, Margaret Hughes, Margo Donohue, Geraldine Curtin, Barry Houlihan, Aisling Keane, Cillian Joy, and Niall McSweeney. Together, you generated time and space for me and my work and so fostered this book and more. Go maire sibh bhur ndílseacht.

At the Library of Congress, my thanks to Mary-Lou Reker, Thomas Mann, Catherine Hiebert Kerst, Todd Harvey, Peggy Bolger, Nancy Seeger, Nancy Groce, Stephen Winick, Jennifer Cutting, Nicole Saylor, Anne Hoog, Joel Sachs, Judith Gray, Elizabeth Auman, Jim Hardin, Jason Steinhauer, Kelly Revak, Maggie Kruesi, Melanie Zeck, and Paul Sommerfeld; and at the Ralph Rinzler Archives and Collections in the Smithsonian Center for Folklife and Cultural Heritage, thanks to Jeff Place, Michael Pahn, Erin Durant, Stephanie

Smith, and Katie Ortiz. It has been my pleasure and privilege to become part of your extended research family.

My research trips to the US were facilitated by the generosity of Patrick and Úna Quinn, Cummin Clancy (1922–2013) and Maureen Clancy, Colleen Dollard, Louisa Bennion, Tim Collins, Scott Spencer, Mio Yamada, Jessica Ziegler, Tom Forhan, and Sheilagh and Henry Smigen Rothkopf.

Friends providing insight, levity, and perspective included Michelle Finnerty, Daithí Kearney, Helen Gubbins, Pádraigín Clancy, Marion Ní Mhaoláin, Breda McKinney, Deirdre Ní Cheallaigh, Freda Nic Giolla Chatháin, Danielle Nicholson, Adrian Paterson, Rebecca Barr, Anne Karhio, Peadar King, Breda O'Connor, and Sarah Kelly.

Sincerest thanks to Máirín MacCarron and Jackie Uí Chionna, whose friendship, guidance, good company, and practical support in good times and in bad have been gifts; and to Lillis Ó Laoire, whose unwavering support, good humor, professionalism, and generosity I treasure—your trust and belief in me have been the ballast of my research life. Go maire sibh triúr.

Finally, thanks to my parents, Máirtín and Máire; and my siblings, Máirtín Éanna, Micheál, Diarmuid, and Rónait, without whose support, understanding, and forbearance this book would not exist.

Any errors are mine alone.

Abbreviations

BB	Bailiúchán Bhairbre
BBC	British Broadcasting Corporation
BLSA	British Library Sound Archive, London
CCÉ	Comhaltas Ceoltóirí Éireann
CSO	Central Statistics Office
EMI	Electric and Musical Industries Ltd.
IFC	Irish Folklore Commission
ITMA	Irish Traditional Music Archive
LC	Library of Congress, Washington, DC
MM	Music Manuscripts in the National Folklore Collection at UCD
MRU	Mobile Recording Unit (Radio Éireann)
NFC	National Folklore Collection, Delargy Center for Irish Folklore in the School of Irish, Celtic Studies, Irish Folklore and Linguistics, University College Dublin
NGI	National Gallery of Ireland
NLI	National Library of Ireland
NUIG	National University of Ireland, Galway
NYPL	New York Public Library
OED	*Oxford English Dictionary*
PRONI	Public Record Office of Northern Ireland

RA   Resettlement Administration

RÉ   Radio Éireann

RF   Rockefeller Foundation

RIA   Royal Irish Academy

RILM   Répertoire International de Littérature Musicale

RnaG   RTÉ Raidió na Gaeltachta

RNLI   Royal National Lifeboat Institute

RR   Sidney Robertson Cowell Ireland Collection, Ralph Rinzler
             Folklife Archives and Collections, Smithsonian Center for Folklife
             and Cultural Heritage, Washington, DC

RTÉ   Raidió Teilifís Éireann

SEM   Society for Ethnomusicology

UBL   Universitaetsbibliothek Leipzig (Bibliotheca Albertina)

UCD   University College Dublin

UL   University of Limerick

WAC   Written Archives Center (BBC), Caversham, Reading

WPA   Works Projects Administration

Notes on Sources and Appendixes

Throughout this book, LC stands for the Library of Congress, except where
it is used to refer to the Sidney Robertson Cowell Ireland Collections at the
Library of Congress, Washington, DC: her Irish sound recordings are housed
in the Archive of Folk Culture in the American Folklife Center (AFC 1959/004);
and other documentation is housed in the Music Division (ML31.C78). NYPL
stands for the Henry Cowell Papers, JPB 00–03, in the Music Division of the
New York Public Library for the Performing Arts. Recordings held in the Rodgers and Hammerstein Archives of Recorded Sound at the New York Public
Library for the Performing Arts are cited in full.

      With regard to the appendixes, decisions to provide or exclude certain mate-
rial were informed by a number of considerations: space, balance, discoverability, accessibility, and the potential to enable further research and collaboration.
The task of providing comprehensive editions of written source material is

beyond the scope of this book. Instead, appendix 1 shares facsimiles and transcriptions of the O'Curry manuscripts held in Leipzig, Germany, to make this previously unpublished material more accessible and to demonstrate the feasibility and challenges of attempting to reunite song airs with their words. Appendixes 2, 3, and 4 share a chronology and tables to aid the discoverability and navigability of the original source materials produced by Séamus Ennis. The scale and detail of the author's catalog of Sidney Robertson Cowell's Irish recordings—numbering more than two hundred individual tracks—demanded a more navigable approach than print could provide. The complete digital catalog—available at the Library of Congress, the Ralph Rinzler Archives, and the Irish Traditional Music Archive—is designed to enable multiple institutions to share data relevant to their respective audio holdings, including duplicates, and so connect collections that span multiple archives. The webpage hosting the catalog online (https://www.itma.ie/blog/sidney-robertson-cowell) also includes lists of Irish and American women collectors compiled by the author. Finally, the cataloging of Bailiúchán Bhairbre remains incomplete, so it is not yet ready to be published in full.

Collecting Music in the

ARAN ISLANDS

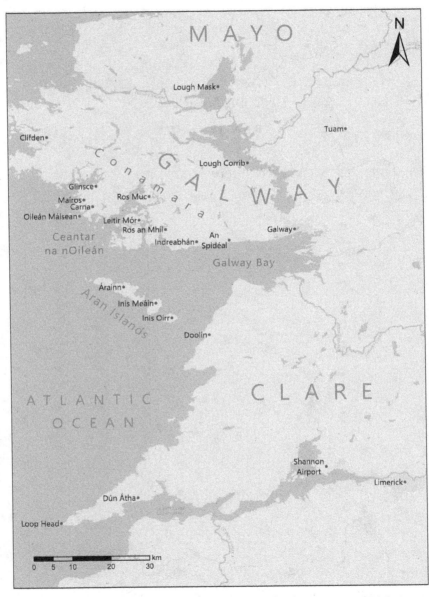

MAP 1. The Aran Islands and the mainland. Used by kind permission of Daphne Pochin Mould; modified by the author and Liam Ó hAisibéil, with basemap data from Esri, HERE.

Introduction

As long as I remember my father rose at or about seven o'clock in the morning, breakfasted, and looked after his letters, of which he daily received a considerable number from all classes. Some wrote about the meaning of certain Irish words, some for information on obscure points of Irish history, some about Irish music. . . . The answers to the various correspondents required much time and research, yet he never looked for compensation. . . . I don't think there ever existed a more devoted, enthusiastic lover of his work than my father. . . .

On Sunday he usually rested and gave himself more to his family. He went to an early mass and had some of us constantly with him. . . . Later in the day he went to Glasnevin to pray at the graves of deceased members of our family; and after that he would go out by Clontarf. During these walks he was always quite cheery, and had a custom of addressing in Irish poor men or women whom he met. If they answered him in the same tongue, as sometimes they did, he would look delighted, take out his large handkerchief, spread it on the nearest stone or dyke, and chat away forgetful of time.

We had often some poor people to spend the evening, either fiddlers or pipers or beggarmen, whom my father discovered somewhere, and from whom he usually took notes about some old Irish airs; and these visitors had to be treated with as much respect as would have been shown to Lord Adare himself.

—SR. MARY [ANNE] PATRICIA O'CURRY, I.B.V.M.,
daughter of Eugene O'Curry (1794–1861)

Why did Eugene O'Curry address random strangers in Irish as he walked through Dublin in the mid-nineteenth century? What inspired him to invite "poor people" into his home, insist they be respected, listen to them perform, and transcribe music and lore from them? And what prompted those strangers to accept his offers and oblige his requests to converse, perform in his home, and collaborate in his transcription work? The precise nature of the hospitality or recompense afforded to the performers is not known, and what awareness they had of O'Curry's reputation as a leading light of contemporary Irish scholarship less so, though the documented experiences of contemporaries such as piper Paddy Conneely may provide some insight.[1]

Sr. Mary Patricia's narrative, written around 1899, sheds some light on these questions.[2] She highlights her father's interaction with both literate and non-literate people, whom she differentiates by class and language. She notes how much time he spent with each correspondent, whether writing letters of a weekday or having a roadside chat in his native language of a Sunday afternoon. Her framing of his moments of labor and leisure enfolds these separate activities in the context of a single emotional pursuit: to connect with and through his native cultural practice. Her testimony echoes her father's own verses, reprinted and translated below, in which he recalls and immortalizes the earliest of such encounters he had growing up in Dún Átha on the Loop Head peninsula in County Clare where his father, Eoghan Mór, was a tenant farmer (map 1).[3] Together with Sr. Mary Patricia's narrative, these verses—now inscribed on a memorial to him in his native village—demonstrate that the choices of Eugene's personal and professional life were informed by a lifelong ethos that was rooted in his cultural inheritance:[4]

> Seo an áit nár iadar riamh a ndoirse
> Ar fhánach riain ná ar dhianbhocht breoite
> Acht fáilte's riar gach mian le cóir mhaith
> álmhach iarla ar aíocht nuair gheobhadh ann.

> Dob áthas cléibh leo aon dem' shórtsa,
> Trácht' na ngaobhar chum léinn do sheoladh,
> Ar scáile niamhdha, ar réim is nóite,
> I gcás gach céim dá n-aosaibh óga.[5]

> [Here is the place where they never shut their doors
> On wayfarers or paupers sick and ill
> But welcome and a well-appointed range of wishes fulfilled
> Such as of an earl's tribe were they there to repose.

A joy to their hearts was one of my like
At opportune times for education,
The lustrous light, the noble rite,
At each step, to their young generation.]

What was it about his cultural inheritance that made it so compelling to O'Curry's life and work? The forces at work were both positive and negative. He was drawn to its beauty, excellence, and purpose. His father, Eoghan Mór (1744–1825), was a noted storyteller, singer, and bearer of local and traditional lore.[6] The farmhouse in Dún Átha also had a library of more than fifty books—consisting certainly of manuscript material, if not also print—and Eoghan Mór taught his sons to read and write Irish.[7] Sarah Atkinson highlights how song, lore, and literature coexisted as performance practice in the O'Curry homestead, generating a touchstone of the cultural milieu of the locality.[8] Brian Ó Dálaigh describes it as "an institute of learning" and marvels at "how rich and fruitful was the environment": "The vigour in which Gaelic learning was pursued in west Clare is all the more extraordinary because it was happening at a time when people were turning away from Irish to English. The people, who engaged in Gaelic learning, the ordinary farmers, tradespeople and schoolteachers of the area, read and wrote the manuscripts in their leisure time only. Irish was not a marketable commodity; one could not make a living from it."[9] In this context, the threat of cultural oblivion—arising, in this case, from the contemporary language shift from Irish to English, the "keystone of fortune"—presented a grave concern.[10] Under threat, the practice of any cultural inheritance can gain a special impetus. The experience of losing some manuscripts in a fire at the farmhouse must have consolidated in young Eugene's mind the value of such documents.[11] Nessa Ní Shéaghdha highlights a later incident when he rescued a manuscript from a pawnshop in Tralee, intending for it to be deposited in an Irish institution only to see it sold to the British Museum.[12]

Collecting documents of cultural or historical significance and creating documents of his own emerge as natural expressions of O'Curry's specific cultural inheritance.[13] In his case, they are manifestations of the phenomenon of *dúchas*, which Peter McQuillan glosses as a semantically rich and culturally significant concept with a corresponding practice: "To paraphrase Bourdieu, we might say that *dúchas* is embodied, internalized history, both individual and collective, which is therefore forgotten as history, until activated by the appropriate context. So *dúchas* here forms a *habitus* in which it embodies and enacts history (*ó aimsir go haimsir*), is thereby naturalized and recursively activated through genealogy, chronicles and traditional lore (*seanchas*). Where *dúchas* occurs in a particular context, speakers apply their understanding of its pragmatics, an understanding that presupposes older contexts of use and potentially entails the creation of new contexts."[14] O'Curry's practice of *dúchas* came to occupy new and atypical contexts. Some instances echoed the intimacy of his childhood home, as did the evenings he spent with fellow Irish speakers and musicians whom he had invited into his Dublin home. Other instances, including his appointment to the chair of archaeology and Irish history in the early days of the Catholic University of Ireland, generated significant platforms that afforded him opportunities to make a more public case for the culture he spent his life documenting, parsing, and sharing.[15] O'Curry's landmark series *Lectures on the Manuscript Materials of Ancient Irish History*, published in the year of his death, embodies a vital convergence of the oral, performance, manuscript, and print modalities that O'Curry employed throughout his life, not simply for the content of the series but also for the multifaceted, lifelong practice that brought it into being. Others, including Pádraig Ó Cearmada (ca. 1833–1909) and Canon Séamus Goodman (1828–96), generated practices of their own.[16]

We cannot know the sounds of the music performed by "fiddlers or pipers or beggarmen" in O'Curry's house in Dublin in the 1840s and 1850s or in the O'Curry homestead in West Clare at the turn of the nineteenth century. Yet we believe we can know some of their elements, that we can encounter traces of their essentially evanescent existence. The participants therein—performers, scribe, and audience—held the same hope. They too imagined transcriptions would enable us, in their future, to come to know something about the sounds they were producing and hearing in our past. Their care and attention to the task at hand demonstrate an understanding shared through the ages: that literacy provides a seemingly impossible and thus magical potential for sound to resound beyond its immediate emanation, to achieve a degree of permanence and, with that, immortality. Our collective effort to connect, to facilitate a séance of sorts, expresses an extraordinary faith in the chosen medium—in this case, literacy. Thomas Forrest Kelly captures the sense of the miraculous that imbues this prospect: "To imagine that one could translate music—which exists in a moment of present time and in sound—into a visual medium that exists outside time is an amazing conceptual leap."[17]

While the potential to counter evanescence and transience and so, in a sense, to cheat death, held a certain allure, it need not have dominated proceedings.[18] The performances themselves demanded a reverence and authority of their own.[19] Then as now, the act of performing occupied a certain privilege in the hierarchy of encounters with music.[20] Singing forms "part of the aesthetics of *gaisce*"; the term "comprises an impetus to excel, and to perform renowned and memorable deeds."[21] The moment of song "creates a time outside of ordinary time that can reconfigure ideas and influence action."[22] At this remove of nearly two hundred years, the performances command an additional authority, one that relies on the presence of witnesses—O'Curry and his young daughter among them—and their capacity and desire for remembering them.[23]

The ephemerality of music echoes the inherent unreliability of memory itself, and so the potential for music to be forgotten, misremembered, or disremembered appears to increase.[24] Correspondingly, efforts to document music and the history thereof are often defined in negative terms of the potential or inevitable occurrence of loss.[25] Questions of access to resources and sustainability can restrict such efforts, compounding the sense of loss. In this uneasy context, the document—in this case, the musical transcription—offers some comfort. While its existence reiterates the irretrievable loss of the original utterance, it also promises to defer or deny the sense of that loss and to deliver the potential to contribute memory to the future practice of the music it records, the chance to deny amnesia.[26] The nature and efficacy of that particular contribution differ from artifact to artifact and from medium to medium.[27] Each medium and artifact can also encounter the threat of obsolescence from one generation of media to another. Fallibility, it emerges, is a defining concern of efforts to document music. It is expressed most frequently in terms of measuring and securing authenticity and authority, qualities often embodied by the enduring cultural phenomenon—conceptual and physical—of the voice.[28] Writing in July 1787, poet and scribe Aindrias Mac Craith considered the challenge: "How is it possible that any man in the kingdom could give a particular true, or satisfactory account of the birth, names, lives, death, parentage, personal description, or places of residence of our ancient bards, of their works, performances, or different compositions in prose or verse, or on what particular instruments they performed their church or other music?"[29]

The interplay of positive and negative emotional forces driving the practice of documenting music is captured beautifully in the representation that appears

in figure 2. In September 1857 the artist Frederic William Burton, born and
reared in County Clare, sketched the scene aboard a Galway hooker as O'Curry
transcribed a song from an Aran woman. At the heart of his mute image is the
sound that engrosses the figures—the scribe and the singer—and the artist
too. The sense of wonder of the acoustic is coupled with a sense of its loss: the
impromptu feeling of the sketch resonates with the ephemerality of the song
performance it documents, the quality that drove O'Curry and Burton to rely
on literacy and life drawing, respectively, to define and challenge its transience.
The hope and magic of deliverance is realized in the existence and survival of
the material artefact itself: it was an extraordinary alignment of circumstances
that brought these two men together in a sailing boat off the Aran Islands with
some local singers, circumstances that generated their respective documents of
local song, written and drawn. Burton's sketch merits the attention it receives
here and in the following chapter as it appears to be the oldest surviving image
of the practice of documenting music in Ireland. It is a welcome addition to the
corpus of surviving material from that encounter, which fortunately includes
some of O'Curry's song manuscripts.

From the earliest days of musical transcription, when the ninth-century
monk and poet Notker—an early contributor to the development of music
transcription—wondered how we might "grasp the wind," music documents
have appeared in collections such as Notker's own book of mnemonic poetic
sequences titled *Liber hymnorum* or, a millennium later, O'Curry's song manuscripts.[30] The materiality of music documents makes dreams of possession and
reproducibility tangible, and their desirability and utility promotes the practice
of collecting, of generating and gathering together individual documents.[31]
Such activity varies in form and intensity according to the motives and means
of those investing in it; their relationship with the objects that are being generated, gathered together, traded, and shared; and their relationship with the
content documented and collated therein.[32] The practice of collecting music
produces archives, the "value, relevance, or meaning" of which can change over
time.[33]

Diana Taylor provides a useful conceptualization and contextualization of
the *archive* in relation to the *repertoire*. She determines that "'archival' memory
exists as documents, maps, literary texts, letters, archaeological remains, bones,
videos, films, CDs, all those items supposedly resistant to change"; and that it

"succeeds in separating the source of 'knowledge' from the knower—in time and/or space."[34] In contrast, the repertoire of "embodied memory" relies on "presence" and includes "performances, gestures, orality, movement, dance, singing."[35] Taylor characterizes the symbiotic relationship between the two domains: "The archive and the repertoire have always been important sources of information, both exceeding the limitations of the other, in literate and semi-literate societies. They usually work in tandem and they work alongside other systems of transmission—the digital and the visual, to name two."[36] In the Gaelic song tradition of Cape Breton Island in Canada, Stephanie Conn observes an example of the interplay between the archive and the repertoire that mirrors the interweaving modalities of Irish traditional music practices: "Objects which prompt memory are adjuncts to the text that is the song, for they help to bridge the distance between the song's origins or past performances and my present one."[37] She also highlights the potential of both the archive and the repertoire to enrich and empower a musician's life.[38] In Ireland, Stiofán Ó Cadhla observes instances where the work of documenting performances is reimagined by the performers themselves as play: "tá na filí seo chun tosaigh ar an mbailitheoir sa mhéid is gur tráth ceiliúrtha agus cruthaitheachta dóibh ócáid an bhailithe féin" (these poets are ahead of the collector insofar as, for them, the collecting event itself is an occasion for celebration and creativity).[39] Each of these examples demonstrates the potential for a musical practice to oscillate between, or to merge, the two domains—the archive and the repertoire.

The potential for play in the practice of music collecting is typically subsumed in a narrative of labor, however, reflecting the institutionalization of the practice over time. The lexicon associated with music collecting molds itself to the activities of professionals who work within the contexts of museums, institutes, libraries, and broadcasters. Where corpuses of musical material emerge—published and unpublished, professional, organizational, and independent—the term "music collection" is attached to them, and to their chief creators, the attribution of "music collector." Such orienting reflects how "the archival . . . sustains power."[40] Acknowledging the dominance of the archival narrative in an Irish traditional music context,[41] and maintaining an awareness of the particular role of language in that positioning, this book seeks to investigate the mechanics and motives of music collecting in Ireland—the how and the why—in order to better understand its special impact.

The purpose of music collecting is to overcome distances of one or more varieties, whether temporal, physical, or cultural, between people and music. The
inherent intangibility of music means collectors and musicians need to collaborate to create transcriptions or recordings of music, objects that will enable
music to move great distances through time and space. With increasing mobility and ease, these objects enable people to negotiate their relationships with
the music in question from any distance. Music collections enable people to
establish what cultural distances, if any, lie between them and the music in
question. They are inherently political arenas in which issues of ownership,
authorship, authority, agency, and control over music are contested at every
turn. They can become touchstones for future generations, canonizing the
music they document, and they can become marking stones of the music they
exclude or marginalize.

Narratives of music collecting typically focus on collections that have been
published, in part or in full, or on collections created by professional collectors.[42] They rarely account for unpublished collections or for the activities
of collectors operating independently of institutions. This is understandable.
Unpublished and independent collections are generally more difficult to access,
so acknowledging their significance has proven to be challenging; but scholars have also lacked an adequate terminology with which to discuss them. In
addition, narratives of music collecting typically center on the instigators of
music collections—song catchers, ballad hunters, and collectors—on people
like Alan Lomax whose extraordinary exploits and achievements are justifiably
celebrated.[43] Nevertheless, these near synonyms are problematic because they
have propounded a myth that the primary motive behind music collecting is
preservation. They do not allow for alternative motives for collecting or documenting music.[44]

This book offers a critical historiographical study of the practice of collecting traditional music in Ireland. It focuses on nineteenth- and twentieth-
century music collections from the Aran Islands off the west coast of Ireland.
Exploring some key themes, including collaboration, canonization, and marginalization, it shares new readings of familiar sources and introduces some
unfamiliar ones. Acknowledging the variety of motives, methodologies, and
perspectives behind each music artifact and its corresponding collection, and
setting aside hierarchies of value within which they might be interpreted, it
frames each archive in relation to the individual practice that produced it.[45]

Eschewing simplistic binary constructions that can polarize perspectives and approaches, this framing reveals a spectrum of activities of engagement, navigation, and negotiation, activities that yield the music collections on which we rely to understand and appreciate our musical pasts.[46] The practice of music collecting emerges as a palimpsest of individual practices of engagement, navigation, and negotiation that yield a varied palette of collaborations—between different collectors and between collectors and performers—wherein each agent becomes a creator and coauthor.

This framing represents a new paradigm for contextualizing and understanding the practice of music collecting, one that presents an opportunity to level the playing field between published and unpublished collections and between professional and independent collections and to acknowledge how independent and unpublished sources have real potential to contribute as much, if not more, to our understandings of music.[47] Making a particular case for collections created by locals, it argues for the contextualization of all manner of sources so that we can make the best and fairest use of them all. This proposal has particular resonance in the twenty-first century, where increased access to media, to digital technology in particular, is growing the potential for democratization— of voices, polities, canons, and expression. With greater efficiency, previously marginalized sectors of society are enabled to create and disseminate their cultural artifacts—to share, transmit, and so perpetuate their "archival" knowledge.[48] Communities are urging institutions to engage in repatriation exercises, whether of physical artifacts or of digital surrogates. Archives that have lain idle are being developed, and new ones are being generated. All this activity provides welcome opportunities to revise attitudes to histories, languages, cultural practices, and their artifacts, and so to disrupt dynamics of power.

Such opportunities are, nonetheless, dependent on the perennial question of adequate resourcing, including access, expertise, funding, and practical support. Understanding the historiographical context helps us to maintain awareness of the impact of the archive on music practices and, ultimately, to help mitigate against neglect or negligence. Such awareness is vital to efforts to protect and cultivate cultural equity.

HISTORY OF MUSIC COLLECTING IN IRELAND

The history of music collecting in Ireland is intertwined with the histories of music collecting in the US and Britain—documented in 1959 by D. K. Wilgus in his *Anglo-American Folksong Scholarship since 1898*—two countries from which a notable number of collectors visited Ireland. Nevertheless, the history of music collecting in Ireland is different from those two jurisdictions. It is also largely unwritten because the practice of music collecting in Ireland has only recently been considered as the phenomenon it represents.[49] In March 2009 there were two events that acknowledged the significance of music collecting in Ireland: Seán Corcoran's TG4 television series titled *Na Bailitheoirí Ceoil* (The Music Collectors) and the fortieth Léachtaí Cholm Cille conference, subtitled "Foinn agus Focail" (Music and Words), which was possibly the first-ever serious consideration given to the subject of collectors of Irish traditional music.[50] Nicholas Carolan has offered more recent expositions on music collecting in Ireland.[51] There have also been many individual studies of collections, of collectors, and of the musics they documented.[52]

Histories of music collecting in Ireland typically begin with print culture. They detail how, in the early eighteenth century, for reasons of commerce and personal ambition, Irish music publications began to appear in some quantity in Ireland, England, and Scotland. Carolan elaborates:

> Within Ireland there were two bursts of publishing Irish music in the course of the [eighteenth] century, and both coincided with an upsurge in political feeling among the members of the colony, a movement sometimes referred to as Anglo-Irish nationalism. The first began in the 1720s, in the period of the Wood's Halfpence affair, and the second in the late 1770s, the period of the [Irish] Volunteers. In both periods there was a disillusionment with and a resistance to the authority of the mother Parliament, chiefly for economic and constitutional reasons. In an effort to create an identity that was neither British nor native Irish, some reached for elements of the older culture that could in some way be detached from the older population, and found that the universal language of music was suitable for their purposes.[53]

In 1724 in Christchurch Yard, Dublin, John and William Neal produced the first published collection of Irish music: *A Collection of the Most Celebrated Irish Tunes*. Later, in the 1780s, scholarly interest in Irish traditional music and in its collecting began to appear in print. Carolan confines his survey to publications from Ireland, England, and Scotland, but contemporaneous publications concerning Irish music may also have appeared in other countries. The first scholarly publications on Irish traditional music were produced by a "post-Vallencey generation of Irish antiquarians" that included Charlotte Brooke, Joseph Cooper Walker, and Theophilus O'Flanagan, three who worked hand in hand to publish and preserve poetry in Irish, including song lyrics.[54] To aid her study of the Irish language, Charlotte Brooke (ca. 1740–93) from Rantavan, Co. Cavan, collected poetry from local Irish speakers and consulted native Irish scholars, including Charles O'Conor (1710–91), Muiris Ó Gormáin (ca. 1720–94), Sylvester O'Halloran (1728–1807), and Peadar Ó Conaill (Peter O'Connell, 1775–1826). Joep Leerssen suggests her "retiring disposition kept her from offering these poems, and her translations into English, to the public."[55] Joseph Cooper Walker (1761–1810), who was Brooke's friend, persuaded her to contribute some of her transcriptions and translations to his *Historical Memoirs of the Irish Bards*.[56] Appearing in 1786, when Walker was "a twenty-four year old clerk in the Irish Treasury," it was the first published book on Irish music.[57] The success of the book persuaded Brooke to yield to the entreaties of Walker and of another friend and mentor, Bishop Thomas Percy, and in 1789 she published a seminal collection of translated poems and songs titled—in a tribute to Percy's famous 1765 volume—*Reliques of Irish Poetry*.

Both Brooke and Walker were assisted by Theophilus or Tadhg O'Flanagan (ca. 1760–1814) of Tulla, Co. Clare, who was one of the most well-known Gaelic scholars of the eighteenth century.[58] *Reliques of Irish Poetry* could not have been published without the input of O'Flanagan and other Gaelic scholars on whom Brooke and Walker and other antiquarians depended "to open treasures so long locked up" in the Irish language, as Muiris Ó Gormáin put it in 1766.[59] The contributions made to the collection and preservation of Irish music by O'Flanagan and his ilk are often overlooked. In O'Flanagan's case, this is surprising considering he is regarded as a pivotal figure in the cultural life of Ireland before and after the Act of Union of 1800.

The achievements of Walker, and especially of Brooke, who is regarded as "the first mediator of importance between the Irish-Gaelic and the Anglo-Irish literary traditions," leads Leerssen to credit them with helping "to lay the foundation of Irish literary history."[60] Their contributions to the foundation of music collecting in Ireland are, nonetheless, often overshadowed by those of a young man from Armagh, the most renowned of Ireland's early scholarly music collectors, Edward Bunting. As a nineteen-year-old organist, he began his career as a music collector by transcribing music from ten harpers who performed at the Belfast Harpers' Festival of 1792. In 1796 he published the result of those efforts in *A General Collection of the Ancient Irish Music*. Bunting, who later employed Pádraig Ó Loingsigh (Patrick Lynch) and Séamas Mhac Óda (James Cody) to transcribe the lyrics of Irish songs, became "the first Irish collector that we know of to gather music from musicians 'in the field.'"[61] He went on to produce two other publications of traditional music in 1809 and 1840.

Compared with his forerunners, the memory of Bunting's work is the most vivid. This status can be attributed to the successes of his numerous publications and to the memory of the auspicious occasion that launched his career as a collector: the patriotic and picturesque Harpers' Festival. Carolan maintains that, in light of earlier publications such as those of Walker and Brooke, Bunting's work should be interpreted "as an important and late flowering of eighteenth-century interest in Irish music, and not, as it sometimes is, as the first flowering of that interest."[62] Expanding on this revision, the contributions of Walker, Brooke, and Bunting together are interpreted here as the earliest published manifestations of an older and long-running written tradition of interest in Irish music, a scribal tradition to which ordinary people contributed. Shopkeepers, merchants, schoolteachers, farmers, priests, newspapermen, publishers, poets, local historians, storytellers, educators, and tradespeople of the eighteenth and nineteenth centuries—including, for instance, the farmer, miller, and businessman from Owning, Co. Kilkenny, Pádraig Ó Néill (1765–1832), and the Protestant minister and musician from Baile Áimín Treantach near Ventry, Co. Kerry, Canon Séamus Goodman (1828–96), as well as the O'Curry family of Dún Átha, Co. Clare—read and wrote manuscripts in their leisure time, manuscripts that contained, among other things, the lyrics of songs in Irish.[63] This written tradition of engagement with traditional music via collecting or documenting music was part of a wider tradition of Gaelic learning that people incorporated into their lives by whatever means available to them, whether written, printed, or oral transmission: "These [manuscripts] were for the most part written by professional scribes and schoolmasters, and being then lent to or bought by those who could read but had no leisure to write, used to be read aloud in farmers' houses on occasions where numbers were collected at some employment, such as wool-carding in the evenings; but especially at wakes."[64] While creating and collating manuscripts that feature an abundance of Irish heritage, including historical treatises, genealogies, mythology, and poetry, the Gaelic intellectual tradition was also producing a wealth of music documents in the form of song transcriptions, usually consisting simply of lyrics without musical notation.[65] The majority of Gaelic scribes were unable to transcribe melody, so many of them appended to their song transcriptions the names of the airs to which the songs were sung, as occurred with contemporary printed ballad sheets.[66]

Taking this longer and broader view of written sources of Irish traditional music makes the practice of collecting Irish traditional music much older and more diverse than its print manifestations. It helps to redress the imbalance that sometimes occurs in the representation of the authors who produced early Irish music publications and the Gaelic scholars who acted as their touchstones and conduits to native musical traditions.[67] More importantly for this book, expanding the parameters of our interpretation in this way helps interrogate our preconceptions about the purpose and practice of music collecting. The present study cannot attempt to give a detailed account of this early history of music collecting in Ireland: though many scholars of the Gaelic manuscript and scribal traditions include in their investigations music documents and music collecting activities, we await a comprehensive collation and examination of the substantial range of evidence supporting the present interpretation of the history of the practice of music collecting in Ireland.[68] That work deserves more time and space than this book can provide. Here, the hope is to inspire others to consider this early history of music collecting in Ireland and to contribute further to the reappraisal.

As music collecting developed during the nineteenth century, the Europe-wide movement of nationalism brought politics to bear on the practice in Ireland. Leerssen observes: "Nationalism places culture and politics into a highly specific mutual relationship; it is by definition idealistic rather than materialist or pragmatist, in that it derives political claims (sovereign statehood) from an abstract principle (national identity)."[69] In the wake of the rebellion of 1798 and the Act of Union of 1800, some of the music collectors of Ireland abandoned eighteenth-century patriotism in favor of a more apolitical antiquarianism. Bunting's work provides the most well-known if tragic example of how this shift of allegiance impacted on music collectors and their collections. After recruiting Patrick Lynch to collect song lyrics for him, Bunting then excluded his lyrics from his publications because of Lynch's complicity, however reluctant, in the hanging of the rebel Thomas Russell. Leerssen suggests another political reason behind the exclusion of Irish lyrics from Irish songs published at this time: "Irish music could the easier be relished since it was so intrinsically a-political—as long as it was instrumental, that is."[70]

Another European movement that influenced music collecting in Ireland in the nineteenth century was Romanticism, which constituted "a reaction to the dogmatic rationalism of the Enlightenment and more specifically to the role of the French and the Industrial revolutions in transforming contemporary European society."[71] The emotional and imaginative power of music made it a primary concern of Romanticism, which valued "the elevation of the emotions above the reason."[72] Diarmuid Ó Giolláin observes: "Sensitivity, spontaneity, historicism, difference and distance are key notions in Romanticism."[73] Romanticism encouraged nostalgia and "emphasized the singularity and specificity of individuals and communities," which led to "a fashion for the exotic."[74] Each of these concepts is predicated on physical and/or cultural distances. Consequently, accepting that the purpose of collecting music is to overcome distances of one or more varieties, whether temporal, physical, or cultural, between people and music, then music collecting found in Romanticism an ideological space in which it would resonate most voluminously. In this climate, Irish traditional music found its fans, including the French historian Augustin Thierry (1795–1856), for whom it was music "which paints the insides of souls."[75] The pervasiveness of the Romantic sensibility in the modern world was observed in 1979 by H. G. Schenk, who then believed it was "still the most recent European-wide spiritual and intellectual movement."[76]

Along with antiquarianism, interest in folklore and philology increased during the nineteenth century, as did interest in the Irish language. Each of these concerns encouraged more collecting of Irish traditional music, as did the concurrent spread of literacy. Music collectors who were inspired by such scholarly pursuits include George Petrie (1790–1866) and Eugene O'Curry (1794–1862), James Hardiman (1782–1855), Seán Ó Dálaigh (ca. 1800–1878), Patrick Weston Joyce (1827–1914), Fr. Richard Henebry (1863–1916), and his student Áine Ní Fhoghlú (1880–1932). In contrast, Canon Séamus Goodman (1828–96) collected music for leisure, as did Carl Gilbert Hardebeck (1869–1945). Improvements to transport networks throughout the country also enabled these collectors to travel to different locations to find the music they sought. As the nineteenth century drew to a close, the number of music collectors and the variety of motives that drove them increased. Although their efforts span decades, they were united by their interest in Irish traditional music and by a desire to gain access to it, to improve their understanding of it, and to preserve it.

The development of sound recording technology eased the task of collecting music for twentieth-century collectors. Some of the earliest recordings of traditional music in Ireland were created in the early years of the twentieth century by the Austrian Rudolf Trebitsch (1876–1918), Fr. Richard Henebry, Fr. Luke Donnellan (1878–1952), and Charlotte Milligan Fox (1864–1916). The increasing portability of sound recording technology and the increasing mobility of people, thanks to further developments in transport, introduced foreign music collectors to Ireland, the majority of whom came from the Anglophone countries of Britain and America. Sound recording also introduced motives of broadcasting and publishing records, each of which impacted on Irish traditional music in different ways.

Some final observations of this short history of music collecting in Ireland from the mid-nineteenth century until the 1970s—the period to which the four collections discussed here belong—include the following: the collectors were predominantly male, which may have limited the profile of the performers and of the material featured in the collections; and their varied social and cultural backgrounds and language capacities affected their choices in relation to where and what material they recorded.

SIGNIFICANCE OF MUSIC COLLECTING IN IRELAND

Given that music collecting in Ireland has only recently been considered as the phenomenon it represents, it follows that its significance has been, until recently, underestimated.[77] Apart from its obvious contributions to our understanding of the music of the past and to our current musical landscape—the contribution with which this book is primarily concerned—music collecting has also contributed repeatedly to the ideological, literary, and historical landscapes of Ireland. Beginning with the ideological landscape, Barra Boydell observes: "Nineteenth-century nationalism encouraged the identification of selected aspects of a country's culture and history as iconic symbols of nationality. Irish nationalism inherited a direct role for music within this imagery."[78] In no small part, Edward Bunting's music collection from the Belfast Harpers' Festival of 1792 combined with the interest of late eighteenth-century and nineteenth-century antiquarians in the harp, and with the imagery of the United Irishmen, to contribute to the growing symbolism of the harp as the emblem of Ireland. Bunting's collections also coincided with "a brief revival of interest in harp playing (although not of the true Irish harp) in the early nineteenth century," which helped popularize his publications.[79] Furthermore, it was from Bunting's published collections of 1796, 1809, and 1840 that Thomas Moore appropriated most of the *Irish Melodies* to which he set his seminal, sentimental, and nationalistic lyrics.[80] In so doing, Moore further mythologized and politicized the music of Ireland, but only to a point; as Douglas Hyde observed much later in 1923: "He had rendered the past of Ireland sentimentally interesting without arousing the prejudices of or alarming the upper classes."[81] Later nineteenth-century music collectors, including George Petrie (*The Ancient Music of Ireland*, 2 vols., 1855 and 1882) and Patrick Weston Joyce (*Ancient Irish Music*, 1873; *Irish Music and Song*, 1888; *Old Irish Folk Music and Songs*, 1909), continued in Bunting's antiquarian and nationalist vein, albeit in different directions. They urged the "national" significance of the music they documented with the words "Irish" or "Ireland" in the titles of their published collections. In collecting, publishing, and popularizing Irish traditional music, albeit in different forms, music collectors sowed the seeds of an ideological symbiosis between traditional music and Ireland that appears today to be stronger than ever.

Turning to the literary landscape of Ireland, during the course of the nineteenth century there were several attempts to bring the poetic riches of sean-nós (meaning "old style") song—a style of unaccompanied, solo, monophonic singing with a corresponding repertoire, mostly in Irish—to an English-speaking literary audience. Some included translations of the lyrics from Irish to English, and all met with "various degrees of failure and success."[82] Breandán Ó Conaire recognizes that these lyric translations were attempts to "bridge the chasm" between Ireland's two literary inheritances—"Gaelic and English."[83] Douglas Hyde's attempts, which included several important collections of sean-nós song lyrics published with verse and prose translations, were the most successful and helped transform the literary landscape of Ireland.[84] John Wilson Foster identifies Hyde's first song collection, *Love Songs of Connacht*, which was published in book form in 1893, as "the source of what has come to be regarded as the most notable and distinctive characteristic of modern Irish drama—the quality of the writing which gave dialect and English as it is spoken in Ireland a new status in world drama."[85] Hyde's prose translations offered an "indefinable Irish quality of rhythm and style" that William Butler Yeats believed would help create "a national literature which shall be none the less Irish in spirit from being English in language."[86] Hyde's book helped John Millington Synge in particular. Synge went beyond the obvious poetic veneer of the "rhythm and style" of the language of sean-nós song to the sensibilities it expressed, the potentially scandalous sensibilities that had earlier been suppressed in Petrie's music publications and that later sparked riots when they were exposed in *The Playboy of the Western World*. Synge enriched the dialogue of his plays with a wealth of imagery from sean-nós song, especially from *Love Songs of Connacht*, but he also recognized the substance of sean-nós song and deliberately appropriated "the images, ideas and intensities of an entire literary tradition" into his plays.[87] Yeats may have delighted in "the coming of a new power into literature," as he wrote about Hyde's song collection in *Samhain* in 1902, but it was Synge who capitalized most fully and spectacularly on that power.[88] He realized some of the potential of sean-nós song to contribute to the new Irish literature Yeats had imagined. In trying to create a song collection of his own in Inis Oírr in 1901 and in publishing his translations of the songs he collected there in *The Aran Islands*, Synge acknowledges the key role that sean-nós song played in his work and the transformative influence of Hyde's seminal song collections.[89]

In *The Aran Islands*, Synge marks his indebtedness to Hyde's book. He recalls an incident that occurred in Inis Meáin in 1899, where a young man read extracts from *Love Songs of Connacht* and an old woman found "her version was often not the same as what was in the book."[90] As Yeats might have done, Synge commends the style in which she "recited the verses with exquisite musical intonation, putting wistfulness and passion into her voice that seemed to give it all the cadences that are sought in the profoundest poetry." But Synge also acknowledges the substance of sean-nós song, the old woman's right to marshal it, and his own deference to the place, the people, and the culture to which it belongs: "The lamp had burned low, and another terrible gale was howling and shrieking over the island. It seemed like a dream that I should be sitting here among these men and women listening to this rude and beautiful poetry that is filled with the oldest passions of the world." This encounter between "the ancient literature" and the modern writer marks one of the moments of literary revelation that Yeats had imagined in 1892 as "a golden bridge between the old and the new."[91] It was, however, Hyde who, through the medium of song, enabled that encounter to occur, an encounter that Richard Fallis described as "the first great discovery" of the Irish Literary Revival.[92]

Except, perhaps, for Synge, each of the music collectors of the nineteenth century and the early twentieth century named above valued Irish traditional music "primarily as a remnant of the past" rather than as "a living tradition."[93] This interpretation continued well into the twentieth century and is evident in the collections of the Irish Folklore Commission, which featured a wealth of traditional music, especially songs. It was, perhaps, the medium of radio—with its potential for immediacy and its ability to transmit the sound of music—that initiated the change in attitudes toward Irish traditional music and toward the music collections that documented it. Music collections were eventually recognized as priceless historical documents, not of "remnants of the past" but of "a living tradition," and Irish traditional music assumed a "defining role . . . in popular perceptions of Irish identity."[94] Some of the most recent manifestations of this shift in attitudes include the establishment of a National Archive of Irish Folk Music within the Department of Education in 1972, which was driven by its director, piper and music collector Breandán Breathnach; the establishment of the Irish Traditional Music Archive (ITMA) in 1987; and the online archival resource developed by Comhaltas Ceoltóirí Éireann (CCÉ). Music collections now contribute to contemporary Irish musical life, to festivals, to music tourism, and to local economies in Ireland and beyond, wherever Irish traditional music is performed and consumed. Some reveal more about the past than others. By highlighting and sometimes refuting the myths of music in Ireland, they make important contributions to its historical landscape.

ARAN

Midway along the western seaboard of Ireland lies a small archipelago called the Aran Islands. Three of the islands—Árainn, Inis Meáin, and Inis Oírr—have sustained populations, and the other three are much smaller and uninhabited (fig. 1). The largest of the islands, Árainn, lends its name to the archipelago as a whole, a name that has since been anglicized as "Aran." In the nineteenth century, the island of Árainn earned the qualifying appellation "Arran More." That was later replaced by "Inishmore," which has since been gaelicized as Inis Mór, a name that is now in common usage. This book adheres to "Árainn" to connote the singular island and the anglicized term "Aran" refers to all three.

The islands lie on a west-northwest–east-southeast axis some sixteen miles long across the mouth of Galway Bay, around five nautical miles from the southwestern tip of Conamara to the north and around six nautical miles from

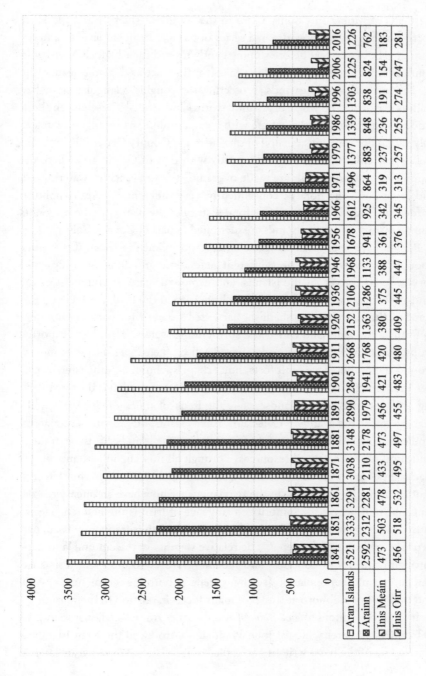

	1841	1851	1861	1871	1881	1891	1901	1911	1926	1936	1946	1956	1966	1971	1979	1986	1996	2006	2016
Aran Islands	3521	3333	3291	3038	3148	2890	2845	2668	2152	2106	1968	1678	1612	1496	1377	1339	1303	1225	1226
Árainn	2592	2312	2281	2110	2178	1979	1941	1768	1363	1286	1133	941	925	864	883	848	838	824	762
Inis Meáin	473	503	478	433	473	456	421	420	380	375	388	361	342	319	237	236	191	154	183
Inis Oírr	456	518	532	495	497	455	483	480	409	445	447	376	345	313	257	255	274	247	281

FIGURE 1. Aran Islands Census Returns, 1841–2016. Graph by the author, with data from CSO.

the Cliffs of Moher in County Clare to the southeast (maps 1 and 2). Their north-northeastern shores rise in a series of terraces from sea level to a maximum height of 406 feet before sloping gently toward their high cliffs and wild uninhabited southwestern reaches. As such, they act as a buffer against the prevailing southwesterly winds, protecting the roughly triangular spread of Galway Bay from the worst of Atlantic storms and swells. These eleven thousand or so acres of karst limestone with some thin but fertile soil and remarkably varied flora are an extension of the Burren in County Clare. The look and feel of this environment contrasts greatly with that of Conamara, where the mountains and stone walls are made of granite, the soil is acidic, waterlogged, and boggy, and the flora is, consequently, very different. As Aran's political borders are founded less on the natural history of the district and more on its human history, today the islands are identified as part of County Galway.

People have been living in Aran since 2500 BC at the latest, if not since 4000 BC, and evidence of how different generations and different groups have survived and thrived in the islands, and exploited them, is abundant in the landscape, history, and culture. People have farmed the land, reared livestock, combed the shoreline for shellfish, harvested seaweed for consumption and to fertilize the land, and fished the surrounding waters. They have exported crops, livestock, fish, stone, and seaweed ash or "kelp."[95] From the stones all around them, they have built forts, huts, chapels, churches, monasteries, castles, monuments, graves, lighthouses, piers, roads, and—what is the most striking element of the built landscape—hundreds of miles of dry-stone walls that crisscross the islands.[96] Chieftains, rulers, saints, missionaries, monarchs, landlords, and tenants have fought for control of the islands, for their strategic value and for their natural resources. Through all this, the inhabitants of this Gaeltacht community have continued to speak Irish and—from the sixteenth century at the latest—English; the two languages now have an uneasy coexistence in Aran, where the minoritized language of Irish is the first language of most islanders but the worldwide language of English is frequently used, particularly by younger islanders.[97] The relative stability of the cultural landscape through centuries of conquest and rebellion, proselytization and resistance, and famine and depopulation (see fig. 1) reflects both the remoteness of Aran and the stoic or stubborn attitudes of many locals in relation to their home.

In 1994 the editors of *The Book of Aran*—artist Anne Korff, historian J. W. O'Connell, and archaeologist John Waddell—introduced the Aran Islands as "surely one of the most written-about places in Ireland."[98] Seven years later, in

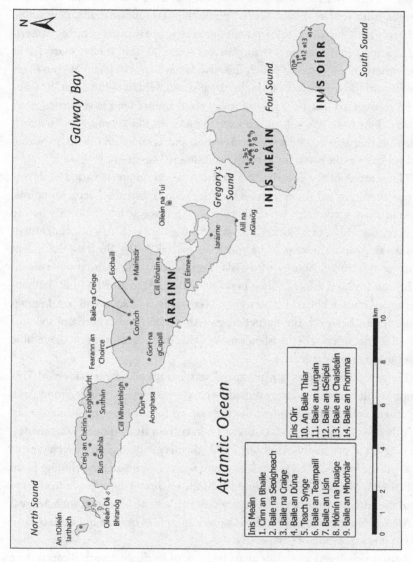

North Sound

Galway Bay

An tOileán Iarthach

Oileán Dá
Bhranóg

Creig an Chéirín

Bun Gabhla

Eoghanacht

Sruthán

Cill Mhuirbhigh

Dún
Aonghasa

Fearann an
Choirce

Baile na Creige

Corrúch

Eochaill

Mainistir

Gort na
gCapall

Cill Rónáin

ÁRAINN

Cill Éinne

Iaráirne

Oileán na Tui

 Aill na
nGlasóg

**Gregory's
Sound**

Atlantic Ocean

INIS MEÁIN

1 •3•5
2•4 6 7 8 •9

Foul Sound

10•
11 •13
•12 •13
•14

INIS OÍRR

South Sound

Inis Meáin
1. Cinn an Bhaile
2. Baile na Seoigheach
3. Baile na Craige
4. Baile an Dúna
5. Teach Synge
6. Baile an Teampaill
7. Baile an Lisín
8. Móinín na Ruaige
9. Baile an Mhothair

Inis Oírr
10. An Baile Thiar
11. Baile an Lurgain
12. Baile an tSéipéil
13. Baile an Chaisleáin
14. Baile an Fhormna

0   1   2   4   6   8   10
km

MAP 2. The Aran Islands. Map by Liam Ó hAisibéil, with basemap data from Esri, HERE.

a review of yet another publication about Aran—Andrew McNeillie's *An Aran Keening*—Tim Robinson found "there is no end to the making of books on Aran."[99] There is a formidable Aran canon featuring a cornucopia of contributions from writers, poets, artists, photographers, antiquarians, naturalists, archaeologists, linguists, folklorists, filmmakers, broadcasters, cartographers, and scientists to name a few. Breandán and Ruairí Ó hEithir have marveled at "the variety of interests" to which the islands have appealed and at "the sheer numbers of those who have thought, dreamt and written about Aran."[100] Robinson recognized that he is one of many contributors who have turned Aran into a palimpsest: "We will all just have to move up, like cormorants on a rock when another arrives with widespread wings, and, without graceless squawking and pecking, make room for a worthy addition to the canon."[101]

The motives of the contributors to the Aran canon are as varied as the interests that have led them to represent the islands, but their representations of Aran share a common tenet: that Aran is "a place apart."[102] Shortly before he died, Breandán Ó hEithir (1930–90), who grew up in Árainn, concluded: "To be an Aran islander is to be someone special."[103] To illustrate the acceptance of this conclusion by other islanders, in all its "restrained narcissism," Ó hEithir invoked a local *blason populaire*: "Baile Átha an Rí a bhí; Gaillimh atá; agus Árainn a bheas" (Athenry was; Galway is; and Aran will be). In pragmatic terms, however, the perpetual growth of the Aran canon and the sustained tourist interest in the islands make Ó hEithir's conclusion more credible if not utterly reasonable.

The notion of Aran as "a place apart" was first mooted by outsiders.[104] This is important because so many outsiders have represented or understood Aran as "other." Patrick Sheeran identifies the reasons for the representation of Aran as "other," as "a place of enchantment": a "recurrent human need for romance, for magic and providential mystery" and "the necessity to ground such desires in a specific locale."[105] Nevertheless, island writers, or insiders, including Liam O'Flaherty, Máirtín Ó Direáin, and Pat Mullen, whose voices began to emerge from the end of the nineteenth century onward, have also located "such desires" in Aran.[106] So, the notion of Aran as a place apart is as much a question of context as it is a question of perspective.

Aran is privileged as a place apart because of its distinctive and captivating combination of topography, culture, and myth. An evocative, liminal, island location on the edge of Ireland, on the edge of Europe, and on the edge of the

Atlantic Ocean sets the stage for a spectacular landscape and a rich culture. Originality, individuality, diversity, authenticity, and antiquity are the key elements of its identity. In Aran, Korff, O'Connell, and Waddell find "something that cannot be found, or at least not easily, elsewhere": "The Aran Islands are unique, in the quite particular sense that there is no other place in Ireland where you will find such a wealth of archaeological and cultural material to hand. Ever since the islands were rediscovered in the 19th century . . . they have exercised a fascination that is as easy to account for as it has been impressive in its results."[107] The powerful allure of Aran encourages the growth of the Aran canon. With each addition to the canon, "Aran is once again a larger place than it was."[108]

The privileging of Aran should be understood not only in a national context but also in a global context. While small island communities and minoritized cultures and languages around the world bow to environmental, economic, and cultural pressures, the Gaeltacht community of Aran remains alive and active. Its resilience suggests that the people of Aran cultivate a strong and rich culture. This, in turn, encourages the identification of Aran as a place apart.

Given the cultural importance attached to the Aran Islands and to Irish traditional music in local, national, and international contexts, and considering the continuous practice of traditional music in Aran over the last two hundred years at least, it is surprising to learn that comparatively little of the rich Aran canon engages directly with traditional music or with any genre of music. Instead, many contributions refer to music in passing. In other representations, music features because it has performed, or continues to perform, a function, often an aesthetic function, for the author: as diversion while in Aran; as color in literature and broadcasting; as an aid to learning Irish; or as a tool of political propaganda.[109] None of these functions or representations focuses specifically on music or on its historical value because, for these contributors to the Aran canon, music was not their chief motivation.[110] Of those commentators who were motivated by the music of Aran, their efforts most often amounted to collection without publication, documentation without dissemination. Consequently, music in Aran has been marginalized within the Aran canon and, by extension, within the wider contexts of Irish traditional music and Ireland. This is reflected in the misinformation and assumptions that continue to be made about music in Aran.

This book is the first to discuss Irish traditional music, or any genre of music, in Aran.[111] As a work of historiography, it questions what inspired, motivated, influenced, and challenged four visiting collectors and one local collector of music in Aran and queries their methods of representing traditional music. It casts a critical eye over these representations of traditional music and over the processes of selection, collection, and publication behind them. It sheds light on the parts that performers, collectors, and publishers play in making Irish traditional music such an evocative and pervasive element of Irish culture. It argues for the contextualization of music sources so that we might better understand the realities they try to represent. The investigation helps us reposition music in the Aran canon and reimagine the place of the traditional music of Aran in the wider discourse of Irish traditional music. Highlighting the marginalization of the music of Aran in this way also leads us to question the integrity of the narratives that have dominated, and that continue to dominate, discourses on Irish traditional music, on Aran, and on Ireland.

BIASES

Although this book is about collections of instrumental music and song in Aran, song features more than instrumental music. This emphasis reflects both the historical prevalence of song in Aran as compared with instrumental music and the bias in favor of song that occurs in sources of music making in Aran. An attempt has been made to frame discussions of song within the context of local music making in general.

While the book is concerned with the music of all three Aran Islands, the majority of contributions to the Aran canon relate to Árainn, the largest of the three islands. The emphasis on Árainn in the Aran canon is understandable considering it has the largest population (see fig. 1) and has had more visitors than Inis Meáin and Inis Oírr. Consequently, in this book the two smaller islands receive less attention than the largest island. Many accounts that discuss the archipelago suffer from a similar imbalance. An attempt has been made to overcome the imbalance by considering traditional music in all three islands while discussing the musical details of individual islands.

MUSIC COLLECTING IN ARAN

Together, the four collections discussed here form a cross section of music collecting in Ireland from the mid-nineteenth century until the 1970s. Drawing this cross section from a single geographical reference point—the Aran Islands—generates for this discussion a useful and instructive focus. The five collectors discussed here were Irish and American; English-speaking and bilingual (Irish and English); male and female; professional and independent; musician and nonmusician; well known and unknown; and foreigner, visitor, and local. They also used different technologies to document music. George Petrie, Eugene O'Curry, and Séamus Ennis transcribed music, while Sidney Robertson Cowell and Bairbre Quinn (the author's aunt) recorded music on magnetic tape. They acted alone sometimes and, at other times, with other people. Petrie and O'Curry worked in tandem, but Ennis, Cowell, and Quinn were frequently solo operators. Nevertheless, Cowell also collaborated with Ennis for a time, and Quinn casually enlisted the help of friends and family.

These collectors bring a complex variety of perspectives to Irish traditional music in the Aran Islands. They are, nonetheless, united, as are the collectors named earlier, across a span of 120 years by their desire to gain access to traditional music, to improve their understanding of it, and to preserve it, albeit by different means. Although few of them discuss or admit a historical agenda to their music collecting in Aran, there is a sense of purpose and a sense of worth in the four collections, leading us to interpret the collectors' efforts as partially if not wholly historical and, thus, as projects of preservation. When we consider the context in which Petrie and O'Curry's work in Aran was conducted— concurrently and in tune with their antiquarian work there and with Sir William Wilde's hopes to salvage and to enshrine the archaeological heritage of Aran— their efforts to collect music emerge as historically motivated. Similarly, the historical purpose guiding Ennis, Cowell, and Quinn is largely unspoken and apparent mainly in the content and in the context of their collections.

The four collections and the insights they provide into the musical traditions of Aran ought to be read in the light of the privileged position in which Aran is held. Themes of endurance and Romanticism and a sense of history permeate the substantial Aran canon, and each of these themes is present in all four sources to one degree or another. Nonetheless, the merits of the featured collections outweigh their prejudices. Questions about the collectors' methodologies and the degrees to which each of them succeeded in the historical endeavor arise, but regardless, the sense of purpose and the sense of worth that is palpable in their collections earn them the right to be considered.

The activities of these music collectors are interpreted here as a series of attempts to overcome the temporal, physical, and/or cultural distances that lie between the collector(s) and the music they collect. This theory might also be applied to other forms of documentation. It eschews the interpretation proposed by Breandán and Ruairí Ó hEithir in their 1991 compendium of Aran writings titled *An Aran Reader*. They account for "the variety of interests to which the [Aran] islands appealed; the extraordinary and abiding potency of the images created by Synge and Robert Flaherty; and above all, the sheer numbers of those who have thought, dreamt and written about Aran" by invoking a phrase from Seamus Heaney's poem, "Lovers on Aran."[112] They propose that the common motive is "to possess Aran."[113] Absolute terms of the presence or absence of possession are avoided here in favor of the measuring of distances of time, space, and understanding. Each collection is considered not as a product of acquisition but as the fruit of engagement, navigation, and negotiation.

chapter 1

The Petrie and O'Curry Aran
Music Manuscripts of 1857

O n Sunday, September 6, 1857, a Galway hooker set out from the pier
in Cill Rónáin, Árainn, for a day's sailing around the archipelago.
Aboard were some of Ireland's leading antiquarians and cultural figures: poet and scholar Sir Samuel Ferguson; physician Dr. William Stokes, his
son Whitley, and daughter Margaret; two renowned artists, Frederic William
Burton and George Petrie, who had his violin with him; and Petrie's former
colleague at the Ordnance Survey of Ireland, Irish-language scholar and historian Eugene O'Curry. They were the stragglers. The rest of their party, originally numbering around seventy people, had left the day before, undoubtedly
exhausted having spent the week attending a major conference of the British
Association for the Advancement of Science, first in Dublin and then in Aran,
where they spent three days cruising and tramping around the rugged islands.
The ambitious event had been "crowned with a glorious success," so this Sunday voyage was surely a celebratory one.[1] Before the conference, Aran represented to many people a "terra incognita," its archaeological wealth having
been witnessed by only a handful of earlier visitors, including Petrie in 1821,
John O'Donovan and William Wakeman in 1839, and Ferguson in 1852.[2] Afterward, Aran would be forevermore represented as an *insula sacra*.[3]

The delicate sketch by Frederic Burton, who had traveled especially from
Munich, captures the events of that fine September day with the immediacy
of a photograph (fig. 2). He depicts a studious O'Curry calmly transcribing
something, most likely a song, from an Aranwoman who is sensitively por-
trayed with stillness and simplicity. The image registers the esteem in which
antiquarian visitors held Aran. It also gives a sense of the time that antiquarians

29

invested in documenting Aran and the generosity of islanders who gave their time and knowledge to such visitors. The livelier image to the right depicts Sir Samuel Ferguson in Victorian attire, manning the helm while his hair and clothes flap in the wind that drives their boat around the islands. This image conveys the desire of the nineteenth-century urban dweller to escape to utopian idylls. Underlining the exoticism and romanticism that colored the experience of the urban-dwelling passengers and helmsman, Burton wrote "Captain Samuel Gulliver" above Ferguson's head in the top right-hand corner of the drawing. He then drew lines through the words "Samuel" and "Gulliver" and replaced them so that the inscription reads "Captain Lemuel Ferguson." The reference to Jonathan Swift's iconic work of 1726, *Gulliver's Travels*, compares with a similarly fanciful reference to Daniel Defoe's *Robinson Crusoe* (published just seven years earlier in 1719) by another, later visitor to Aran, Mary Banim.[4] Consequently, this drawing is not only an early representation of the act of song collecting in Ireland in the nineteenth century. It is also a multilayered

FIGURE 2. Frederic William Burton (1816–1900), *Eugene Curry, Historian (1796–1862), a peasant woman and Sir Samuel Ferguson, left to right*, September 6, 1857. Graphite on paper. NGI.2638. Courtesy of the National Gallery of Ireland.

depiction of an unusual contemporary encounter between visitors and island-ers. This interpretation of the image prompts us to question photographers' and artists' silent representations of people who may be singing.

Lady Ferguson confirms that this voyage was a musical one: "They sailed from island to island, taking with them on board the hooker all the local singers of whom they could hear. The music they sang was noted by Petrie and ren-dered on his violin—the Irish words recorded by Curry. . . . As the autumnal days became shorter, the musical *séances* were held on *terra firma* and in the evening."[5]

The transcriptions that Petrie and O'Curry created during their fortnight in Aran in 1857, which include up to forty songs, constitute the oldest surviv-ing source of music from any of Ireland's offshore islands. This chapter assesses this substantial body of music, as well as Petrie and O'Curry's representation of it, in particular Petrie's idiosyncratic treatment of Irish song. Building on the work of Breandán Ó Madagáin, it presents an opportunity to consider in greater detail their musical work as the collaboration it truly was—a collaboration that produced a store of traditional music and songs from all over Ireland—and to redress the marginalization of O'Curry's contribution to their work (see appen-dix 1).[6] Specifically, it shares the results of my efforts to reunite the texts and airs of songs the duo collected in Aran, a project enabled by the archival discoveries of Ciarán Ó Con Cheanainn and Dáibhí Ó Cróinín. Ó Con Cheanainn identi-fied two Aran songs amid O'Curry's Royal Irish Academy manuscripts, and Prof. Ó Cróinín uncovered some of O'Curry's Aran song texts in the Universi-taetsbibliothek Leipzig (UBL) in Germany and shared them with me in 2007, just in time for the 150th anniversary of the occasion that Breandán Ó hEithir dubbed "Aran's coming-out into the modern academic world."[7]

GEORGE PETRIE AND EUGENE O'CURRY

Born in Dublin of Scottish parentage, George Petrie (1790–1866) was a poly-math and an innovator (fig. 3). He was a renowned artist and collector of Irish music and "one of the most important antiquarians of the 19th century."[8] He has been called "the father of sound Irish archaeology."[9] His comrade in arms Eugene O'Curry (1794–1861), or Eoghan Ó Comhraí (fig. 4), was a native of Dún Átha on the Loop Head peninsula in County Clare, where his father, Eoghan Mór Ó Comhraí (1744–1825), was a *seanchaí*, storyteller, singer, poet, and a "scholar of high repute."[10] O'Curry, who learned English in his teens, is

FIGURE 3. George Petrie. RIA C/24/5/B. By permission of the Royal Irish Academy.

FIGURE 4. Eugene O'Curry.
RIA C/24/5/B. By permission
of the Royal Irish Academy.

described by Brian Ó Dálaigh as "a self-taught man, who came from one of the remotest and most poverty stricken areas of west Clare" to become "one of the true giants of Irish historical scholarship."[11]

Petrie and O'Curry first met in 1835 when O'Curry was appointed to the staff of the Ordnance Survey of Ireland, where, from August of that year, Petrie directed the Topographical Department. Petrie recognized in O'Curry "a kindred spirit," and the pair struck up a lifelong friendship.[12] Writing in 1869, journalist and historian Maurice Lenihan (1811–95) described the "perfect congeniality of feeling" that existed between the two men around 1852:

> Dr. Petrie was some years older than O'Curry; in person, he was more spare than his illustrious fellow labourer in the cause of Irish Archaeology; age indeed, appeared to have made a sharper impression on his classical features, which bore the traces of deep thought and study. O'Curry in many respects was of a different mould and calibre. Stout and robust, he looked better able to bear the wear and tear of the student's laborious life than Petrie; his features broader and more massive, possessed stronger characteristics of the Irishman than those of his friend; but between both there existed a perfect congeniality of feeling; they had

sympathies in common, and the love they bore their respective pursuits was vehement. . . . [O'Curry] was ever genial, warm, good humoured, full of anec- dote "racy of the soil"—anxious to communicate as freely as possible all he knew of whatever subject enquiry was made of him.[13]

COLLECTING IRISH TRADITIONAL MUSIC

Throughout the nineteenth century, Irish traditional music was practiced in towns and villages, in urban and rural settings, and by different classes of people from lower to upper classes, but most of the people who practiced it were un- educated, nonliterate, and poor, and many of them lived in rural communities. Although there is probably little chance of accurately quantifying the practice of traditional music in Ireland in the nineteenth century, if we consider the con- temporary distribution of wealth, traditional music must surely have then been the most prevalent genre of music in Ireland. As a young, middle-class, classi- cally trained amateur musician, Petrie took an early interest in jotting down some of the traditional tunes that were all around him, and though he came to have "a wide knowledge of music in general," Irish music soon became his main interest.[14] It was part of his consuming passion for the history and native heritage of Ireland. He believed Irish traditional music was the "greatest but most dilapidated monument of our national character" and that it was impor- tant to "preserve" it.[15] From about 1807 to his death in 1866, his musical jottings developed into more deliberate and industrious collecting, and he amassed more than two thousand traditional tunes, which can now be found in his music manuscripts in the National Library of Ireland and Trinity College Dub- lin. To transcribe tunes and to create manuscripts was, however, not enough, Petrie felt, to preserve them, so in 1855 he published some of his collection with piano accompaniments and arrangements that were written mostly by his daughter Marianne. A posthumous second volume appeared in 1882, without any material from Aran.

Having little or no Irish himself, Petrie came to depend on O'Curry for translation and communication with their Irish-speaking informants. More sig- nificant than his native fluency was O'Curry's unique combination of talents. A singer, a composer of verse, and a music collector in his own right, he also combined an insider's understanding of the Irish language, folklore, history, and music with an unrivalled knowledge of Irish manuscripts. Their friendship enabled Petrie to draw on O'Curry's authoritative expertise to enrich his music collection, frequently citing him "as the source of a melody or Irish lyric, a translation, a textual gloss or an opinion."[16] Petrie was the driving force behind their collaboration. He asked O'Curry to transcribe song lyrics for him. He then employed O'Curry's transcriptions to idiosyncratic effect in his *The Ancient Music of Ireland*. As Ó Madagáin observes: "This Petrie-O'Curry partnership was a lasting and very fruitful one, providing Petrie with a proficient insider source, fully at home with the Irish language (of which Petrie knew very little), and giving O'Curry the stimulus of working with an accomplished musician and fellow-enthusiast, as well as providing him with an outlet for the publication of his material. When Petrie published the first part of his great collection *The Ancient Music of Ireland* (1855), a work of critical importance to the present day, he could not have achieved it without O'Curry."[17] O'Curry was crucial to Petrie's mission. He was not simply Petrie's translator. He was his interlocutor, guide, and touchstone. Petrie admitted his reliance on O'Curry for his musical work in a letter to him dated August 28, 1855: "I am getting on . . . as well as I can, without having you beside me. But in truth . . . I can do nothing of consequence till I have you again to aid me."[18]

This comment probably refers to the musical work that Petrie and O'Curry did together in the little back parlor of Petrie's house on Great Charles Street in Dublin. It was from there that Petrie orchestrated the work of the Topographical Department of the Ordnance Survey of Ireland in which O'Curry was involved. O'Curry sometimes brought musicians whom he met on his travels and around the city to Petrie's house, where they could then transcribe music from them. He also contributed to the work by recalling memories of his father's music. Beyond the parlor, Petrie and O'Curry corresponded about music. They also received manuscripts from correspondents around the country, some of which contained music and songs. Petrie traveled around the country for the Ordnance Survey more than O'Curry did, and he collected music as he went. It is unclear whether O'Curry did likewise with song texts. Interestingly, there is little evidence that they accompanied each other on their respective journeys. There is only one account of musical fieldwork that they conducted together. It was created in 1868 by Dr. William Stokes, who accompanied them to the Aran Islands in 1857. As the only surviving account of their modus operandi, it is frequently cited and appears later in this chapter. Briefly, Stokes describes a seemingly well-worked formula: Petrie notated the air from the singer, stopping them at intervals to transcribe each phrase, and O'Curry then followed, transcribing the lyrics. Their music fieldwork in the Aran Islands may well have been exceptional, but the methodology Petrie and O'Curry adopted there was probably the same as that employed in Petrie's parlor in Dublin.

In all likelihood, meeting and befriending O'Curry inspired Petrie to spend more time collecting and working on traditional music. Marian Deasy observes how "Petrie's main work in Irish folk music ... was accomplished in his later years," having devoted his youth "almost exclusively to art."[19] Nonetheless, there were other, tragic reasons that spurred Petrie to change direction. Quoting him, Deasy observes that he was moved to focus more of his energies on collecting music by "the loss of a large portion of our native culture, as a result of the calamities of 1846–47, which 'had struck down and well-nigh annihilated the Irish remnant of the great Celtic family.'"[20] In the aftermath of the Great Famine, as Deasy writes: "He [Petrie] still believed it possible ... to gather from the survivors of the old Celtic race innumerable melodies that would soon pass away for ever. He stressed the urgency with which this should be done, as he believed that even though the new generation would continue to supply songs, they would have lost many of the peculiar characteristics of their forefathers as a result of being subjected to different influences."[21] Petrie was fortunate to find in O'Curry someone who could enable him to surmount the temporal and cultural distances between himself, an English-speaking classical musician from Dublin, and the music closest to his heart—Irish traditional music. As Ó Dálaigh notes: "[O'Curry] provided that link between the periphery and the centre, the bridge between the time when everything was broken and scattered to a time when the heritage of Ireland was nurtured and cherished. Without his contribution Irish society would have been very much poorer."[22] To date, however, O'Curry's part in their joint effort to preserve what John Boyle O'Reilly imagined were "the disconnected jewels of a queen's necklace" has been somewhat overlooked.[23]

Publishing Irish Traditional Music

Petrie modeled his music publications on those of earlier collectors of traditional music like Edward Bunting (1796; 1809; 1840), for whom, David Cooper writes, the piano was a "vehicle" of his "high-art aspirations" and whose arrangements were "the synthesis of ancient Gaelic and modern European practices."[24] Petrie tried to create arrangements that were more suited to what he called "the simple character and peculiar expression of the airs."[25] Cooper likens his simple arrangements to "harmonised hymn-tunes" that are "generally more musically neutral and passive than those of Bunting."[26]

In providing these publications, Petrie was satisfying a growing demand. Cooper—who is the most recent editor of Petrie's published collections—describes how, in the late eighteenth and nineteenth centuries, there was "a burgeoning interest in, and enthusiasm for, 'the music of the people' that fuelled, and was itself fuelled by, the development of literary Romanticism."[27] We should add to this artistic Romanticism, nationalism, utopianism and exoticism, elements that are apparent in a painting Petrie created around 1827 titled *Dun Aengus Fort, Inismore, Aran Islands*. J. W. O'Connell describes how, in the nineteenth century, "older and more 'primitive' civilisations were seen as having a value of their own, and . . . the study of the language, the folklore, and the manuscripts of these cultures not only had an intrinsic value, but . . . much of importance could be learned through such study."[28] Petrie was interested not only in studying Ireland's native culture but also in creating opportunities for a broader spectrum of society—from the educated to the literate to the working classes—to access it. His efforts to facilitate access included illustrating and painting the natural and built landscape of Ireland; writing for the *Dublin Penny Journal*, for the *Irish Penny Journal*, and his numerous and acclaimed essays; and opening the penny Gaslight exhibitions at the Royal Hibernian Academy. In this context, Petrie's published music volumes emerge not simply as acts of preservation. His piano arrangements of traditional music were, rather, translations from one musical genre to another, from one world to another. The provision of piano accompaniments made traditional music "performable in the front parlours of the bourgeoisie who, reassured by the reification of the artefact, were able to sing and play what they could now regard as 'their' national music."[29] These publications enabled educated classes to access and to appropriate "the music of the people" but in a mediated and sanitized form, "fashioned," as Cooper writes about the efforts of Bunting and James Macpherson, "to be congruent with contemporary taste and prevailing notions of antiquity."[30]

PETRIE'S MELODIES

Petrie's idiosyncratic approach to collecting and setting folk music springs from a long philosophical tradition concerning song and singing that Marina Warner traces to Aristotle's *De Anima*, noting "that voice above all is the physical, outer expression of the inner being: 'Voice is the sound produced by a creature pos-sessing a soul.' He [Aristotle] weaves voice into the very nature of conscious-ness and personal identity, writing: 'For, as we have said, not every sound made by a living creature is a voice ... but that which even causes the impact, must have a soul, and use some imagination; for the voice is a sound which means something.'"[31] Petrie's interest in Irish traditional music is defined by a fascina-tion with the particular capacity of melody—the solo musical voice—to mean something beyond words and to express something individual. Believing Irish melodies were beautiful and that they distinguished Ireland from the rest of the world, he became a founding member and president of the Society for the Preservation and Publication of the *Melodies* of Ireland (my emphasis) that ini-tiated the 1855 publication of his collection. His search for Ireland's melodies constituted a search for Irish identity: "For Petrie, ... Irish identity was most strongly encoded by the 'purest' melodies found in the Gaelic-language songs of the, often dispossessed, Catholic peasantry."[32]

In an Irish song, the Irish language served Petrie as a mark of the authenticity of the accompanying air. According to song collector Tom Munnelly (1944–2007), a "distaste for ... practically all English ... texts is universally evident" throughout Petrie's work on Irish traditional music.[33] In transcribing the airs of songs in Irish, Petrie often required the lyrics to establish the rhythm of its melody, to ensure the accuracy of his musical notation, and to authenticate its background or origin.[34] In this instance, language and lyrics were subservient to melody.[35] He was also concerned by the creativity of instrumental musicians—"pipers, fiddlers, and such other corrupting and uncertain mediums"—who, he felt, were prone to altering melodies too much, preferring instead to collect airs from singers, "their proper depositories."[36]

The heavenly association between the voice and the soul informing this aesthetic is all the more compelling for the potential of its hellish inversion, which Petrie and his compatriots experienced in Ireland during and after the famine of the 1840s. Encountering the absence of voice, specifically the absence of song, save for the keening that framed occasions of grief, Petrie was filled with dread. In 1855 he gave this depiction: "'The land of song' was no longer tuneful; or, if a human sound met the traveler's ear, it was only that of the feeble and despairing wail for the dead. This awful, unwonted silence, which, during the famine and subsequent years, almost everywhere prevailed, struck more fearfully upon their imaginations, as many Irish gentlemen informed me, and gave them a deeper feeling of the desolation with which the country had been visited, than any other circumstance which had forced itself upon their attention."[37] The soul of the country appeared to have departed its stricken agrarian heartland. Petrie renders the mute absent and the mourning disembodied, their unmusical cries belonging only to the air that carries them to the "traveller's ear," to the interloper bearing witness.

Petrie spoke only of the melody, the air of a song, as "the clue to so many traits for which we [Irish] have been distinguished."[38] The clues that lyrics might hold to national traits did not interest him. Indeed, profanity in song lyrics intensified the perceived purity of melody and so reinforced the polarity of his aesthetic of song wherein song lyrics represented the singing angel's feet of clay. When it came to publishing Irish songs, the potency of native lyrics, alive with currency in contemporary Ireland, intimidated Petrie, and he altered some of the offending songs so that they might be more readily accepted in urban drawing rooms. Blinded by moral prejudice, he manipulated and sometimes excluded lyrics of songs in English and in Irish that were, to his Victorian sensibility, intolerable. Munnelly gives several examples of Petrie's selective treatment of songs and characterizes it thus: "[Petrie] may deny subservience to the genteel world of the musical soiree, but he certainly gives the impression that one eye never left the polite society among whom he moved. He may have mixed with the purveyors of traditional music, but he was perennially aware of his own social order and constantly on guard lest he offend bourgeois respectability. Furthermore, he was prudish to a staggering degree."[39] Continuing his critique, Munnelly contrasts Petrie's work on traditional music with his other outstanding achievements: Petrie was certainly a "meticulous antiquarian" and a "charismatic leader," but "in the field of folksong scholarship, he displayed a level of amateurishness that he certainly would not have tolerated from colleagues in the many other fields in which he shone."[40] For these reasons, Munnelly finds Petrie's work to be "hugely flawed."[41] Munnelly's robust criticisms are, however, unfair. Petrie's work should be understood in the context of the milieu in which he acted. His actions should be understood in the context of his motives. Of these, his desire to preserve his aesthetic was vital. Petrie may have understood Irish song as well as O'Curry did, as Ó Madagáin suggests— "they were both passionate about Irish song and understood its all-embracing functions in the daily lives of the people"—but he was simply more interested in melodies.[42] His treatment of song lyrics was functional. Song served his purpose of preserving the best of the melodies of Ireland via the human voices of Ireland.

Were Petrie's publications solely acts of preservation, O'Curry might have impressed upon him the significance of the lyrics and persuaded him to include them in their entirety and in their original settings, at least in the 1855 publication when they were both still alive; but being also translations from one musical genre to another, Petrie's publications ultimately followed the trend of nineteenth-century publications of Irish traditional music. Petrie was not alone in his treatment of lyrics, in which he sheared traditional songs of their relevance and of their emotional impact and offered instead a censored distortion, sometimes a caricature, of Irish traditional song, styled for urban Victorian consumption. Other collectors, including John Edward Pigot (1822–71) and, in Wales, Maria Jane Williams (1795–1873), followed this trend.[43] Consequently, in spite of his shortcomings as a collector and publisher of Irish traditional music, his achievements in music must be regarded as nonetheless remarkable and important.[44]

Except for those cited by Petrie, O'Curry's opinions in relation to the songs they collected are largely unknown. O'Curry, whom Muiris Ó Rócháin called "the neglected scholar," is often cited as an important influence in Petrie's musical work, but the extent or true nature of his influence, or the lack of it in the case of Petrie's musical publications, awaits further investigation.[45]

THE MANUSCRIPTS

There are three volumes of Petrie's manuscripts of Irish traditional music in the National Library of Ireland.[46] They contain over two thousand airs that Petrie transcribed from musicians from all over the country, including his Aran material. There are additional music manuscripts held in Trinity College Dublin.[47] Petrie's collection was edited and published by Charles Villiers Stanford between 1902 and 1905. In the 1950s Veronica Kennedy made an attempt to enumerate the collection.[48] In 1982 Marian Deasy created a new edition of the collection for her doctoral dissertation. The present study draws on Deasy's unpublished edition of the collection. The indices she created are particularly useful for identifying which of Petrie's airs accompany O'Curry's song texts.

Locating the words of the songs O'Curry transcribed is more difficult. The song texts have not been collated nor have they been enumerated. They occur in at least four different archival collections of nineteenth-century manuscripts,

including the O'Curry manuscripts in Maynooth University; the Petrie manuscripts in the Library of the Royal Irish Academy (RIA); the Bunting manuscripts
in the library of Queen's University, Belfast; and the Stokes notebooks in the
Universitaetsbibliothek Leipzig. The song texts are sometimes catalogued as
poems. None of the O'Curry manuscripts consulted in the course of the research for this study contain the original transcriptions that were created in Aran.
Instead, all the Aran transcriptions that emerged from these sources appear
to be fair copies.

While it is currently impossible to compare O'Curry's Aran manuscripts
with the rest of his collection, Petrie's Aran manuscripts represent less than
2 percent of his entire collection of transcribed melodies. Small though this
selection would seem, it is, nonetheless, a valuable one, in particular because,
in comparison with other airs in his music manuscripts, Petrie's Aran airs
appear to be exceptionally well identified. Since it became possible to combine
some of them with O'Curry's manuscripts, the value of Petrie's Aran manuscripts has increased further. From this relatively small sample of a much larger
body of work, there is much that we can learn about their music collections in
general and about the collaborative work of the illustrious duo as well as about
the music of Aran.

CONTEXT AND MOTIVES

The 1857 trip appears to have been O'Curry's one and only visit to Aran. It
was Petrie's second visit; he went to Aran in 1821 and produced drawings and
writings that enriched studies he published later, evidence that is among the
earliest published representations of Aran. This led William Stokes to call Petrie "the discoverer—at least in an antiquarian point of view"—of Aran.[49] His
assessment appears to have stood the test of time. It might well be said that the
visit of the British Association for the Advancement of Science, which brought
Petrie and O'Curry to Aran in 1857 and which marks a pivotal event in the
history of Aran, would not have occurred but for Petrie having visited Aran in
1821 and published descriptions of the place that drew new attention to it, particularly from antiquarian and scholarly quarters.

There is no record of Petrie collecting music during his first visit, perhaps
because of his lack of Irish or because he did not have his violin with him or
both. In 1857, however, he brought his violin with him. In doing so, he signaled his intent to capitalize on O'Curry's company and collect music there.

O'Curry was probably just as motivated to collect music in Aran as he had been in Dublin.

Petrie and O'Curry's motives for collecting music in Aran should be understood in the context of the contemporary fascination with islands.[50] Inspired by utopianism and Romantic ideals of cultural purity among peasants, antiquarians were attracted to islands because they believed their relative isolation impeded unwanted cultural assimilation of outside lifestyles, cultures, and language and preserved an older, more authentic way of life. J. W. O'Connell highlights the special relationship between Aran and this contemporary perspective: "The Aran Islands offered a perfect example of a people and culture that had remained apparently untouched by what many were now starting to describe as the 'defects' of a too-cultivated civilisation."[51] The notion of Aran as a cultural sanctuary must have motivated Petrie and O'Curry to collect traditional music there. The potential for a relatively unadulterated musical culture, protected by Aran's islandness, would certainly have attracted Petrie.

Petrie and O'Curry's motives should also be understood in the context of the relationship between Aran and contemporary antiquarianism, a movement that dominated intellectual life in Ireland for much of the nineteenth century. In the built and natural landscape of Aran, many nineteenth-century antiquarians saw the apparent permanence of ancient stonework and the continuity of the cultivation of soil amidst stone as expressions of man's triumph of survival over the forces of nature in a wild and remote place. Together, the singularities of nineteenth-century Aran—the Irish language, the people's costume, their ancient currachs, and their Gaelic culture—suggested to antiquarians that a unique, different, ancient, and stable community, a singular identity, inhabited the place. They imagined the local inhabitants as a stoic community descended directly from those who created the monuments and churches so abundant around them. The theme of resilience resonated with the contemporary air of romantic nationalism, and antiquarians interpreted Aran and its archaeological and cultural wealth as emblematic of precolonial Gaelic Ireland. The integrity of this image of Aran rested not least on Aran's islandness but also on its geographical and cultural remoteness from urban, industrialized, and modernized centers, especially Dublin where many of the antiquarian authorities on Aran were based. Nonetheless, Aran was like the rest of rural Ireland, subject to change, and the antiquarian urge to document and so preserve its archaeological and cultural wealth was an acknowledgment of that fact.

In creating their transcriptions of the music of Aran, Petrie and O'Curry were undoubtedly motivated to continue their individual and joint efforts to collect Irish traditional music. Nevertheless, the manner in which Petrie recorded the details of his Aran airs suggests they had other motives too. We have seen that, in comparison with other airs in his music manuscripts, Petrie's Aran airs appear to be exceptionally well identified. Specifically, they list the location, the name of the contributor, the title, and sometimes the exact date of each contribution. Petrie may have recalled this information at a later date in Dublin, which could explain how inaccuracy arises, but his intention to identify the music of Aran so clearly suggests a concern for that music or for the place where it originated or both. In light of the regard Petrie and his compatriots felt for Aran, in light of their interest in the conservation of its built heritage, and in light of their interpretation of Aran as representative of Ireland, the concern Petrie shows for his Aran airs suggests that the music of Aran may have represented to him, if not to O'Curry too, the music of precolonial Gaelic Ireland or, at the very least, the music of an older form of native Irish culture. Their attempt to collect traditional music in Aran might, therefore, be interpreted as an attempt to preserve Aran and, thereupon, Ireland.

It is possible that the care with which Petrie identified his Aran airs simply indicates that he found time to document them with greater attention than was afforded to other airs in his collection. It may also simply reflect the esteem in which he held the performers and their music. Considering the contexts in which they operated, it seems more likely that, in Aran, Petrie and O'Curry were ultimately engaged in a search for identity and difference: a native Irish identity that was different from urban, industrialized Dublin. This motive explains the color and content of their Aran collection, which focuses, as we shall see later, on Irish-language song and, to a lesser extent, on traditional dance tunes and eschews English-language songs, which were almost certainly sung in Aran in the mid-nineteenth century.[52]

THE ARAN FIELD TRIP

The visit to Aran by the British Association for the Advancement of Science was organized by the group leader Sir William Wilde, who was president of the association's ethnological section. Wilde wanted to put Aran on the historical pedestal he felt it deserved by enabling as many antiquarians and scholars as possible to acquaint themselves with its archaeological riches.[53] He also hoped that such a large scholarly gathering would impress upon islanders the national and international significance of the ruins among which they lived, because up until the excursion of 1857, local attitudes toward the ruined forts and other stone structures amounted to indifference or superstition. He chose the impressive Bronze Age stone fort Dún Aonghusa as the pantheon in which to stage the climax of the event—an open-air banquet on the edge of a three-hundred-foot sheer cliff overlooking the expanses of Galway Bay and the Atlantic Ocean—because he was particularly concerned for the fort itself, which was showing signs of damage where islanders had been engaged in hunting for rabbits to eat. While the spectacular nature of the site impressed the antiquarian visitors, the speeches given at the banquet in English, Irish, and French appear to have won over the islanders: by the late nineteenth century, they were working under the stewardship of the Office of Public Works on the restoration of the damaged archaeological ruins of Aran, including Dún Aonghusa.[54] It is unclear whether Petrie or O'Curry played specific roles on this excursion. They were then around sixty-seven and sixty-three years of age, respectively. It is likely that they participated because they supported Wilde's vision for the archaeology of Aran. As two of the most eminent scholars present, they undoubtedly lent gravitas to the occasion too.

In an atmosphere of exploration and discovery (and fine weather), Petrie and O'Curry prolonged their visit to Aran in order to indulge their interest in documenting subjects of antiquarian interest, including Irish traditional music. While most of the seventy antiquarians left Árainn two days later, on September 5, at least seven of them—Ferguson, Burton, Petrie, O'Curry, and William, Whitley, and Margaret Stokes—stayed behind. Ferguson and William Stokes both summoned their wives, families, and a servant with a "well-stocked hamper" to join them in a "roomy cottage" they had secured.[55] For a fortnight, they sketched, described, and so recorded the island's archaeological remains by day, and by night Petrie and O'Curry collected music and songs from the islanders. William Stokes recalled that the spirit of the whole occasion made it "a time of great enjoyment."[56]

> In the autumn of 1857 it was the writer's privilege to spend a fortnight in the Islands of Aran along with Petrie and several of his friends, when he often accompanied him in his search after the old Irish music, of which not less than twenty-eight airs were collected. It will be well to describe the method by which the airs

were obtained. Inquiries having been made as to the names of persons "who had music," that is who were known as possessing and singing some of the old airs, an appointment was made with one or two of them to meet the members of the party at some cottage near to the little village of Kilronan, which was their head-quarters.

To this cottage, when evening fell, Petrie, with his manuscript music-book and violin, and always accompanied by his friend O'Curry, used to proceed. Nothing could exceed the strange picturesqueness of the scenes which night after night were thus presented. On approaching the house, always lighted up by a blazing turf fire, it was seen surrounded by the islanders, while its interior was crowded with figures, the rich colours of whose dresses, heightened by the fire-light, showed with a strange vividness and variety, while their fine countenances were all animated with curiosity and pleasure. It would have required a Rembrandt to paint the scene. The minstrel—sometimes an old woman—sometimes a beautiful girl, or a young man—was seated on a low stool in the chimney-corner, while chairs for Petrie and O'Curry were placed opposite; the rest of the crowded audience remained standing. The song having been given, O'Curry wrote the Irish words, when Petrie's work began. The singer recommenced, stopping at a signal from him at every two or three bars of the melody to permit the writing of the notes, and often repeating the passage until it was correctly taken down, and then going on with the melody, exactly from the point where the singing was interrupted. The entire air being at last obtained, the singer—a second time—was called to give the song continuously, and when all corrections had been made, the violin—an instrument of great sweetness and power—was produced, and the air played as Petrie alone could play it, and often repeated. Never was the inherent love of music among the Irish people more shown than on this occasion; they listened with deep attention, while their heartfelt pleasure was expressed, less by exclamations than by gestures; and when the music ceased, a general and murmured conversation, in their own language, took place, which would continue until the next song was commenced.[57]

That Petrie and O'Curry should go to some lengths to find the best sources of music and songs—those "who had music," as Stokes put it—is unsurprising; in Dublin, Petrie had often drawn on authoritative sources like Tadhg Mac Mathúna and Mary Madden.[58] In this effort, they were no different from other collectors. They were kept relatively busy during the first few days or nights in

Árainn between September 7 and 10. As the novelty wore off, fewer people
came to contribute, and the collecting finally finished on September 19.

THE SINGERS

It is supremely difficult to retrieve information about individual islanders in
the nineteenth century, but one islander named Patrick Mullen of Cill Rónáin
made such an impression on Petrie and O'Curry and their contemporaries
that he emerges from the shadows of anonymity to become a presence in this
story. Mullen is identified in a number of sources as "the guide and antiquary of
the island."[59] Indeed, his services were retained by the 1857 party. Given the
amount of contact he had with the islands' most illustrious contemporary visitors, it is likely that he spoke both English and Irish. Being bilingual would have
made him an ideal candidate to act, as he did, as the antiquarians' emissary.[60]
He was the only islander invited to speak at the banquet in Dún Aonghusa:
"Paddy Mullin, the Guide, was then called on, and made a short speech in Irish,
very much to the purpose. He reminded his fellow-islanders that for the sake
of their honour as well as their interest, they should endeavour to preserve
their ruins."[61] Mullen was also a singer, Lady Ferguson recalls. Her revealing
anecdote about him merits its unabridged inclusion here:

> Our Aran guide, Paddy Mullan, at a subsequent period finding himself out of
> health, felt that he would do well to consult Dr Stokes. He got in a friend's boat to
> the mainland, and walked thence to Dublin, and presented himself at Ferguson's
> house. Here he was invited to take up his abode while under Dr Stokes's treatment.
> He got on well in the kitchen, from whence sounds of hilarity frequently were
> heard, both song and laughter. On his restoration to health, a purse was made up
> for him to pay his travelling expenses, and weighty bundle of garments contrib-
> uted by those who had been under his guidance on Aran. We found subsequently
> that he had saved the money, and had walked all the way to Galway, and on reach-
> ing Kilronan—his native village—had described our hospitality in such glowing
> colours—"lashin's and lavings" were among the terms employed—that another
> islander appeared on the scene, who had walked to Dublin to seek employment.[62]

Given Mullen's resourcefulness, his ability as a singer, and his apparent amia-
bility, his role as local guide to the antiquarians is likely to have extended to
assisting Petrie and O'Curry in their search for people "who had music."

The other men who contributed music were James Gill, Pat Folan, Pat O'Malley, Peter Mullin, Peter Cooke, and John Dubhany (Devaney) of Casla, Conamara, who was possibly a visiting boatman, potentially the skipper of the boat the antiquarians had hired. The women were Mary O'Malley, Mary O'Donoghue, and Mary O'Flaherty, who was married to one John Dillane. We have little information on these performers. Both Petrie and O'Curry noted their names and Petrie sometimes noted their location or origin ("Arran-More") as well as the title and date of their contribution. Though the pair based their collecting work in a cottage near or in the village of Cill Rónáin, islanders may very well have traveled from other villages to perform for them or from the neighboring islands of Inis Meáin and Inis Oírr, of which Petrie and O'Curry visited at least one if not both of them.[63] I tried and failed to identify the contributors by consulting censuses and marriage and baptismal records. There are also few clues as to the standard of performance, but judging by the volume of their contributions, Mary O'Donoghue and Mary O'Malley were probably good performers. Both women gave seven airs or songs each, and some of their airs had a wide range of pitch and were more difficult to sing. The quality and quantity of their contributions combine to suggest that these women were particularly able performers.

THE COLLECTION

Thirty-four airs from Petrie's manuscripts have thus far been identified as being from Aran, but of the ten O'Curry song transcriptions Dáibhí Ó Cróinín uncovered in Leipzig, I could match only six of them satisfactorily with accompanying airs.[64] This suggests that Petrie and O'Curry collected more than thirty-four airs and songs. In a letter to his friend Kuno Meyer written some decades later, Whitley Stokes remembered Aran in 1857: "There were as many folksongs and folk melodies as wild flowers."[65] His picturesque hyperbole prompts us to question just how many songs and airs Petrie and O'Curry collected in Aran over a fortnight.

The tune titles that appear in Petrie's manuscripts were translated from Irish to English by O'Curry. The question of the accuracy of those translations is discussed later in this chapter. Without an encyclopedic knowledge of sean-nós song, it is difficult to identify what songs they collected from the English titles of the airs alone. A title like "The Enchanted Valley" (D.824) might be "An Gleann Draíochta" or "An Gleann Sí." Some imaginative investigation into the English titles alone has thus far yielded the identity of four songs that appear to have been sung in Aran in 1857: "Dónal Ó Dálaigh" ("Donnell O'Daly" D.724); "Gleanntaí Mhac Cochláin" ("O'Coghlan has a glen" D.702); "Séamas Ó Murchú" ("Alas that I'm not a freechaun on the mountainside" D.700); and Antoine Ó Raiftearaí's "An Ciníneach" ("We'll Drink the Health of Keenan" D.534).

The recent and timely appearance of the O'Curry manuscripts was the key to solving the puzzle of the remaining English titles in Petrie's manuscripts. Combining O'Curry's text "Tógfaidh mé mo sheólta go dubhcheodhúch ar maidin" (p. 131) with Petrie's air "I will raise my sail black mistfully in the morning" (D.1009), for example, confirmed the identity of the air and the song.[66] Today, it is known as "Tógfaidh mé mo sheolta go Dúiche Sheoigheach ar maidin," which translates as "I will raise my sails toward the Joyce Country in the morning."[67] The difference between the titles is understandable because, in the Aran dialect, "go dubhcheodhúch" and "go Dúiche Sheoigheach" can sound alike.[68] It is unclear whether the difference is an example of the dynamic variation that occurs in orally transmitted cultures or an example of how collectors can misinterpret and then misrepresent what they hear.[69]

Collating the manuscripts also showed up some errors, usually on the part of Petrie, who was communicating via translation from Irish to English and whose manuscripts contain more information on individual performances. His manuscripts are thus statistically more likely to contain errors. Looking again at the question of song titles, the air that accompanies the song "Má Bhímse Beo in Éirinn" (p. 130) was left without a title, and Deasy later took a title from a variant from another source and named it "Gaily we went and gaily we came" (D.1317).[70] Petrie had incorrectly attributed the translated title "If I'm alive in Ireland" to a different tune (D.1300) and to a different singer (Peter Cooke). The task of reuniting the texts and the airs helped identify the error and reinstate the air's correct identity—"Má Bhímse Beo in Éirinn" or "If I'm alive in Ireland" sung by James Gill (D.1317) (see appendix 1).

It is conceivable that, from 1855 until his death, Petrie continued to forward music to his publishers with a view to publishing more volumes of music.[71] In any case, his Aran airs were not published until 1877, and even then, Francis Hoffmann's book of piano arrangements of Irish airs contained only fifteen of them.[72] A lack of time and his age may have prevented Petrie from publishing his Aran airs before he died in 1866.

Petrie and O'Curry's collection appears to be a faithful representation of contemporary music making in Aran. Dominated, as it is, by Irish-language song and holding a small number of dance tunes, it reflects the contemporary reality of a poverty-stricken population that could little afford musical instruments and for whom Irish was the vernacular. In light of the contextual information gathered here, however, the representation created by Petrie and O'Curry emerges as a partisan Irish antiquarian record of music in Aran in the nineteenth century. The absence of English-language song from the collection confirms this bias. English-language song was almost certainly sung in Aran at the time, but because it did not interest Petrie or O'Curry, because it did not meet the needs of their music-collecting work in Aran, there was little chance that they would have documented its occurrence there. In fact, any English-language songs that might have been part of the contemporary repertoire in Aran are likely to have been neglected by the majority of those who documented life in Aran in the nineteenth century, a majority that was primarily interested in and concerned for the native elements of Aran culture, especially Gaelic or Irish-language elements. Nonetheless, as the questioning of the absence of English-language song from Petrie and O'Curry's Aran collection ultimately amounts to conjecture, so the value of their collection, which provides an unrivaled opportunity to assess the state of Irish traditional music in the Aran Islands in the mid-nineteenth century with some accuracy, remains intact.

ASSESSMENT OF THE TRANSCRIPTIONS

The following assessment of the transcriptions is based on a preliminary examination of the manuscripts and not on a complete paleographic study, which is beyond the scope of this investigation. O'Curry's transcriptions appear free of blotted errors, suggesting the Leipzig and Dublin manuscripts are not the original transcriptions. Looking at the song "Tógfaidh mé mo sheólta go dubhcheodhúch ar maidin" (p. 131), the use of "dham" and "dom" in the line "A's ní léir dham na bóithre, atáid na deora dom dhalladh" suggests that O'Curry transcribed some words phonetically. He follows such phoneticisms with explanatory notes: for instance, he deciphers "sían" as "sidheán" and "duibhicain" as "dubh-aigéin" or "black abyss" (his translation).

Two different translated titles emerge for "Tógfaidh mé mo sheólta go dubhcheodhúch ar maidin" (p. 131). Petrie's manuscript gives "I will raise my sail black mistfully in the morning" (D.1009), but O'Curry's own manuscript in the RIA gives "I shall raise up my sails, black-gloomy in the morning."[73] Indeed, O'Curry translates the whole of the first verse in this manuscript. It is presented here along with his Irish transcriptions from both the Leipzig and the Dublin manuscripts so that we might assess his style of transcription.

> Tógfaidh mé mo sheólta, go dúbhcheodhúch ar maidin
> Ar cuaird go mo mhíle stóirín a's go deó deó ní chasfad;
> Mar do gheall mé go bpógfainn a rós-bhéilín meala,
> A's ní léir dham na bóithre, atáid na deora dom dhalladh.
>
> (UBL NL 291/634, 131)

> Tógfaidh mé mo sheólta go dubhcheódhach ar maidin,
> Ar cuaird ag mo mhíle stóirín, is go deó deó ní chasfad;
> Do gheall mé go bpógfainn a rós-bhéilín meala,
> Is ní léir damh na bóithre, táid na deóra dam dhalla.

> I shall raise up my sails, black-gloomy in the morning,
> To visit my thousand storeens, and never, never to return
> I promised that I would kiss her rose-honeyed mouth
> And I perceive not the roads, for the tears are me blinding.
>
> (Dublin, RIA, 12 N 5, 178)

O'Curry's translation for Petrie—"I will raise my sail black mistfully in the morning"—was potentially created immediately, in the field, as they listened to the song. It is a more direct translation than "I shall raise up my sails, black-gloomy in the morning." For one thing, "I will" seems a literate translation as compared with the more literary "I shall." Moreover, O'Curry could have chosen to write "black-gloomy" in response to the melancholy of the song, he having come to that understanding of the term "go dubhcheodhúch" later, after some consideration of the meaning of the song, possibly after their return from Aran. This interpretation of O'Curry's different translations suggests that the Leipzig manuscript is older than the Dublin manuscript. The changes applied to the Dublin version of the verse—including the removal of aspirated syllables including "mar" and "a"—support this assessment. At the very least, the double translation of the term "go dubhcheodhúch" confirms that the term O'Curry heard in Aran was "go dubhcheodhúch" and not "Dúiche Sheóigheach" as occurs in other versions of the song. If "go dubhcheodhúch" represents a misinterpretation of "Dúiche Sheóigheach," it is an artful one that adds to the emotion of the song. Overall, O'Curry's translation of this verse seems direct and considered. In it, he preserves the structure of the expression and the meaning of the song. This glimpse of O'Curry's style of translating songs from Irish into English confirms that the English titles he provided to Petrie are of some use when trying to establish the original Irish titles of Petrie's airs. It combines with his relatively detailed annotations and with Burton's sketch to suggest that he was thoughtful and careful in his song collecting.

In her edition of Petrie's airs, Deasy made grammatical changes to key and time signatures where necessary, but she found the "majority of changes" that she made to his transcriptions were "of a rhythmic nature."[74] As the most recognizable of the thirty-four airs, "Táimse i mo Chodladh" (D.560) presents a ready example of how Petrie's training as a classical musician led him to impose Western art music sensibilities on the traditional music he transcribed. At the time, most Irish traditional music thrived on oral transmission, and most of its practitioners would not have gained musical literacy. To this day, the free and individualistic style of sean-nós singing in particular, to which "Táimse i mo Chodladh" belongs, often resists accurate transcription. With "Táimse i mo Chodladh," Petrie applied a $\frac{3}{4}$ time signature and bar lines to his transcription that straitjacket what was more likely to have been a much freer air. Similarly, the natural arcs of the airs D.569, D.1266, D.1331, and D.1358 all seem to conflict with the barlines of Petrie's settings.

Questions relating to Petrie's representation of tonality also arise. Deasy found "doubtful notes in the melody" and ignored changes introduced by him "except where: (a) they appear to be an improvement on the original or (b) provide a good alternative in which case the alternative is given after the tune."[75] Deasy questioned the tonality and thus the transcription of the song "I will raise my sail black, mistfully in the morning" (D.1009)—specifically the appearance throughout of atypical major sevenths (D♯) in a minor mode (E minor)—by placing a natural sign followed by a question mark over each D♯. In 1975 Breandán Breathnach severely criticized Petrie's "lack of understanding" of the tonalities of Irish traditional music: "Enthusiasm he had in abundance but his knowledge of the music, as exemplified in his editorial comments, is largely encompassed in the word, sentiment, which he appeared unable to desist from using; and his strictures on pipers for their ignorance of the major and minor modes betray a lack of understanding of even the basic elements of the music. Without O'Curry's transcription and notes, Petrie's volumes would be somewhat of a curiosity, affording us an insight into the social and political sentiments of its compiler."[76]

We await the potential appearance of accompanying notes relating to Aran by either O'Curry or Petrie to provide more conclusive evidence of their opinions of tonality, rhythm, and other features of contemporary Aran music. Petrie's manipulated transcriptions do not lend themselves easily to an analysis of musical style (some would argue no transcription can). Also, modern aesthetics will no doubt color any interpretation of his transcriptions. Nevertheless, the pairing of six of the song texts O'Curry collected with their accompanying airs as noted by Petrie that is presented in appendix 1 allows us to assess, with a degree of fairness, Petrie's attempts to transcribe the rhythm of traditional airs. The six restored songs demonstrate how O'Curry's song texts helped Petrie notate rhythmic values correctly. The vowel sounds of O'Curry's texts appear to meet longer notes in Petrie's airs, giving the melodic lines a singing quality. Therefore, although Petrie is criticized for altering his transcribed melodies, in particular for changing the modality of airs, his attention to rhythm, highlighted here and by Deasy, appears to have been hard won and, in the case of the six restored songs from Aran, somewhat successful.[77]

chapter 2

Séamus Ennis and *Amhráin as Árainn*

On Tuesday, August 28, 1945, Séamus Ennis spent the morning updating his fieldwork diary and mending his shoe. Having spent a frustrating week in Árainn, he had resolved to intensify his efforts to collect the music of Aran for the Irish Folklore Commission. After a lunchtime swim at Port Mhuirbhigh near his lodgings in Fearann a' Choirce, he walked six miles to Cill Éinne in the east end of the island in search of a well-known singer named Tomás "Tyrell" Ó Briain. There his tenacity was rewarded. His meeting with Tyrell, his sister Máirín, and her daughter Máire marks the turning point of his time in Aran:

> Bhí eolas agam 'sa teach agus cuiriú síos tae domh ar a' bpoínnte. Cúpla óráin dhe chuid Chaoidheáin aduairt mé oidhche an chéilidhe 29-6-'45 i gCill Rónáin b'éigin dom iad a rádh aríst dób anois mar bhí Máire agus a máthair (Máire eile) an-mhór 'n-a ndiaidh.
>
> Ach ó ba oncail "Tyrell" seo go Mháire (dreithiúr [deartháir] g'á máthair) ní rabh agam ach fios a chur amach air. Chua' Máire amach ghá thóraíocht agus dhiún dhá chraic go ra' sé isteach in-éindigh léithe.
>
> Feairín beag ciúin é Tyrell, stúmpa beag, gan mórán déanamh air, a chuid éadaigh gan a bheith righte air agus caipín anuas ar a shúile nach rabh aon bhlas nuaichte a' pléidhe leis. Croimbéal beag dorcha air agus loinnir an tsuilt in-a shúile (c. 60).
>
> Ní ra' sé bhfad 'n-a dhia' sin go ndeacha muid a' cárdáil órán, agus ní rabh an fear is fearr a casú ariamh liom níos sásta ná "Tyrell" ghá gcur india' a chéile. 'S é chaoi mbeadh dúil aige mé fanacht go maidin a' cárdáil leis agus ba dh' é a

fhearacht ag a dhreithiúir [dheirfiúr] é agus ag Máire óg. Bhí glór binn aige agus thaithneochadh liom a bheith ag éisteacht leis agus a' scrí' uaidh. Maidir le Máire óg, feicthear dhom gur feabhsuighthe atá sí ó chualas cheana í. Bhí sí fhéin agus a máthair agus "Tyrell" a' cuimhniú ar óráin agus ar phíosa beaga fánacha suimiúla go dtí go rabh liosta beag deas breacaithe agam uathab agus cupla ceann scríobhtha. Ar a h-aon ar maidin a d'fhágas an teach agus bhí mé an-bhuidheach ar fad go'n triúr seo. Shíltheá nach rabh tada ar domhan uathab ach congnamh a thóirt dom-sa oiread 's fhéadfaidís. Bhí fear a' tighe [Maidhcilín Ó Dioráin] ó bhaile 'sa "Webster" agus bhí drithiúr óg eile le Máire [Bríd] amuigh a' cuartaidheacht. Gaedhilge uilig atá 'sa teach sin agus ins gchuile theach i gCill Éinne, cé is moite dhe thrí chinn creidim a bhfuil daoiní pósta íonntab as tír amuigh.

Rinne mé mo shé mhíle siar go Fearann a' Choirce gan stróbh, agus mé sásta go dtugas cuaird ar Árainn, rud nach rabhas go dtí anocht.[1]

[I was known to the household and tea was put on for me immediately. A few of [Colm] Ó Caoidheán's songs I said the night of the *céilí* 29-6-'45 in Cill Rónáin I had to say them again for them now because Máire and her mother (another Máire) were very much after them.

But seeing as this "Tyrell" was Máire's uncle (her mother's brother) all I had to do was to summon him. Máire went out looking for him and before long he was in with her.

Tyrell is a quiet little man, small, stumpy, slightly built, his clothes loose on him and an old cap down over his eyes. A small dark moustache on him and the twinkle of fun in his eyes (c. 60).

It was not long after that that we went carding songs, and the best man I ever met was never happier than "Tyrell" putting them after each other. It was the way that he desired me to stay until morning singing song after song with him and it was like that with his sister and young Máire. He had a sweet voice and I liked listening to him and writing from him. As for young Máire, I see that she has improved since I heard her before. Herself and her mother and "Tyrell" were remembering songs and other little stray interesting pieces until I had noted a nice little list from them and had written a few. At one in the morning I left the house and I was most grateful to these three. You would think that they wanted nothing more in the world than to help me as much as they could. The man of the house [Maidhcilín Ó Dioráin] was away on the "Webster" and another young sister of Máire's [Bríd] was out visiting.[2] It is all Gaelic [spoken] in that house and in every house in Cill Éinne, except for three houses I believe in which there are people from the mainland who married into them.

I made my six miles west to Fearann a' Choirce without exertion, happy to have visited Árainn, which I was not until tonight.]

Over the course of four days, Ennis transcribed fourteen songs from Tyrell (1890–1962). It was the largest selection he got from a single performer in Aran and is particularly valuable because it represents one of only three known records of Tyrell's singing (see appendix 3).[3] Nevertheless, Ennis's entire collection of "Songs from Aran" ("Amhráin as Árainn," as he titled them) is not without its anomalies or absences (see appendix 4). He makes no mention, for instance, of Tyrell's older brother Pádraigín (1889–1979) or his younger brother Antaine (1902–89), both of whom were singers, nor does he mention that Tyrell and Antaine, and Pádraigín too, were song makers. Antaine may or may not have begun to compose songs by this time, but by 1935 the brothers had together composed "Amhrán an Dole" (The Song of the Dole)—also known as "Amhrán na Feola" (The Song of the Meat)—a song that Ennis failed to collect or that Tyrell neglected to share with him.[4] Furthermore, Ennis was apparently unaware that in the summer of 1934 Tyrell and Antaine had collaborated with Irish film director Norris Davidson to make a short, now lost, sound film titled *Damhsa Árann* or *Aran Dance*, an opposition piece to Robert Flaherty's *Man of Aran*; Tyrell served as assistant director and Antaine sang in the film. Contextualizing the encounter between the fifty-five-year-old islander and the twenty-six-year-old music collector from County Dublin (fig. 5), who went on to become one of the most celebrated figures in Irish traditional music, raises questions about Ennis's Aran collection—one of the earliest substantial sources of the music of Aran in the twentieth century—and about his work in general.

The collecting work that Séamus Ennis did for the Irish Folklore Commission (IFC) has been scrutinized to varying degrees by a number of commentators, including Mícheál Briody, Christopher J. Smith, and Ríonach uí Ógáin, and has been the subject of various radio and television programs.[5] Nevertheless, only uí Ógáin has conducted a detailed examination of Ennis's interaction with his contributors and with the places where he collected for the IFC. Her editions of Ennis's field diaries—the second being an English translation of the first, Irish-language edition—contextualize his outstanding achievements as a

FIGURE 5. Séamus Ennis transcribing from Colm Ó Caodháin, Glinsce, Carna, Co. Galway, 1945, M010.01.00017. Courtesy of the National Folklore Collection.

music collector for the IFC and present Ennis's own almost day-by-day account of his fieldwork during the formative years of his professional career. Where uí Ógáin's editions of Ennis's field diary contextualize his account of his work in Aran, this chapter presents a closer analysis of that work and considers its contribution to our understanding of the entirety of Ennis's work, of the music of Aran, and of Irish traditional music in general. The only comparable analysis is uí Ógáin's detailed study of Ennis's collaboration with his most celebrated contributor, Colm Ó Caodháin.[6] Valuable as it is, that analysis is of limited use because their outstanding collaboration is an exceptional example and does not reflect the variety of Ennis's experiences of music collecting for the IFC.[7] The analysis of Ennis's Aran collection presented here, which discusses a more everyday example of the collecting work he did for the IFC, enables us to question the ordinary in light of the extraordinary and so to understand better the full spectrum of Ennis's achievements, from his failures to his successes to his triumphs, and how they have impacted on Irish traditional music.

Produced under the auspices of the IFC, the representation that Ennis generated in his Aran collection was molded not just by the creator and his contributors but also by the policies and principles of that institution. There follows a short explication of the formation of the IFC—a more comprehensive account of which can be found in Mícheál Briody's 2007 book *The Irish Folklore Commission, 1935–1970: History, Ideology, Methodology*—and of its relationship with Irish traditional music. This chapter considers how the needs and the prerogatives of the IFC influenced Ennis's collecting in Aran. It introduces Ennis, his background, how he came to be a music collector for the IFC, and how he came to collect in Aran. It analyzes the work he did there and details his involvement with the music of Aran afterward (see appendix 2). It considers how Ennis engaged with other music collectors and reflects on the implications of those liaisons for traditional music. It concludes with some remarks on the necessity of further engagement with Séamus Ennis and his outstanding contribution to Irish traditional music.

THE IRISH FOLKLORE COMMISSION AND IRISH TRADITIONAL MUSIC

When the Irish Free State was established in 1922 in the wake of a decade of critical social, political, and economic unrest—including the Dublin Lockout of 1913, World War I of 1914–18, the Easter Rising of 1916, the War of Independence of 1919–21, and the Civil War of 1922–23—one of the priorities of the new government was the cultivation of a sense of national identity. The task was complicated by a number of political and cultural factors, including the disputed partition of the island of Ireland; the existence of many different religions and denominations, most notably Protestantism, alongside the Catholic majority; the existence of two languages—colonial English and native Irish—

not to mention dialects such as Ulster Scots and cant; and the fact that the majority of the population was based in rural and not urban areas. Amid these pluralities, the state chose to adopt many of the Gaelic League's policies in relation to identity, language, and culture. In choosing this particular ideological path, the Free State government indicated that it sought to cultivate a national identity for a new postcolonial era that was based on an old notion of a truly native Ireland, a Gaelic Ireland.

Of all the policies the state adopted from the Gaelic League, the most ambitious was the extension of Irish as a spoken tongue throughout the entire country. This policy manifested itself ultimately more in rhetoric than in action. The government exhibited a largely positive and often sympathetic attitude toward the Irish language, but constructive steps toward resurrecting Irish in areas where it had been lost, or toward supporting the typically economically deprived areas where Irish was still the vernacular, were rarely taken.[8] As the language continued to decline, the dream of a postcolonial restoration of a Gaelic Ireland faded, and state policy in relation to the Irish language shifted from salvation to salvage.

The Free State's focus on the Irish language was a boon to the folklore of Ireland. Mícheál Briody explains how folklore was enrolled in the project of rebuilding the nation:

> When the Folklore of Ireland Society was founded in 1927, the Irish Free State had no national collection or archive of folk traditions. This did not place it in an anomalous position when viewed from the perspective of Europe as a whole, as no such archive existed anywhere in Britain or in Northern Ireland, and on the Continent archives of folk tradition were, for the most part, only to be found in northern Europe, particularly in Scandinavia and the Baltic States. However, viewed from an Irish perspective, the situation appeared to certain people quite different. Ireland was believed to possess a folk tradition, particularly in the Irish language, incomparable in its richness to anywhere else in western Europe, with the exception of Gaelic Scotland, and relatively little Irish folklore had been collected up to that time. Furthermore, the fact that Irish was in rapid decline as a spoken language meant that unless something was done soon to initiate extensive collecting the bulk of these traditions would be lost for ever.
>
> The Folklore of Ireland Society, established in 1927, endeavoured to make a last-minute effort to save as much of the riches of Irish folklore for posterity

before they were irretrievably lost. .... Efforts by [Séamus] Ó Duilearga and fellow members of the Folklore of Ireland Society to get state support for the mammoth task of collecting systematically the folklore of Ireland within a few years bore fruit, and in less than twenty years the South of Ireland would be able to boast of possessing one of the largest folklore collections in the world, assembled by the Irish Folklore Commission.[9]

It was on the back of the government's policy in relation to the Irish language that the Irish Folklore Commission first received government support. Founded in 1935, the IFC was envisaged by the government as a vehicle through which it could advance its policy of preserving, if not restoring, Irish traditions. Nevertheless, while government officials saw the work of the IFC as "a source for linguistic and cultural regeneration," the staff of the IFC believed they were creating "a resource for international scholarship."[10] The scholarly motive often challenged the comprehension of officials who held the government's purse strings and who questioned what they interpreted as the inefficiency of the IFC's exhaustive methodology of folkloristics.

With regard to Irish traditional music, the Board of the Commission understood that it was—as stated in the terms of reference—part of the "oral and written folklore" of the country, which it hoped to collect, collate, catalog, and possibly edit and publish.[11] But, as Briody observes, although the director of the IFC, Séamus Ó Duilearga, or James Hamilton Delargy (1899–1980) from Antrim, "had referred to the need to collect folk song in his memorandum to [Éamon] de Valera in May 1933, the Terms of Reference of the Commission made no explicit mention of folk song nor folk music."[12] It was not until late August 1938 that the IFC finally acquired confirmation of the government's support for the Commission to extend its activities to include folk music and song. Considering that traditional music was then such a vital part of traditional culture and folklore, this initial "oversight" by the Commission—as Briody suspects it to be—may surprise some people; it is certainly a surprising oversight by León Ó Broin (1902–90), the man who drafted the Terms of Reference, because he had a lifelong and wide interest in music.[13] It represents an example of the ways in which contemporary rhetoric about the merits of cultivating and preserving Irish culture abounded but did not always translate into action.[14]

In the same year that the Commission was founded, another unfortunate and more destructive neglect of traditional music at a national level occurred when the Public Dance Halls Act was passed. This act effectively ended house dances throughout Ireland. Briody believes there is "surely more than irony" in the fact that the IFC was founded in the same year that the act was passed.[15] The act was intended to "control the countryside."[16] While it certainly introduced into the informal practice of dancing a new notion of authority—within their parishes, many Catholic priests infamously took it upon themselves to exercise a perceived moral authority in relation to communal dancing—in actuality the act was not intended to ban communal dancing. Its negative impact on the practice of traditional music and dance was simply not foreseen when the legislation was being drafted and ratified.[17] The passing of the Public Dance Halls Act was simply another contemporary oversight in relation to traditional music. It is another example of the ways in which contemporary rhetoric about the merits of cultivating and preserving Irish culture, even in the face of its destruction, rarely translated into action. Nonetheless, the Public Dance Halls Act dealt such a devastating blow to the fabric of rural life in Ireland that Briody is rightly compelled to question the inaction of those who witnessed its negative impact and who were potentially in a position to do something about it: "One might have expected bodies such as the Folklore of Ireland Society, the Irish Folklore Institute, and the Irish Folklore Commission to have warned of the possible effects of this Act on the culture of rural Ireland, or to have appealed for it to be amended when the negative consequences of the Act should have been clear to all. As far as I am aware, none of these bodies appealed to the authorities on behalf of 'the country people.' For the most part an older world was what they were interested in."[18]

This assessment of the attitudes of the IFC and its related bodies is revealing and particularly relevant to traditional music. At the time, as most of the population of Ireland lived in rural areas, traditional music, song, and dance were arguably the most popular forms of entertainment in the country. The IFC was not, however, concerned with what was most popular nor was it concerned with what was current unless it related directly to the past.[19] Instead, the IFC was chiefly concerned with what was old and endangered. The Commission's director, James Delargy, vividly captured this attitude in this often-quoted analogy: "As I saw it as I got to grow older, especially when I went to the Aran Islands in 1919 and took folktales down there in Inis Meáin, but particularly in Kerry, I realized that the old house was on fire, you know, and it was about time some of the furniture was taken out before the whole thing went up."[20] Delargy delivered another, similar analogy when he recalled sailing back to Ireland after a tour of the Nordic countries, an analogy he may have first encountered in those jurisdictions: "I went right out to the bow and I saw the Irish hills. That is a long time ago—1928—and I said 'the tradition of Ireland is behind those hills and we've got to rescue it before it's trampled into the dirt' . . . because it was a jewel of great price and one had to see that it was given a refuge and an appreciation by the Irish people."[21] The notion of rescuing, which was a common motive in contemporary folkloristics, is echoed in the motto that appears on every issue of *Béaloideas*, the journal of the Folklore of Ireland Society: "Colligite quae superaverunt fragmenta ne pereant" (Gather up what fragments remain lest they perish). This particular desire to salvage the remains of traditional Irish culture had a major influence on the IFC's conceptual and practical approaches to the preservation of Irish traditional music.

For much of its life, the IFC focused on two separate but related issues: the Irish language and folk texts. The focus on the Irish language is understandable given the contemporary reality of the decline of the language, the political and cultural implications of that decline, and the responsibility conferred on the IFC to collect and document Irish traditions. The focus on texts can be attributed not least to the focus on language but also to the methodology of study employed by the Commission: namely, the historic-geographic or Finnish method of folkloristics developed by Kaarle Krohn and Antti Aarne. The assimilation of this particular methodology is unsurprising as the collections of the IFC were "amassed at a time when comparative studies were in vogue in folkloristics."[22] The Finnish method "required that as many variants of a particular tale be collected as possible in order to determine the 'proto-tale' (or ur-form) and place of origin."[23] Significantly for traditional song, in this method songs were accepted as folk texts.

Delargy, who was "by any estimation the central figure in Irish folkloristics" from the mid-1920s to his retirement in the early 1970s, shared the chief concerns of the IFC.[24] Crucially for traditional music, however, collecting music "was never his top priority."[25] Instead, his focus was more on the endangered Irish language and on the folktales and traditions contained within it: "For Ó Duilearga, . . . while the presence of survivals added to the intrinsic importance of Ireland as an object of study, this was overshadowed by the tremendous sense of loss he felt at the decline of the Irish language and the rich traditions enshrined in it."[26] In 1933 Delargy revealed that he believed the case of folktales and folklore to be more urgent than the case of traditional music. He wrote: "A good deal of unnecessary material such as Songs, etc. had to be taken down in order to humour the old people and this constituted a certain waste of time."[27] When the IFC's mandate to collect traditional music was confronted with political, financial, and practical obstacles—namely the continuous battle to maintain government support for the work of the Commission, the cost of purchasing "a suitable recording apparatus," and the challenge of finding suitably qualified music collectors—Delargy sometimes displayed a lack of sufficient motivation to overcome them.[28]

There were a number of collectors working for the IFC, including Seán Ó Cróinín (1915–65), who were not charged specifically with collecting music but whose interest in and passion for music offset Delargy's attitude.[29] They contributed a significant collection of music to the IFC archive by transcribing song lyrics or, later, by making sound recordings. Their lack of musical skills and knowledge sometimes affected the quality of their music collections. Their numerous contributions to the IFC collections reveal that Delargy's sense of urgency may have been somewhat confined or even misguided. In the case of Irish song at least, the IFC collections show that, just like folktales and folklore, a wealth of music was disappearing. Many of the songs in the collections are rarely heard today, and others might have been lost forever had they not been transcribed or recorded for the IFC.[30] The memory of that music has survived thanks not just to the appointed music collectors Liam de Noraidh and Séamus Ennis but also to the musically inclined collectors who took it upon themselves to collect traditional music for the IFC.

Unsurprisingly, Delargy's inaction in relation to traditional music frustrated those for whom its preservation was a greater concern, including the following members of the board of the IFC: the song collectors Fionán Mac Coluim (1875–1966) and Fr. Lorcán Ó Muireadhaigh (1883–1941); Séamus Ó Casaide (1877–1943), who was particularly interested in piping and in historical and literary aspects of music; and Éamon Ó Donnchadha (1876–1953), who was especially interested in the song tradition of his native Munster. They frequently tried to pressure Delargy into action, but he "resisted these attempts, feeling that the Commission, with its limited budget, had other priorities."[31] Even when the IFC acquired a mobile recording unit in 1947—which made the task of collecting music in particular much easier technically and far more efficient—"it mainly concentrated on recording samples of tales and lore."[32]

The music collecting done by the IFC's mobile recording unit and, contemporaneously, by Radio Éireann and the BBC may have seemed to alleviate somewhat the IFC's responsibility for preserving traditional music, but as Briody observes, they "simply skimmed the surface" or "sampled tales, lore and song in order to have an acoustic record."[33] It was only a matter of time before Delargy would be urged yet again to appoint a full-time music collector. Consequently, despite the admirable achievements of the music collectors and the musically inclined collectors, as compared with other aspects of traditional culture, the IFC ultimately displayed a level of disregard for traditional music.[34]

In relation to the traditional music that was preserved by the IFC, the focus was more on song lyrics than on melodies or airs, and more on the Gaeltacht than on other parts of Ireland.[35] Considering the political purpose behind the foundation and operation of the IFC, and considering the contemporary emergence of sean-nós singing as a powerful symbol of the Irish nation, it was inevitable that, whatever time the IFC spent on traditional music, much of it would be spent on sean-nós song.[36] Both of the music collectors appointed by Delargy—de Noraidh and Ennis—were fluent Irish speakers, and he encouraged them, and sometimes sent them, to collect in the Gaeltacht where, along with many other folk traditions, songs in Irish were most prevalent. Angela Bourke details the brief given to Ennis: "to collect songs, not tunes alone, but tunes with words to them, and preferably words in Irish."[37] As a result, although the IFC was, in theory at least, concerned with preserving authentic or native Irish traditional music whether instrumental or vocal, that concern extended mostly toward songs in Irish. Instrumental music and songs in English were often overlooked and thus marginalized.[38]

In the end, it is clear that Delargy's priorities became those of the Commission and that traditional music was, consequently, rarely at the top of the IFC's agenda. When he chose to ignore or defer the question of the IFC's responsibility for the collection and preservation of traditional music, Delargy revealed himself to be an Irish folklorist of his time, concerned mainly with the decline of the Irish language and with the resulting disappearance of a wealth of lexicon and lore. Although Irish traditional music was recognized by all concerned as an element of the "oral and written folklore" that the IFC was charged with protecting, it was ultimately marginalized within that institution for want of resources, for want of suitably qualified or interested staff, and for want of some of Delargy's "steely determination," which he chose to apply more to other elements of Irish folklore.[39] It should be noted, however, that the neglect of traditional music by the IFC was due less to disinterest and more to the considerable practical and financial difficulties it faced in trying to appoint suitably qualified music collectors, factors over which the IFC had little control because government funding was limited by a stagnant economy and suitable candidates were almost impossible to find. The IFC and its inconsistent treatment of traditional music emerge as products of their time.

Séamus Ennis

Séamus Ennis (1919–82) is widely recognized as a central figure in the history of Irish traditional music in the twentieth century. His influence on his contemporaries is beyond doubt and continues today via recordings of his music, which have helped to make him "an icon of modern piping"; via the performers whom he guided, including Liam Óg O'Flynn (1945–2018) upon whom Ennis bestowed his uilleann pipes; and via the understandings and narratives of Irish traditional music that he propounded and perpetuated throughout his career and that have since entered the idiom of Irish traditional music.[40] Ríonach uí Ógáin qualifies his achievement in this regard: "In all his endeavours in music he reached high standards, and his collections are a source heavily relied on by students of traditional music."[41]

Breandán Breathnach believed Ennis's legacy as a piper was "his most valued contribution to the cultural life of his country."[42] Indeed, when Na Píobairí Uilleann was founded in 1968 to promote the playing of uilleann pipes, Ennis was elected patron of the organization along with Leo Rowsome. In focusing on his piping prowess, however, Breathnach neglected Ennis's other achievements as a collector and as a broadcaster. His greatest legacy must surely be the decisive role he played in raising the profile of Irish traditional music in the twentieth century. He achieved this feat by combining his talents as a multi-instrumentalist, singer, storyteller, raconteur, collector, broadcaster, and mentor and, most crucially, by actively occupying a position of influence in Irish music.

Ennis was acutely aware of his position in Irish music and of the power that came with it. At times, he played with that power: Breathnach observed that he "possessed a well-developed streak of showmanship," and Liam Óg O'Flynn stated that he could "play to the gallery at times."[43] At other times, he took advantage of his position to share his skill and wisdom with others, in particular with musicians. Here Breathnach recalls numerous occasions at meetings of Na Píobairí Uilleann from the late 1960s on, when Ennis's bravura performances were, simultaneously, occasions for musical instruction: "As ever he would dramatise his arrival at our annual meeting, select some exotic mixture—at the last but one it was a 'dog's nose' consisting of a large bottle of stout with a glass of vodka in it—and thus primed would place himself at the disposal of the audience, face this way or that as requested and then wait 'til all [recording] machines were in action. All the favourite tunes would be played, requests invited and forms of decoration or ornamentation repeated on demand. He had no trade secrets when among pipers. These performances continued, with regular primings, for three or four or more hours, until daylight brought an end to them. They are now part of the Society's history."[44]

Breathnach's recollections reveal two key points in Ennis's story. First, under the veneer of showmanship, Ennis was concerned with sharing his music and his knowledge with present and future generations, and he consciously used his elevated position to influence Irish music. Second, he has been mythologized.[45] Stories such as the one relayed above often combine with his extraordinary achievements to make Ennis more of a myth than a man. This is problematic, as his colleague Seán Mac Réamoinn (1921–2007) observed in 1988. For him, Ennis was "the sort of man who is blessed or cursed by having legends attached to him."[46] Mac Réamoinn goes so far as to suggest that Ennis was "treated perhaps more as a character, than as ... one who has done something solid."[47] Whatever its extent, the mythologization of Ennis has implications for his work and for our interpretation of it. It shapes the notions people have about him and about his aesthetics. It has the potential to privilege his work over that of others. It also affects our understanding of the narratives of Irish traditional music, to which Ennis contributed so much. The legacy of Séamus Ennis is best approached with caution. We should weigh up his achievements carefully and be mindful of the mystique that surrounds him and his oeuvre.

BACKGROUND

Séamus Ennis was born into a musical family. His father, James Ennis (1885–1965), from Naul, Co. Dublin, and his mother, Mary Josephine McCabe (1890–1977), from Monaghan, were both musicians. James Ennis also had a lifelong interest in the Irish language. From 1900 at the latest, he was involved with the Gaelic League, and in the succeeding years, he played numerous instruments and danced at many of the League's functions, including concerts and competitions such as Oireachtas na Gaeilge. He also played football and hurling and he cycled. When the music collector and chief of police in Chicago, Francis O'Neill, met James Ennis in Ireland around 1911, he remarked: "If there's another such all-round artist knocking about I haven't met him."[48]

Séamus appears to have taken after his father in his musical ability, his athleticism, and his interest in Irish language and culture. From a very young age, he showed a keen interest in music. James fostered his talents, teaching Séamus to play the pipes and cutting for him "a pair of sticks as make-believe pipes."[49] He also taught him how to read musical notation. In addition, James regularly brought his young family to Conamara, to Ros Muc in particular, where they were given the opportunity to experience the Irish language as a vernacular in everyday life and the traditional music of the locality. This early introduction to the Gaeltacht, and especially to Conamara, would prove invaluable to Séamus in the early days of his career as a music collector.

His father was the first of a few key individuals in Ennis's life who noticed and nurtured his unique set of talents and guided him through the early years of his career. A family friend named Colm Ó Lochlainn (1892–1972), with whom James Ennis exchanged piping lessons for Irish lessons, was responsible for the next decisive move in Séamus's life. After he completed his schooling in 1936, Ennis studied at a college of commerce and sat an examination to enter the civil service. In 1938, hearing that Ennis had missed out on a civil service position by the narrowest of margins, Ó Lochlainn gave him a job at his printing and publishing house, At the Sign of the Three Candles.[50] In preparing music for printing and publication, Ennis perfected his calligraphic skills and developed what his schoolmate Dr. Kevin McCann called "his superlative penmanship."[51] He joined an Irish-language choir called An Claisceadal, of which Ó Lochlainn was then the director, and at Ó Lochlainn's behest prepared sheet music for the ensemble.[52] Ennis's training at this time went far beyond the printing and publishing trade. He himself recognized it as an apprenticeship in Irish traditional music. In an interview with Mícheál Ó hAlmhain in 1973, he stated: "It was in Colm Ó Lochlainn's printing house that I got my first experience of writing Irish songs and music. My job was to do the musical notation and write in one verse neatly by hand under the music. . . . The time I spent in the 'Sign of the Three Candles' proved very important to me later."[53] In 1979 Ennis credited Ó Lochlainn with awakening his interest in Irish-language song:

"Nuair a bhíodh an ceacht ceoil agus an ceacht Gaeilge agus gach uile shórt críochnaithe, shuíodh Colm isteach ag an bpianó a bhí sa bhaile agus bhíodh na seanamhráin ar bun aige agus sin mar a músclaíodh mo spéis sna seanamhráin" (When the music lesson and the Irish lesson and everything else was finished, Colm would sit at the piano at home and perform old songs and that is how my interest in the old songs was stirred).[54]

As World War II took hold of Europe, and the Emergency came into effect in Ireland, printing materials became scarce, and Ó Lochlainn was forced to lay off some of his workers, among them Ennis. He was not unemployed for long. Ó Lochlainn knew the Irish Folklore Commission was then looking for a full-time music collector to take the place of Liam de Noraidh, who was forced by ill health to reduce his involvement with the IFC. Ó Lochlainn recommended Ennis for the post. The director of the IFC, James Delargy, became the third person to have a decisive effect on the course of Ennis's life. He was very pleased to have come upon Ennis, who represented so suitable a candidate for a position that was proving difficult to fill.[55] As a young, able-bodied man, Ennis would be up to the long hours and arduous journeys to isolated parts of the country.[56] He also had the essential and rare combination of musical, linguistic, technical, and personal skills needed for the task of collecting traditional music. De Noraidh took a part-time position as a collector in March 1942, and on June 1 Ennis took up his new position as full-time music collector at the IFC. Briody observes that the work of de Noraidh and Ennis represents the peak of the IFC's achievement in relation to the collection of Irish traditional music: "The Commission had been extremely lucky to get music collectors of the calibre of de Noraidh and Ennis. It was not to be as lucky again. The vacancy left by Ennis's departure was never filled."[57] Uí Ógáin concurs with this assessment: "In 1942, his appointment ... as fulltime collector of music and song was to prove inspired, and Ennis' legacy in this capacity is unsurpassed. ... During his five years with the Commission, Ennis collected almost two thousand items of song, music and lore, which now form part of the National Folklore Collection at University College Dublin."[58]

EARLY CAREER

Ennis spent his first weeks at the IFC familiarizing himself with the growing collection of folklore in the archive and transcribing music from wax cylinder recordings created by Luke Donnellan. Independent observers, including

Donal O'Sullivan, Prof. Aloys Fleischmann, and Prof. John Larchet, commended the quality of his transcriptions. The IFC lost no time in deploying him to the field. On July 2, 1942, at twenty-three years of age and armed with "pen, paper and pushbike,"[59] Ennis left Dublin for Conamara to begin his first incursion. Having little firsthand experience of collecting music, Ennis lacked confidence in the early days of his fieldwork, but he quickly became "highly skilled at his job."[60] His outstanding achievements as a music collector were enhanced immeasurably by his musical prowess and interpersonal skills. He also attracted attention wherever he went, as uí Ógáin observes: "He is remembered in his prime as a tall, handsome man of independent character, witty, erudite and frequently charming."[61] His greatest gift was his ability to communicate with people, through language and through music, as Seán Mac Réamoinn recounted: "He could literally speak to people in their own language. This was one of his great gifts. He could speak, as I say . . . to the man from Maínis in the language of Connemara. He could speak to the man from the Blaskets in the language of Corca Dhuibhne. Now, but as well as that, he could speak to them . . . in terms that were of their own experience and culture. He wasn't the big fellow coming from outside. He could exchange, he could share with them their culture and then ask them to, to give him some. You know, . . . here was a side of it that he didn't know about. And that was a tremendous gift."[62]

For Ennis, communicating with people about Irish traditional music—whether he was learning from people in the field or sharing with others all he had learned—was a strong desire. As Liam Óg O'Flynn, who shared accommodation with Ennis for a time, recalls: "Anytime I took out the pipes to play, I would be just playing for minutes, and the door would open very quietly and this, this vision would appear in the doorway in the form of Séamus. And he'd just sit and listen and offer advice and whatever, and he was . . . not wanting to be critical or anything—he was just really interested in helping."[63] Breandán Breathnach too recalls Ennis's strong urge to communicate and to share his knowledge of traditional music: "The folklore of piping has many stories of pipers jealously guarding their favourite tunes, of wives being stationed at kitchen doors to ensure no rival sneaked up who, with an ear to a keyhole, sought to acquire some treasured tune by stealth. Séamus' generosity in sharing tunes and technique was a complete break with tradition."[64] Working for the IFC was something that Ennis enjoyed. His great friend Johnny Joe Pheaitsín, or Seán 'ac Dhonncha (1919–96), of Carna said it was "the job that suited him best."[65] It provided him with opportunities to indulge in his consuming interest in traditional music and to communicate with people about that music.

Crucially, as a full-time music collector for the IFC, Ennis was also gaining the experience, expertise, and renown that would help make him a recognized authority on traditional music.[66] Uí Ógáin describes how he performed his duties with dedication and style:

> Faoi mar a mhínigh Johnny [Joe Pheaitsín], ní raibh aon chlog ann agus dhéanadh Mac Aonghusa a oiread in aon lá amháin agus a thógfadh seachtain ar dhaoine eile. Bhíodh Mac Aonghusa ag obair gan stop agus ansin thógfadh scíth cúpla lá. Bhí a fhios aige an chaoi le labhairt le daoine agus an chaoi le déileáil leo. Bhí bealach faoi leith aige agus chuir sé daoine ar a suaimhneas.[67]

> [As Johnny {Joe Pheaitsín} explained, there was no clock and Ennis would do as much in one day as would take other people a week. Ennis used to work nonstop and then would take a few days' rest. He knew how to talk with people and how to deal with them. He had a certain style and he put people at their ease.]

Having committed his once-in-a-generation constellation of talents to the IFC's urgent mission, Ennis was now poised to take center stage in the unfolding narrative of Irish traditional music.

COLLECTING MUSIC IN ARAN

The mission of the IFC was not to present a geographically balanced and plural survey of the country's store of folklore—including music and song—but to collect the riches of that store. The staff of the IFC, including Séamus Ennis, were particularly interested in the places that represented the more extraordinary enclaves of Irish folk culture. They were also keen to stretch their limited resources as far as they could go. They could not afford to indulge too much in pursuing folklore that was, perhaps, more ordinary, nor did they often have the luxury of spending time traveling to and from more remote places such as offshore islands. As a result, they were more likely to visit places that were relatively accessible and that boasted a concentration of folk culture on which they could draw with relative ease and efficiency.[68]

It was inevitable that, of all the time he spent collecting for the IFC in Ireland, Ennis would spend most of his time in Conamara.[69] Conamara was then, as it is now, in both geographical and demographic terms, Ireland's largest Gaeltacht, so in the eyes of the IFC, it merited attention. Ennis was sent there for his first assignment by Delargy, who believed that the Conamara parish of Carna was the richest source of folktales and that it was rich in the other oral arts of music and song too.[70] As well as being sent to Conamara, Ennis was also naturally drawn to collect there not least because of his boyhood visits to Ros Muc with his family but also because of the camaraderie he experienced in the company of local communities and later because of the relationship he formed with Colm Ó Caodháin (1893–1975). Indeed, Ennis revealed a sense of belonging in Conamara in his diary entry for September 5, 1945, the last day of his collecting trip to Aran, when he described how he swam out to some boats from Conamara that had anchored in Port Mhuirbhigh to enquire if any of them could "bring him home": "A' féachaint a bhí mé a' rabh aon bhád as Cill Chiaráin ann a tiúrfadh abhaile mé agus bhí Johnny Lally romham amuigh, duine go mo lucht aitheantais fhéin agus duairt sé liom go mbeith sé réidh ar a ceathair" (I was looking for any boat from Cill Chiaráin that might bring me home and Johnny Lally was there in front of me, one of my own acquaintances, and he said he would be ready at four o'clock).[71] (Uí Ógáin identifies the boatman as Johnny Casey.[72]) Most importantly, Ennis was drawn to the wealth of material he found in Conamara, and much of that from Ó Caodháin. Toward the end of his life, Ennis told Éamon de Buitléar: "The greatest repository of songs and tunes in their background in fact and fable I found in a little pocket of north Conamara, on the south shore of Cuan na Beirtrí Buí, the bay of the yellow oyster bank, in a place known as Glínsce [*sic*], 'clear water' in English. It was there that I met Colm Ó Caoidheáin and I wrote 212 items straight from his memory."[73] Apart from the quality of the material Ennis gleaned from Ó Caodháin and others in Conamara, the sheer abundance and concentration of it ensured that he was well occupied there between July 1942, when he first went to collect music in Conamara, and August 1945, when he eventually began collecting music in neighboring Aran. In that time, he also collected in Cavan, Donegal, and Mayo.

The Aran Islands were then, as they are now, commonly regarded as part of Conamara. Delargy's instruction to collect in Conamara might be interpreted as an instruction to collect in Aran as well. Delargy had visited Inis Meáin in 1919 to improve his Irish, collected folktales in Árainn in the early 1930s, and orchestrated the production of the first Irish-language talkie, *Oidhche Sheanchais*, which featured Seáinín Tom Ó Dioráin of Sruthán, Árainn.[74] He was, then, aware of how little of the folklore of Aran had been documented since the turn of the century and of how little of the collected material had been published.[75] Regardless, Ennis probably planned a trip to Aran at some stage, not least because of its status as a Gaeltacht but also because of its proximity to and its connection with Conamara. Nevertheless, considering that he delayed his first visit to Aran until his ninth collecting trip to the district, over three years after he first began collecting in the west, it appears that Ennis was in no great rush to collect in Aran. This may be because he had such an amount of material to collect in Conamara. The notion that Aran was culturally a part of Conamara may also have led him to believe that he would simply find more of the same kind of music on the islands. His collecting trips to Aran were not only delayed; they were also "comparatively short visits."[76] In the end, of the sixty-two weeks Ennis spent collecting in County Galway, he spent just over two weeks trying to collect music in Aran.

After two short introductory excursions to Aran in June and July, Ennis began to seriously collect music there on his third visit in late August 1945 (see appendix 2). At the end of that trip, he stated that he was very happy with his visit. He liked the place very much but, in the same breath, acknowledged that he had been lucky to have had fine weather. He was particularly impressed by the song melodies he heard from Seán Mhurchadha de Bhailís and from Máire Ní Dhioráin (see appendix 4). He may even have prompted Máire to attend if not to compete in Oireachtas na Gaeilge in Dublin later that year, an occasion upon which he recorded her singing four songs. Ennis also expressed a wish to return to Árainn for a fortnight to collect more songs from Seán Mhurchadha and from Tomás "Tyrell" Ó Briain. Nevertheless, in light of his rather noncommittal two-day visit at the end of June 1946, during which he tried but failed to collect music, it appears that he was simply not sufficiently motivated to act on that wish. Indeed, after July 1946 Ennis never returned to Aran in a professional capacity, most notably when he was a collector and broadcaster for Radio Éireann (RÉ) and later for the BBC. Instead, his subsequent visits to Aran were as a holidaymaker. Tomás Bhaba Pheige Ó Miolláin of Sruthán recalls that Ennis visited Árainn around 1950. He recalls hearing Ennis playing the pipes on the rocks below Beairtle and Peaits Sheáin Bheairtle Mac Donnchadha's house in An Sruthán and on top of the flat roof of the house in which he was staying, Tí Éamoin Uí Choncheanainn in the neighboring village of Eoghanacht, on which Éamon's large family of twelve children sometimes danced.[77]

The shortness of Ennis's visits to Aran and his noncommittal attitude to returning to collect music there could simply have been the result of time constraints and questions concerning access and transport, issues that frequently affected visitors to the islands. Aran certainly represented to him a challenging place to work. He had cause to complain about expensive accommodation—costing his entire week's wages of three pounds—and he sometimes found traveling to and on the islands arduous: when he first sailed to Aran, his return to Conamara was delayed by a storm; on the return leg of his second voyage to Aran, he and Pat Cheoinín had to sail hard against a headwind; and, on his third voyage to Aran, the vessel was becalmed so he had to help row the boat ashore. In addition, the local population was smaller than the mainland population, which meant the local repertoire was smaller. He had difficulty in tracking down singers—he failed to catch Peadar Mac Coistealbha of Inis Meáin and Peaits Bheartla Mac Donnchadha of Creig an Chéirín—as a result of bad timing or because his host in Aran insisted on serving dinner at the relatively late hour of three o'clock.[78] He also spent a day evading men who had been drinking and who merrily sought his musical company. When he finally caught up with Matt Neainín Ó Maoláin of Eoghanacht, Matt chose to observe the local custom of abstaining from singing while in mourning, on this occasion for his recently deceased mother. All of these factors may well have combined to persuade Ennis that collecting in Aran was too challenging a prospect to bother with further attempts.

The shortness of Ennis's visits to Aran and his lack of commitment toward returning to collect music there should also be considered in the context of the work he conducted on the neighboring mainland around the same time. Throughout his engagement with the music of Aran, Ennis was preoccupied with recording the larger and, to him, more satisfactory repertoire that lay within easier reach all around him in Conamara. Until August 1, 1945, at least, he was certainly preoccupied with collecting Colm Ó Caodháin's remarkably extensive repertoire of more than two hundred songs.[79] He was also beginning to acquaint himself with the music of West Clare, which he later praised in a declarative fashion that is strikingly similar to the way in which he praised the song tradition of Carna: "In the early 1940s I had been over many miles on my bicycle for the Irish Folklore Commission. Dublin to Connemara, to Donegal, Mayo, Leitrim, Cavan, Connemara again, and where my present yarn's location for me was in West Clare. That for sure will make ears for Irish music especially attentive because it is there we have today the richest repository of instrumentalists. Fiddle, flute, pipes, accordion and concertina-playing are in no way so concentrated in any other part of the country."[80] Ennis's interest in the music of Carna and West Clare continued throughout his career after he left the IFC. On November 5, 1949, in his capacity as Outside Broadcasts Officer with RÉ, he returned to Clare to record Bobby Casey, Willie Clancy, Martin Talty, and others, some of whom he had met in 1945. In 1951 he brought the American music collector Alan Lomax and his companion Robin Roberts to visit Carna. In contrast, in the aftermath of his 1945 and 1946 visits to Aran, Ennis appears to have said little about the music he encountered there, with the exception of his collaboration with Sidney Robertson Cowell (see chapter 3). His behavior in relation to the traditional music of Aran after 1946 can be characterized in general terms as a disengagement from that music. Of course, this disengagement must be viewed in light of subsequent developments in his personal and professional life, which changed considerably in the 1950s and 1960s. It should also be viewed in light of the fact that Aran is flanked by what Ennis believed to be the two most extraordinary enclaves of Irish traditional music, not just in the west of Ireland, but in the whole country: Carna and West Clare. It was inevitable that he would spend more of his time in the west in those places on the mainland where he could collect more music more efficiently. Efficiency was important to Ennis. In his field diary entry of October 19, 1944, he reflected on his attempts to collect in Mayo and Donegal in the preceding weeks: "Mé beagán míshásta le mo chuairt ó Iúil i leith; níor éirigh liom oiread a fháil is gheobhainn i gConamara, ach níl neart air sin" (I am a little unhappy with my tour since July; I failed to get as much as I would get in Conamara, but it cannot be helped).[81] His behavior in relation to the traditional music of Aran after 1946 represents a natural distancing from one music in favor of deliberate attempts to draw closer to other musics.

Ennis himself provided evidence of his disengagement from the music of Aran in an interview he gave to Dublin piper Mícheál Ó hAlmhain (now married and living in Inis Oírr) on March 27, 1973, from which the relevant extract appears below.[82] While he was creating his 1945 collection, Ennis gave very little direct analysis or criticism of local music. There are just two instances: he found Nóra Pheaits Sheáin Ní Chonghaola's rendition of "Nóra Ní Chonchubhair Bháin" to be "truaillighthe" (corrupted); and, in a note he appended to his transcription of "Siúil a Rúin," he inferred his doubt about the authenticity of

Máirín Uí Dhioráin's rendition of the song by saying, "These (Gaelic) words are those of 'An Craoibhín' as published in An Lóchrann, March 8th 1902."[83] The opinion Ennis expressed in 1973 in relation to the music of Aran was an empirical judgment based not just on his firsthand experience almost twenty-eight years earlier but also on his experience of listening to and commenting on Sidney Robertson Cowell's 1955 tapes over eighteen years earlier. This extract and its apparently negative conclusion are more a reflection of the remoteness of his relationship with the music of Aran in later life than a reflection of the reality of that music in either 1973 or 1945:

MÍCHEÁL: And in which area now did you find the greatest wealth of song?

SÉAMUS: Connemara. North Connemara. The parish of Carna. The parish of Carna is known/notable [unclear], among folklorists, as being the richest area per head of population or per square mile (if it goes to that); the richest folk repository in Western Europe. That is recognized fact.

M: And was there any particular trait in the people that you can attribute that to? Or was it just that there were so many people living in a small area and they were so isolated . . .

S: There are *three* traits, three reasons why, I should say. Well, one would guess, so many people concentrated in one area. They can also guess at the intelligence of a fish-fed community; that was largely their diet—fish. And also, the fact that they were so isolated. You don't go through Connemara to go anywhere. There's no traffic going through Connemara. Connemara is out on a limb.

M: And it probably hadn't very many connections apart from the Aran Islands.

S: [The] Aran Islands were part of it.

M: But I would have distinguished between the Irish of the Aran Islands and . . .

S: You'd be right.

M: Connemara.

S: You'd be right. [The] Aran Islands are an approach to Munster Irish from Connemara Irish. They really mingle each [unclear] down to Clare.

M: And, did you find that the songs of the Aran Islands were related fairly closely to Carna or to Clare?

S: More to Connemara. Related more to Connemara, but even at, eh, in Aran you only got fragments of the whole of which you found at Connemara.

Ennis's apparently negative conclusion seems remarkable considering that, just over five months earlier at Oireachtas na Gaeilge 1972, Treasa Ní Mhiolláin of Sruthán, Árainn, won Comórtas na mBan and Corn Uí Riada. She won Comórtas na mBan with "Cúirt Bhaile Nua" and "Sagart na Cúile Báine," and she won Corn Uí Riada with "Tá an Oíche Seo Dorcha" and "An Sceilpín Draighneach."[84] She learned each of these songs at home in Aran, though her version of "Tá an Oíche Seo Dorcha" was partly influenced by that of Joe John Mac Con Iomaire of Cill Chiaráin, Conamara. Furthermore, two months before that, in August 1972, Treasa and her brother Tomás, respectively, won the women's and men's competitions for singing in Irish at Fleadh Cheoil na hÉireann in Listowel, Co. Kerry. For Treasa, it was the first of three All-Ireland titles in a row in the same competition. She also won third place in the women's competition for singing in English in 1974.[85]

Engaged as we are in a process of contextualizing his Aran collection, it is worth tempering Ennis's apparently negative statement on the music of Aran in comparison with the music of Conamara with some caveats about his work in Aran, caveats like that given at the beginning of this chapter in relation to the Ó Briain family of singers and song makers. For instance, Ennis did not stay in Aran long enough to hear a broad spectrum of local musicians and repertoire. There were also many other good singers in Aran at this time, some of whom—including Petairín a' Bheagach Ó Maoláin (1910–2003) of Bun Gabhla and Pat Pheaidí Ó hIarnáin (1903–89) of Cill Mhuirbhigh—knew locally composed songs such as "Creig Sheáin Phádraig" (Seán Phádraig's Rock) and "An Mhíoltóg" (The Midge) that would have interested Ennis had he heard them. He makes no reference to these singers or to the repertoire of local songs in his accounts of his work in Aran, even though he had already transcribed verses of two Aran compositions from contributors in Conamara.[86] Furthermore, he attended four, if not five, céilithe in the recently opened dance hall, but he made no comment on the music he heard there. Clearly, it would be inaccurate and unfair to interpret Ennis's Aran collection as a representation of a musical tradition that was, at that time and as compared with that of the neighboring mainland communities, less impressive or more ordinary. Instead, the circumstances outlined above—Ennis's disengagement from the music of Aran and the shortcomings of his work there—suggest that this collection represents a more everyday example of his fieldwork for the IFC, hindered as it was by various practical and logistical challenges and unsatisfying in its failure to capture music from some worthy local sources. It is, nonetheless, a valuable example. As one of the earliest substantial sources of the music of Aran in the twentieth century, it helps us better understand the changes incurred by the musical traditions of Aran during that century. It also confirms the extent to which Ennis's methodology in Aran was shaped by the agenda of his employers, the IFC. Finally, it helps contextualize Ennis's more extraordinary achievements in relation to the music of other places.

THE COLLECTION

Ennis's Aran collection reflects the focus of the IFC on songs in Irish and the resulting marginalization of other aspects of traditional music. Nevertheless, local circumstances—including the absence of a strong tradition of instrumental music and a lack of variety in the type of musical instruments then available—also contributed to the pattern of this collection. Furthermore, collections of song transcriptions frequently illustrate a focus on text not least because the work of transcribing airs is typically slower and more taxing than transcribing lyrics, even for someone with Ennis's famed skills of musical dictation. A transcription of a song's lyrics appended with the name of the accompanying air is often regarded as a sufficient record of a song, and Ennis employed this shorthand in Aran.

With the exceptions of a well-known folk saying and a rendition of the bilingual song "Siúil a Rúin," every one of the items Ennis collected from seven contributors in Aran is a song in Irish.[87] Including "Siúil a Rúin," there are twenty-six songs in the collection, one from Inis Meáin and the rest from Árainn. The exclusion of the songs in English that were part of the contemporary Aran repertoire is also unsurprising because, to Ennis, the vast majority of them did not seem to fit his IFC brief to collect the authentic traditional music of the locality. In the majority of Gaeltacht areas where he collected, including Aran, authentic local or native music was more likely to be in Irish than in English. Furthermore, in speaking Irish with his informants, he was more likely to get songs in Irish.

METHODOLOGY

Ennis makes no mention of having any musical instruments—such as his uilleann pipes—with him in Aran as he did in other localities. Nevertheless, he is likely to have had a tin whistle in his pocket. In most other aspects, his methodology in Aran was generally consistent with the rest of his fieldwork for the IFC. He was liable to collect music wherever it occurred. In Aran he heard music and song in the dance hall, in the pub, and aboard a Galway hooker, and he collected songs in people's homes and while sitting on the seashore. Uí Ógáin describes how he was generally received in the field: "His acquaintances were people for whom music and song were a natural part of their everyday lives at a time when Irish music had only just begun to make a very tentative public appearance beyond its indigenous environment. In most instances, an aspiration to collect, record, broadcast, archive, photograph or film had not impinged on the lives of the traditional singers and musicians, and they welcomed Ennis into their world, giving freely of their music, song and lore."[88]

Ennis was not only a fluent Irish speaker; he could alter his speech to the local dialect. His diaries sound the accent of whatever district they describe. This ability to "speak to people in their own language," as Seán Mac Réamoinn described it, encouraged people to accept him.[89] Ennis did not bring an Ediphone with him to Aran in 1945 or in 1946. He had used one in Carna in June 1944, but in those early days, Briody observes that Ennis appeared "initially at least, to have been somewhat reluctant to use it."[90] He may have been reluctant to bring it on a relatively long voyage across unpredictable waters to Aran for fear of damaging the apparatus.

Most of the people from whom Ennis collected were older men. In Aran, the average age of his seven contributors—four men and three women—was around fifty-three years, at least twice his own age. His preference for collecting from older performers is understandable given that he was looking for the native musical heritage of each locality.[91] He was attracted to such performers because their company and traditions sometimes made him feel like he was experiencing another, older world.[92] Such encounters also reminded him of the urgency of his work. He gravitated toward Tomás "Tyrell" Ó Briain in particular because he represented to him a star informant: "D'fhéadfainn fanacht go maidin ann ag scríobh dhá dtogróinn é, agus duine den chineál é 'Tyrell'" (I could stay there until morning transcribing if I decided, and "Tyrell" is that sort of person).[93] He also avoided material he felt was unworthy of his efforts.[94]

There is one important difference between Ennis's work in Aran and his work in other districts. When he collected in Tory Island, Donegal, and Mayo, he often had the help of fellow collectors and local schoolteachers. Uí Ógáin observes

that, in Mayo, Ennis "relied a great deal on the folklore collector Pádraic Ó
Moghráin for guidance."[95] Similarly, his friendship with Sorcha Ní Ghuairim
contributed to his work in Conamara. In Aran, however, he had to make his
own way. This is surprising considering his colleague Máire Mac Neill (1904–
87) had spent some of her childhood in Árainn and had known islanders—
Maggie Dirrane of Eoghanacht and her niece Méiní Tom Uí Mhaoláin of Creig
an Chéirín—who had been in the employ of the Mac Neill family in Dublin.[96]
Máire had also spent July, August, and September of 1944 collecting folklore
from eight people in the west end of Árainn, among them the singers Petairín
a' Bheagach Ó Maoláin (Méiní Tom's husband)—from whom she transcribed
the lyrics of "An Caisdeach Bán"[97] [*sic*]—and Peaits Bheartla Mac Donnchadha
(1871–1962). She did recommend lodging in Fearann a' Choirce with Bairbre
Pheait Uí Fhlaithearta but appears not to have given Ennis any names of potential contributors or informants. Where the path was prepared somewhat for
him in Donegal, Mayo, and Conamara by Seán Ó hEochaidh, Ó Moghráin, and
Ní Ghuairim, respectively, Aran presented to him a relatively unknown prospect. When he first arrived to collect music there, Ennis felt he was a stranger to
the place. On Wednesday, August 22, he wrote: "Is mór an nidh cáirde áirthide
a bheith i n-áit choithiach ag duine" (It is good to have certain friends in a place
where one is not known).[98]

The Singers

Ennis could not have achieved his successes in Aran without some good fortune and the goodwill of his contributors.[99] His first encounter with a local—
with Matt Neainín Ó Maoláin on June 29, 1945—was untimely in that Matt
was precluded from contributing to Ennis's work by the death of his mother;
but it was fortuitous in that Matt, a singer, poet, and song maker, was later able
to give Ennis the name of an impressive singer, Seán Mhurchadha de Bhailís
(ca. 1877–1964) from Bun Gabhla, whom Ennis tracked down on his last day of
collecting in Aran. Tuesday, September 4, 1945, was so calm that the chimney
in Seán's house in Sruthán would not draw smoke from the fire and the house
soon filled with smoke.[100] Being somewhat shy of the work of song collecting,
the smoking chimney provided Seán with an excuse to lead Ennis down to the
seashore some distance from the house, out of earshot and out of sight of the
villages and the main road. There, seated on a cliff, Ennis proceeded to notate
two songs from Seán: "Bhí bean uasal seal ghá luadh liom" and "Máire Ní

Thaidhg Óig."[101] Ennis liked his airs and succeeded in notating one of them.[102] When he returned to Aran in June 1946, Ennis went in search of Seán so that he might write more songs from him, but when he eventually found him wandering on the shore half a mile from his house, Seán was in no mood for singing. They spoke, instead, for some time about music and song on the island:

Chaith sé tamall fada ag cur síos ar shagart [an tAth Tomás Ó Cillín] a bhí ann ag stopadh ceolta is damhsa i gach uile theach a dtosaídís ann. Deir sé liom go dtáinig an séiplíneach [an tAth Pádraig Ó Dubhshláine] atá anois ann gur thosaigh sé damhsaí sa seanteach scoile [i 1944], "Agus cuirfidh mé do rogha geall leat nach stopfaidh an seansagart iad sin," a deir sé.[103]

[He spent a long time describing how a priest {Fr. Tomás Ó Cillín} there was stopping music and dancing in every house in which they would begin. He told me that the current curate {Fr. Pádraig Ó Dubhshláine} began dances in the old schoolhouse {in 1944}, "And I will bet you anything that the old priest will not stop those," he told me.]

Ennis had better luck in the eastern end of the island. It was on his first night in Aran on June 29, 1945, at the céilí in Cill Rónáin that he first heard Máire Ní Dhioráin (1922–2007) of Cill Éinne, who impressed him greatly. When he found himself back in Aran two weeks later, he took the opportunity to seek her out and set about transcribing the air of a song from her: "Duairt sí órán ar báll dúinn—'B'ait liom bean a d'imreóchadh beart' ('Peigí Mistéal') agus fonn an-áluinn aice leis, agus go deivin níor thada a áilneacht le h-ais an ghlóir cinn atá aig Máire fhéin. 'Sí is breaghtha chuala mé go dtí seo bhfuil glór aice" (She later said a song for us—"Strange to me a woman who would play a move [trick]" ("Peggy Mitchell") and she had a very beautiful air to it, and indeed her beauty was nothing to the singing voice Máire herself has. She has the finest voice I have heard yet).[104] Unlike Seán Mhurchadha de Bhailís, Máire was not shy of the work of music collecting. She herself had transcribed songs from her uncle Tyrell and from her father, Maidhcilín, for the IFC's Schools' Scheme of 1937–38. Under the direction of the schoolmaster at Scoil Chill Éinne, Séamus Pádraig Ó Domhnalláin (for whom Máire later worked in Aran and in Galway), the children of Cill Éinne created a collection of fourteen songs—the largest number of songs collected by any of the schools of Aran that participated in the scheme—and Máire collected two if not four or more of them.[105] She transcribed her uncles' composition "Amhrán an Dole" (also known as "Amhrán na Feola") and "Amhrán an Phúca" and may also have transcribed "Amhrán na bhFataí" and "Péarla Deas an Chúil Bháin."[106] Máire undoubtedly understood the historical function of Ennis's efforts and the opportunity that he was presenting to her and her fellow islanders. She enabled Ennis's interaction with his most significant contributor in Aran, her uncle Tyrell, by introducing them and, later, by helping Ennis create the ideal environment for collecting songs from him.[107] Ennis described Tyrell's style of singing as he sang "Bhfuil sé n-a lá?," which opened, accidentally or otherwise, with a verse from "Na Gamhna Geala":[108] "Ba bhreagh uaidh é rádh, nó d'fhághadh sé blas breá air fhéin a' tosuighe dhó agus bhíodh a phléisiúir fhéin le feiceáil ag an saoghal 'n-a éadan agus 'n-a shúilí nuair a lomadh sé ar a' gcéad churfá; cuireadh [sic] sé castaíacha breaghtha 'sa bhfonn agus choinuighith sé nóta annseo is ann siúd tamall le sult as" (He performed it very well, or he accentuated particularly in the opening, and his pleasure was plain to see in his face and in his eyes as he launched into the first chorus; he ornamented the tune well and he sustained notes here and there as pleased him).[109] Ennis was most impressed by Tyrell, his sister Máirín Uí Dhioráin, and her daughter Máire. He spent half of his collecting time in Aran with this family: Tuesday, August 26, and the next three available days, Saturday, Sunday, and Monday, September 1–3. He enjoyed their company and felt obliged to them for their generosity; of young Máire, he later wrote: "Ar ndóigh, cailín an-bhreá í Máire Ní Dhireáin, múinte, geanúil, fial le strainséirí" (Of course, Máire Ní Dhioráin is a very fine girl, mannerly, affectionate, generous to visitors).[110] Later, in Lahinch, Co. Clare, on September 11, he wrote them a letter of thanks for showing him a "sweet time" and included transcriptions of two songs he had promised them.[111]

Máire Ní Dhioráin provided Ennis with his only opportunity to record the music of Aran when, in October 1945, she visited Dublin for the first time ever. Her stay was something of a holiday—she attended a hurling match at Croke Park and visited the Houses of the Oireachtas—but she also sang at Oireachtas na Gaeilge, which was then going on in the capital. Although it is unclear whether she competed or simply performed at An tOireachtas, she may well have gone to Dublin specifically to compete in its singing competitions.[112] Considering Ennis's high opinion of her singing and considering that few if any Aran islanders appear to have competed in the singing competitions of An tOireachtas before then, he may well have encouraged her to attend and to compete.

Oireachtas na Gaeilge 1945 began on the evening of Saturday, October 20, and ran for a week. The stage competitions took place in the Abbey Theatre. The occasion brought a celebratory atmosphere to the Irish-language community in Dublin, which included enthusiasts and native speakers from all over the country who lived and worked there. The occasion also attracted many people who traveled from the Gaeltachtaí to compete and participate in the competitions.[113] It was then a common occurrence for the musicians and singers who had traveled from different parts of the country to Dublin to attend or compete in An tOireachtas to be invited to the headquarters of the IFC, where they might record their music onto acetate discs. Ennis spent some of the Oireachtas week in 1945 recording competitors, including Máire Ní Cheocháin of Baile Bhuirne and Tadhg Ó Cuanaigh and Diarmuid Ó Ríordáin of Cúil Aodha, Co. Cork; Seán Jeaic Mac Donncha, Seosamh Ó hÉanaí, and Beartla Ó Conghaile of Carna, Co. Galway; and Conal Mhicí Hiúdaí Ó Domhnaill from Rann na Feirste but who then lived in Donaghpatrick, Co. Meath.[114] Ennis and his colleagues were glad of the chance to create these recordings. For many years, up until 1947 when the IFC launched its mobile recording unit, the Ediphone was the only sound-recording equipment available to collectors in the field, and as Briody observes, it was troublesome: "De Noraidh did not realise the problems of recording song and music by means of the Ediphone. It had to be explained to him that the needle of this apparatus 'was unsuitable to the high notes, and in such cases the singers sounded as if they were screeching.'"[115] Considering that the performers who visited Dublin to compete in An tOireachtas were often the musical stars of their respective localities, the gathering represented a golden opportunity for the IFC to collect and preserve on record some of the best traditional music in the country with the best available sound recording equipment.

On the afternoon of Wednesday, October 24, 1945, in the IFC headquarters on Earlsfort Terrace, Ennis recorded Máire singing four songs onto ten-inch acetate discs. Ennis had transcribed the airs to all these songs from Máire when he was in Aran, but only three of those transcriptions survive; his first, "Peigí Mistéal," is missing. When he transcribed Máire's air to "Siúil a Rúin," he took the lyrics of the song from her mother.[116] He did the same for "Cúirt Bhaile Nua."[117] Only once did Ennis transcribe song lyrics from Máire (for the song

"An Sagart Ó Domhnaill"), and on that occasion he neglected to name or to transcribe the accompanying air.[118] This pattern of collecting suggests that Ennis was more interested in Máire's song airs than in her song texts. The short-ness of the Dublin recordings, which amount to a verse or two of each song, may also indicate that he was focused more on her song airs. It is also possible that their shortness represents a limitation of the ten-inch acetate discs.

In 1946 Máire emigrated to England, where she married Leslie Arnsby. She died in 2007. As it is not known whether her singing was ever recorded by anyone else, Ennis's recordings of her represent a valuable contribution to the Aran canon.

ASSESSING ENNIS'S ARAN COLLECTION

Ennis must be commended, first of all, for reaching the Aran Islands. There were many other places that he could have visited instead. Considering the numerous challenges he faced in trying to collect music in Aran, the relatively small collection of twenty-six transcriptions of song lyrics—for which there are eleven surviving transcriptions of accompanying airs—is no mean feat. More-over, his recordings of Máire Ní Dhioráin, which are among the earliest record-ings of any musician from Aran, are particularly valuable documents. Apart from preserving Máire's singing, they also legitimize Ennis's music transcrip-tions by illustrating the accuracy of his dictation in terms of pitch, rhythm, phrasing, and the correct alignment of the notes with the text. The recordings and the transcriptions combine well to provide rare and valuable insight into some of the repertoire, melodies, and singing styles of Aran in the first half of the twentieth century. His focus on Tomás "Tyrell" Ó Briain is a particularly valuable contribution because it constitutes the most substantial record, and one of only a handful of records, of this noted local singer and poet.

Ennis's collection indicates that, in 1945, there were some songs and some melodies sung in Aran that are no longer heard there today, reflecting the amor-phous and vulnerable nature of the local music repertoire. The collection also indicates a variety of singing styles, specifically among the three singers from whom he transcribed airs and recorded songs. Two of the slower songs sung by Tomás "Tyrell" Ó Briain and Seán Mhurchadha de Bhailís, "Níl sé ina lá," or "Na Gamhna Geala," and "Máire Ní Thaidhg Óig," respectively, are, for in-stance, more ornate than some of the other songs in the collection.[119] By com-parison, Máire Ní Dhioráin's singing is quite direct and free of ornamentation except for some glissandi. The variety between these three performers offers a glimpse of the stylistic individualism that is a trait of the local music tradition.

The collection is, nonetheless, confined to such a small number of singers that it cannot possibly reflect the full variety of contemporary singing in Aran. Furthermore, as we saw earlier in this chapter, Ennis missed out on potential contributors and on a body of local compositions that would certainly have interested him had he heard them. His visits were ultimately too short for him to create a satisfactory collection of the music of Aran. His Aran collection thus constitutes a limited representation of what Irish traditional music was performed there in the mid-twentieth century.

A Position of Influence

Ennis entered the world of broadcasting at a time when Irish traditional music lived, as Mac Réamoinn recalls, "underground": "this was [*sic*] the days before the Fleadh Cheoil, before Comhaltas Ceoltóirí Éireann, and Irish traditional music, while immensely alive, lived, if you like, in the quiet places. . . . It was almost invisible or inaudible to a lot of people in the country, and it was—a lot of people had a very dismissive attitude to it, you know? 'Trad.'"[120] Within a few years, however, the profile of Irish traditional music in Ireland and beyond had grown. Ennis's work for RÉ and the BBC played no small part in this revival of interest.[121] Indeed, Smith believes his broadcasting work "helped define the role of traditional music in the mass media."[122] Becoming a broadcaster enabled Ennis to establish for himself a position of influence. He could also privilege, disseminate, and canonize the music of one place over the music of another as he could never have done before.[123] Moreover, becoming a broadcaster raised Ennis's own profile and stature. Even though he was already known throughout the country for his exceptional ability as a performer and for his achievements as an IFC collector, it was his work in broadcasting that effected his transformation into a touchstone of Irish traditional music.[124] Late in 1950, when the American collectors Alan Lomax and Robin Roberts consulted with Brian George of the BBC about going to collect traditional music in Ireland, they were told Séamus Ennis was "the man to see in Ireland."[125]

Ennis was certainly the right person in the right place at the right time when Radio Éireann launched its new mobile recording unit (MRU), and he was fortunate that such an enterprise was being launched just as he was asserting his authority in the world of traditional music; but he also pursued the position

of outside broadcasts officer during his fifth year of working for the IFC. He
left the IFC on July 31, 1947, and joined the MRU just over two weeks later on
August 18.[126] Though his decision to move was encouraged by the prospect of
a pay increase, it was ultimately inspired by his strong desire to communicate
with people about traditional music. Broadcasting gave him an opportunity
that was too rarely provided at the IFC, an opportunity to share on a more
regular basis and with as wide an audience as possible—to publish or to air—
the knowledge that he was harvesting. It also made the most of his unique capa-
bilities, in particular his talent for storytelling. At the heart of this move to
broadcasting was his concern for the creative legacy he would leave behind. His
desire to seize all such opportunities to indulge in and share his passion for
music is evident in the series of career choices he made after leaving the IFC.
He spent the next ten years working for RÉ and the BBC and, thereafter, was a
regular contributor on radio and television.

In many respects, the MRU was very like the IFC. It was not chiefly concerned with presenting a geographically balanced and plural view of Ireland.
Instead, it was confined by its budget to recording and broadcasting the best
and most suitable material available.[127] The brief given to the MRU was, according to Ennis's colleague Seán Mac Réamoinn, "to seek throughout the country,
including the Gaeltacht, material suitable for recording and suitable broadcasting."[128] So when Ennis moved from the IFC to RÉ, the pattern of his collecting work and the values that guided him changed very little. Throughout
his time with RÉ and, from 1951 to 1957, with the BBC, he revisited some of the
people he met during his IFC years.[129] In this way, his IFC work became the
foundation upon which his career as a broadcaster was built.

In his new position as a touchstone of Irish traditional music, Ennis was
often approached by people who were interested in traditional music and who
were looking for guidance in their efforts to record it. He sent them to performers and districts that he held in high regard, often to people and places
he encountered during his time with the IFC. When he assisted two American
collectors, Jean Ritchie and George Pickow, as they traveled around Ireland collecting music between 1952 and 1953, he directed them to visit Bess Cronin,
whom he had met and recorded in 1947. Nicholas Carolan describes how the
aforementioned Lomax and Roberts "followed the Ennis trail" during their
monthlong tour of Ireland in January and February 1951.[130] When producing
an album of their Irish field recordings for Columbia Records titled *Ireland*,

volume 2 of The Historic Series: World Library of Folk and Primitive Music, which included earlier recordings by the BBC, Lomax went so far as to attribute the 1955 release to Ennis: "The recordings were made by Robin Roberts and myself in January 1951, and by Brian George and Maurice Brown of the BBC in 1947. All of us travelled with Seamus Ennis, a great piper and son of a great piper, a fine singer of ballads, and a man known and loved wherever Gaelic is spoken and music made in Ireland. This collection is his."[131]

The sense of authority and the power that this new status conferred on Ennis are well illustrated by Roberts, who observes how some commentators believed his contributions could actually negate the shortcomings of those with whom he collaborated: "Later there were those who complained that Alan [Lomax] had roared through Ireland like Atilla [sic] the Hun, had trod rough-shod over other folklorists' special territories. He had not spent enough time with the people to understand them properly, and he did not speak Irish. But he did have the imprimatur of Seamus Ennis, without whom he might easily have been led astray."[132] Not only does Roberts's description give a sense of the respect accorded to Ennis—and, thereupon, to the music he valued—by his contemporaries, it also confirms the enduring quality of that respect. Furthermore, it represents an example of the mythologization of Ennis's abilities and achievements, a mythologization that continues to contribute to his status as a touchstone of traditional music.

By the late 1940s, and especially during the 1950s when he presented the seminal BBC radio series *As I Roved Out*, Ennis was in a unique position of influence in relation to Irish traditional music from which he could propound and perpetuate his understandings and narratives of Irish traditional music.[133] This is not to say that Ennis was solely responsible for the narratives of Irish traditional music that emerged during this period, but as Daithí Kearney argues, his opinions certainly contributed to those narratives: "The musicians recorded by Ennis were to become reference points for the musical distinctiveness of their regions and reinforced the perception of these 'regions' as primary locations of 'authentic' Irish traditional music."[134]

To illustrate this point, we return to Ennis's opinions of the musics of Carna and West Clare and his contrasting opinion of the music of Aran, which were outlined earlier. Given his position of influence, and given the fact that the wealth of music in Carna and in West Clare continues to be lauded and admired today, we might deduce that Ennis's favorable opinions of the musics of Carna and West Clare and his continued engagement with them throughout his later career contributed to the privileged positions they now enjoy in narratives of Irish traditional music.[135] We might also conclude that Ennis's disengagement from the music of Aran contributed to its marginalization within the same narratives. This conclusion is supported by the fact that Ennis had nothing to do with the decisions made by various music collectors, including W. R. Rodgers and David Thomson of the BBC and the Americans Jean Ritchie and George Pickow, Sidney Robertson Cowell, and Diane Guggenheim, to visit Aran in the period 1949–56. Although Ennis met and/or advised some of them, all these collectors made their decisions to visit Aran independently of him.

In the end, it is difficult to determine the degree to which Ennis's disengagement from the music of Aran contributed to the marginalization of that music in narratives of Irish traditional music. Nevertheless, his work in Aran does provide us with an example of how the successes and failures of each music collector can have a significant effect on the music they document and on their choices to praise, criticize, or ignore it. It encourages us to consider each music collection in its context in order to better understand its import and its impact. It also heralds a need for a closer, and perhaps more comprehensive, examination of Ennis's work in relation to traditional music in all its varied forms, from collecting to broadcasting to performing to mentoring. Whatever it reveals, such an effort can only serve to further highlight the significance and setting of his star in the traditional music firmament.

chapter 3

Sidney Robertson Cowell
and *Songs of Aran*

I n New York in October 1934, the American composer Henry Cowell had a
group of islanders from Árainn illustrate one of his lectures on "Music of
the World's Peoples" at the New School for Social Research. He was introduced to Maggie Dirrane, Micilín Dillane, and Coleman "Tiger" King by his
friend, the American director Robert Flaherty, in whose film, *Man of Aran*, the
trio had starred. Cowell chaperoned them in the Big Apple at Flaherty's request
and performed alongside them at a dinner at the Ritz-Carlton hotel organized
by the Architects Emergency Committee to support destitute architects and
draftsmen of the Great Depression. He also persuaded them to sing and dance
onstage at the Broadway premiere when they were introduced between reels
of the film.[1] At the New School, they recorded some songs onto aluminum
discs using a recording machine built by Charles Seeger (1913–2001), the eldest
son of Cowell's colleague Charles Seeger.[2] Cowell's wife, the ethnographer and
folk-music collector Sidney Robertson Cowell, recalled that Henry "never had
time or patience really to go around recording himself," so his efforts to record
the islanders are notable.[3] They yielded some of the earliest recordings of music
from Aran, among them one of the earliest known recordings of the Irish practice of lamentation known as *caoineadh* or keening.

Twenty-one years later, before embarking on a European tour during which
Henry gave concerts and lectures, the Cowells holidayed in Ireland. While they
both wanted to see Aran, Sidney wrote that "the one person Henry wanted to
see was Maggie Dirrane."[4] They arrived in Ireland on May 31, 1955, and went to
Árainn, staying in Conneely's guesthouse in Cill Mhuirbhigh around two miles

east of Maggie's home in Eoghanacht.[5] Sidney wrote: "Maggie was touchingly happy to see Henry again, and she and her son Sean both sang for us,—Sean with a remarkably decorative old style learned from an ancient singer when he was a boy."[6] It was Sidney's first time hearing sean-nós singing, and the experience changed the course of her life for the next two years. Within a week, she turned their vacation *à deux* into a solo music-collecting trip and became one of the first people to bring sound recording equipment to Aran. For many of the islanders she met, she was the first to record them. She created a collection of sound recordings, writings, and photographs that is pioneering and little known in the field of Irish traditional music.

Sidney's work on the music of Aran was pioneering on a number of fronts.[7] Her collection is one of the earliest sound records of music and song in Aran. In Ireland, the field of music collecting was then dominated by men from Ireland and Great Britain, so Sidney stands out for being one of the first women collectors and one of the first American collectors to work there.[8] In 1957 she published some of her 1955 field recordings on *Songs of Aran*, an album she produced for the American company Folkways Records. It was the first commercial music record from Aran and includes a rare commercial release of caoineadh. It was also one of the earliest US releases of sean-nós singing on record.[9]

Sidney's early exposure to a wide range of different musics throughout America and her work as an ethnographer and music collector combined to give her a perspective on Irish traditional music that was then uncommon among collectors from Ireland or Great Britain.[10] This chapter examines the juxtapositions that arose in contemporary collecting practices and raises questions about the motives and methodologies of professional collectors who have the power to canonize the music they collect via broadcasting, archiving, or publishing. It highlights the need to examine how the elements of power, authority, and responsibility contribute to the work of collectors of traditional music. Finally, this study—in particular, the discussion of Sidney's documentation of keening—showcases a rare fieldwork achievement and illustrates well the benefits of ethical fieldwork, which can create an atmosphere of dialogue between the collector and the performer. Such an atmosphere enables a potentially fruitful exchange in which the performer is enabled to contribute via recording to the permanent record and the collector can create a representation that is fair and faithful to the performer and their practice.

Sidney Robertson Cowell

Sidney William Hawkins was born in San Francisco on June 2, 1903, to Charles Albert Hawkins and Mabel "Muz" Morrison, the eldest of their four children.[11] Catherine Hiebert Kerst, who has conducted extensive research on Sidney's work, describes her relatively privileged childhood:

> Her family appears to have been quite well off. As a child, Sidney was bright, articulate, and inquisitive. Her upbringing reflected an independent and rather unstructured, but open-minded educational philosophy, progressive in character, but definitely high-cultural in texture. She was given piano, violin, dancing, and elocution lessons from an early age. She had French tutors, riding and polo lessons, children's cooking classes and more.
>
> From the ages of 10 to 14, Sidney accompanied her piano teacher each summer on "Cook's Tours" of Europe. Sidney seems to have been present at many memorable early 20th century high cultural events and to have run into or met royalty and famous artists, authors, and musicians frequently. She claims to have attended the premier of Stravinsky's *Sacre du Printemps* in Paris. She was in Rome at the outbreak of World War I and in Paris when German troops moved into Belgium. And she wrote and spoke about her experiences with flair and in detail.[12]

After obtaining a degree in Romance languages and philosophy at Stanford University in 1924, Sidney married philosophy student Kenneth Greg Robertson.[13] They moved to Paris, where she took piano lessons with Alfred Cortot in the École Normale de Musique.[14] They also studied with Carl Jung in Zürich. They returned to California in 1926, where Sidney taught music in the Peninsula School for Creative Education in Menlo Park until 1932.[15] At the same time, she studied counterpoint and analysis with Ernst Bloch at the San Francisco Conservatory of Music and received a formal introduction to "the music of non-European cultures" from Henry Cowell (1897–1965), who would later become her second husband.[16] Sidney had known Henry since she was fourteen years of age and began taking piano lessons from him in 1927.[17]

By this time, Sidney had already begun to transcribe and collect music informally, including Spanish and cowboy songs that she then taught to her pupils. In her taped reminiscences of the 1980s, now housed at the Library of Congress, she recalled how this experience proved to be formative: "I had for some time been worrying the question of folk song, like a dog with a bone, and particularly I was curious about American Folk songs—what was American about it? I knew only the Lomax *Cowboy Songs* and a few tunes from my parents, but I had been so struck by the wild enthusiasm and persistence engendered among the youngsters at the Peninsula School by "Home on the Range" that I was convinced that there was some special affinity between the character of this song and the youngsters who went after it so hard."[18] This question of identity and music sparked Sidney's lifelong interest in folk music and coursed through her entire career as a music collector and ethnographer.

MUSIC WITH A PURPOSE

Around the same time, Sidney began to exhibit a related concern for the social purpose of music. America in the 1930s was characterized by social activism and progressivism that had emerged in the late nineteenth century and became more urgent during the Great Depression.[19] After she and Kenneth divorced in 1934, Sidney decided she was leading too "self-indulgent" a life in California and moved to New York in 1935 to serve as director of the Social Music Program at the Henry Street Settlement on the Lower East Side.[20] The program "offered large-scale recreational music activities" such as choirs, choruses, and other ensembles.[21] Its purpose was "to help tenement workers forget, if only temporarily, their deplorable living and working situations."[22]

While visiting friends in Washington, DC, in 1936, Sidney went to the Archive of American Folk Song at the Library of Congress to ask the question regarding the identity of American folk songs that had arisen during her time at the Peninsula School. There, she was encouraged to visit Charles Seeger (1886–1979), who had become centrally involved in the efforts of President Franklin D. Roosevelt's government to capitalize on the social benefits of music via a radical new series of programs known as the New Deal. Seeger had traveled a path similar to Sidney's, charting his own "musical odyssey" from California to New York in 1919 and then to Washington, DC, in 1935.[23] His appointment that year to the position of head of the Music Unit of the Special Skills Division of the Resettlement Administration enabled him to begin the realization of his personal vision for the role of music in people's lives. He sent his staff of ten fieldworkers, including Margaret Valiant (1901–81), Herbert Haufrecht (1909–98), and Herbert Halpert (1911–2000), into various resettled communities to collect folk music and to use music to ease tensions and cultivate a sense of community.[24] Seeger was "in his element, having finally met his goal of meaningfully relating music and society, a goal which his personal odyssey of twenty-five and more years had sought to satisfy."[25] Although his ambitions for the Resettlement Administration (RA) and for the subsequent organizations with which he was involved, including the International Music Council and the Pan-American Union, were not fulfilled, the legacy of his socially conscious conception of music has since been borne out by his children Pete (1919–2014), Mike (1933–2009), and Peggy and by his grandnephew Anthony: "Each Seeger has contributed to the intellectual and musical culture of their generation and its zeitgeist."[26]

The meeting of Sidney Robertson and Charles Seeger was crucial for both of them. She exhibited a rare and useful set of linguistic and musical skills and had a burning interest in folk songs. He promptly recruited her to work for him. She recalls in somewhat exaggerated terms that Seeger quickly "latched" onto her: "I was the only person that he'd ever met who knew what a folk-song was, and understood what he wanted to do with it. I had been doing something like it at the Henry Street Settlement House, . . . and when Charlie had such fascinating things to suggest, going around with a machine and recording songs, . . . I couldn't resist this. And it was a fascinating experience."[27] Seeger realized that Sidney was "someone who could actually carry out the theoretical notions about the character of traditional music and music-making" in her fieldwork.[28] Sidney may also have been glad to move on from the Henry Street Settlement to escape the atmosphere there, which was still fraught with recrimination after the dismissal of the controversial director of music, Hedi Katz, in June 1935.[29] David C. Paul suggests Sidney left because of ill-health.[30]

DEVELOPING A STYLE OF COLLECTING

Sidney revealed herself to be an exceptionally talented and innovative music collector (fig. 6). Early discussions with Seeger helped her "forge her notions and techniques" of music collecting.[31] She recalled that his instructions to her were to "record EVERYthing. . . . Don't select, don't omit, don't concentrate on any single style. We know so little! Record *everything*!"[32] While the remarkable diversity of her oeuvre suggests she took this advice to heart, Kerst justifiably questions the extent of Seeger's influence on Sidney. Focusing on Sidney's wide-ranging choice of material—in particular on her work in Minnesota, Wisconsin, and the Chicago area in 1937 on Croatian, Finnish, French, French Canadian,

Lithuanian, Norwegian, Polish, Serbian, Scottish Gaelic, and Swiss music as well as songs of English and Irish origin, and on her work in California in 1938–40 on the music of Armenian, Basque, Croatian, Finnish, Hungarian, Icelandic, Italian (including Sicilian), Norwegian, Russian Molokan, Scottish Gaelic, Spanish, Mexican, Puerto Rican, and Portuguese people from the Azores—Kerst observes that, "before the field recordings [Sidney] made in the Midwest in 1936–37 and then in California, there are few examples of ethnographically documented recorded ethnic music made in the United States that include much beyond African American, Native American, French, or Spanish music."[33] Kerst emphasizes the originality and innovation of this early work and highlights the initiative Sidney showed in instigating and undertaking it, drawing attention to her worthy but failed attempt to expand the remit of her California work to include the music of non-Western peoples, including the "Chinese, the Japanese, the Pacific Islanders, the South and Central Americans, the Persians, the Assyrians, the Syrians, and the Sephardic Jews."[34] Assessing the relationship between Sidney and Seeger, Kerst suggests that Sidney "carried out many of

FIGURE 6. Sidney Robertson Cowell, South Haven, Cape Breton Island, August 1953. Photographer unknown. Sidney Robertson Cowell collection, Music Division, Library of Congress. Courtesy of the David and Sylvia Teitelbaum Fund Inc.

the ideas that Seeger merely wrote or spoke about."[35] The diversity of Sidney's oeuvre and the other admirable qualities of her work appear less the result of her mentor's influence and more part of an organically formed, personal style of collecting.

Tracing the development of this style, Sidney first understood the historical importance and potential impact of sound recording, factors that became touchstones of her work: "Recording is not necessarily a museum thing, of course (in case that was implied) but is the only true way of knowing—preserving the knowledge—of what native culture is, in a form that can then be circulated with truth. The old is being snowed under so fast at the moment, and people will want so badly to know what it actually was in another generation or two, it needs an extra support at the moment."[36] Her concern for documenting the actuality of musical performance demonstrates that she was also "keenly interested in documenting folk musical performance in its ethnographic context—not merely in recording individual songs as separate items, as had been done by many early collectors."[37] Kerst praises Sidney's ability to capture in writing "details reflecting the cultural background of the groups she recorded, the environment in which the music was performed, and the functions it served in community life."[38] According to Nicole Saylor, she was among the earliest American collectors "to employ the use of extensive note taking, a field technique that gives her work an integrity notable in its time."[39] She also became an avid photographer.

Sidney's ability to communicate well with people was another cornerstone of her field technique: "I wanted to convince people that I shared their tastes and values and that I liked and understood them. This is what has made a wide variety of people willing and even anxiously determined that I should know and record the best they had. It carried often past the language barrier to simple people who knew only that I found their music beautiful and important and that I wanted it preserved as it truly was for future generations to hear."[40] Sidney soon learned that her winning abilities to communicate with people about music as she was recording them and to put performers at their ease were invaluable—indeed, necessary—to Seeger's RA project because, as she said in her interview with Peter Goldsmith in 1992, she believed "Charlie had a lot of good ideas but he wasn't very adaptable to people."[41] To illustrate this point, she related the following story:

I had a couple of Union representatives who had come for a Congressional hearing, two black men one of whom was a preacher who wore a shawl over his head. And they were in Washington, the man who brought them there knew about our program and said they had made up some songs and would we want to record them? Charlie was not in the office, so I asked them to meet me at the warehouse where the equipment was, met them there, and they sang some wonderful songs, one of them had made up some wonderful songs. And they were [the] nicest, most modest people, nothing surprised, the recording machine they took like the weather. They were migrant farmers from Tennessee, I think, and they had to take a train back at a certain hour. I left a note for Charlie at the time where I was, and he came charging in after I had only about an hour with these men, and he took over. And began to tell them, he wished to make it perfectly clear that he was not racist, and he was not condescending. And to make this clear, he explained how the recording machine worked. Well, they couldn't have cared less.

They were interested in the songs, and I was interested in the songs, and obviously I enjoyed them, and they were perfectly happy singing. But Charlie couldn't stop talking about the mechanics of the thing. And it came time for them to go and they had sung only 3 or 4 songs out of the repertory of 30 or 40, and they had to go. And that was so characteristic of him because he had no sense of people.[42]

Sidney demonstrated an independence of mind, skill, and the courage to challenge the assumptions and superiority of her colleagues, mentors, and contemporaries. Criticism of their methodologies emerged on her very first professional field trip to North Carolina in July 1936 with John Avery Lomax (1867–1948) and the folklorist and professor of English at Duke University, Frank Clyde Brown (1870–1943).[43] (Significantly for her later work in Aran, the trip introduced her to unaccompanied melismatic singing, "a singing style that was to be the chief attraction for her in any folk or traditional music she heard thereafter."[44]) In her first official government report following the trip, Sidney described her primary objective in undertaking it and how her identity as a woman presented her first obstacle: "To get training and experience in running the recording machine and in the rough-and-tumble of folksong collecting under the wing of a veteran in the field, John A. Lomax. Once Mr. Lomax recovered from the notion that a woman is a fragile thing, to be waited on hand

and foot, I was able to relieve him with the driving and recording and lugging odds and ends about, recharging batteries, etc."[45] Soon after, Sidney would go on to work alone "in areas that other single women at the time might have found to be too risky": in lumberjack camps, in dance halls, and with chain gangs.[46] Her identity as a single and independent woman collector continuously challenged contemporary social mores: "[Folklorist] Vance Randolph, in particular, never could understand why I didn't have an assortment of unpleasant experiences: he was scandalized that I would register alone at a motel cabin along the road, explaining that these were notorious places for a couple to make a three-hour stop. . . . I also made some contacts that alarmed him, to the point of offering to lend me a revolver."[47]

After just two weeks in the field with Lomax and Brown, she became dissatisfied with the patronizing and, in her opinion, misguided and damaging methodologies of her colleagues and mentors. Citing her report of the trip, Kerst describes how Sidney was "openly annoyed by Dr. Brown's single-minded interest in finding song and text variants for items he had already collected—always looking for the earliest version possible, she felt, and intimidating performers in his search for new material. . . . Her report concludes with a long-winded critique of Brown's total disregard of the younger generation's singing and dancing traditions as 'irrelevant' and as a 'waste of precious time.'"[48] Sidney was riling against a long-standing antiquarian school of song collecting in America that was established and legitimized by the Harvard literature professor Francis James Child (1825–96).[49] Child collected songs from old manuscript collections that predated the inexpensive printing of "commercial ballads and printed music, which together, Child believed, had polluted the oral tradition."[50] His search for purity in and of folk songs laid a template for later scholars and collectors. His successor at Harvard, George Lyman Kittredge (1860–1941)—who later taught John A. Lomax—believed "the text is the thing."[51] Sidney imagined her "training as a musician conditioned her interest in the music and the singing styles that belong to traditional singing and playing, at a time when other folksong collectors in the US were for the most part interested only in gathering texts."[52]

Sidney also criticized Lomax's and Brown's discriminatory attitudes toward the people from whom they collected songs. In particular, she criticized the way they had tried to lead her to believe that "mountain people" were "difficult and strange folk."[53] The newfound "awareness of folk traditions" may have represented "a kind of evolution from and beyond the leftist political aesthetic agenda of the 1930s," but many of the contemporary collectors of folk music were simply blind to their own discriminatory ways.[54] The best-known example of this is the relationship between John A. Lomax and Huddie Ledbetter, which Sidney witnessed:[55]

> Lead Belly was so remarkable. The way [John A. Lomax] got the black singers was to go to the Chain Gang camps in the prisons. Everyone was gathered together and was crazy to sing, it was very handy. And I went with him to two or three of those places. But he was very patronizing to the men, the whole thing was kind of sickening. It is true that Lead Belly sang himself out of prison, with John's help, because John wanted him to travel and help illustrate his lectures. John Lomax sort of took on the behavior of the Southern large land holder, which he wasn't at all. And he told me once when Lead Belly got impatient with him after he got more experience with other people and living in New York and so forth, he said, "I don't see how he could do this; I treated him just like my own son. He slept in the same room with me right on a pallet by the door." . . . He didn't see at all.[56]

In contrast to some of her colleagues and mentors, Sidney's style of music collecting was respectful, relatively holistic, and remarkably broad-minded. Over the course of her twenty-one-year career as a collector, she collected from star performers with substantial repertoires, including singers Warde Ford of Crandon, Wisconsin, and Emma Dusenberry of Mena, Arkansas, as well as children who had learned their songs either at home or at school.[57] She collected dance music, ritualized music such as keening, children's songs, charms, old compositions, and new ones.[58] She collected work or occupational songs, whether it was among the lumberjacks of the Great Lakes states or at milling frolics in Cape Breton Island, Canada.[59] She was also interested in the song traditions of individual families, which offered a chance to observe the changing functions and fashions of a song tradition over time. Over fifteen years, she found several opportunities to study one midwestern family.[60]

From the beginning, Sidney's style of music collecting was founded on a modern understanding of musical traditions as being "contemporary, dynamic and alive" and not "antiquarian" as demonstrated to her by Brown. In her report of the 1936 North Carolina trip, she illustrated that understanding vividly:

"And here we are, struggling to make our way into the main current of contemporary culture, which we conceive as dynamic and alive, drawing its force from a thousand tributaries which flow forward with a perpetual meeting of the waters, into the future!"[61] Her style of music collecting was based on a fundamental belief that, as a music collector, she was—in her own words—part of a symbiotic process of "sharing the music ... with people who liked the music and appreciated that I liked it. So I was part of the scene."[62] She explained further the principles on which her successful style of collecting was based:

> I could get singers to sing without paying them, because our objective was the same. I said, "These songs are disappearing, and the government wants to help preserve them." And that was their objective, too. So there was no question of my hiring them to do anything for me, which was hard for Alan [Lomax {1915–2002}] to understand. He gave people the feeling that they were doing something for him, personally. And I never felt that way, and was careful to avoid the appearance of it. So that people sang for me quite readily; I think in all the time I was collecting, people refused only twice. Sometimes they were shy, it would take a while to get them refusing, but it was only twice that people said no and they stuck to it. Out of several thousand informants. So I thought that was not doing too badly.[63]

Kerst observes how her perception of the "folk"—a perception she shared with other "New Deal radicals"—helped "pave the way for our current understanding of the doing of ethical fieldwork—including the fostering of respect for performers' rights and the acceptance and acknowledgement of the active and very adaptable living character of expressive traditional musical culture."[64]

MORE MUSIC COLLECTING

After the Special Skills Division of the Resettlement Administration was liquidated late in 1937, Sidney began fieldwork that transformed into a pilot project known as the California Folk Music Project.[65] In October 1938, with funding from the Works Progress Administration, the Music Division of the University of California at Berkeley, the Archive of American Folk Song at the Library of Congress, and the California State Relief Agency, Sidney's staff of twenty commenced work at Berkeley.[66] Kerst observes that the project was "ahead of its time in documenting a representative collection of English-language and

European ethnic folk music from Northern California."[67] Sidney hoped the collection would "provide a prototype for a national folk music collecting effort," but it was closed in 1940 due to a lack of funds.[68] She then began, as she wrote, "looking for some way of financing the continuation of my field collection," but she had little success: "Until Charlie Seeger made me his office assistant at the Pan American Union in June 1941, the only income I had was a couple of $50 payments, very kindly made me by Alan Lomax, for setting up the bibliography of American Folk Song that some music teachers' organization had asked him for. . . . At the end of September, my three-months' Pan American Union contract job ended. Henry Cowell and I were married September 27 [1941]."[69]

Following her second marriage, Sidney made fewer field recordings. In the mid-1940s, she recorded in their homes singers she heard at the White Top Festival in Marion, Virginia.[70] In September 1950 she took "great pleasure" in recording with Maud Karpeles in the Appalachian Mountains where Karpeles and Cecil Sharp had collected between 1916 and 1918.[71] In 1951 Sidney wrote notes to accompany Moe Asch's Folkways album of shape note singing titled *Old Harp Singing by the Old Harp Singers of Eastern Tennessee*. Between 1955 and 1957, she released three albums of the music she collected during the early 1950s, also on Folkways. In 1955 she released some of her recordings of Gaelic singers from the North Shore on *Songs from Cape Breton Island*. From 1950 to 1954 she continued to record members of the Ford-Walker family intermittently in Wisconsin, California, Wyoming, and Germany; three generations feature on the 1956 release *Wolf River Songs*.[72] Her Aran recordings of 1955 appear on the 1957 release *Songs of Aran*. Sidney's final field recordings were made in the Middle East and Asia in 1956 and 1957.

After Henry died in 1965, Sidney occupied much of her time preserving his memory.[73] In 1980, Brett Topping described how Sidney lived in the Cowells' second home in Shady, New York: "She leads a busy life responding to requests for information about her husband's work as well as her own, and remains a zestful woman of indomitable spirit."[74] Sidney Robertson Cowell died in New York on February 23, 1995.[75] She is remembered as "a talented, productive, capable woman, with a highly original personality and lively sense of humor."[76] For James P. Leary, Sidney's "frank and witty correspondence and memoirs reveal a politically engaged, independent-minded, anything but naive, spunky 'new woman.'"[77] According to Leary, "She was remarkably open-minded not only for her time but for all time. Her work in California, the seeds of which were starting to grow in Wisconsin and Minnesota, was unprecedented in the 1930s."[78] Finally, Alan Jabbour (1942–2017), head of the Archive of Folk Song (now the Archive of Folk Culture at the American Folklife Center) in the Library of Congress from 1969 to 1974, contextualizes her achievements:

> My close-up impression of her as an older woman was that she was assertive, strong-willed, and tenacious in pressing for whatever she wanted to do. She was cheerful and curious, but there was also a kind of determination in her spirit that lingers in my recollections, even when the details giving rise to the impression have faded. That firsthand impression coincides with my impression of her through her correspondence with Alan Lomax and others at the Archive. She might have become more emphatic with age, but I think the same tenaciousness was there all along. It was that tenaciousness that first captured my imagination reading her early correspondence. It must have been difficult for a young single woman as a fieldworker in rural America during those earlier decades, but if she complained aloud, it was about the petty aggravations of fieldwork (balky equipment, blank discs in short supply, etc.), not the existential drama of what she was daring. But of course she was then a young person writing her peers, not a senior figure talking to a young person like me later in life. And she was writing people upon whom she was dependent for assistance. So the tone was more open and solicitous. But what is most memorable to me about the early correspondence is the lively engagement of her full spirit with the ethnographic present in all its fascinating and bewildering detail. She is one of those great correspondents who, you might say, didn't leave anything out.[79]

MARGINALIZATION

Between 1936 and 1957, Sidney Robertson Cowell created a large collection of recordings and fieldwork on ethnic music in America, Canada, Iran, Pakistan, Thailand, Malaysia, and Ireland that is "among the most extensive ever gathered and includes some of the earliest documentation of ethnic music in the United States."[80] This work has been marginalized—surprisingly so, considering the esteem in which she was held by her peers.[81] Reasons for her marginalization include her being a woman working in a male-dominated field; conflicts with peers and superiors regarding her opinions on how music collecting ought to be conducted; the fact that, except for her Folkways projects and the *California Gold* digital collection at the Library of Congress, the majority of her work remains unpublished; and the scarcity of published accounts of her life and work.[82]

Referring to herself in the third person in an undated publicity document, Sidney writes: "SRC is a Californian whose adventures as a 'government song woman' in pursuit of folksongs would fill several books. Before she married the composer Henry Cowell in 1941, she had worn out 3 automobiles, traveling over 300,000 miles in 17 states, alone with her recording machine, her sleeping bag, and a companion once described in her hearing as 'the lady-about-the-songses' dog.'"[83] There were times during her marriage to Henry when Sidney was able to pursue field collecting activities but, as "Mrs. Cowell," she appears to have refrained from indulging in her passion for music collecting.[84] It is difficult to reconcile the image of Sidney Robertson, the woman whose "wit, character, determination, spunk, and expertise" enlivened her solo fieldwork, with the image of Sidney Robertson Cowell, the wife of the famous composer in whose shadow she seemed to live even after he passed away.[85] The contrast makes Sidney's work of the 1950s all the more remarkable.

In Ireland, Sidney's work is remembered mainly for the unique recordings of keening, excerpts of which feature on the album *Songs of Aran*. Her complete collection of Irish field recordings is relatively unknown, standing in the shadows compared with that of her peers Séamus Ennis, Brian George, Peter Kennedy, and Ciarán Mac Mathúna (1925–2009), who, between them, worked for the Irish Folklore Commission (IFC), Radio Éireann (RÉ), and the BBC. These contemporaries often collaborated and intertwined, ranging over great areas for relatively long spells, thereby building substantial bodies of work. Their work earned a lasting, almost mythic reputation through that enviable tool of dissemination and influence—radio. They have also been the subject of study.[86] In contrast, Sidney worked independently in Ireland. She had a limited, short-term collaboration with Séamus Ennis. Her collecting trips were short and intense and, in Aran, she focused on a relatively small area that was then being effectively ignored by other music collectors. The album *Songs of Aran* had a limited impact, and her recordings and papers in Washington, DC, and in New York have remained, until now, largely untouched by Irish music researchers. Sidney's independence appears to have pushed her to the margins of Irish memory.

Motives in Aran

Sidney was first motivated to begin recording in Aran when she discovered that no visiting collector had recorded Maggie Tom Dirrane (1899–1995) or others, including her son John Beag Johnny Ó Dioráin (1925–2004)—whom Sidney called Seán Dirrane—and Pádraig Mhurchadha de Bhailís (1927–2005): "When I learned that both Maggie and Seán had refused to sing for a visiting collector earlier, I reproached them, and when we left Maggie offered her singing and Seán's if we would only return soon. This seemed perfectly impossible at the time, but only a week later, to my great surprise, I was back on Aran, equipped by [the] BBC with a portable EMI tape recorder (thanks to the intervention of the International Folk Music Council), and my clothes planned for continental concerts and summer visits, exchanged for very necessary woolen underwear, a waterproof cape and heavy shoes."[87] Sidney's friend Maud Karpeles (1885–1976), who had visited and collected some music in Aran in 1937, was then secretary of the International Folk Music Council and also worked with the BBC's Folk Music and Dialect Recording Scheme (1952–57) along with her nephew Peter Kennedy (1922–2006) and Séamus Ennis.[88] She expedited Sidney's acquisition of a recording machine from the BBC.[89] It was to be Sidney's first time recording outside of North America, and she relished it as a rare opportunity to collect once again and in new terrain: "I was making arrangements for life in a wheel chair, with no hope of further collecting; but that dire moment seems a little farther off than it did 18 months ago. You should have seen me in fishermen's boots and sweater on a bicycle on Aranmore!"[90]

While Sidney was motivated initially by the novelty and significance of recording previously unrecorded musicians in Árainn, she was also motivated by her attraction to sean-nós singing. With an enduring interest in melismatic singing, she was understandably captivated by some of the sean-nós singing she heard in Aran.[91] She tried to record as much of it as possible, but she also accepted other varieties of singing styles, songs in English, and songs learned in school. As such, her body of recordings focuses on sean-nós singing and catalogs some of the musical variety of Árainn.

The novelty and pleasure of recording such music were later eclipsed by a third motive concerning American folk music. Early in her collecting trip of June 1955, Sidney began to make some musical connections between Irish traditional music and American folk music. In the notes for *Songs of Aran*, she describes the melodic and structural connections she had made and included examples of them. She was keen to document such connections for an American audience because "the music lies very close behind much of the folk music of the United States" and because she believed that there were "no recordings of this [sean-nós] material now in the US at all."[92]

Sidney became interested in a particular stylistic connection she was making between the folk musics of both countries. She connected the more embellished forms of sean-nós singing she heard in Aran and Conamara with the melismatic singing she recorded almost twenty years earlier in America's South. She first disclosed this observation on September 10, 1956, when she sent her 1956 tapes to Harold Spivacke: "You might be interested in listening to Sean Dirrane and the family of Sean Colm McDonogh [Seán Choilm Mac Donnchadha] in Carna, Connemara, to hear (if you have n't heard it before) the decorate [*sic*] musical style that lies behind our oldest singers in the South. Nora Maher [Nóra Uí Mheachair] on Inishmaan is also a fine singer."[93] The content of her collection suggests that this stylistic connection had become a concern for her, at the latest, before she began recording in Ireland in 1956.

Between 1955 and 1956, Sidney made time for some research. She learned that the culture of Gaeltacht communities, including Aran and Conamara, was associated with the country's most ancient cultures. Echoing the growing orientalization of Irish music and of sean-nós singing in particular, she identified the culture of An Ghaeltacht as Celtic in origin and drew attention to similarities with Mediterranean, Balkan, and Middle Eastern cultures—citing the Iberian peninsula, Italy, Persia, "the Orient," and even gypsy culture—but often without indicating specific correlations.[94] In drawing such conclusions and comparisons, which are frequently vague but not necessarily inaccurate, she was emphasizing the antiquity of the music she heard in Aran and in Conamara.[95] She also learned of the esteem in which Aran and Conamara were held as bastions of ancient Irish culture. For Sidney, sean-nós singing was not only the oldest, most enduring, and most authentic local style of singing in Aran and in Conamara; it was also the oldest style of singing extant in Ireland: "At least in the west of Ireland, such singing was a long-established folk style, inherited from a singing style once widespread throughout the Mediterranean."[96] Her understanding of the antiquity of sean-nós singing and of the mobility and mutability of musical traditions enabled her to imagine that sean-nós singing was related to, and even an ancestor of, the singing style of the southern United

States. By May 1956 she had drafted a proposal for the provision of recordings of Irish traditional music that would enable research into just such a stylistic connection with American music, research that no transcription could satisfactorily sustain.[97]

At the heart of this investigation was the question of identity and music that first came to her attention in California in the 1920s and that piqued her interest in folk song: "How was it American?"[98] Her investigation into the Irish ancestry of American folk music represents a search for American identity. As a motive for her work in Aran, this one was at least as significant as her wishes to record sean-nós singing for her pleasure and for posterity.

A MODERN STYLE OF MUSIC COLLECTING

Sidney's search for an Irish contribution to American musical identity is revealing of her understanding of American folk music and, more generally, of traditional music the world over. In searching for the roots of American music in contemporary Irish traditional music, she accepted a dialectical conceptualization of musical traditions as entities that are both static and moving in time and in space. The element of stasis encouraged her belief in the conservatism of sean-nós singing through the ages while the element of movement allowed her to imagine that some of the roots of the singing style of the southern United States lay three thousand miles away in the oldest style of singing in Ireland. This conceptualization of musical traditions was typical of modern American collectors who were casting off the long shadow of the antiquarian school of music collecting and who were trying to refute the myths propounded by Cecil Sharp and his contemporaries. They disavowed the class-ridden, archaeological, and flawed narrative of a long-dead art being unearthed in the manuscripts of England and Scotland or in the mountains of Appalachia and replaced it with a narrative befitting the aspirations of their times, a narrative of a living tradition characterized by resilience and renewal and by greater tolerance, acceptance, and plurality.[99] This narrative was, nonetheless, not without its own faults.[100]

Coming from this shifting American milieu into Ireland in the mid-1950s, Sidney found that music collecting in America and in Ireland shared some commonalities, including an antiquarian urge to preserve the past and a patriotic urge to celebrate it. Nevertheless, she also found that the contemporary Irish narrative of folk music did not reflect the spirit of the modern American narrative of folk music, which she compared—as cited earlier—to a river, "dynamic and alive, drawing its force from a thousand tributaries which flow forward with a perpetual meeting of the waters, into the future!"[101] The Irish narrative of traditional music in Ireland was generally characterized by loss, despair, and marginalization. Many contemporary Irish traditional musicians experienced "indifference, dismissiveness, criticisms of 'inferiority' and hostility" toward the music they played.[102] This climate gave the work of contemporary Irish music collectors a particular urgency. Until the mid-1950s, music collecting in Ireland had been, in essence, a cultural salvage operation, present in the Gaelic manuscript tradition and in the eighteenth-century efforts of Walker, Brooke, and Bunting, perpetuated during the hemorrhage of the Great Famine by antiquarians and scholars such as Petrie and O'Curry, and given a greater political and spiritual potency during the Gaelic Revival. From the inception of the Irish Free State government in 1922, there was government support for initiatives that included music collecting, but in the early cash-strapped decades of the Free State—through the Economic War with Britain of the 1930s, the Emergency of the 1940s, and rising emigration in the 1950s—those who were motivated to collect music in Ireland faced a greater struggle than their American counterparts to gain fiscal support for their endeavors.[103] Resources were more limited and sound recording equipment was scarce. Economic constraints combined with political needs to train the focus of music collecting in Ireland on preserving the culture that was still regarded as the country's most significant, on a national and global scale, and, at the same time, as being in the gravest danger of extinction: the culture of An Ghaeltacht. Alan Lomax witnessed this emphasis on Gaeltacht culture during his monthlong music collecting trip around Ireland with Robin Roberts in 1951. In a typically subjective but vivid description of the work of staff of the Irish Folklore Commission among the Irish-speaking "cottagers in the West"—a description that both echoes and contrasts with Sidney's metaphoric depiction of the work in which she, Lomax, and other collectors in America were engaged—he captured a sense of the "special urgency" of their work there: "They see an entire culture traced on the sands of the western beaches. They must recover what they can, before the next wave washes the beach smooth of the old words."[104] The pessimism of 1950s Ireland combined with the continuing decline of An Ghaeltacht to further entrench the views of contemporary Irish music collectors.

Into this Irish milieu, Sidney brought a modern style of collecting. She took care to document not just the music and the context in which it was collected, as many Irish collectors including Séamus Ennis already did, but she also took care to document the process of negotiation between the collector and the performer that led to each performance.[105] It can be argued that Sidney was enabled to indulge in ethnographic detail because she had a winning combination of resources, including abilities, time, and money. For want of such resources, many of her Irish contemporaries were unable to emulate, or could not afford to entertain, the relative holism and pluralism that characterized her approach.[106] Nevertheless, Sidney was less forgiving of the inadequacies she saw in contemporary professional Irish music collecting. For her, its postcolonial focus jarred with the increasing pluralism of the modern American style of music collecting, and her interpretation of contemporary Irish attitudes to folk music and to music collecting was that they awaited modernization.[107]

Sidney drew particular attention to the marked difference between the ways in which Irish and American collectors treated song. All collectors of Irish music, including Sidney, used orality as a mark of authenticity in seeking a localized and thus unique and authentic folk music. In Ireland, however, she found a rigid interpretation of the connection between oral transmission and authentic folk music, based on the process of oral transmission but focusing on its content, its product—in this case, the song text—and questioning its purity or authenticity, its loyalty to the original text. She wrote: "Divergence from the original creator's intentions is not considered a virtue."[108] Contemporary American attitudes were more liberal. "In America," she wrote, "our confidence in the new and the individual seems to have led us to welcome variation, so that we have developed great interest in the whole *process* of variation, which we think of as an unconscious selection that produces regional styles."[109] Where people like Séamus Ennis found Aran's contemporary songs "truaillighthe" or "corrupted," Sidney could accept the same songs that were—in her words— "textually imperfect" because she was interested in the process of oral transmission and in "the interest and beauty of their melodies and their singing styles."[110] The contrast between Irish and American approaches to collecting music is, of course, tempered by collaborations between both parties.

Sidney's criticism of the methodologies of Irish music collectors extended to other issues.[111] Of the IFC, she wrote to Rae Korson: "They are preparing, and doing, a lot of publication themselves; but you'd have thought that the

concept of publishing [audio] *records* was completely new and unheard-of, as
was obviously the idea that notation is a short-hand, not a full publication. Dear
me."[112] She tried to contribute to the field of traditional music collecting and
scholarship in Ireland. In the proposal document previously mentioned, she
shared with Séamus Ó Duilearga, head of the IFC, her personal recommenda-
tions for, among other things, the improvement of field recording in Ireland:[113]
"Delargy," she wrote, "is an immensely adroit man, and I think he is aware that
Ireland greatly needs contact with the best modern techniques in many fields,
and that an 'expedition' from a great University that has functioned successfully
in connection with other aspects of Irish history and tradition, would have the
proper weight to make its standards contagious."[114]

Throughout her time in Ireland, and in the aftermath of her visits, Sidney
encouraged a change in Irish attitudes to the purpose and use of sound recordings and attempted to rebuild bridges between Irish and American folk song
scholars and institutions, bridges that had previously been burned by tactless
gestures:[115] "I offered to let [Radio Éireann {RÉ}] copy my stuff, indeed I urged
it, so everybody is now very relaxed. [Pádraig Ó Raghallaigh] is a nice man,
but not a collector nor student; he would feel, I think, that it would be highly
advisable from several points of view for R.E. to cooperate with you [at the LC]
in making Irish music available to scholars in the U.S. (R.E. is largely subsidized
but I believe not formally a gov't [government] station.)."[116] Her efforts to promote dialogue between concerned parties in Ireland and the US may not have
had a direct impact on the modernization of music collecting in Ireland, but in
sharing her experience and opinions with her Irish counterparts, she brought a
fresh perspective to the field of professional music collecting there.

METHODOLOGY IN IRELAND

Although her focus on a particular style of singing, namely sean-nós, marked
a purposeful departure from her omnivorous collecting for the RA and the
Works Projects Administration (WPA) California Music Project, in Ireland
Sidney tried once again to collect from men and women of all ages, and sometimes from specific families, a broad and diverse repertoire ranging from occupational songs to keening.[117] In recording, Sidney aimed to collect sean-nós
singing and sean-nós songs in a manner that was fair and faithful to each performer. Recognizing that successful recordings are born of a relationship of
understanding and trust between the collector and the performer, she took

time to gain the confidence of potential performers. The few surviving photographs that she took echo the ethnographic style of her writings.[118] She produced revealing accounts of her fieldwork and of the music and musicians she encountered, acknowledging actualities that other collectors failed to capture for want of an opportunity, a sense of purpose, or the desire to do so.

Sidney faced difficulties in finding traditional singing because people did not always agree on what constituted "traditional" music. In Carna in August 1956, she wrote: "I can't go everywhere, alas, so must choose according to local reputation for large repertory, popularity, prevalence of sean-nós (*old* songs, traditional ones), and most active singing trad[ition] in the home."[119] In Inis Meáin her song collecting triggered a discussion about what was traditional: "Father Benedict, a visiting personality from Dublin, kept things in order outside, and was kind enough to say I had greatly helped forward the "cause of truly Irish music" by refusing some songs on the ground that they were not traditional, and thus stirring much dispute as to what was, and what was not, an Irish song. Actually, the only things refused were non-traditional *singers*; but the distinction between singing styles, apart from texts and tunes, seems impossible for most people in Ireland to grasp."[120]

As compared with other collectors, Sidney was at a disadvantage because of her lack of familiarity with sean-nós songs and with the Irish language. She attempted to overcome it, improving her knowledge of sean-nós songs and learning Irish so she might understand and communicate better with sean-nós singers.[121] Her shortcoming in this regard may have focused her attention more on the musical aspects that fill her writings including ornamentation, vocal style and delivery, and how the voice was used or projected. In her efforts to contextualize and to qualify the music she recorded, Sidney consulted printed works, including Douglas Hyde's *Love Songs of Connacht*, Fr. Tomás Ó Ceallaigh's *Ceol na nOileán*, Eibhlín Bean Mhic Choisdealbha's *Amhráin Mhuighe Seóla*, George Petrie's *Complete Collection of Ancient Irish Music*, Colm Ó Lochlainn's *An Claisceadal*, Donal O'Sullivan's book on Irish folk music (presumably *Irish Folk Music Song and Dance* of 1952), and Róis Ní Ógáin's *Duanaire Gaedhilge*.[122] She also contextualized the music she heard in Ireland by comparing it with American folk music and by actively pursuing airs and tunes she thought were related to American tunes.

With respect to the authority of the versions of songs she collected, Sidney tried to balance the opinions of collectors with those of local singers. She sought the opinions of people who were authorities on the subject of traditional sing-ing, including Séamus Ennis: "He is much the best collector here, a wonderful guy."[123] Following her 1956 trip, an unnamed peer or peers in Ireland compli-mented her recent recordings: "These tapes are all done in the west of Ireland, in the Aran Islands and Connemara, and some of the stuff is very fine, *I am told here* [my emphasis], from every point of view; some of it is textually im-perfect; but all but one or two things are of real musical interest."[124] She some-times disagreed with authoritative opinion. When Séamus Ennis questioned the authenticity of some of the songs Sidney recorded—saying that many of them "were the identical versions (as to text, but seldom as to tune apparently) that have been published with school circulation in view"—she responded: "None of these songs can have been learned in this way."[125] The singers themselves had told her they learned them orally from other singers in the community.

For want of time or, perhaps, for want of another opportunity, Sidney's investigation into the Irish ancestry of American folk music was incomplete. By the time *Songs of Aran* was released in 1957, she appears to have disengaged from, or even lost faith in, some of the theories that spurred and steered that work. Regardless, her thorough, understanding methodology of collecting music yielded an admirable record of contemporary traditional music making in Aran and, more especially, of contemporary sean-nós singing in Aran and Conamara. Her peers at the IFC later "approved the material on the record [*Songs of Aran*], simply as a 1955 report on singing on Aran, with the exception of the last part of the caoine done by the anonymous croonan."[126] They also "felt the material was old but that they could find better to represent Ireland."[127]

THE COLLECTION

Sidney's two recording trips to Aran and Conamara in 1955 and 1956 produced up to eleven hours of relatively good-quality recordings; around two hundred tracks have been cataloged by the author.[128] It is a considerable haul bearing in mind the ways in which time, weather, illness, technical hitches, and bad luck impeded her efforts. Though Alan Lomax criticized the "tall-tale" quality of some of her accounts, her abundant and evocative writings on Aran—including field diaries, letters, and notes to accompany and identify the contents of tapes—contextualize and enhance her recordings.[129] Her field notes give invaluable insight into the conditions of recording, performance, and musical practices in Aran, and when her tape machine did not let her down, her recordings were generally good too. While there is a fair range of material in the collection, including Irish and a few English songs, a little mouth music, accordion, har- monica, dancing, and keening, it contains far more songs than instrumental music. This reflects the contemporary inclination in local music making toward singing and also Sidney's specific interest in local singing. Through its focus on the singing traditions of individual families—the Dirranes in Árainn, the Ó Fatharta siblings in Inis Meáin, and the Mac Donnchadha family in Carna— and on keening, which she witnessed and documented both in Árainn and in Inis Meáin, Sidney's Irish collection demonstrates her interest in "the processes of oral transmission, cultural interaction and change."[130]

1955: Fieldwork Challenges

Between Saturday, June 11, and Wednesday, June 22, 1955, Sidney stayed in Conneely's guesthouse in Cill Mhuirbhigh. She traveled around Árainn by horse and trap, by bicycle, and by foot.[131] She recorded sixteen five-inch reel-to- reel tapes.[132] Out of ten days, she spent at least five days recording around seven hours of material in the villages of Eoghanacht, Sruthán, and Cill Mhuirbhigh in the western end of the island and in the villages of Eochaill and Cill Éinne in the eastern end of the island. She does not describe in detail how she came to record the people she recorded, but presumably they were recommended to her as she went along.

Upon returning to Árainn to commence her music collecting, Sidney im- mediately visited Maggie Dirrane to discuss recording.[133] Maggie was willing to record, but Sidney met with resistance from other candidates, including Maggie's neighbor Tom Jamesie Ó Flaithbheartaigh: "Tam [*sic*] is a man 54 who came bounding to the door with a lilted fragment of song on his lips—a step danced on the door step not knowing I was there. His embarrassment wore off sooner than I expected and he told Maggie in Gaelic that I seemed a fine common and sensible sort of woman—but his singing awaits the moment that whiskey gives him 2 hearts."[134] The following day, Maggie went to see Sid- ney at Conneely's guesthouse to tell her that her son John Beag Johnny and Tom Jamesie were too "ashamed" to sing. Sidney feared that the whole project might fail, but on June 13, she succeeded in recording Maggie and her daughter- in-law's sister, Máirín Bheairtlín Aindí Ní Mhaoláin, known later as Máirín Lucas (1940–2019), of Sruthán:[135] "Arriving at Maggie's—much talk of the heifer that died some weeks ago—Maureen (aet 15) brought Seán in to hear her song and when I asked him 'Don't you want to try your voice' he smiled assent and sung [sic] a flood of songs—Maggie greatly relieved when I asked admiringly if there are many like Sean on the islands she said, 'Oh almost everybody can do something!'"[136]

Curiosity was not the sole motivation for John Beag Johnny's change of heart. He articulated to Sidney his desire to better his family's current economic circumstances: "He would like to have a [commercial] record made to make up for the heifer that died, but it is hard for him—alas curious neighbors keep dropping in. . . . 'If only I went out on the rocks I'd remember songs fast enough!'"[137] Much later, Sidney recounted that the death of the cow was the catalyst for the making of *Songs of Aran*: "When their cow died, I wrote Moe [Asch] said firmly I wanted $150 for this recording. And Moe immediately sent it to me. . . . I just informed Moe that he owed that to him, and without any argument he just sent it to me. He wouldn't have sent it if I had suggested it was payment for singing, I think."[138] She may have been prompted to suggest the making of an album to John by the fact that, at the back of her Aran field diary, she was then writing preliminary drafts of the album notes for her Folkways release, *Wolf River Songs*.[139]

Máirín's nineteen-year-old brother Beairtle or Vailín Bheairtlín Aindí Ó Maoláin (1935–2010) joined the party that Monday, as did Pádraig Mhurchadha de Bhailís (1927–2005). Excepting "Amhrán an Tobac," all of John's performances that day were included on the album, reflecting Sidney's high opinion of him and of his singing: "It will be a long day before I forget his snapping eyes and gay laughing way of swinging hands with me as he sang."[140] She wrote to Harold Spivacke: "Do listen to the Irish singing of Sean Dirrane—so beautiful, and some of it so Near Eastern."[141]

On Tuesday, June 14, with the assistance of Willie Choilm Liaim Ó Coisdealbha, Sidney went in search of Maidhlín Mhaidhcilín Seoighe (1914–96), whom she called Miles Joyce, and his brother, probably Tommy, who was also a singer.[142] They called to the Joyces' home in Cill Éinne.[143] "Dead for sleep" after a fishing trip, Maidhlín agreed, after much cajoling from Willie, to record in the nearby pub Tí Fitz.[144] Men were already singing there by the time they arrived. Sidney sat behind the bar with the machine on the floor and the microphone on the counter between her and the singers. Willie unwittingly inhibited her efforts to secure satisfactory recordings from the men, not least because, in a spirit of generosity and assumed cooperation, he kept buying drinks for them: "Mr. C—is a perfect dragoon, makes any natural recording situation impossible by telling singers not to sing too loud, or too high, or hold the notes too long, or tap their feet,—and if anyone gives the conventional exclamations of applause that I like so much and which I'm sure gives support to the singers, Mr. C—shushes them loudly and if they thereafter forget he playfully plunges about with a threatening fist, making a stir that arouses the singer."[145] Pádraigín Ó Briain (1888–1979) of Cill Éinne was present and he sang a song he learned from his brother Antaine (1902–89), "Amhrán na Trá Báine":[146] "Pat O'Brien, Kileany, is a very old man, obviously a great singer in his day, a kind of 'bank' on which the others at Fitz's pub drew for reminders of songs or bits of text or tune. The whiskey and porter unfortunately put him right under but I liked this first song,—his style of singing anyway—the song ['Amhrán na Trá Báine'] is not a rare one however."[147] All of Maidhlín's songs were included on *Songs of Aran* except for the last one. Although others sang, including Cóilí Pheaitsí Mhéiní Conneely of Baile an Fhormna, Inis Oírr, the men admitted that "the songs had got too wet," so Sidney abandoned the pub as soon as she could.[148] She planned a repeat expedition to Cill Éinne the following Sunday to record Maidhlín Mhaidhcilín and his brother in more satisfactory conditions but was prevented from doing so because, by then, she was suffering from "bronchitis."[149]

Later that Tuesday night, Sidney went to Willie Choilm Liaim Ó Coisdealbha's house, where she had an appointment to record Peige Jóín Uí Fhátharta (1920–82), whom Sidney called Margaret Flaherty of Eochaill but who was originally from Inis Meáin.[150] Willie's nephew Peter Pheaits Ó Fátharta (1910–95) of Corrúch, who was married in Sruthán, joined them—unexpectedly, it would appear. Having been recorded along with his wife, Céitín, by the BBC in 1949, he may have expected that Sidney was recording for a radio station. Peige Jóín was "really tired" after a long day's work:[151] "She sang in a thin firm skirly voice rather like a corncrake, very lovely in its way. Terribly shy, and unable to recall more songs, she said if she were in her garden or beside the cow she'd remember more in a moment. Mr. Costello was unfortunately recommending faster songs to the drawling Mr. Peter Faherty (relation—or at least not her husband) who had come with her, so when she suddenly replied to my query about milking songs with a cradle song ['Seoithín Seotho'], she sang it too fast, with a great effort. But it's a wonderful song."[152] The cradle song was the only one of Peige Jóín's contributions that featured on *Songs of Aran*. Playing host to the work in his own home, Willie was liberal with the alcohol and so Peter "soon got too drunk to sing, alas."[153] While Sidney recorded Peter again later in the week in his own home, none of his performances feature on *Songs of Aran*.

Musical Style

Sidney found a variety of singing styles in Aran including sean-nós singing, though she did not use the term sean-nós in relation to Aran; the term first appears in her Carna diary.[154] She described the "astonishing melismas" of sean-nós style in detail and with accuracy: "The vocal arabesques are not fixed, but are added spontaneously to a tune skeleton, and they vary considerably from performer to performer, from performance to performance. With the older singers they often grow more elaborate, with more decorative notes between the notes of the tune, as the song goes on and the singing increases in intensity and excitement."[155] She wrote that John Beag Johnny Ó Dioráin, one of her younger singers, "superbly exemplified" this style.[156] She included seven of his nine songs and some of his lilting on *Songs of Aran* and excluded his harmonica tunes.

Sidney assessed the authenticity of a song performance according to the singing style, the choice of song, the process by which the performer learned the song, and the song's independence from printed and published sources. Two singers in particular appeared to her to have assumed stylistic traits from singers they heard on the radio. On Saturday, June 18, she recorded Céitín Sheáinín Aindí Uí Fhátharta (1917–91)—whom Sidney called Kate Faherty—the wife of Peter Pheaits Ó Fátharta, in their house in Sruthán:[157] "Very good light soprano—she goes back and forth from the old flat tonal production to the bel canto someone has taught her, and she winds up some of her songs with a high octave, Irish tenor style."[158] As Céitín's style of singing was not traditional enough for Sidney, she excluded almost everything Céitín performed from the album: "Mrs. Kate Faherty sang a couple of years ago for Radio Eireann and received so many compliments on her pretty voice that she has been learning songs from visitors, teachers, and any place else that she can. (She has one of the few battery-run radios on the island, protected from the damp air by a fitted tea-cozy.) She had great expectations of the opportunities she mistakenly thought I could offer, and her singing-style is as concert-like as she could make it. However, the lullaby I was able to use on the record is beautiful, and a traditional one."[159] Of Cóilí Pheaitsí Mhéiní Conneely, she wrote: "This boy has a lovely voice but only fairly good style—faintly bel canto in spots. If he has a large enough repertory various Irish radio programs in the States would love him."[160]

Finding the right songs proved challenging, particularly when people misinterpreted what exactly she sought. For example, Sidney enjoyed Peter Pheaits's performances—"[his] first song ['A Ógánaigh Aeraigh'] was a wonderfully sustained slow bit of the 'great music'"—but Willie Choilm Liaim hampered a successful recording session with Peter by interjecting with his unhelpful opinion: "This is a bit of the 'great music'—very slow, fine melismas—(all much disapproved by Mr. Costello, who kept asking for a really old song, a comallye [*sic*]. I was really ready to wring his neck, wonderful as he has been to me!)"[161] There were some instances of unwelcome songs. The recording session with Peter Pheaits's wife, Céitín Sheáinín Aindí, got off to an unexpected start: "She has a very pretty voice and radio aspirations and has got various teachers here to teach her songs. I declined the one she offered first and tried for simpler songs. We settled on a comallye [*sic*] but when I started the machine she gave me a rebellious look and then went back to her operatic piece. My prime horrible example!!"[162] Sidney identified this piece as "an operatic aria in Irish taught her by a school teacher," but it was, in fact, a sean-nós song named "Eochaill," which was commonly sung in Aran at the time.[163] Sidney did succeed in avoiding an unwanted song from Céitín: "Mrs. Kate Faherty, Schrawn, Aran, sings another song I did not want! About the war and the bombs falling (to an old tune) text by her sister who is a nun at St. Louis (in Ireland), and must not be mentioned. I did successfully evade another song by a priest, a eulogy, lament on his own loneliness written upon the death of his brother priest on Aran (I probably missed something!)."[164] The song about the war was "Amhrán an Chogaidh," which was composed by Céitín's sister Mary Sheáinín Aindí Ní Ghoill (ca. 1920–94), who, as a Sisters of St. Louis nun, was also known as Sr. Benan.[165] The second song—an elegy that opens "Scéal gan cuimhne a shroich ar ball mé"—concerned Fr. Mícheál Ó Flatharta, an islander who was based in Sligo at the time of his death.[166]

Together, Sidney's reaction to Céitín's performances of these songs and the difficulties she faced in trying to communicate with people about songs and in trying to collect songs in a foreign language demonstrate how her lack of familiarity with the Irish language and with sean-nós song had a negative effect on her assessment of a performer and on her collection. By interpreting Céitín's style of singing as untraditional, she ended up neglecting some local compositions that she might otherwise have collected. The manner in which she dealt with Céitín in particular suggests that, although she was concerned about the repertoire she collected, she was ultimately more concerned about collecting what she recognized as the genuine style of sean-nós singing. She recognized that her lack of familiarity with the Irish language and with sean-nós song was a disadvantage and how it was affecting her collection: when she consciously ignored some of Céitín's repertoire, she admitted that she "probably missed something." Although Sidney thought Céitín's voice was beautiful, the cradle song "Thobha Mo Leanbh" is her only piece to feature on *Songs of Aran*, reflecting Sidney's wariness about the authenticity of Céitín's style of singing and choice of song.

Other singers attracted Sidney with their large traditional repertories because such repertories were often examples of a pedigree of orally transmitted traditional songs that were uniquely localized and potentially independent of printed and published sources.[167] For example, although Maidhlín Mhaidhcilín Seoighe was not the best traditional singer she heard—"Joyce is in the 'good typical class'—good singing style of its kind and could sound well"—Sidney was attracted to "the great store of songs he has in his head."[168] Collecting a singer's repertory depended, however, on having a reasonable knowledge of the Irish language and of sean-nós song, neither of which Sidney could satisfactorily claim. Recognizing her disadvantage, she hoped that someone who was better equipped than her would pay heed to such notable singers or song carriers whose repertories were more impressive than their singing. She hoped Séamus Ennis in particular would "spend some time quietly" with Maidhlín Mhaidhcilín and with Pádraigín Ó Briain; "Mr. O'Brien I'm sure has a really large repertory."[169] Her attention to such singers reflects an understanding of how musical ability and musical memory do not always come together in one singer and that to experience a musical tradition more fully prompts consideration of its carriers as well as its performers.[170]

1955: Coda

With the last tape she recorded in Árainn in 1955, Sidney was introduced to the prospect of recording elsewhere in Ireland. On June 21, she recorded a woman from Ros an Mhíl, Máiria Pheaitín Terry Nic Dhonncha, or Marie McDonough (1926–2019), who was working on the island at the time and staying in Conneely's.[171] Máiria sang six songs that she learned mostly from her mother and from her grandmother.[172]

After her departure from Aran, Sidney returned the recording machine to the BBC, left sixteen tapes there for safekeeping, and followed Henry to Europe.[173] She was glad to hear that the IFC requested copies of her tapes be made for its archive: "I'm hell-bent on breaking down these various kinds of scholar-in-isolation worlds."[174] For the BBC archives, Séamus Ennis made copies of some of the material.[175] All of the duplicate recordings appear to have survived. The original recordings were later sent to Sidney in America. She then approached Folkways Records where Moe Asch accepted her proposal to issue *Songs of Aran*.

1956 Trip

Sidney's second trip to Ireland was prompted by Henry's wish to study Arabic music.[176] Their initial plan to spend six months in Damascus, Syria, turned into a tour of ten countries, including Turkey, India, Pakistan, Burma, Thailand, Indonesia, the Philippines, Japan, and Korea, with sponsorship from the Rockefeller Foundation:[177]

> When word got around that we were going to the Near East, John Marshall of the Rockefeller Foundation [RF] asked whether Henry would investigate applications to the RF for various kinds of funding, and make recommendations about the reality of the situation, since such requests were often based on dreams of future competence, without too much basis in realization. Requests began to come in for financial assistance with folk song collecting projects after visiting foreigners had visited the Archive of American Folk Song at the Library of Congress. Everybody wanted one of these of his own, from Istanbul to Singapore and beyond, and I was asked to report on the viability of these requests, too. Ours were not study grants. We were paid salary and expenses, as employees of the RF. I was encouraged, however, to record myself when I could. This was not often possible, but I did bring back some recordings for the Library of Congress, which was generous with letters of introduction.[178]

Sidney decided to preface the trip with a summer spent in Ireland combining fieldwork with some leisure time. She spent three months there in 1956 and planned to spend June 20 to August 18 recording in the west.[179] Before leaving New York, she described her sound recording equipment: "I shall have a tape recorder with me, a Magnemite independent of house current, which does not quite match the quality of my Magnecorder, but the new model is engineered to meet the [National] Association of Broadcasters' specifications and to my ear is extremely good . . . 7½ ips [inches per second] twin-track, claims up to 8,000 vbs [bulk-to-source voltage], which is more than enough for most folk music."[180] Unfortunately, the Magnemite was troublesome. It broke down twice at the most inopportune moments. She lost over five and a half weeks and spent just over one week recording: three days in Árainn, two days in Inis Meáin, and at least three days in Carna: "It was maddening to have the machine go wrong just as I had 3 wonderful musical centers well developed."[181] In spite of these difficulties, she produced more tracks in 1956 than she did in 1955.

Sidney recorded eleven five-inch double-track tapes in at least eight days.[182] The documentation for these recordings is less detailed than her 1955 recordings because they were generated during periods of transience and upheaval. She was uniquely fortunate to witness two funerals in Inis Meáin in 1956 and produced a particularly vivid account of the practice of keening to complement the recordings she produced in 1955, all of which material is examined later in this chapter. After her second trip, she intended to return to record in Ireland again, but never did.[183]

Pádraig Ó Raghallaigh

Sidney landed in Shannon on Tuesday, June 12, 1956.[184] She arrived in Árainn in time for the annual St. John's Eve bonfires on June 23 that she wanted to witness, having missed them the previous year. She did little recording in her first few days in Árainn: "Radio Eireann [*sic*] has a team here recording takes and dances and interviews with old people and children, so I'm biding my time and letting them locate good singers for me."[185] The RÉ team included radio producer Pádraig Ó Raghallaigh and an unnamed assistant, probably a sound engineer.[186] They were sent there by the head of programs in RÉ, Roibeárd Ó Faracháin, to gather material for a series titled *Gaeltacht na nOileán;*[187] RÉ had broadcast material recorded in the Aran Islands only once before, around 1950, and that material was collected in collaboration with BBC producers who had provided the equipment. Ian Lee, former broadcaster and archivist at RTÉ, believes the material Ó Raghallaigh recorded in Aran was not all that rich:

Bhí guth álainn craolta ag Pádhraic agus chuir mé roinnt aithne air i ndeireadh a shaoil agus ba fear uasal geal-gháireach é agus iontach oilte i mbun agallaimh.

Ach is léir ó na taifeadaí nár thuig sé saibhreas agus saoifiúlacht Árann nuair a chuireann tú é i gcomparáid le [Proinsias] Ó Conluain, [Séamus] Ennis, [Seán] MacRéamoinn agus [Ciarán] MacMathúna ach is maith ann na taifeadaí ar scor ar bith.[188]

[Pádhraic had a beautiful broadcasting voice and I came to know him a little at the end of his life and he was a pleasant gentleman and highly skilled at interviewing. But it is clear from the recordings that he did not understand the wealth and distinctiveness of Aran when you compare him to [Proinsias] Ó Conluain, [Séamus] Ennis, [Seán] Mac Réamoinn and [Ciarán] Mac Mathúna but it is good to have the recordings in any case.]

The first program that Ó Raghallaigh produced after their trip to Aran indicates that RÉ recorded in Eoghanacht, Árainn, and in Inis Oírr.[189] The second program appears to be lost along with the material that constituted it.[190] The surviving material consists mainly of current affairs interviews discussing the need for mains electricity in the island, the infrequency of the ferry service (the ferry voyage to the mainland then ran twice a week typically and could be three to six hours in duration), the new vocational school, and the blessing of a boat. Lee is critical of what he sees as Ó Raghallaigh's failure to capitalize on the opportunity he—the first producer to bring an Irish radio team to record in Aran—was afforded to record some of the wealth of local music:[191]

Sílim gur chaill Ó Raghallaigh deis a d'aimsigh Cowell agus ní thuigim cad chuige a raibh an oiread sin de na paidreacha i Laidin ar an téip agus ábhar fíor shuimiúil ar fáil ach an taighde ceart bheith déanta aige. Barúil agam go n-aontódh sé féin leis sin dá mbeadh sé beo.[192]

[I think Ó Raghallaigh missed an opportunity that Cowell found and I do not understand why there were so many prayers in Latin on the tape and really interesting material available if he had only done the proper research. I imagine he himself would agree with me if he were alive.]

Ó Raghallaigh's most significant surviving music recording is of the song "Amhrán na Ringers," composed by Antaine Ó Briain and probably sung by Martin John Thady Dillane, both of Cill Éinne.[193] Ó Raghallaigh also recorded a number of songs that were sung by the choir in Scoil Rónáin in Cill Rónáin. In the dining area aboard the steamer *Dún Aengus* as they sailed from Galway to Aran, he recorded Antoine Tónaí Ó Flátharta of Cill Rónáin singing "Baile Uí Laoi" and a visiting fiddler named Dónal Ó Conchubhair of County Kerry playing "Miss McLeod's Reel."[194] The chance nature of these last two recordings reflects the secondary importance of music to Ó Raghallaigh's mission.

Breakdown

Sidney's exact movements between July 1 and 24 are unknown. The Magnemite broke down shortly after she began recording in Árainn and she brought it to Galway to have it repaired: "I lost at least 3 weeks when I might have recorded nearly every day."[195] During this period, she was based in Geraghty's American Hotel in Galway and spent her time completing the album notes for *Wolf River Songs*, preparing to collect songs in Árainn and Conamara, and learning more about Irish traditional music from listening to it and talking with people. She suggests that, by Thursday, July 26, at the latest, she recorded Seán 'ac Dhonncha or Johnny Joe Pheaitsín (1919–96) of An Aird Thiar, Carna. On that day she wrote: "I have 4 or 5 wonderful bits of singing by Seán McDonagh."[196] The details of where and when this recording was created and what songs Seán sang on this occasion are not known because the recording appears to be missing.[197]

During this period, Sidney paid what was possibly her first of at least three visits to Carna to attend the annual local feis on Sunday, July 15, arriving from Galway the evening before.[198] Monday, July 16, was Lá Fhéile Mhic Dara (Macdara's Feast Day), the annual pattern day in Carna. It remains an important occasion for the people of Carna and for the surrounding communities. It entails sailing to Oileán Mhic Dara (Macdara's Island), where a mass is celebrated, and entertainments including music making and dancing. It is surprising that Sidney did not mention Lá Fhéile Mhic Dara and that she returned to Galway on the Monday morning, missing the biggest day of the year in Carna.

In a letter written to Henry on Tuesday, July 17, she described the feis, the hinterland of Carna, and in particular, the local attitude to singing, which impressed her: "The singing is often elaborately melismatic, and some of the children and young people are proud of Carna's position as the central point for retaining the old traditional style, and they sing quite wonderfully. I am going back there the first week in Aug. for a few days. One of the sons of the family where I stayed (much like the Conneelys) [Seán Ó Gaora (b. 1930), also known as Jackie Geary] is a teacher of Irish in the college at Kilkenny, and knows everybody, and will help me. But we must go back so you can meet some of these people when you come."[199] The people she heard and met at the feis made her hopeful for future recording in Carna: "So many places to stay for songs are opening up to me, I am beginning to feel crowded for time. I am not actually recording all I might."[200] She would later focus on the singers she heard at the Carna feis.[201] She found Carna a place "VERY Gaelic speaking, and singing," to which she planned to return so that she might record plenty of "authentic" sean-nós singing.[202] Of Seán 'ac Dhonncha's singing she wrote: "Seán McDonogh is both beautiful and authentic, quite wonderful."[203]

Sometime during those first three weeks of July, Sidney also visited Eibhlín Bean Mhic Choisdealbha (1870–1962) in Tuam. The meeting between these two song-collecting women arose via a chance encounter in Aran between Sidney and an unnamed doctor who knew Eibhlín's recently deceased husband, Dr. Thomas Bodkin Costello.[204] The doctor brought Sidney to meet Eibhlín, who was then eighty-six years of age. She found her a "wonderful character" and praised her book *Amhráin Mhuighe Seóla*: "It is valuable because it is completely oral tradition. . . . Very fine job. Mrs Costello was [a] friend of Hyde, and Yeats, and Lady Gregory, and the Chestertons, and so on—and is a great beauty still. (But sure her stuff is being pirated in the U.S. She paid for the publication herself in 1923; cost £500.)"[205] Sidney recommended the Library of Congress buy a copy of the book, adding the prompt: "It has some of our northern tunes in good transcriptions."

By Wednesday, July 25, Sidney's machine was repaired. That day, she sailed from Galway to Inis Meáin, where she stayed with the publican Séamus a' Bhéarla Ó Fátharta.[206] She had intended to be in Inis Oírr from Wednesday until Saturday, "but flu intervened."[207] Shortly after arriving, the Magnemite broke down again: "After 3 days of casual visiting and introductions I made dates for recordings, only to find the spring-motor refusing to work when the tape is threaded—a trouble I had earlier but had thought corrected."[208] She was also stranded, the weather being too bad for the ferry to sail from Galway where she might be able to have her machine repaired. Via telegraph, "radio phone," the fishermen's radio frequency, and word of mouth, she tried to find alternative means of transport to the mainland.[209] She accepted her lot: "This now probably means I cannot get back to Inismaan [*sic*] to record except after Henry comes, when I shan't lose much time. However, island life is shaped by winds and tides, and 'impatience serves nothing.'"[210]

Sidney eventually sailed from Inis Meáin to Galway on August 4. Around August 9, "Sean Walsh, a kind of mechanical genius in Galway, got the Magnemite working and even lengthened by 2 minutes the period it runs without rewinding."[211] She next went to Carna. In choosing to go to Carna at this point, she may have felt safer in the knowledge that, should the Magnemite break down for a third time, she was better off being there than in Aran because she would be more conveniently placed to reach her repairman in Galway. She also had only one week left for recording before Henry's arrival.

Preparations and Irish Lessons

While her machine was out of action, Sidney spent time building rapport with local people. She wrote of the importance and the challenge of that exercise: "To get people to give me a whole evening at home so I can get a real idea of their repertory and the relation of the singing to their lives and to the many-sided tradition requires familiarity first of all."[212] She admitted that "it takes a great deal of apparent waste of time to bring this about, before songs are mentioned at all."[213] She also spent time taking Irish lessons from fifteen-year-old Seán Ó Conghaoile in Cill Mhuirbhigh, Árainn, from twenty-six-year-old Jackie Geary in Carna, and, in Inis Meáin, from the Dublin scholar Giollacríost Ó Broin (1878–1973) who regularly holidayed there.[214] In late July she wrote: "My Irish won't take me much forever altho' I begin to understand much of what is being said and can read the newspaper and so on."[215] By the second week of August, she had enough Irish to understand an animated debate overheard in Carna about where and who she was recording.[216] Nevertheless, she did not learn enough Irish to be able to question fully the authenticity of the songs as she was recording them. On her return to America, she compared printed versions with her recorded songs to assess their authenticity and consulted Dr. John P. Hughes of Columbia University and Joseph Davitt (Seosamh Daibhéid, 1903–74) in New York.[217]

Árainn

Sidney spent three days recording in Árainn in 1956; two days in late June and one day in late August. On Friday and Saturday, June 29 and 30, she recorded

Petairín a' Bheagach Ó Maoláin (1910–2003) of Bun Gabhla, whom she called Peter Mullen, and Pat Pheaidí Ó hIarnáin (1903–89) of Cill Mhuirbhigh, whom she called Pat Hernon.[218] The accompanying notes for their performances are sketchy, and Sidney's 1956 field diary begins in late July in Inis Meáin, so neither source gives any insight into her opinion of these singers. Of Pat Pheaidí, Sidney noted that he sang "with his eyes closed."[219] Both men recorded local compositions for her: Peter sang "Creig Sheáin Phádraig," which was composed by Páidín Póil (ca. 1840–1923) of Eoghanacht; and Pat sang "An Mhíoltóg," which he attributed to a poet from his native village, Séamus Ó Caoluighe (ca. 1793–1875).

Sidney's final day of recording in Árainn was somewhat pressed for time. The Cowells sailed from Inis Meáin to Árainn on Saturday, August 25, to stay for just one night. Henry wanted to meet Maggie Dirrane once more, and Sidney wanted better recordings of Maggie to add to the album *Songs of Aran*. Having recorded Maggie and John Beag Johnny before, they were a safe bet in the time available. Sidney wanted to allow enough time to record a little more in Carna and for Henry to see Conamara on their drive up the west coast, so the Cowells left Aran for the last time on Sunday, August 26.[220]

Carna

In Carna, Sidney recorded over at least three days. She recorded families, including the Ó Caodháin and Mac Donnchadha families, as well as remarkable individual performers like Colm Ó Caodháin and Seán 'ac Dhonncha. Considering Sidney understood Carna to be a "center" for sean-nós, and considering the purpose of her 1956 trip was to record the best sean-nós singing she could find in the west of Ireland, it is unsurprising that she was advised to visit the parish.[221] She does not identify the source of that advice. She was impressed by the singers she heard and recorded there. Recording in a different district opened her eyes to some of the diversity of sean-nós song throughout Ireland, which contributed to her theories on the Irish origins of American folk music. In a letter to Harold Spivacke at the Library of Congress dated July 20, Sidney wrote:

> It has been something of a surprise to me to find that the voices of many Irish peasants, like those of beggars and boatmen in Italy, are really surpassingly beautiful by cultivated concert standards, although they may sing nothing but songs

from the oral tradition, in the old curving vocal style,—very surprising from a fellow in hip boots digging peat in a Connemara bog. Many of our ballad tunes are current here, as you know; and some of our sea songs and highwayman songs. And the fiddle tunes for Irish dancing seem to have been transported bodily to our square dance tradition.[222]

Around August 9, and with only one week left to record in Ireland, Sidney returned to Carna to collect music:

This is my last week for concentrating on Irish [i.e., sean-nós], so I have plenty to do! The singing is much rarer of course than it was; but what there is of it is magnificent, so I feel good. Also for the past 3 days the machine has behaved extremely well. It now goes 5 minutes without winding instead of 3, and I have a fine 5-minute egg timer to gauge it by, as I am no good at remembering to wind it during a song [without] some such visual reminder. . . . I certainly was right in choosing Carna when I had only 1 week left for work.[223]

As compared with recording in Aran, Carna presented an altogether different prospect. The population in Carna was then larger than in Aran so, statistically, Sidney was likely to find more singers there. More important than demographics was Carna's identity as a hotbed of sean-nós singing, and Sidney was aware of the significance of this identity: "Some of the kids—Pádraig and Seán [Ó Gaora (Jackie Geary)],—sing fairly well in the winding-about traditional style of which this is the center."[224] She was also aware of how some Carna singers, including Seán 'ac Dhonncha, were known throughout the country and that other collectors had collected there before her.[225] People in Carna were arguably more accustomed to collectors and recording machines than people in Aran. A display of "personal ambition" that Sidney witnessed in Carna— when she overheard a discussion between locals about whom she ought to record—supports this suggestion.[226] Most significant of all was the impressive and undeniable strength of the local singing tradition that Sidney witnessed and recorded. On August 13 in An Aird Thoir, she recorded Seán Choilm Mac Donnchadha (1895–1968) and four of his twelve children—Cóilí (1928–77), whom Sidney called Colman; Barbara (1933–); Peige (1937–); and Michael (1938–)—singing twenty-one songs.[227] "I spent a wonderful evening with a singing family in Carna Parish in Connemara—father, 2 sons and 2 daughters, all with fine voices and wonderful singing style—the men came in, sat down and burst immediately into song, head back and eyes closed, without paying the slightest attention to strangers or machines: we could like it or not; this was their home and their music and *they* liked it."[228]

Earlier that day, in Geary's of Carna where she was staying, Sidney recorded three men: Stiofán Choilm Ó Cualáin (1925–2003), whom Sidney called Stiofán Folan, and Pádraig Ó Gaora (1939–) from the village of Carna; and Johnny Joe Pheaitsín or Seán 'ac Dhonncha from An Aird Thiar, Carna.[229] Eighteen people had congregated in the house that day, and although the recordings of Stiofán and Pádraig are relatively free of background noise, such interference became a worry for Sidney.[230] Relocating to the relative quietude of the car outside, she recorded another thirteen songs from Seán 'ac Dhonncha.

On August 15, Sidney recorded Pádraig Mháirtín Thomáis Ó Caodháin (Pádraig a' Bhláca', ca. 1907–97) of Glinsce; his wife, Sarah Mháirtín Aindriú Ní Churraoin (1915–69), of Oileán Máisean; and their eleven-year-old daughter, Barbara (1945–) in their home in Dumhaigh Ithir, Maíros.[231] Jackie Geary acted as Sidney's interpreter. Sidney left Carna on Saturday, August 18, to meet Henry in Shannon. After eight or nine days, three of which were spent recording in Aran, they drove to Carna together with Seán Ó Conghaoile of Cill Mhuirbhigh, Árainn, and Jackie Geary in order to stay with his family for a few days and "to record Bairbra Keane's uncle [Colm Ó Caodháin] at his home on a low point of the Connemara coast, with the water lapping the stones of its foundations . . . such lovely people."[232] This final visit to Carna was a deviation from her original plans. Colm Mháirtín Thomáis Ó Caodháin (Colm a' Bhláca', 1893–1975) of Glinsce was recognized in his own community and by Irish song collectors as a star informant. Considering Sidney was among the earliest collectors to bring a tape recorder to the west of Ireland, she may have been prompted to make an effort to record him with the latest sound technology by Colm's friend Séamus Ennis, who collected more than two hundred songs from him.[233] In the notes she made to accompany her last Irish tape, Sidney wrote: "Colm Keane said several times that he learned *all* his songs from his father who had them from his grandfather. Seamus Ennis has recorded 180 songs from him."[234]

From Carna, the Cowells and Seán Ó Conghaoile drove to Achill. Sidney and Seán then took the train from Westport to Dublin while Henry drove to Derry and then to Dublin. The Cowells left Ireland for London on September, 12, 1956.

Inis Meáin

Sidney's initial efforts to record in Inis Meáin were thwarted by the breakdown of her machine and also by the occurrence of two deaths in the community that would likely have silenced some island singers for a period. She prepared to record there in the hope that she might be able to return in late August. In a letter to Henry, she wrote: "Darling, you should be here, it's the old old island world. . . . This is [John Millington] Synge's island, and less changed than either of the other islands. Almost all the women wear red flannel skirts with 1–3 black borders like Italian tarentella [*sic*] skirts, plaid men's Seans Rochelle shirts and gay many-colored crocheted shawls."[235] Her diary and letters are similarly occupied with descriptions of the singularities of life in Inis Meáin, by which she was immediately struck upon arrival on July 25: "The now-familiar image of grey stone walls of the islands and the wide view of sky and sea and Connemara [Mountains] that is peculiar to Inishmaan, the brilliant grey light and the scudding clouds, the quiet child at my side, and the donkey, I led with my 2 bags slung across his back and the women in red appearing busy in their doorways to observe the stranger—all struck me to the heart somehow, and I caught myself thinking, as only a few times in my life before: 'This is to be remembered forever.' There is an intensity of awareness [that] comes over one so that one feels the victim of magic."[236]

The antiquity and uniqueness of local culture was encapsulated in the keening she witnessed at the first funeral sometime in July. She felt it offered her "a real glimpse of the antique pagan world."[237] It inspired an extraordinary eyewitness account that will follow presently. The only other musical activity she witnessed in Inis Meáin was a nightly céilí—"a ceilidh, (kayly) a figure-dancing and singing gathering"—that ran "every night, from 9–11"; it was part of the "one man camp program" organized by her Irish teacher from Dublin, Giollacríost Ó Broin, for his grandchildren and for the young Irish-language students in his charge.[238]

Henry arrived in Shannon on Saturday, August 18, and on August 22, they sailed to Inis Meáin with Seán Ó Conghaoile and Jackie Geary. Sidney spent Thursday and Friday recording Colm Saile Ó Conghaile (ca. 1898–1978), Máire Pháidín Bheartlaí Uí Fhátharta (1910–93), Máirín Thomáis Uí Dhomhnaill *née* Ní Chonghaile (1934–2020) and siblings Peige Dara Pheigín Uí Chonaola (1905–90), Nóra Dara Pheigín Uí Mheachair (1915–94), and the poet Dara

Beag Ó Fáthartaigh (1920–2012).[239] She also recorded some children, including Peigí Mhéiní Ní Fhatharta (b. 1944) and Máirín Mhicí Conneely (b. 1943) of Baile na Craige, who was the daughter of Peige Dara Pheigín:

> I had two good recording sessions, the last with a family of really wonderful singers, 2 sisters [Peige Dara Pheigín and Nóra Dara Pheigín] and a brother [Dara Beag], the latter the local bard who has learned, or made up, long songs about the island steamer ["Amhrán an Dún Aengus"] and various wrecks and other local events. This went on till late in the evening and 50 or 60 people gathered at the door to listen. Seeing the crowd, old Kathi Beag [Ceaite Bheag], a great Island figure who once knew Padraic Pearse, came staggering in to ask who was getting married. She was too deaf to understand the explanations and wanted to know who was the husband. I produced Henry and she sat down, satisfied, to listen to the music. (Songs are part of every wedding celebration, which is nowadays their chief ritual occasion.)[240]

On August 23, in Baile an Mhóthair, probably in the dining room of the public house where she and Henry were staying, Sidney recorded Colm Saile and Máire Pháidín Bheartlaí.[241] She then recorded Máirín Thomáis in her own home.[242] Later that day in Tí Sheáinín Thomáis, the Faherty siblings provided Sidney with the strongest local performances.[243] Dara Beag sang a song he called "Mná Spéiriúla Inis Oírr," which he then attributed to the Inis Oírr poet Mícheál Ó Meachair, but which he later attributed to a man from Conamara who was in love with a young woman from Inis Oírr.[244] Meaití Jó Shéamuis Ó Fátharta identifies this song as a version of "Mná Spéiriúla Ros an Mhíl," composed by Paidí Beag Ó Conghaile of An Caorán, Conamara.[245]

The Faherty siblings provided Sidney with a valuable collection of local songs, some of which were being recorded for the first time.[246] Dara sang "Céibh Chill Rónáin," the author of which is unknown.[247] He also sang his own compositions "Amhrán an Dún Aengus," "Dún Chonchubhair," and "Amhrán an Bhearach" [sic], which he also called "Amhrán an Mhíl Mhóir."[248] Nóra sang "Amhrán Inis Meáin," which is also called "Fáth Mo Bhrón," composed by a schoolmaster from southwest County Clare, Bernard Lennon, who had taught in Inis Meáin. She also sang "Aill na nGlasóg," composed by 1924 at the latest by Tadhg Seoighe (1857–1945) of Ballyloughane, Galway, who had worked in Aran from 1910 to 1929.[249]

A group of young girls recited "Rann na Brídeoige," and one of them, Peigí Pheadair Ní Mheachair, recited "Rann an Dreoilín."[250] Peigí Mhéiní recorded "Eanach Dhúin" and "An Spailpín Fánach." The following day, Friday, August 24, in the dining room of the public house in Baile an Mhóthair, Sidney recorded Peigí Mhéiní and Máirín Mhicí.

CAOINEADH 1955 AND 1956

Keening is an ancient Irish tradition of lamentation that reaches as far back as pagan times when its function was, as Breandán Ó Madagáin explains, "to transfer the spirit of the deceased from this world to that of the spirits."[251] Ó Madagáin elaborates: "With the passage of time there came a change of emphasis in the function of the keen: to that of emotional release, although echoes of the older supernatural function persisted down to our own time."[252] Keening is no longer practiced in Ireland, but it is still remembered in some parts of the country.[253] It was practiced in Aran until the 1960s, and Sidney witnessed and documented it there in 1955 and 1956.[254]

The emotional and magical functions of the caoineadh ensured it was rarely performed out of context, and it was dying out when improvements in recording technologies might have eased its capture on record. In addition to the four recordings from Aran featured here, around sixteen other significant recordings of keening survive; these were performed by eight men and four other women, and each of them was recorded by men. Around twenty recordings in total span a period from 1934 to the late 1970s.[255] The final one is a surreptitious recording taken from an unidentified woman at a funeral in Carna around 1979 and, as such, is the only one to have been created in the usual context.[256] The rest were created specifically for the recording machine. It is notable that so many of the surviving recordings of keening originate from Aran; the circumstances surrounding their emergence are revealed here.

From the mid-nineteenth century, instances of keening in Aran were documented by a number of visitors to the islands.[257] These visitors took a special interest in it because it represented an extraordinary element of what was, for many of them, an exotic life. Sidney probably first heard about keening via Henry's experience of recording Maggie Dirrane keening in 1934. Sidney was, by her own admission, "not one to refuse anything rare and interesting" when collecting music.[258] She understood keening to be an ancient element of the musical culture of Aran, so in the context of her work in Aran, it merited documentation.

Keening may have contributed to Sidney's theories on the origins and history of sean-nós singing. She does not draw an explicit parallel between the origins of sean-nós singing and the origins of keening, nor does she suggest that the two forms of musical expression are related, but there is a striking similarity between her observations in relation to keening and the manner in which she qualified the origins of sean-nós singing. Just as Sidney believed sean-nós singing was related to the singing of Mediterranean, Balkan, and Middle Eastern lands, her observations in relation to keening evoke the same geographical area. She compared keening with "a similar ritual . . . found in other Celtic enclaves in the Balkans" and with "a similar ceremonial among the Molakani (Russians from near Van in Armenia, in Asia Minor)" that she witnessed in San Francisco in 1938: "A young woman had been murdered and a half-dozen mourners (who were not members of the family) knelt and beat their heads on the floor as they wailed in much this way, the congregation sitting around with the women covering their heads with their shawls."[259] The Indo-European roots of the Irish language may have encouraged Sidney to make these comparisons with two vocal expressions indigenous to Aran. Nevertheless, she makes no definite statements about the origins or history of keening. While she demonstrates an interest in its musical and performative aspects, in the main she simply reiterates its antiquity. Considering the importance of historicity to her arguments for a musical connection between sean-nós singing and American folk singing, Sidney's efforts to document keening and the manner in which she documented it might be interpreted as attempts to historicize the local musical tradition and so to legitimize her search for authentic Irish music in that musical tradition. Nevertheless, it is more likely that she was motivated to document keening simply because it represented to her another element—primal and fascinating—of the local music tradition.

As an ethnographer and collector of folk music, Sidney was particularly well placed to comment on keening. Her 1955 tracks from Árainn are unique for being contextualized with an eyewitness account of the keening she saw and heard in Inis Meáin in 1956. It is unclear whether Sidney was ever aware of the rarity of her achievement. Among the many collectors who have tried over the years to capture this performance practice, her efforts appear to be the most comprehensive and so are arguably among the most valuable.

Sidney's chief collaborators in this effort were two islandwomen: Bríd Iarnáin, the last professional keener of Aran; and Maggie Dirrane, who was not a professional keener. Sidney first discussed keening with Maggie on June 17, 1955, at the end of their third day of recording:

> After [John Beag Johnny] left, Maggie sang the spinning song again as if spin-
> ning—as she did for Henry and me—then I folded shut up the machine—as it
> grew dark and we sitting there alone—and then had another idea and asked about
> the caoine. To my great surprise she consented to sing it—first going around the
> house to look up and down the road, and then, barring the door against eaves-
> droppers—so fearful of being overheard—She sang very quietly, her hand on my
> knee, rocking slightly, for a long time, going right into the world of the song, as
> I had praised Seán's gift for doing—it was very wonderful. Oho ochone—grief
> grief at night and in the morning—(words that to my surprise I understand!)
> When she finished she said I would not please let anyone who knew her either
> here or in the 'States,' know she had sung me this (it is very bad luck, of course
> for one thing). "This is just a whisper between you and me," she said. "Do not
> sound it by my name" she said.[260]

Sidney wrote that "it has a beautiful 'atmosphere' certainly."[261] Upon witnessing keening in Inis Meáin in 1956, she noted: "The sound is unique and hair raising, a real glimpse of the antique pagan world."[262]

Maggie's experience of recording the caoineadh in New York in 1934 for Henry Cowell—possibly in front of a classroom or lecture hall full of students at the New School for Social Research—emerges as a vital prompt for her to record the caoineadh twenty-one years later.[263] The nature of her 1934 record-ing suggests it was easier for her to perform the caoineadh in New York, far away from home where her performance for the recording machine, and pos-sibly for an audience, would have been unthinkable.

After recording Maggie keening, Sidney was referred to Bríd Iarnáin (ca. 1866–1965) of Sruthán, whom she called by her married name, Bridget Mul-len.[264] Bríd's father, Peaits Mhicil Ó hIarnáin (1841–ca. 1908) of Eoghanacht, was a poet, and her brother Colm was also known for composing songs.[265] Her professional keening services were, by then, rarely required because Fr. Thomas Killeen, or Tomás Ó Cillín—parish priest from 1935 to 1948—had effectively put an end to the practice. In 1972 Pádraig Ó hEithir of Cill Rónáin remem-bered that, earlier, there were better keeners than Bríd on the island, whose voices were sweeter.[266]

Bríd's position as keeper of the flame granted her a special authority, enough to inspire her to perform the caoineadh out of context on several occasions. The first of these reported out-of-context performances dates from the early 1930s when Robert Flaherty was making *Man of Aran*. Flaherty expressed interest in the Irish wake, so Bríd and fellow islander Pat Mullen, who was Flaherty's right-hand man, staged a mock keen to demonstrate one of the wake's components. Pat's account of the macabre episode and his descriptions of Bríd elsewhere in his book capture her wit and humor, attributes that are not immediately associated with keepers of lament.[267] Together with Frances Flaherty's photographs of Bríd, these resources help color the generally black-and-white image of a woman defined by her singular profession and also to vary the timbre of a voice defined by grief, the classic memory of Bríd that became the focus of collectors later.

The prospect of negative reactions among locals did not dissuade Bríd from performing the caoineadh out of its normal context once again, this time for a recording machine. The second report of an out-of-context performance dates from 1949 when she recorded a sample of the caoineadh for the BBC and Radio Éireann as they collaborated to produce a series of recordings that were later broadcast on both stations.[268] In a house thronged with friends and neighbors, Bríd later listened with pride to the broadcast. By the time Sidney got to record her in 1955, the third known out-of-context performance, Bríd had sustained a hip injury that aged her and her voice, and she repeated at intervals qualifications for her performance as it was sometimes strained. In the near sixteen minutes of interview captured on tape, Sidney wisely focuses specifically on Bríd's keening instead of her singing of songs and, realizing the significance of context to this special performance, allows Bríd time to compose herself. With that, we hear Bríd seeking to source the appropriate energy, summoning memories of loved ones now gone and delivering a litany of her personal sorrows before beginning her caoineadh, and then sometimes interrupting herself to narrate her emotional states past and present. Sidney pressed Bríd as far as she could and encouraged her, stopping and restarting the tape to secure as much of the improvised caoineadh as possible. Together, they co-created and committed to the archive an arresting, reflexive portrait of human creativity and vulnerability.

Sidney included two samples of caoineadh, one each from Maggie and from Bríd, on *Songs of Aran*. They are, arguably, the *pièces-de-resistance* of the album.

In the album notes, Sidney qualifies the rarity of her recordings of keening emphasizing that, in Aran, performing the caoineadh out of context was taboo: "It is of course risking bad luck to 'wail' or 'cry' at random what is a solemn ceremonial expression of grief, and one's relatives might well be alarmed at it. But I gathered there was also some question of presumption, since 'crying the dead' is a professional thing."[269] Maggie and Bríd agreed to perform the caoineadh out of context for Sidney's recording machine because of its unique-ness, its musical interest, and because they realized that keening was a local practice then in decline; for all this, it merited special recognition and preser-vation. In the album notes, Sidney stipulated that listeners should honor the exception the women had made in making the recordings: "The singers agreed that I might use [the caoineadh] if I thought it would be heard with respect."[270]

Except for the decline in her voice, there is little difference between Bríd's two recordings of caoineadh. Maggie's two recordings are, however, strikingly different. Her 1934 recording is performative and extrovert and her 1955 record-ing is quiet and understated. The relatively reserved and introverted nature of the latter recording was probably caused by Maggie's fear of local opinion and by the prospect of publication; a fear of being "overheard" caused Maggie to sing "very quietly," and a fear of drawing censure from family and friends inspired her to request anonymity.[271]

Sidney's honest and persuasive approach yielded invaluable and ethically created examples of this artistic funerary rite and ritual of grieving. It might be suggested that it was Sidney's status as a woman that enabled her to record these women keening; but both women had recorded the caoineadh before for men. So in this case, Sidney's good rapport with Maggie was of greater signifi-cance than her identity as a woman.

In 1956, with more time in the west of Ireland than on her 1955 visit, Sidney succeeded in witnessing in-context performances of keening. She found the experience of witnessing two funerals in Inis Meáin "unforgettable."[272] She also heard keening on the mainland, probably in Conamara, and a lament: "A lament is a more elaborate and personal expression of loss, usually done by the be-reaved. An expression of loss, a description of grief. It does not have the ritual character of the *Caoine*, nor does it tell over the virtues of the deceased as the poetic elegies do. I heard such a lament from a woman sitting at the door of a roadside cottage with her head covered with her shawl, near Lisdoonvarna in County Clare. It went on for half an hour, with no one else near."[273]

Sidney attended the funerals in Inis Meáin with the express hope or intention of witnessing keening. When she heard the first funeral was about to take place, she delayed her planned departure from Inis Meáin. When there was no keening at the second funeral in late July or early August, she documented and contextualized its absence:

> For this [second] funeral "the white horses were up" so that it was too rough for the priest, who serves the 2 small islands and lives on the other one [Inis Oírr], to make the trip by curragh for the service; he had come over the day before to administer the sacraments, and would say a requiem mass when next he came. So, a rosary was said, in the evening before the coffin (which was left all night in the church because the dead man's brother objected to being alone with it in the house. As both men were a little odd, and not popular, I was told, no one offered to keep him company, and there was no caoining since there was no one to feel him any great loss.)[274]

She gives the following vivid account of the first funeral she witnessed, which appears here almost unabridged. It is remarkable as a comprehensive ethnographic description of keening on the cusp of its decline as a ritual practice in Ireland. It provides insight into the everyday, emotional, ritual, religious, and historical contexts of the performances, their melodic, rhythmic, and dynamic structures, and the timbre and tone of the caoineadh:

> On an earlier occasion I delayed leaving the island when I heard all the island women going down to meet the boat, their faces concealed this time in the folds of the second red petticoat, the patter of hurrying feet along the stones and a curious moan in their voices giving an impression of acute agitation and urgency. One could hear some unidentifiable bad news running from door to door up from the quay, in rapid spates of speech and rising voices quickly quelled, to be renewed from the next house. I started down with my bag as I had intended, but near the quay I could hear the unmistakable sound of the caoine—the "Irish cry"—a kind of wailing ritual lament with a few words beyond—"Oh, woe,—woe—grief at night and in the morning—Och, ochone—ochone." A coffin was being carried ashore from the *Dún Aengus* that of a young woman much loved on the island, and I parked my bag under a bush and went down as close as I could without being conspicuous and settled among the donkeys waiting for their loads

of flour and porter against a stone wall. The bare coffin was up-ended from the
curragh to the slippery narrow steps of the pier, and 2 women, one the postmis-
tress, at once threw themselves full length upon it, beating the ground with their
fists and wailing. Others joined in, kneeling on the pier and rocking to and fro in
a tearless but profound complaint at the harshness of life and the bitterness of
death—an age-old Celtic ritual, so pagan in its revolt against the human condi-
tion that it is no wonder that many priests object to it, many Irish people are
embarrassed to have so primitive a bit of antiquity surviving, and it is apparently
still done in this public way only under stress of extreme shock and grief.[275]

In a letter to Henry, she describes how women at the wake "cover their heads
with a second red skirt, and all the caoining is nearly invisible[,] women draped
in yards and yards of bright red."[276] Her field diary account continues:

I heard the Caoine going on in the house where the dead woman was lying, in
the evening and before the coffin was taken to the church the next day. Except for
2 old women who came in to caoine before the service began, while there were
yet only half a dozen people present, the service was seemly and only the young
priest's admonitions to calm and resignation produced any tears. I did not feel
I should go to the graveside as I was still so much a stranger but after the priest
left the graveyard I heard (from a nearby beach) the Caoining renewed by at
least a dozen voices, starting high and loud, winding about in a protesting sort
of wail and then falling in pitch and volume, only to be renewed with a deep
long, breath. The voices seem never to coincide except by accident—it is a series
of cries of varying pace, pitch and words, individuals starting and ending at random. All I could make out of the form (and this thanks chiefly to last year's
recording of individual voices alone) was that there seemed to be a long single—
descending—phrase version, another of 2 phrases with men then twice as much
o-ochoning as detail text (this may have been a kind of ABA form, beginning
and ending with the ochone—"woe, woe!") and then there was a seemingly,
much more sophisticated form with 2 lines of text of unequal length, muttered
fast like a religious formula, followed by a violent outburst och, ochone—in
which several people (including some men) joined, although they did not even
then sing exactly the same thing. It was only after a second visit some weeks later
that I felt able to inquire about the words from one of the women; but she was
so puzzled by the question despite perfect goodwill—so unable to conceive of

words apart from the actual "crying" and its occasion, that she could n't answer my question. If my machine had been working properly I might possibly have run it in the dark outside the dead woman's house, but it was too heavy for me to carry so far up hill and across stone walls into a dark corner for concealment, and I dared not ask for help—I would have been run off the island, and quite properly too. I would know better how to manage another time, and with the teacher back on the island I would have help; sometime I will try again, as the sound is unique and hair raising, a real glimpse of the antique pagan world. It fits well with other glimpses one gets on the island for instance the survival of the coracle of Mediterranean antiquity which is identical with today's island curragh—a keel-less canoe for 1–4 men. This is a lath skeleton whose modern tarred canvas cover replaces the skins of 2000–3000 years ago; but the shape and the method of handling with long bladeless oars are the same.[277]

Sidney echoes the antiquarian sentiment of this final statement in the cover of the album *Songs of Aran*, which shows a black-and-white photograph of Aranmen in currachs.[278] As the traditional seafaring craft of the islands for generations, currachs have been an icon of ancient Aran since the nineteenth century. In the album notes, Sidney writes: "These are small canoe-like affairs, still built exactly like the coracles of antiquity except that tar-covered canvas has replaced the skins of early Mediterranean use."[279] The image of the currach would have reminded many Americans of *Man of Aran*, which made heroes of the currach men; the album notes mention the film four times, drawing particular attention to the fact that both Maggie Dirrane and Bríd Iarnáin appear in it.[280] The coupling of the image of the ancient currach with a description in the album notes of how the "age-old ritualistic plaint" of Bríd Iarnáin and Maggie's keens were received—people "felt that the Caoine *is* Ireland, a window into antiquity," and a man in New York declared, "Why that one recording has all Irish history in it!"—historicizes the "antique pagan" act of keening and identifies it as ancient and uniquely Irish.[281]

COLLABORATION

Between 1955 and 1957, Sidney consulted with Séamus Ennis to create *Songs of Aran*. Their interaction prompts us to examine more closely the independence of Sidney's work in Ireland and also presents a revealing opportunity to assess a collectors' collaboration. Though their respective Aran collections are separated by just ten years, Ennis and Sidney collected music from different people there. The only connection between their individual endeavors in Aran is the Ó Briain family of Cill Éinne: Ennis collected songs from Tomás "Tyrell" Ó Briain (1890–1962), and Sidney recorded songs from his older brother Pádraigín.

In return for the use of their EMI tape recorder and tapes, the BBC wished to secure copies of some of Sidney's 1955 recordings and engaged Ennis to identify the material to archive. Amid Sidney's papers, there is a five-page recording log that shows how Sidney and Ennis graded the 1955 material. It was compiled to help them decide what to duplicate, what to archive, and what to publish. The selection criteria that Sidney and Ennis used were essentially the same: the highest possible standard of technical and artistic qualities and the uniqueness of the material.

Sidney marked the performances as a schoolteacher would, with A+, B-, and even NG. Ennis's selection of certain pieces was indicated simply by the note "BBC." Significantly, Ennis made comments to inform Sidney as to the origin of songs—for example, "school learnt"—or remarked on their quality: "good singing, mixed text."[282] For the most part, Sidney followed his lead when she chose what material to include or to exclude from the album. In this way, although he did not create the original recordings, Ennis had an opportunity to influence what examples of the traditional music of Aran should appear on record and what should survive in the BBC archive. Although he never again collected in Aran after his 1945 trip, his collaboration with Sidney presented him with a chance to "revisit" Aran. Ten years on, his choices were characteristic.

In duplicating a relatively high number of John Beag Johnny Ó Dioráin's more successful performances, Ennis appears to have been particularly attracted to John's singing, just as Sidney was. In contrast, the relatively small number of samples from each of the other five singers suggests that he was less interested in their singing than in their choices of song. He probably copied Pádraigín Ó Briain's slightly inebriated rendition of "Amhrán Pháirc an Teampaill" in order to preserve this little-known song. In duplicating just the first of Maidhlín Mhaidhcilín Seoighe's four performances for Sidney, Ennis's intention might have been to keep the best available record of the man's singing; alternatively, his interest may have been piqued by Maidhlín's particular version of that song ("An Cailín Fearúil Fionn"). Ennis appears to have duplicated some of the performances of Peige Jóín Uí Fhátharta ("Liam Ó Raghallaigh," "Seoithín Seotho," "Cúirt an tSrutháin Bhuí") and Céitín Sheáinín Aindí Uí Fhátharta ("Seoithín Seó,

Thobha Mo Leanbh") in order to have a record of their singing as much as to have a record of their respective renditions of the songs in question. In relation to Maggie Dirrane's performances, he appears to have focused more on her unusual versions of the songs than on her singing. Ennis chose to preserve Maggie's anonymous version of the caoineadh rather than that of Bríd Iarnáin, which was, arguably, more authentic given that Bríd was a genuine keener. Sidney may not have disclosed to Ennis the identity of the anonymous keener or the fact that she was not a professional keener as Bríd had been. Ennis's choice may have been influenced by the fact that Maggie's recording is melodically and lyrically more distinct than that of Bríd, whose voice and ability to sing had deteriorated.

Sidney included all but two of the performances Ennis marked for BBC duplication on *Songs of Aran*. She excluded Pádraigín Ó Briain's "Amhrán Pháirc an Teampaill" because, although it was "rare," it was "hardly usable for reprod[uction]."[283] She excluded Peige Jóín Uí Fhátharta's "Cúirt an tSrutháin Bhuí" for a number of reasons: Peige made one or two mistakes, and the tape wobbled at different points in the performance and ran out before she concluded the song.

ASSESSING SIDNEY'S ARAN COLLECTION

The present assessment of Sidney's Irish collection is limited to that which she collected in Aran because a comprehensive assessment of Sidney's work in Conamara is beyond the scope of this chapter. While Sidney failed to collect from some notable singers and song makers of mid-twentieth-century Aran, including, for instance, Maggie Dirrane's neighbors Matt Neainín Ó Maoláin and Cóilín Bheairtlín Ó hIarnáin of Eoghanacht, Ceaitín Neaipe Uí Chuacach of Bun Gabhla, Baba Pheige Uí Mhiolláin (1898–1992) of Sruthán, and Antaine and Tomás Ó Briain of Cill Éinne, her entire collection of Aran recordings presents a good selection of what traditional music was practiced there in the mid-1950s and illustrates some of the diversity of the musical traditions of Aran. Her field notes tell us much about a contemporary musical milieu that was in flux as it assimilated influences from gramophones, radios, printed sources, and oral transmission. The album, however, is a limited record of traditional singing in Árainn in 1955 and so does not best represent the contemporary musical milieu of Aran or indeed the "Songs of Aran." It focuses heavily on the singing of Maggie Dirrane and her son John Beag Johnny and it eschews most of the English repertoire that was then steadily growing in Aran.

The fact that Maggie Dirrane and her son John Beag Johnny dominate the album is unsurprising considering the rapport Sidney had with Maggie and the regard she had for John's singing. *Songs of Aran*, which contains seven performances by John—a substantial contribution that was outnumbered only by his mother's nine performances, often of shorter, simpler songs—provides the earliest record of his singing. It does not, however, provide the best example of his singing.

Apart from the technical difficulties that afflicted some of his recordings, John found it difficult to perform to the best of his ability in what were new and extraordinary circumstances. It being his first time in front of a microphone, he was initially intimidated by the prospect of recording his singing; when he was first asked to contribute, he refused. The prospect of changing his family's economic circumstances may have combined with the persuasive encouragement of his family, in particular that of his mother, to change his mind; but Sidney still found it "difficult to get anything but comallye's [*sic*]" from him, songs that were not in a sean-nós style.[284] John was then busy with farm and shore work, and he sometimes used that work as an excuse to evade the machine or to escape the attention of inquisitive callers. Compared with his performances of "An Caiptín Seoirse Ó Máille" in 1962 for Bairbre Quinn and in 2001 for me, his performance of the same song for Sidney was atypical.[285] In 1955 he sang it to a quicker and slightly different version of the same tune, a choice that is suggestive of his desire to escape the recording machine and get back to work.[286]

Sidney's album notes to *Songs of Aran* are long and somewhat detailed but are inconsistent in comparison with the shorter album notes for *Wolf River Songs*. They feel rushed in parts and sometimes inconclusive. This is, perhaps, understandable considering that, when Sidney first approached Folkways Records, she lacked expertise in Irish traditional music, in particular in relation to Irish song. Nevertheless, between 1955 and 1957, her familiarity with Irish traditional music increased. She learned much about Irish music from books and from people in Ireland and in America. The album notes name Dr. John P. Hughes and Joseph Davitt in New York and James Ross at the School of Scottish Studies of the University of Edinburgh as three of her sources. In her letters, she also names James Delargy (Séamus Ó Duilearga) and Seán Ó Súilleabháin of the IFC and Donal O'Sullivan (1893–1973) and his collaborator, soprano Veronica Kennedy (1931–2018), of whom she wrote: "Very able gal. Much better than Davitt or Hughes in the U.S."[287]

While her album notes are pragmatic and perceptive if somewhat rushed, her unpublished field notes and letters are more revealing. Outside influences like the radio or songbooks are mentioned only twice, and fleetingly so in the album notes, so as not to distract from the image of a mainly local, deep-rooted, independent, if not autonomous, tradition of music. Sidney excluded from the album the song she regarded as an "operatic piece"—"Eochaill"—sung by Céitín Sheáinín Aindí Uí Fhátharta (Mrs. Kate Faherty) of Sruthán, along with Céitín's younger sister Sarah Ní Ghoill (b. 1930), who tried to introduce songs that she had learned from literary sources, songs that were from another musical genre altogether: "Young Sarah with her US notions is making things worse. . . . [She] wanted to sing a song about Galway Bay which everybody knows—written by a pair of radio stars—Sarah had the sheet music for it, and some printed texts of other popular songs. 'Galway Bay' is the equivalent of our synthetic rodeo cowboy ditties. Chickens wandered in and out—Mr. F and I approved of this but Sarah did not."[288]

Sidney's unpublished diaries and letters throw up such colorful instances of the contemporary musical milieu in flux. In the context of her collected Aran recordings, these descriptions seem startling and even alien, but in the context of other contemporary recordings and collections, including those of Bairbre Quinn, these descriptions ring true. Where the unpublished elements of Sidney's work reveal some of the changes that were then occurring in the musical milieu of Aran, they show up the published element—the album *Songs of Aran*—as a representation of an ideal of Aran music rather than of the actual musical milieu of Aran, an ideal that focused on that which was deemed to be most authentic to Aran.

This attempt to historicize the music of Aran was driven as much by Sidney's investigation into the Irish roots of American music as it was by the commercial needs of the album. For her part, by the time the album was released, her theories concerning those Irish roots had either faded or faltered. Her familiarity with English-language song and instrumental music in America enabled her to qualify with some certainty the melodic connections she was making between Irish traditional music and American folk music. In the album notes, she wrote: "Not only have Celtic melodic styles penetrated our song and dance tunes, but actual melodies still sung in western Ireland with Gaelic texts can be found in the northern United States, used with topical lumberjack and miners' song texts and all sorts of other songs in English; and innumerable fiddle tunes are played and named alike in both countries."[289] She gave specific examples, such as comparing Maggie Dirrane's version of "'Twas Early, Early in the Spring" with versions of the same song collected by Cecil Sharp and Maud Karpeles in the Appalachian Mountains, and this comment on a tune sung by Céitín Sheáinín Aindí Uí Fhátharta of Sruthán: "Her 'tune for going around the house' was *Way Up on Old Smoky,*—a far cry from Bascom [Lamar] Lunsford who first put this song into circulation from North Carolina."[290] In trying to prove her theory of a stylistic connection between sean-nós singers and "our oldest singers in the South," however, Sidney faced some difficulty. In her unpublished correspondence, she is direct. She marks a clear line of influence between sean-nós singing and the singing of the southern states.[291] Later, in the album notes, her description of this stylistic connection is vague: "The astonishing melismas (several tones to a syllable), which had nearly disappeared in the United States when I began recording traditional music twenty years ago, and which are superbly exemplified in the singing of Sean Dirrane, were a commonplace of concert singing in the eighteenth century, deliberately learned and often described. From sophisticated musical circles there may well have been some influence on the oral tradition. But it seems more likely to me that, at least in the west of Ireland, such singing was a long-established folk-style, inherited from a singing style once widespread throughout the Mediterranean."[292] By 1957 Sidney had either lost some faith in her theory about the stylistic connections between sean-nós singing and the singing of the southern states or failed to secure enough evidence to support it.

The dichotomy between the published and unpublished elements of Sidney's work in Ireland illustrates two important points. First, comparing the published and unpublished elements of any documentation or recording is a worthwhile exercise. It can reveal some of the issues with which the author or collector has grappled, such as authenticity, loyalty, and truth. It can also reveal the power the author or collector has to affect people's perceptions of the world around them. Second, commercial albums of field recordings do not necessarily provide an accurate representation of the music they mean to represent. No matter how earnest an album producer may be, commercial needs can often come before documentary needs.

A REVEALING COMPARISON

The differences Sidney observed between the singing practices of Aran and Carna in the mid-1950s are striking: "People here [in Carna] sing much more easily than on Aran on the whole. They know me much better, having seen me at the Feis; at the bus drive and the Gearys and the local Garda all promote my interests and answers for me, with the result that now people come around pressing me, not me them."[293] The differing attitudes related less to local singing practices and more to the prospect of singing for a recording machine.

Sidney found that Carna had a critical mass of singers, which cultivated among locals a strong sense of confidence in their own singing tradition and in their abilities as singers. Their confidence was bolstered by the experience of competing in music competitions at local and national levels and also by the experience of encountering other music collectors, some of whom brought recording machines with them to Carna or brought Carna singers to machines elsewhere, as did Séamus Ennis in Dublin in 1945. In addition, Sidney encountered an active acknowledgment across the whole community of the musical prowess of the parish.

In contrast, by the mid-1950s the depopulation of Aran had deprived the islands of a critical mass of musicians who would have encouraged more occasions for music making and, as a consequence, a greater sense of confidence among islanders who wished to perform for a visiting collector and her recording machine (see fig. 1). Furthermore, by 1956 few islanders had competed in music competitions, either at local or national levels, and music collectors were rarely encountered at home or away from the islands. Consequently, islanders rarely had the opportunity to gain such experiences. These factors contributed to the reticence she encountered and go some way toward explaining why some island performances appeared by comparison to lack a sense of authority.

The contrast between the contemporary attitudes to performing for a recording machine in these two neighboring, rural, and traditional communities reveals the positive impact that proactive participation in competitions can have on the musical practices of a community that is struggling to maintain its traditions in the face of depopulation and other pressures. It also illustrates the contribution that music collectors can make to the music they document. Sidney's observations not only present further evidence of how the work of music collectors can help to legitimize and canonize music; they also demonstrate how such a transformation breeds confidence and cultivates a sense of identity among the musicians whose tradition is being represented and, on some occasions, disseminated.

ASSESSING THE COLLECTOR

Sidney's interest in documenting the singing practices of both Aran and Carna, regardless of the differences between local attitudes to performing for a recording machine, is an important aspect of her work. Her attitude toward documenting the music of the two districts is dissimilar from that of other collectors who focused on Carna and other parts of Conamara, where they found more impressive musical traditions, where local people were more accustomed to hosting music collectors and were perhaps more easily persuaded to contribute, or where it was easier to travel.[294] For want of time and resources, many of Sidney's peers in Ireland could not afford to document anything other than the most impressive musical traditions or those that were most accessible. They may also have lacked an interest in, and an appreciation for, documenting what was less impressive or less extraordinary. They may have lacked the vision to do so.

In contrast, Sidney's work in Aran and in Carna demonstrates a more catholic and, perhaps, a more farsighted approach. The advancements in sound-recording technology, especially in the portability of recording equipment, enabled her to indulge her broad interests and to document music of varying quality in different places. Her acceptance of the ordinary as well as the extraordinary reveals a modern attitude to documenting traditional music that some of her peers did not, or could not, emulate. In accounting all at once for the music of two different places, the ways in which those musics have been documented, and the differences between them, she yielded a more nuanced portrait of traditional music practices in the west of Ireland in the mid-1950s and the documentation thereof than is to be found in the work of peers who were chiefly concerned with preservation and broadcasting.[295]

Sidney's Irish collection indicates that she was a diligent, conscientious, tenacious, and talented collector with a modern methodology. Viewed in the context of her earlier work in America, her Irish collection suggests her methodology was consistent up until 1956 at least. The quality and overall consistency of the work examined in this study suggests that her entire oeuvre deserves more attention. It also encourages us to consider other American collectors who worked in Ireland, including Alan Lomax, Jean Ritchie and George Pickow, Diane Guggenheim, Artelia Court, and Rita Weill Byxbe, to name a few—in particular women collectors, many of whom have been marginalized in the history of folk music collecting.[296]

chapter 4

Bairbre Quinn and
Bailiúchán Bhairbre

On Tuesday, June 21, 1955, as Sidney Robertson Cowell sat in Conneely's guesthouse in Cill Mhuirbhigh, Árainn, and recorded Máiria Pheaitín Terry Nic Dhonncha of Ros an Mhíl singing, the eldest of the nine children of the household, twenty-year-old Bairbre, was manning the shop downstairs (fig. 7).[1] It was the first time a recording machine had been brought into the house. It may also have been the first time a tape recorder was used in Aran. Soon after, when portable reel-to-reel tape recorders appeared on the domestic market in Ireland, Bairbre—the author's aunt—was inspired to acquire her own apparatus and begin collecting music. By 1958 she had a Philips EL3541 reel-to-reel tape recorder, becoming the first islander in Árainn to own sound-recording equipment (fig. 8). The experience of hosting and witnessing Sidney's work as music collector emerges as a likely catalyst for Bairbre's own collection of tape recordings, which now constitutes the most substantial and probably the most significant body of field recordings of music ever to emerge from Aran.

Bailiúchán Bhairbre (Bairbre's Collection) is a distinctive and remarkable collection of forty-four tapes containing an estimated thirty-two hours of recordings, mostly of song but also of instrumental music.[2] It spans almost twenty years, from the late 1950s to the mid-1970s. Bairbre recorded mostly in Árainn but also in Leitir Mealláin and Ros Muc in Conamara and with her relatives in Tipperary and Dublin.[3] She did not record in Inis Meáin or in Inis Oírr nor does she appear to have recorded people from those neighboring islands. She emerges as the single most productive collector of music in Aran. The overall good sound quality of Bailiúchán Bhairbre and the preservation of the

FIGURE 7. Bairbre
Conneely, late 1950s.
Courtesy of Mary
Conneely.

collection are also considerable feats for an untrained collector operating independently of any organization.

Bairbre's work—more accurately, her recording practice—is particularly
significant for both its content and its context. She created an exceptional collection of recordings that captures in sound, and especially in music, a sense
of the complex variety of the cultural landscape of Ireland and especially of An
Ghaeltacht at the time. Her collection also captures a sense of the movement
that characterized the contemporary cultural landscape—from the increasing transience of life that accompanied modernization to the contrasting stasis
that appeared to many to characterize the traditional way of life—and reveals

FIGURE 8. Bairbre Quinn with husband, Paddy; mother-in-law, Nell; and unidentified visitor. Courtesy of Mary Quinn.

some of the nuances of negotiation that were part of that movement, from acceptance and assimilation, to diffidence and resistance, to neglect and desertion. It achieves an unrivaled historical accuracy at a time when music in Aran was being ignored or marginalized by other collectors. Where the efforts of visiting collectors were thwarted by difficulties arising from issues concerning access, time, and cost, Bairbre was more favorably positioned to overcome such logistical challenges.

Bailiúchán Bhairbre is most significant because it is radically different in its motives, methodologies, and style to other contemporary collections, in particular the work of professional music collectors. Bairbre's strikingly different representation of music in Aran in the mid-twentieth century springs from her identities as a local and as an independent collector. Her collection adds to the canon of music in Aran a welcome, alternative representation, a comparatively pluralistic and democratic view of music in Aran from the mid-1950s to the 1970s. It also raises questions about that canon and about current narratives of Irish traditional music. Her collection makes a strong and important case for music collecting that is conducted "outside the conventional institutional framework" of universities and other organizations, which can thus offer, as Hugh Cheape argues, "a freshness of approach."[4]

MILIEU

Bailiúchán Bhairbre was created during a time of unprecedented change in local life and music making in Árainn. The people whom Bairbre recorded witnessed the steady decline of the population of Árainn throughout the twentieth century. Between 1901 and 1956, the population fell by more than half, from 1,941 to 941 (see fig. 1). It continued to fall as Bairbre recorded: 864 in 1971 and 848 in 1986. Emigration and migration were integral parts of life because the local economy of small-scale seasonal tourism, farming, inshore fishing, and small-scale trawling could not sustain all the islanders born during this period. The dramatic downward shift in the island's population within two generations, which was echoed in Conamara and in Clare, impacted negatively on local music and songs, which were subsequently lost.[5] The local repertoire was, however, supplemented during the same period with material assimilated from the gramophone, the radio, and the record player, material that enriched and helped sustain the traditional practice of communal music making.

Under the pall of depopulation, positive improvements to life in Árainn also appeared throughout the period during which Bairbre recorded. Radiotelephone, bottled gas, running water, and telephone lines were introduced throughout the island in 1954, 1956, 1957, and in the 1960s, respectively, and the first commercial flight with Aer Árann occurred in 1970. More significantly for local music making, the installation of mainline electricity throughout the island began in 1975, although some businesses used generators before then.[6] Bairbre's recording practice spans the period before and after the introduction of television. She witnessed how the eventual proliferation of television sets contributed in no small part to the decline of the communal practice of house visiting in Árainn, a practice that encouraged communal music making.[7] Communal music making continued, moving to the pub along with a generation of women whose social-izing entered that former bastion of male leisure.[8] Bairbre witnessed and par-took in that move.

During the period, the genres of music that interested islanders diversified dramatically, thanks to the growing popularity and local assimilation of mod-ern music. Nevertheless, accessing modern, mediated music in Aran then was not at all straightforward. Until 1975 wet and dry batteries for electrical appli-ances had to be shipped from time to time to Galway on the twice-weekly ferry to be recharged. Replacing them was also costly.[9] Touring musicians rarely vis-ited the islands and, excepting commercial records and radio and player devices, there was no physical embodiment of modern music in Aran at the time, ex-cept for the odd guitar brought in by a visitor. Consequently, islanders—young people in particular—often traveled to the mainland and stayed over for a time to attend dances and concerts in Galway, Na Forbacha, and elsewhere.[10] Con-sidering the challenges faced by young islanders who wanted to access popu-lar, country, and showband music, whether live or mediated, and considering their efforts to attain that access, the popularity of these genres of music in the local community at the time is remarkable. It hints at the novelty and attraction of this new music, the music of elsewhere, and also at the persuasive powers of commercial recordings, radio, and television, the media that first brought these musics to Aran. Some of the repertoire and style of this newly acquired music were incorporated into the local practice of communal music making and so helped to sustain that practice, albeit in a new fashion.

This development in local music making constituted a sea change in the musi-cal traditions of Aran. The era in question was marked by the birth of a distinct youth culture, which was separate from traditional culture, a culture in which young islanders felt a desire to participate and in which older people generally did not. Like the move of the local practice of communal music making from the house dance to the pub, this development introduced an element of ex-clusivity into a society that was previously comparatively inclusive. While the assimilation of modern music in Aran helped sustain the traditional practice of communal music making, paradoxically it also played its part in the decline of that practice. Its negative effect was, however, less significant than that of the change of venue from the home to the pub.

Bailiúchán Bhairbre bears witness to this paradox and to the music that has since been lost. It contributes to, and shares in, the sense of loss that imbues the history of traditional music in Aran and, more especially, the history of this particular era, during which Gaeltacht communities like Aran felt increasingly marginalized and embattled. There remains some question as to the degree to which that sense of loss affected Bairbre's methodology as it did the work of other music collectors because she had another, different motive for recording, which was not about documenting the endangered and dying elements of local cultural life. Each of her motives and methodologies are investigated and contextualized in this chapter.

BAIRBRE QUINN

Remembered locally by her married name, Bairbre Quinn, Bairbre Ní Chonghaile was born on March 29, 1935. She was the eldest of nine children born to Maidhcilín "Twenty" Ó Conghaile and Máire Gill. A currach fisherman, Maidhcilín (1901–86) was the youngest child of laborers Micil Sheáin Eoghain Ó Conghaile (ca. 1861–1957) and Bairbre Tom Burke Ní Chonghaile (ca. 1856–1940). Their household in Cill Mhuirbhigh was Irish speaking.[11] Máire Gill (1913–99) grew up in Cill Rónáin, where many spoke English as an everyday language. Her father, Robert (1885–1961), was a shipwright who served in the Royal Navy during World War I. When her mother, Bairbre Tónaí Ní Fhlatharta (ca. 1884–1926), died, Máire stayed home from school to care for her younger siblings until her father married Mary Mullen two years later. In the early 1930s, Máire was preparing to leave for England to begin nursing studies when she was approached by Pat Mullen (1883–1972), aide to the recently arrived American film director Robert Flaherty who had begun work on *Man of Aran*.[12] Mullen asked her to come to Cill Mhuirbhigh to cook for Flaherty and his family. Máire accepted the position, which lasted a year and eight months. During that time, she met Maidhcilín. They married in August 1933 and set up home in Cill Mhuirbhigh, where they opened a small guesthouse that came to be known as Conneely's.[13]

Máire had met and fed the many guests who stayed with Robert Flaherty during the shoot, among them Tom Casement (Roger's brother), the folklorist, scholar, and author Robin Flower, and the London critic Cedric Belfrage. Some of them, including Séamus Ó Duilearga, later referred visitors to her guesthouse.[14] At the time, there were few places for visitors to stay in Árainn, so the business expanded. Maidhcilín and Máire extended their house at intervals until they were able to keep around forty guests.[15] They also opened a shop and, later, a post office. They employed locals and people from else-where, including Séamus Murphy, who came to live on the island for a time.[16] The guesthouse ran for more than fifty years until Maidhcilín passed away in 1986. It was a busy and hardworking household that, for a long time, oper-ated without central heating, running water, or electricity. Irish was the spo-ken language of the household, but thanks to their guests, Bairbre and her siblings had more exposure to English than did their peers.[17] Indeed, in com-parison with many other households on the island, the young Conneelys had a relatively cosmopolitan upbringing. Government ministers, presidents, TV personalities, sportsmen, and writers were among the guests, including Earnán de Blaghad and his family: Mitchell Cogley, his wife, and son Fred; Cearbhall Ó Dálaigh and his wife, Maureen; Éamon and Maureen Kelly; Des and Maureen Kenny; Máirín de Valera; Ria Mooney; Maura Uí Chatháin; Augustine Martin; Tony Barry; Pat Baker; Stuart Hertington; Simon Weafer; Mick Reynolds; Enda Colleran; Seán Beecher; Edna O'Brien and her two sons; and Brendan Behan.[18]

Throughout the 1940s, 1950s, and 1960s, the Conneely homestead was a magnet both for business and for pleasure. It attracted the communities of the west end of the island in particular. Bairbre's brother Stiophán (1936–2008) recalled: "Bhí aghaidh na ndaoine uilig i gCill Mhuirbhigh an t-am sin" (every-body was heading to Cill Mhuirbhigh that time).[19] Locals came to use the shop and the post office and resident holidaymakers brought a pleasure-seeking atmosphere that encouraged music making and dancing among guests and islanders. Stiophán remarked: "Ba dream mór spóirt iad na strainséaraí" (the visitors were great fun).[20] One visitor of the 1950s, Pierre Travassac, bore wit-ness to that atmosphere:

On aime beaucoup danser en Irlande, et peut-être davantage encore à Aran. On y danse en tout lieu et à toute occasion, dans le "salon" ou même tout bonnement dans la cuisine de la petite "guest house" de Kilmurvey, au son du plus moderne électrophone, aussi bien que dehors, au clair de lune et aux accents de l'accordéon, sur la grande dalle de pierre qu'on trouve au tournaut du chemin, en haut du vil-lage.[21] Que par hasard un musicien vienne au "pub" où l'été les touristes résidents ont couture de se rendre aprés dîner, en haut de la côte Cowrugh sur la route de Kilronan, et aussitôt commenera la "ceilidhe";
    Et tout cela, c'est Aran.[22]

[In Ireland people really love to dance, and perhaps even more so in Aran. They dance everywhere and at every opportunity, in the living room, or even quite simply in the kitchen of the little "guest house" in Kilmurvey, with its modern electrophone. They dance by moonlight, to the accents of an accordion, on the big flagstone by the turn in the road at the top of the village. When a musician happens to stray into a pub where summer residents congregate after dinner, at the top of the Cowrugh coast on the Kilronan road, the "ceilidhe" will begin right away.

And all of that, that's Aran.[23]]

Though the tourist season was then much shorter, holidaymakers were often annual visitors who stayed for a fortnight at a time or even longer. They built up relationships with local people who looked forward to their return each summer. Bairbre's mother wrote: "We had people to stay with us from all over the world and they all loved the island because many of them came back and back again. All the people seemed to feel at home as that was our pleasure."[24] Bairbre later recorded some of the parties that were sparked by holidaymakers.[25]

After attending primary school in Scoil Fhearann a' Choirce, Bairbre went to boarding school on the mainland in Coláiste Chroí Mhuire in An Spidéal. This move signaled the beginning of her lifelong relationship with Conamara, a place she visited most frequently in her youth and where she recorded on numerous occasions. Upon completing her secondary education, she accepted a temporary teaching position as a junior assistant mistress (known as "JAM") in Scoil Leitir Mealláin. She worked there from November 8, 1955, to July 6, 1956.[26] She lived in a house known as Tí Joe Neainín but spent much of her time in the household of Tí Pheaitín Mháirtín Bheairtlín—which was also a shop—because it lay between her residence and the school where she worked. Bairbre then moved home to help with the family business. In 1960 she returned to Conamara to teach for a year or so in Scoil an Ghoirt Mhóir in Ros Muc along with Bríd Ní Fhátharta.[27] In Ros Muc, Bairbre befriended Máire-Áine Nic Dhonnchadha from Leitir Ard, Carna, who was teaching in Scoil an Turlaigh Bhig, and together they stayed in Tí Mháirtín Thomáisín. They were friendly with Meaití and Nóra Mannion in Cill Bhriocáin. Máire-Áine recalls that the Mannions were particularly fond of Bairbre:

Cuimhním uirthi mar, duine an-deas ar fad, a bhí cainteach agus a bhí i gcónaí ag gáire agus bhíodh sí ag imirt chártaí linn agus bhí an-eolas aici nó caint aici le

Bairbre Quinn and Bailiúchán Bhairbre   149

muintir an tí freisin agus bhí an-mheas acu uirthi sin agus an-fháilte roimpi. Agus . . . bhí sí an-spraíúil agus an-ghealgháireach i gcónaí agus bhíodh sí ag caint le muintir na háite agus le fear an tí, bhíodh scéal, go leor eolais aige sin ar Árainn agus, le Meaití Mannion freisin, tá sé sin caillte anois freisin agus, Nóra a bhean, tá sí beo fós. Agus, thaitnigh sise go mór leothab, mar bhí sí ar nós dhuine acu fhéin.[28]

[I remember her as, a very nice person altogether, who was talkative and who was always laughing and she used to play cards with us, and she knew the people of the house very well or talked with them too and they had a great respect for her and a great welcome for her. And . . . she was very playful and always so full of joy and she used to talk to the people of the house and with the man of the house, he had stories, he knew a lot about Árainn and, with Meaití Mannion too, he is dead now too and, Nóra his wife, she is still alive. And, they liked her a great deal, because she was like one of their own.]

At the weekends, Máire-Áine and Bairbre drove to Galway or Clifden. On a number of occasions, they visited Máire-Áine's mother in Carna. Bairbre once brought her tape recorder along with her and recorded Máire-Áine's brother, Johnny Mháirtín Learaí Mac Donnchadha, who is now a well-known and award-winning sean-nós singer. Johnny recalls it was the second time he had ever been recorded:

Bhí deis taifeadta aici, agus ba rud an-nua an t-am sin é, ceann a raibh na *spool*annaí air. Agus, ar ndóigh, nuair a bhí a fhios aici go raibh mise in ann amhrán a chasadh, bhí sí ag coinneáil i mo dhiaidh, chaithfeadh mé a dhul ag casadh amhráin dhi. . . . Bhíodh muid inár gcónaí an t-am sin thíos ag an bhfarraige, bhí mo mháthair beo ag an am, agus, ó bhíodh an-fháilte roimh. . . . Bhí sí thiar cúpla babhta nó trí agus bhíodh an-fháilte againn i gcónaí roimhe nuair a thagadh sí, mar bhí sí an-ghéimiúil ag caint agus bhíodh an deis taifeadta amuigh i gcónaí aici.[29]

[She had a recording machine, and it was a very new thing that time, one with spools on it. And, of course, when she knew that I was able to sing a song, she kept after me, I would have to sing a song for her. . . . We lived that time down by the sea, my mother was alive at the time, and, oh she [Bairbre] was so welcome. . . . She was there a few times or three and we always had a great welcome for her

when she came, because she was very sportive in talking and she always had the
recording machine out.]

Bairbre returned to Árainn in 1961 or 1962 to work once again at home. In
1965 she married Paddy Quinn (1935–2014) of Cill Rónáin. They settled there
and had four children. Paddy later had a fishing boat called *Barbara Maria*, and
Bairbre worked in the electronics factory in Eoghanacht for a time. In February
1987 the family moved to An Lochán Beag in Indreabhán just across the bay in
Cois Fharraige where they bought a house. Bairbre took ill and died on November 25, 1987, at fifty-two years of age.

CHARACTER

Bairbre's personality is a key element in the story of her collection of recordings. Family and friends remember that, although she could not play or sing, she
loved music and song. On many of her recordings, she can be heard at the end
of a recorded performance commending a musician as "good" to acknowledge
their contribution or, perhaps, to be diplomatic. She once chided a gathered
party for not showing their appreciation to two mediocre musicians who had
just finished playing Tommy Coen's reel, "Christmas Eve": "Shílfeá go dtabhar-
fadh sibh *clap* dóibh; cén sort daoine sibh fhéin?!" (Wouldn't you think you
would give them a clap; what kind of people are you?!).[30] Her delight in playing her recordings for others is further evidence of the enjoyment she gained
from sharing music with those around her. Within her own family, her father,
Maidhcilín, was known to sing a song ("Amhrán an Lifeboat" or "Brídín Bhéa-
saigh"), and his mother's people, the Tom Burkes, are known to be musical; her
maternal grandmother Bairbre Tónaí was also musical, as were her kin; and
Bairbre's husband Paddy was an accordion player.[31]

Bairbre was also a dancer and a good cardplayer and was highly regarded in
the community as an actor.[32] In the 1970s she took part in a film, part of which
was shot in Inis Oírr.[33] Later she developed a passion for sea angling and participated in angling competitions in Galway Bay and in Aran.[34] Her favorite
popular singer was Jim Reeves, and she loved his rendition of "He'll Have to
Go." Her brother Stiophán described her as "barrúil" (funny).[35] Paddy Quinn's
American cousin John Folan called her "a swell girl."[36] Johnny Mháirtín Learaí
remembered her as "a sportive woman who was always smiling"[37] and whose
speech was "tráthúil" (witty) and full of "nice sayings"—"bhíodh an-leaganachaí

deasa cainte aici." She had an infectious laugh.[38] When recording, her gift of the gab put people at ease.

Stiophán's description of her as "duine den sean-saol" (a person of the old life) is revealing: the "old life" that he envisages is the traditional way of life that was in decline in Aran and throughout Ireland during the mid-twentieth century, a life that he described as "better by far"—"b'fhearr an saol i bhfad é."[39] His testimony suggests that Bairbre's character lay close to that of the older generations around her, that she had an uncommon ability to relate to them and to communicate with them. The content of her collection demonstrates that she also had a special interest in recording the older people around her. Complementing her affinity with "the old life," and encouraged by the fact that older people were more likely to stay at home than go to the pub, Bairbre also enjoyed the local, traditional practice of house visiting. Stiophán recalled: "Bean mhór chuartaíochta a bhí inti" (she was a great woman for visiting). Her sportive personality, wit, and appreciation of music were a gift to gatherings of this nature, which thrived, as Henry Glassie observes, on witty chat, bids, and the appreciation of art.[40] Bairbre's love of music, song, and dance, and the central role that these activities played in the local practice of house visiting— a practice she embraced and to which she contributed a flair for company keeping—together ensured that she would exhibit a strong desire to participate in the traditional local practice of communal music making. This desire emerges as a cornerstone of her recording practice.

The Collection

After Bairbre's death in 1987, her husband, Paddy, preserved her collection. The current count of forty-four reel-to-reel tapes does not represent its entirety. There may be a few more tapes that have yet to emerge. Thirty-eight tapes were loaned to me in September 2003 and six more in December 2008. Most were unlabeled (which hindered the completion of my cataloging), so I numbered them randomly from 1 to 44. Tape 24 is a red herring: it is a letter home from Patsy Ó Tuathail (also known as Pádraig Bhid Bhile) of Bun Gabhla, Árainn, which he recorded in Africa in the 1970s on his own machine.[41] How it came to be among Bairbre's tapes is not known.

The magnetic tapes Bairbre used are three inches in diameter. Domestic tape recorders then offered a choice of speeds at which one could run tape. A higher speed gave a better quality of sound but less recording time. In the interests of economy, Bairbre chose a recording speed of 4.7 inches per second, which gave her around twenty-five minutes of recording time on each side, amounting to around fifty minutes per tape. Discounting the hundred minutes or so of poor-quality recordings on Tapes 22, 23, and 36, which constitute only 5 percent or so of the entire collection, around thirty-two hours and sixteen minutes of audible recordings survive on forty-three tapes.[42] Of these, around two hours and fifteen minutes of material from Conamara—including a whole tape of singing and lilting recorded in Scoil Leitir Meallái—survive, along with a tape of the Gill family of almost twenty-two minutes' length, which was recorded in Dublin.[43] The whole of Tape 27 was recorded in Tipperary with Bairbre's aunt, Mary Larkin, and her family. Two of the surviving tapes were recorded in America and sent to Aran by Paddy's cousin John Folan in Boston and other cousins; they are included in this estimation because they represent Bairbre's consideration of the diasporic experience of Aran Islanders and their American relatives.[44] A substantial number of tapes were recorded in Árainn in Conneely's, Tí Daly, and Bairbre's own house, but it is difficult to give exact figures because it is often impossible to verify the exact location in which the recordings were made. Nevertheless, by listening to the accents of those present, the choices of repertoire, and the ambient sounds, it is possible to establish the geographical areas of the island—specifically, the western and eastern ends of the island—in which she recorded (fig. 9).[45]

Bairbre did most of her recording in Árainn. In the west end of the island, she recorded in the following locations: her parents' guesthouse (in the shop and the kitchen); An Cuan; Matt Neainín Ó Maoláin's house in Eoghanacht; and Micil Saile Ó Miolláin's house in Sruthán.[46] Other possible but unconfirmed locations in the west end of the island include Pat Pheaidí Ó hIarnáin's house in Cill Mhuirbhigh and the pub Tí Chreig in Fearann an Choirce.[47] In the east end of the island, she recorded in the following locations: in Cill Rónáin, her own home, Nell Quinn's house, where she and Paddy lived for a time, and the pubs Tí Daly and the American Bar; and in Cill Éinne, the pub Tí Fitz.[48] Over eight hours of recording time in Árainn is split somewhat evenly between the west and the east of the island: around seven hours and fifty minutes in the west and around seven hours and twenty-five minutes in the east. This reflects how she lived at intervals in Cill Mhuirbhigh and Cill Rónáin. The collection emerges as a relatively fair representation of contemporary music making throughout the island.

Bailiúchán Bhairbre shows a remarkable range of musical styles and repertoire from performers of all ages and of variable ability and talent. It shares what

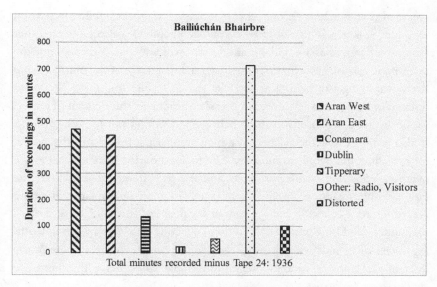

FIGURE 9. Geographical distribution of Bailiúchán Bhairbre recordings. Graph by the author.

appears to be a faithful representation of the actuality of the contemporary musical milieu in Aran and, to a lesser extent, in Conamara. None of the collections documenting the music of Aran that were created before or since match its breadth of variety. Bailiúchán Bhairbre is all the more remarkable for presenting its panoramic view of local music making solely through the medium of sound. The overall good quality of the recordings marks a vital and admirable contribution to her achievement.

MOTIVES FOR MUSIC COLLECTING

Bairbre's motives for collecting music emerge from a close examination of her collection and of the testimonies of those who witnessed her recording activities. First, Bairbre sometimes regarded herself as a music collector. This is evident in the content of her collection and also because, from time to time, she called herself "Ciarán Mac Mathúna."[49] This self-styled comparison with one of Ireland's most well-known contemporary collectors and radio broadcasters of traditional music, whose programs *Ceolta Tíre* and *Job of Journeywork* were very popular when Bairbre was collecting, is significant. At the time, Mac Mathúna was treated as a celebrity by Irish traditional musicians and was regarded as an oracle or chronicler of that music.[50] Bairbre's public comparison with him emerges as a strategy to encourage people to welcome her and her tape recorder just as he and his machines were welcomed throughout the country. It also suggests that Bairbre imagined that some of the music around her was in danger of being lost and that she, as a collector, might be able to document it. Her strategy indicates that she recognized the element of preservation in the practice of recording and deliberately set out to collect music. It also suggests that she set herself a high standard, a professional standard, for recording the people around her. She focused on the stars of local music making, as any music collector might, and also tried frequently to capture the best possible quality of performance in the best possible quality of sound recording. As a collector, Bairbre sensed the purpose and value of such work and understood how best to achieve her collecting objectives. Consequently, regardless of its independent status, her collection is considered here in the light of the work of contemporary professional collectors with whom she shared some key goals.

Second, Bairbre had another motive that is fundamentally different to that of the music collector. It can best be understood in terms of Henry Glassie's depiction of the traditional performing arts of Ballymenone—which resonates in Aran and other parts of Ireland—where "artistic performance achieves engaged union on a base of aristocratic reciprocity."[51] One of the primary purposes of collectors who record music is to document performances. While Bairbre recognized the documentary potential of the recording machine, she also saw it as an instrument with which she could deepen her involvement or participation in the local practice of communal music making. As an audience member, her frequent introductions of the recording machine into the local practice of communal music making represent repeated efforts to engage once again with performers, to acknowledge their "talent, fortitude, wit, strength and duty," but in a new fashion.[52] She also realized the dual outcome of recording those around her: she was creating more opportunities for people to share and enjoy live music (through additional performances as well as through the acts of creating and listening to recordings); and she was providing them with a novel opportunity to hear the sound of recorded local performances, an opportunity they had rarely had before.[53] By helping to create these new and additional opportunities to appreciate local artistry, she—a nonmusician—became a performer within that milieu. By recording those around her, she inserted herself into the local aristocracy of performance and so contributed more to the local practice of communal music making.

Considering that local music-making events depended on the contributions of participants for them to come into being, it is unsurprising to find that Bairbre and her collaborators believed her acts of recording could contribute to the proceedings; the purpose served by local music-making events in Aran was, like the ceilis of Ballymenone observed by Glassie, vital: "Meeting the night's dark threat, people work together building ceilis out of visits, stories out of ceilis. Their attentive goodmanning witnesses to the performer's difficulties while encouraging him to overcome his natural and proper reticence to sacrifice himself to keep them engaged, safe, and passing the time. For a long time I misunderstood. I thought of time as a series of periods and of action that passed the time as filling those periods like water poured into so many cups standing in a row. But the good meal or tale elevates time so that it momentarily pleases you, then carries you on. It is like a wave on an endless ocean that lifts and rides you over the trough that inevitably follows."[54] Bairbre's role in these cases is termed here as that of a recordist, a person who enjoys the operation of recording and the experience of listening to and sharing the resulting recordings, and for whom the documentary purpose of recording is, in that moment, a secondary concern.[55] Evidence to support this interpretation of Bairbre's other motive for collecting music is abundant in her collection, particularly in the recordings that demonstrate her frequently generous and opportunistic, sometimes chaotic, and apparently carefree attitude to recording.

The difference between a collector and a recordist is best determined not by the apparent thoroughness or quality of their work or practice but by their respective relationships with time. The collector's purpose is to document the present for posterity so that future generations might know what the music of the past sounded like. This is an example of what Benjamin Filene calls "memory work," in his words, "an effort to string lines between past, present, and future."[56] The recordist, on the other hand, is less concerned with the future or the past than with the present. For them, the purpose of recording is to enjoy and to contribute to the current moment. That future generations might also be able to enjoy and benefit from such recordings is, for the recordist, a secondary concern.

Bairbre played each of these roles—the collector and the recordist—at different times and sometimes simultaneously, specifically when she made historically

significant recordings in less than desirable conditions.[57] Her collection demonstrates that being a recordist was more important to her than being a collector: the number of recordings created by Bairbre the recordist outnumbers the
number of recordings created by Bairbre the collector.[58] Although there were
times when she strove, as a collector would, for the best possible quality of
sound, and times when she succeeded in producing good-quality recordings—
usually when she could exert some influence over the setting—there were many
more times when she acted as a recordist, times when her lack of control over
an unwieldy setting did not stop her from recording, times when she demonstrated a carelessness that, in a collector, would warrant criticism. For instance,
she was not particular about documenting contextual information for each recording. The vast majority of tapes in the collection are unlabeled and undated,
so it is difficult to determine the order in which she recorded things and to
identify the contents of each recording. In her primary role as a recordist, however, documenting such details was ultimately less important to her than the
actual act of recording. Being a recordist was about living in the moment, not
about manufacturing memory.

Being a recordist was also more vital to Bairbre than being a collector.
While she regarded music collecting as a worthy pursuit and capitalized on the
golden opportunity she had to collect local music, she felt the need to participate more keenly than she did the urge to document. Long after her machine
broke down and her tapes were temporarily silenced, the personal and collective memories of the occasions upon which she recorded her family, friends,
and neighbors sustained her and them. Her ultimate motive for recording music
in Aran and Conamara was to connect with the people around her, to make
the journey, as envisioned by Glassie, "from separation to social accord."[59] For
a great part of her life, recording was a consuming passion, as her brother
Stiophán describes:

> B'iontach an rud ag an am é, mar a déarfá, dise. Fuair sí an-spóirt ann. Agus tá sé
> chomh maith dom a rá gur mhair sí leis, thóg sí greadadh amhráin. Amhráin nach
> bhfuil le fáil ar chor ar bith anois, cuid mhaith acub. *So*, e, sé'n trua mór ... go
> bhfuair sí saol gearr. 'Sé, mar bhí a croí is a hanam aici ann.[60]

> [It was a marvelous thing at the time, you might say, for her. She had great fun
> with it. And I might as well say that she lived with it, she recorded plenty of songs.

Songs that cannot be got now at all, a good few of them. So, eh, it's a great pity ...
that she got a short life. It is, because her heart and soul was in it.]

The combination of the motives of the collector and the recordist—both
driven by related human emotions: the hope of belonging, of achieving "oneness," and the fear of loss or "lonesomeness"—makes Bailiúchán Bhairbre
particularly compelling.[61] Their merging in a local collector is especially significant because the intensity of Bairbre's relationship with the local practice of
communal music making, honed and enriched as it was by her deep and emotional connectedness with that practice, could not be matched by a visiting
collector.[62]

STYLE OF COLLECTING

Bairbre's use of her tape recorder depended on the willingness of her fellow participants to collaborate with her and on her powers of persuasion. She understood that the prospect of being recorded could raise feelings of apprehension
among her potential contributors. Having only encountered the recording
machines of professional collectors—visitors whose tight schedules forced a
degree of urgency and formality on their work—and those only once or twice
before, if ever, many islanders were intimidated by Bairbre's machine. Bairbre's
decision to introduce the notion of recording to people while they were in the
traditional performance arena may have been somewhat calculated: in that
setting, reticent performers might find it easier to perform for her, and also difficult to refuse her. To achieve her two objectives—to collect and to record—
Bairbre adopted a seemingly casual, playful style of collecting music that reflected her down-to-earth personality, a style that tried to undermine the potential seriousness of the work of recording by encouraging performers to relax
and to indulge in the experience of being recorded. This casual, playful style
mirrored the inherently playful nature of the setting in which communal
music making occurred most frequently and in which she most often chose to
record—the traditional performance arena—a milieu that closely resembles
the schoolhouse dance described by Lillis Ó Laoire as "the locus of play *par
excellence* of Tory [Island]."[63]
    One of the most obvious elements of the playfulness that characterized the
behavior Bairbre experienced and performed in the traditional performance
arena was humor. This element is, according to Ó Laoire, "crucially necessary":

"[Humor] influences attitudes and persuades people either to accept or reject particular points of view. It also gives pleasure. It establishes a cheerful atmosphere, assists in the relief of anger, aggression, and interpersonal tensions."[64] Humor also has an inverse effect, a serious side that completes its contribution to communication: "Humor underlines seriousness and fulfils its meaning by rejecting monolithic, fossilized sterility. Humor acts like yeast upon seriousness, leavening and raising it, so to speak, thereby adding to its expressive power."[65] As a participant and as a performer within the traditional performance arena, Bairbre was not just inclined to use humor—she was also obliged to use it. The atmosphere of fun therein encouraged her fellow participants to have a go at recording some music onto her tapes and so helped her achieve her objectives, whether as collector or as recordist. She was not the only person with a recording machine to take advantage of the spirit of informality, generosity, entertainment, and enjoyment that characterized the traditional performance arena. Professional collectors likewise saw the benefits of recording in such convivial settings or, at the very least, in emulating their favorable conditions.

The extent to which professional collectors could indulge in documenting the variety of performances that emerged in such informal settings was, however, usually curtailed by the demands of the archive, the broadcast, the clock, the calendar, or the budget. In contrast, Bairbre was—as a local and as a recording enthusiast—relatively free to entertain her preference for recording in such settings. While professionals focused on recording the products of the traditional performance milieu, Bairbre typically concentrated on enjoying the process at work therein, a process that served to bring the community together and to effect the transformation to which she and other participants ultimately aspired—the conversion "from separation to social accord."[66] The play in which she engaged served to encourage people to collaborate with her to create good recordings, just as it served collectors, but she was also interested in enjoying the game itself; a palpable sense of fun and enjoyment leaps from the recordings. Her approach—along with her practice of playing back her recordings to her contributors to reciprocate their efforts to oblige her—won her the trust of her community. Some people thoroughly embraced the opportunity she provided to engage in this novel pastime as well as document their performances.

Bairbre's style of collecting was an organic creation that sprang from the milieu it documents and from Bairbre's desire to deepen her involvement in that milieu. Appearing unsystematic and sometimes chaotic on the surface, it marks a consistent and coherent effort to touch the full spectrum of music experienced and performed by Bairbre's family, friends, and neighbors in Aran and Conamara from the late 1950s to the 1970s. It emulates and captures the spirit of the local musical milieu, which was, and still is—at heart—democratic, pluralistic, and open-minded. By reflecting the playful essence of the contemporary musical milieu both in the content of her collection and in her style of collecting, Bairbre contributes a great deal to the success—specifically to the historical accuracy—of her representation of that milieu and thus to our understanding of it.

METHODOLOGIES: BAIRBRE AS COLLECTOR

Just as Bairbre had two motives for creating Bailiúchán Bhairbre, she had two corresponding methodologies: that of a collector and that of a recordist. Her two methodologies share some core characteristics. She usually recorded the music that the people around her performed regularly, and she typically did not try to influence their choice of material. She was attracted to good performers, especially good singers, and preferred to record them in their natural habitat—at informal gatherings, parties, and in the pub or at home. In such settings, where people were relaxed and often in good humor and even in the mood for performing, she was more likely to get many consecutive, authentic, and successful performances onto her tapes. Where Bairbre's methodologies differ is the degree of seriousness with which each type of recording was created.

The most important characteristics of Bairbre's methodology as a collector are encapsulated in a single episode of recording that was documented on Tape 18. In 1962 Bairbre went to the house of the poet Matt Neainín Ó Maoláin in Eoghanacht to record him and his cousin, neighbor, and fellow poet Cóilín Mhicilín Ó hIarnáin.[67] Both were revered in their own time for their poetical prowess and are still held in the community's regard. In his first performance on the tape—a recitation of his new composition "Oileán Glas Árann na Naomh"—we hear Matt addressing his audience, which includes his wife Maggie Jeaic, Cóilín Mhicilín and his son Pádraig, Bairbre and her brother Mícheál, and an unidentified man named Tomás. Some other quieter individuals may also have been present. The quality of the recording—the clarity of Matt's delivery and the relative silence of the audience—indicates that they were all aware of the presence and purpose of the machine. Matt's preamble and postscript to his song demonstrates his self-awareness and his intention to record with pride his new composition before an appreciative and critical audience. The setting evidently enhanced his performance. He addresses Cóilín, his poetic peer, directly:

MATT: Ar airigh tú é seo atá déanta agamsa faoi Árainn?
CÓILÍN: Ó ar ndóigh, cas go fóill é . . .

[MATT: Did you hear this that I have made about Árainn?
CÓILÍN: Oh sure, sing it a while . . .]

Matt coughs and clears his throat, at which point Cóilín laughs (in recognition, perhaps, of his fellow poet's self-awareness), and then Matt delivers his performance. When he finishes, Cóilín chuckles in enjoyment, some audience members give their verdicts of "go maith" (good), Bairbre says "very good," and Matt proclaims "Anois! Sin é anois an dán nua!" (Now! That now is the new poem!). In an effort to spare tape, Bairbre often tried to record songs with minimal commentary before or after them, but in this case she broke from her usual practice. She recognized that Matt wanted to add a coda to the end of his performance. This instance of recording was a deliberate effort to document Matt's new composition and its context, to record his voice, his delivery, his explanation of the performance, and the reaction of his immediate and informed audience. In preserving it as she did, Bairbre recognized the significance of the moment and created a record of a good and natural performance.

This episode indicates three distinct characteristics of Bairbre's methodology as a collector. First, she wished to document the performances of good performers. She also made efforts to record in quieter, more intimate, and more deliberate settings with specific performers; the resulting recordings constitute proactive attempts to preserve the contributions of particular performers in the best possible quality of sound.[68] Of the recordings that were created in this way, three tapes focus on solitary singers who sang one song after another, singers who impressed Bairbre: a young woman named Fionnuala recorded seven ballads or popular songs in English, including "The Hills of Donegal," "The Shores of Amerikay," "Mother Machree," "Green, White and Gold," "The Home I Left Behind Me," "All I'm Guilty of Is Loving You," and "Whispering Hope" as well as the Irish song "Cruacha Glasa na hÉireann"; Mary Folan, a cousin of Paddy Quinn, recorded nine country songs, including "Bury Me Out

Under the Stars," "World of Our Own," "Let Alone in This World Anymore," "The Wild Side of Life," "Geisha Girl," and "Anna Marie"; and a young woman or, perhaps, a girl—possibly from Conamara—recorded six sean-nós songs, including "Mainistir na Buaile," "An Abhainn Mhór," "Sé Fáth Mo Bhuartha," "An Draighneán Donn," "Tá na Páipéir dá Saighneáil," and "An Cailín Bán."[69] Similarly, the whole of Tape 6 was recorded with the Gill family in their home in Dublin: Bairbre's uncle Bobby (1923–85) sang eight songs—ballads and sean-nós songs—including "Amhrán na Trá Báine," "Sail Óg Rua," "Galway Bay," "Sean South of Garryowen," "The Queen of Connemara," "The Old Bog Road," and "The Green Fields of Ireland"; his wife, Katie (1925–92), lilted a little and sang two songs, "Amhrán na Trá Báine" and "B'aerach aréir a shiúl mé fhéin an trá"; and their young daughter, Marian, sang four sean-nós songs, "Neilí Bhán," "Bríd Óg Ní Mháille," "Tiocfaidh an Samhraidh," and "Baile Uí Laoi." Bobby and Katie also duetted on "The Bunch of Violets" and Bobby and Marian duetted on "My Bonny Boy Is Young and He's Growing."

The second characteristic of Bairbre's methodology as a collector was her awareness of the historical significance of some of the music around her and her desire to document it. The substantial number of recordings of local and contemporary compositions in Irish—many of which were composed and sung in a sean-nós style—that occur in the collection indicates that Bairbre recognized the reality of the decline of the Irish language and its oral culture. Despite the contemporary currency of their songs, local poets who practiced an oral tradition of song composition that thrived on vigorous and vociferous exchange seemed then to be without heirs. Bairbre's intention to recognize, record, and so preserve their art is demonstrated well by another example concerning three local songs discussing an unfinished road below the village of Creig an Chéirín. She recorded the first of these compositions, Neidín Sheáin Neide Ó Tuathail's "Bóthar Gharraí Nua," from John Beag Johnny Ó Dioráin as well as two individual responses to that song from the poets themselves, Matt Neainín Ó Maoláin and Cóilín Mhicilín Ó hIarnáin, quite soon after their composition.[70] To have recorded such topical repartee between poets is an uncommon achievement. The decline of such poetic exchanges on local issues in Aran since then makes its occurrence in Bailiúchán Bhairbre all the more noteworthy and indicates that Bairbre's decision to record them was that of a collector: it was conscious, deliberate, historically aware, and founded on a sense of impending loss.

The final characteristic of Bairbre's methodology as a collector is her desire to record authoritative renditions. Her efforts to record songs from the composers themselves or from someone close to them—such as Joe Antaine Ó Briain singing the compositions of his father Antaine and his uncle Tomás, "Amhrán an Hero" and "Amhrán na Miotógaí"—show a concern for putting the original or correct version "on record," so to speak.[71] There were occasions when the performances she recorded were not authoritative renditions. Matt Neainín, for instance, inadvertently mixes "Bríd Thomáis Mhurchadha" and "Póg Bhid Óig."[72] Singers who were aware of their inaccuracies were apologetic, and Bairbre usually consoled them or diplomatically praised their efforts. Nevertheless, in a rare but not unkind outburst recorded on Tape 32, Bairbre voices her frustration at one such shortcoming. We hear Malachaí Ó Biadha of Leitir Mealláin trying to record some recitations. When his memory fails him mid-performance, he demurs and tries to quit: "Sin é a dheireadh" (that's the end of it). Bairbre objects: "Ní hé" (it's not). The entire performance is eventually recorded but in fits and starts. As she reaches once more for the pause button, she remonstrates, "Aw, blast you!"

METHODOLOGIES: BAIRBRE AS RECORDIST

As a recordist, Bairbre was less concerned with capturing an unblemished performance than with enjoying the process of recording. This is evident in her apparently carefree attitude to recording, which sometimes yielded recordings of poor quality: recordings featuring feedback and muffled sound, for instance; recordings where the microphone was too close to the performer or the recording level was too low; and recordings of concurrent conversations that are difficult to follow.[73] Sometimes she persisted in recording even if the machine was malfunctioning or even if there was background noise such as a hiss, or the sound of a radio, television, car engine and windscreen wipers, crying children, or the chirping of day-old chicks being warmed in a Carna kitchen.[74] Even more revealing, perhaps, of her frequently blithe attitude to recording is the fact that she rarely if ever cut short the performances of contributors whose offerings were badly affected by their shyness or reticence or by insobriety, however much their performances might have seemed a waste of tape or battery power.[75] Such instances reflect Bairbre's primary purpose in creating her collection, which was to deepen her involvement in the local practice of communal music making by contributing to it: she could not have cut short such performances because to do so might have insulted her contributors and upset the status quo of the milieu in which she operated. Of course, she was in a position to tape over mediocre or bad performances if she so wished, but doing so increased the risk of operational errors impacting recordings.

Bairbre's methodology as a recordist is characterized by the varying quality of her recordings and by the wide range of content. She recorded conversations in houses, in pubs, in a school, in the car, and on the roadside; conversations about the weather, potatoes, cattle and piglets, about friends, and about songs. She recorded people of all ages in English and in Irish. She recorded a visitor who sang a song in French called "Suzanne."[76] In the guesthouse in 1962 she recorded a prank that played on Baibín Mhurchadha de Bhailís's reluctance to be recorded.[77] People rarely got the opportunity to turn the tables on Bairbre but, at a party in Leitir Mealláin, Malachaí Ó Biadha teased her by recording verses and stories about her infamous uncle, Fr. Connolly, a Redemptorist missionary.[78] She recorded card games and her children reciting the English alphabet.[79] She recorded a little of a cuckoo's song on a windy day.[80]

Bairbre later recognized that some of the recordings she had created as a recordist were worth preserving.[81] At such moments, the recordist transforms into a collector. The collector's historical imperative invests the singular occurrence that has been captured by the recordist's impulse with a consciousness of time and place, a consciousness of context, and thereupon, the recorded moment is memorialized. The last track on Tape 30, which is one of Bairbre's earliest tapes, is one such recording. It suggests that, as a recordist, Bairbre wanted to surprise the Conneelys' neighbor Winnie Cheaite Uí Iarnáin by giving her the novel opportunity of hearing her own voice on tape for the first time but that she also wanted to experience the fun of catching Winnie unawares. As a collector, however, Bairbre appears to have realized later the value of documenting the wonder of a local woman viewing the new machine for the first time and so she preserved the recording. We hear Winnie entering a room in the guesthouse sometime in the late 1950s to look at the machine. Bairbre tells Winnie to approach the machine, and Bairbre's mother, Máire, explains that it is currently recording. Winnie marvels at the magic of it. It is an unusual example of the moment of discovery upon encountering a new technology, a moment that occurred at a time when technological advances were less rapid than they are today. It is remarkable that Bairbre the collector recognized its significance and preserved this recording created by Bairbre the recordist.

It is difficult to say how many of Bairbre's recordings were, like Winnie's wondering at the marvelous machine, created by the recordist and then preserved by the collector.[82] This difficulty persuades us not to take for granted the overall informality of the collection. Despite her apparently casual style, Bairbre was frequently conscious of the element of documentation and preservation in her recording practice. Each time she brought her tape recorder with her to a party, to the pub, or when she visited people's houses, she indicated an intention to record and brought with her the potential to capture that moment in time, or, perhaps, to collect and preserve a worthy performance, and to share her recordings with distant or absent friends as well as with those who were present.

Bairbre's brother Stiophán describes her typical methodology as a recordist:

DEIRDRE: *So* bhíodh Bairbre ansin ag dul ag cuartaíocht mar a deir tú. An ngabhfadh sí go teach áirid anois le duine a téipeáil a' bhfuil a fhios agat?

STIOPHÁN: *Well* dá gceapfadh sí anois—bíodh thusa thoir Tí Daly nuair a phós sí mar a déarfá—dá gceapfadh sí go mbeadh lucht amhráin ann, thabharfadh sí síos an téip léi, agus leath a raibh sa teach ósta, Tí Bhríd Ní Dhálaigh, ní raibh a fhios acub a' raibh a leithéid aici, 'bhfuil a fhios agat. Bhí P. J. Lynch anois, ba dheacair amhrán a fháil uaidh. 'S é a bhí sa teach ósta, thoir ann a' freastal ann. Agus chasfadh sé "Trá Inisheer" 'gus sin é 'n bealach a bhí aige le na daoine . . . go raibh sé in am acub a dhul abhaile.

D: A ruaigeadh. Iad a sheoladh abhaile!

S: Iad a sheoladh abhaile.[83]

[DEIRDRE: So then Bairbre used to go visiting as you said. Would she go to a particular house now to tape someone do you know?

STIOPHÁN: Well if she thought now—say you were east in Tí Daly when she married—if she thought that a song crowd would be there, she would bring the tape down with her, and half of them in the pub, Bridie Daly's pub, they did not know she had such a thing, do you know. P. J. Lynch now was, it was difficult to get a song from him. He was in the pub, east there serving there. And he would sing "Trá Inisheer" and that was the way he had for people . . . that it was time for them to go home.

D: To get rid of them. To drive them home!

S: To drive them home.]

Bairbre allowed the entertainment to unfold naturally and then recorded what music was performed and so captured the rhythm and pace of the contemporary practice of communal music making. These recordings document its pattern, where many of those gathered were expected to contribute at least one party piece, and individual performances thus alternated from one person to the next, as demonstrated on Tape 11, which was recorded in Tí Daly. Almost a third of the tapes, including Tapes 2, 4, 8–11, 14–15, 31–33, and 37, follow the same pattern, indicating the frequency with which Bairbre employed this methodology. Sometimes there was a particularly fine performer who was called on to contribute more than others; Coilmín a' tSeoighigh, who recorded twelve songs for Bairbre in one sitting, is one such example.[84] It is through these recordings, through her methodology as a recordist, that Bairbre provides her unrivaled perspective on the range of the contemporary practice of communal music making. She presents gallant efforts alongside star performances in their sometimes chaotic, sometimes messy, and typically unpredictable, shared contexts. She thus captures the timbre and texture of this musical milieu. However outstanding her achievement in this regard, this assessment must also consider her adoption of the methodology of surreptitious recording described by Stiophán, where she avoided drawing attention to the recording machine or sometimes hid it while recording.

SURREPTITIOUS RECORDING

Until the late 1950s, a relatively small number of islanders had come into intermittent contact with sound-recording equipment.[85] Despite their growing familiarity with sound technology in the form of gramophones, radios, and record players, many of Bairbre's contemporaries were unfamiliar with sound recorders, and many were initially reluctant to record music or speech for her. Stiophán recalls the varied reactions of islanders to tape machines when they first came out in the 1950s, reactions that affected Bairbre's methodologies:

STIOPHÁN: *Well*, tháinig siad amach agus, fuair sí é agus, bhíodh sí, 'tógáil daoine a thiocfadh isteach agus, ní raibh a fhios ag na daoine a raibh siad ar chor ar bith air.

DEIRDRE: I nganfhios dóibh, ab ea?

S: *Yeah.*

D: Ó an ndéanadh sí é sin?

s: *Yeah.*

d: *Agus, e, an mbíodh daoine ansin a dhéanfadh é fiú agus fios maith acub?*

s: *Á bhíodh a, á bhí cuide sásta é a dhéanamh.*

d: *Yeah.*

s: *A ní mórán a bhí . . .*

d: *Cé nach raibh?*

s: *. . . ag éisteacht, ag iarraidh a nglór a aireachtáil nó ag iarraidh go ndúirt'dar tada.*[86]

[STIOPHÁN: Well, they came out and, she got it and, she used to take [record] people who came in and, the people did not know that they were on it at all.

DEIRDRE: Unbeknownst to them, is it?

s: Yeah.

d: Oh did she used to do that?

s: Yeah.

d: And, eh, were there people then who would do [record] it knowingly even?

s: Ah yes, ah some were happy to do it.

d: Yeah.

s: There were many who were not . . .

d: Were there not?

s: . . . listening, wanting to hear their voices or wanting to have said nothing.]

To achieve her goal of capturing good, natural performances, Bairbre sometimes recorded people surreptitiously. As time went on and people got used to the machine and to the idea of recording, the number of people she recorded increased and the instances of surreptitious recording dwindled.[87]

It is difficult to assess how her surreptitious recordings impacted on islanders at the time or on Bairbre's collecting, because so many of the people she recorded have now passed on. Any other untrained independent collector who was similarly unaware of standard ethical recording practices and thus flouted them might be forgiven for recording surreptitiously, but Bairbre is herein compared with professional collectors whose ethical standards do not condone surreptitious recording, as Anthony Seeger outlines: "Entirely unethical recordings, made in secret or against the desire of the group recorded, should probably not be submitted to archives at all. They should not be made in the first place."[88] Bairbre's surreptitious recordings were not entirely secret because

she often played the recordings back to the performers themselves.[89] Nevertheless, professional collectors, archivists, and ethnomusicologists might wish to
discount or suppress them. The decision to accept and analyze them here,
despite Seeger's reservations, is driven by the will to discover more about Bairbre's motives and methodologies. More importantly, locals today accept and
welcome Bairbre's collection, however it was created.[90] They do not criticize her
sporadic practice of making surreptitious recordings. Their understanding is that
being recorded often makes the best of performers nervous, which can hinder a
good performance and so prevent the creation of a fair record of the performer's
talent. In this case, they recognize the essential honor in the wish to preserve
well the memory of a good performer, to bear witness to their gift or art. On the
surface of it, surreptitious recording is a deceit against the performer, but where
it is conducted in a manner that achieves the best possible record of the performer's ability, it can be interpreted as a service to that performer. Admittedly,
it is easy for locals to be ambivalent or even positive about something that hap-
pened to somebody else more than fifty years ago, the result of which has since
achieved widespread admiration.[91] One imagines they might react less favorably if they themselves were the subjects of this ethically questionable practice.

OTHER USES FOR THE RECORDING MACHINE

On Tapes 3, 7, 12, 16, 18, 22, 25, 28–29, 31, 35, and 39, we hear how Bairbre found
other uses for her machine, including recording her favorite music off the radio,
bootlegging commercial recordings, and recording weather forecasts from the
radio (from Radio Éireann and the BBC) so that her fisherman husband Paddy
might hear them later.[92] She recorded most of Mícheál O'Hehir's live commentary of the 1964 All-Ireland football final between Galway and Kerry and appears
to have kept the tape as a memento of that historic first win of a three-in-a-row
streak.[93] She recorded a twenty-minute address by President John F. Kennedy
on the Cuban missile crisis in 1963, and in the wake of his assassination later that
year, Thanksgiving greetings from the newly sworn-in president Lyndon Johnson.[94] Describing some of these other uses, Paddy recalls how the tape recorder
seemed to be "a small miracle"—"Ó míorúilt beag a bhí ann an t-am sin":[95]

   Bhí sé an-luath an t-am céanna, 'bhfuil a fhios agat, agus b'iontach an rud é.
   Agus dá dtaitneodh ceol leat, d'fhéadfá a bheith a' téipeáil, dá ngeobhfá ar an
   radio é nó ar rud eicínt eile nó dá mbeadh *party*, 'bhfuil a fhios agat, bhí tú in ann

é a bheith agat aríst. Amhrán anois a thaitneodh leat 's na focla *and so on*. A bhí sé
iontach. Bhí sé go maith cinnte. Mar roimhe sin, a' bhfuil a fhios agat, mura raibh
tú ann, bhí sé thart, ach má bhí sé téipeáilte agat, d'fhéadfá éisteacht arís leis. Á bhí
sé, bhí sé thar cionn ar an gcaoi sin.

[It was very novel that time, do you know, and it was a marvelous thing. And if
you liked music, you could be taping, if you got it on the radio or on something
else or if there was a party, do you know, you could have it again. A song now that
you liked and the words and so on. Ah it was wonderful. It was good, surely.
Because before that, do you know, if you weren't there, it was over. But if you had
taped it, you could listen to it again. Ah it was, it was excellent in that way.]

In sharing recordings with absent and distant friends, Bairbre also enabled
communication in sound with relatives abroad at a time when telephone calls
from Aran to America were reserved for emergencies.[96] Tapes of recorded parties were sent to Paddy's uncles and the extended Quinn and Folan families in
America, either by post or in the luggage of a returning emigrant, where they
could listen to them on their own machines.[97] Sometimes they would then
record over the same tape with their own party, or poignant letter, or choice
of music, and then post it to Árainn.[98] Audio letters like these became more
common in Árainn throughout the 1960s and 1970s as more people, among
them Maidhcí McDonagh (1944–82) of Cill Mhuirbhigh and Patsy Ó Tuathail
(1938–2015) of Bun Gabhla, acquired tape machines.[99] The practice died out
as telephones became more common and less expensive to use.[100] The surviving audio letters are remarkable firsthand documents that vividly record how
music was used by islanders—whether resident, migrant, or emigrant—to overcome distances of time and space.

    The impact of these apparently incidental uses for the recording machine
on Bairbre's methodologies should not be underestimated. They yielded an
alternative perspective on how contemporary islanders incorporated music
into their lives. They reaffirmed the ability of recording technology to contribute to the lives of individuals, family, friends, neighbors, community, and
the locality. They also strengthened the possibility that the recording machine
and the act of bringing it into the traditional performance arena could contribute to the local practice of communal music making and so come to yield, in
time, a most significant harvest.

A Historiographical Appraisal of
Bailiúchán Bhairbre

Bairbre's two methodologies of recording, her other uses for the recording machine, and the novelty of the experience of recording, for her and for her contributors, all combined to yield an extraordinary variety of recordings of both live and mediated musics. This variety is one of the most significant attributes of Bailiúchán Bhairbre because it helps demonstrate the colorful spectrum of the contemporary local musical milieu and enables the unrivaled historical accuracy of her representation of that milieu.

Bairbre's live field recordings give a good cross section of contemporary traditional music in Aran and, to a lesser extent, in Conamara. They include forty-eight sean-nós songs from some noted local singers, among them John Beag Johnny Ó Dioráin, Pat Pheaidí Ó hIarnáin, Joe Antaine Ó Briain, and Matt Neainín Ó Maoláin in Árainn and, in Conamara, Johnny Mháirtín Learaí Mac Donnchadha, a young woman named Máirín, Coilmín a' tSeoighigh from Leitir Calaidh, Leitir Móir, and Paidí Choilm Learaí Ó Conghaile of Corra Bhuí, Leitir Mealláin.[101] Among the instrumentalists whom Bairbre recorded were Pádraig Dharach Peircín Ó Conghaile of Cill Éinne, John Joe Jóin Ó Fátharta of Eochaill, Vailín Bheairtlín Aindí Ó Maoláin of Sruthán, Éamon Eddie an Táilliúra Ó Domhnaill of Leitir Mealláin, and a man named (George or Willie) Horneybrook of Galway who played the then popular "Cuckoo Waltz" and other tunes in the guesthouse.[102] Each of these musicians played the button accordion, reflecting the popularity and ubiquity of the instrument in Aran at the time. There is some lilting by Katie Gill, Matt Neainín Ó Maoláin, and some schoolchildren in Leitir Mealláin.[103] There is also some whistling by an unidentified man on Tape 32 and by Matt Neainín Ó Maoláin on Tape 18. On Tape 19 a visiting fiddler played "Christmas Eve," "My Love Is in America," and other tunes in Conneely's, sometimes in the company of a visiting tin-whistle player. Bairbre's husband Paddy features a lot in the collection. His accordion playing can be heard on Tapes 2, 3, 5, 13, and 21, and he may also feature on Tapes 7, 11, 14–15, and 20. His repertoire included several local favorites: "The Stack of Barley" and "Johnny," "The Frost Is All Over," "The Boys of Blue Hill," and "The Little Beggarman."[104] Contemporary standard tunes like these, especially "Miss McLeod's Reel," reoccur frequently in the collection, reflecting their popularity as well as the limited repertoire of local musicians.

The range of more modern genres of music that appear in Bailiúchán Bhairbre gives a good indication of their increasing popularity in Aran during the
period from the late 1950s to the 1970s. Individual singers recorded ballads
("The Galway Shawl," "The Shores of Amerikay") and comic songs ("Nine-
teen Years Old") as well as country songs ("Forty Shades of Green"), American
songs ("Bury Me Out Under the Stars"), contemporary releases ("The Shoals
of Herring"), and showband songs ("All I'm Guilty of Is Loving You"); it was
the heyday of the showband era and islanders went to Galway especially to
attend dances at the Hanger Ballroom in Salthill.[105] Songs made popular by the
Clancy Brothers feature, reflecting their growing fame; in the jam-packed community hall, Halla Rónáin, islanders congregated to witness their Irish television debut in 1963 on a small black-and-white television that was specially
installed onstage for the occasion.[106] The same is true of songs performed by
the Dubliners.[107] The popularity of this material is demonstrated further in the
surviving remnants of Bairbre's radio listening (in the economically driven process of recycling tapes, Bairbre frequently taped over much of the material she
recorded from the radio). These include popular music by the Beach Boys,
Cliff Richard, and Irish showbands; Acker Bilk playing his 1962 hit "Stranger
on the Shore"; the innovations of Ceoltóirí Chualann and Darach Ó Catháin;
and an orchestral rendition of the Irish national anthem.[108] Bailiúchán Bhairbre
demonstrates vividly the impact of mediated music in Aran. It documents how
many islanders were attracted to the music of elsewhere and how some of them
tried to emulate the professional performers they encountered, usually via various media and sometimes in person. Some, including the young unidentified
woman on Tape 3 who sings "Geisha Girl," assimilated country-style singing.
Some others, including Cóilí Gill who sings "I'll Take You Home Again Kathleen" on Tape 33, imitated stage singers of Irish songs. Some imitated well-known
Irish musicians like the Clancy Brothers and Delia Murphy.[109] These islanders
understood that their newly acquired music and/or musical styles would be
recognized and accepted as contributions to the local practice of communal
music making and so were assured of the merit of their efforts. Assimilation and
change were, after all, a natural part of their local musical milieu.

Nevertheless, Bailiúchán Bhairbre was created at a time when the cultural
landscape of Aran, An Ghaeltacht, and other rural parts of Ireland was under-
going a fundamental shift, one that marked the latest changes to the local musical milieu as seismic. The shift is depicted here by Ríonach uí Ógáin:

Bhí an Ghaeilge ag dul i léig go tréan agus ag meath mar ghnáth-theanga labhartha sna 1940idí cé is moite d'iarthar na hÉireann, den chuid is mó. Thagadh daoine le chéile ina gcuid tithe sa mbaile le ham a chaitheamh agus ag airneáil. Bhí cluichí cártaí, scéalaíocht, seanchas, ceol, amhráin agus damhsa ó dhúchas acu. De réir a chéile tharla athruithe ar mhórán gnéithe den saol nach raibh mórán athraithe tagtha orthu roimhe sin. Bhí athrú suntasach tagtha ar réimsí den saol a bhí gan athrú leis na céadta bliain agus chuaigh an Ghaeilge agus an saol a bhí ceangailte léi ó aithne, beagnach.

[In the 1940s Irish was in an intense decline, and it was dying out as a normal vernacular except for the west of Ireland, for the most part. People used to come together in each other's houses at home to pass the time and to visit. Card games, storytelling, lore, music, song, and dance were their native heritage. Gradually many aspects of life that had changed little before then transformed. Ranges of life that had not altered for hundreds of years had incurred remarkable change, and Irish and the life that was linked to it became unrecognizable, almost.][110]

This cultural shift was one of the most significant of the islands' history because it gave rise to a new and—for music in Aran—influential element of local life: a cultural gap between the generations. The new cultural differences between older and younger generations were embodied in the new venues for socializing that emerged during this period, specifically the pub, which was now frequented by women as well as men, and the ballroom, the mainland home of mainstream music and of showbands in particular. While these venues attracted specific cohorts—young single people were common to both venues—others, including children, married women, the elderly, and the infirm, were effectively excluded. Time that had previously been spent with local music (and comparatively limited media resources) was now being spent with new musics in new spaces. As a result, local music became marginalized. Johnny Joyce of Cill Éinne, Árainn, demonstrates this marginalization graphically when he describes how, in his youth, he and his siblings paid little attention to his father's singing, an occurrence he now regrets:

Ní mórán atá acu agam [amhráin ar an sean-nós], a' dtuigeann tú, agus bhí siad ag m'athair [Maidhlín Mhaidhcilín Seoighe], 'bhfuil 's agat, bhí cúpla ceann maith acu ag m'athair ach níor chuir muinn aon suim ariamh [iontu]. Bhí sé thoir

sa mbaile anois b'fhéidir ar, deireadh na seachtaine b'fhéidir, théis seachtain ias-
cach a bheith déanta agus, b'fhéidir théis an dinnéir go bhfeicfeá, ghabhadh sé
síos sa gcathaoir agus thosaigh sé ag casadh an amhráin agus, is minic a deireadh
muinn leis: "ára, dún do bhéal!" 'dtuigeann tú, 'mb'fhéidir bhíodh sé ag cur isteach
ort, a' bhfuil 's agat. Ach, ní, ní dheirfinn leis inniu é, ná ná ná ar aon duine eile ach
oiread a bheadh ag casadh an amhráin Ghaeilge.[111]

[I don't have many of them [sean-nós songs], you understand, and my father
[Maidhlín Mhaidhcilín Seoighe] had them, do you know, my father had a good
few of them but we never took an interest [in them]. He was east at home now
maybe on, a weekend perhaps, after a week's fishing was done and, perhaps
after dinner you would see, he would go down to the chair and he began singing
the song and, we often used to say to him: "Arah, shut your mouth!" Do you
understand, maybe he was disturbing you, do you know. But I, I wouldn't say it
to him today, nor to anyone else either who would be singing a song in Irish.]

Bailiúchán Bhairbre maps this cultural shift particularly well. It documents
the concurrent use of the home and the pub for communal music making
and the profile of the people who performed in these venues; the recordings
Bairbre made in pubs, for instance, rarely if ever feature very young or very
old people, and only a few women.[112] The collection records how the popularity of house visiting and of dancing at parties and in Halla Rónáin continued to
be the primary means of communal socializing throughout the period during
which Bairbre recorded, even while the popularity of the pub and of modern
music grew, among young islanders in particular. The striking counterpoint
between the local traditional music culture and the contemporary popular,
ballroom, and showband music culture that we hear in Bailiúchán Bhairbre
represents a record in sound of the different identities that inhabited, or related
to, or emerged from Aran at the time: local youth and their elders, visitors,
returned emigrants, and relatives born overseas, in this case Americans.[113]
Bairbre herself presents an example of how young islanders were then negotiating identity—whether personal or communal, in regional, national, or global
contexts—through music. As a young, outgoing woman with a broad taste in
music, she represented her own generation of islanders for whom participation
in local traditional culture and in popular youth culture was simultaneous. In
seeking out "an sean-dream" (the old people) and local poets, she represented

her background, her environment, and her own affinity with a traditional and local culture of speech and song, but at the same time, she also acknowledged that she was, in spite of her brother's description of her as "duine den sean-dream" (one of the old people), different from them in many ways.[114] In recording such people and in seeking to preserve their memory, Bairbre recognized and observed their unique identity. In the deliberate act of recording the stars of local music making, she indicated that she knew she was documenting a way of life that was then passing. Bailiúchán Bhairbre thus documents the transformations of contemporary identities in Aran and how they were expressed in music. It captures in music, in speech, and in sound a unique sense of the variable and of the constant in the contemporary identities of islanders. It also demonstrates Bairbre's awareness of, and participation in, the contemporary cultural shift.

The wealth of variety of Bailiúchán Bhairbre contributes a great deal to the efficacy of Bairbre's representation of the contemporary musical milieu. It details what music was performed in Aran in the period in question and how it was performed. It provides insight into how islanders came to perform such a broad range of music. It presents to listeners the first substantial perspective on the impact of modern music in Aran; the assimilation of modern music is barely touched on in other collections by comparison. It gives some indication of the extent of islanders' efforts to access mediated music. It also presents a perspective in sound on how contemporary islanders were negotiating their place in a world that was, in a sense, growing smaller. Most significantly, perhaps, Bailiúchán Bhairbre documents how the stage was being set for the influential decline in music transmission that would occur over the following thirty years or so and that would eventually weaken the presence of traditional music in Aran and threaten its survival there. The sheer number of contributors, many of whom shared several pieces, and the variety of styles and repertoire they present indicate the level of confidence among contemporary performers, even where their contributions were ordinary. This evidence supports Treasa Ní Mhiolláin's assessment of how that confidence has since waned and local performance aesthetics have since shifted: "Ní bhíodh gá iarraidh ar aon duine fadó *stave* a chasadh, ní hionann agus anois nuair a thógann sé leathuair a' chloig amannta sula mbeifeá in ann amhrán a bhaint as duine" (Long ago there was no need to ask someone to sing a stave, unlike now when it takes half an hour sometimes before you can get a song out of someone).[115] Variety may be one of the most significant attributes of Bailiúchán Bhairbre, but so too is its timing.

Bailiúchán Bhairbre was created just as the tide was turning. It documents a key moment in the history of the music of Aran, a moment when islanders changed how they socialized and changed their use of public and private spaces for making music together, a moment when the traditional musical milieu began to be replaced by the modern musical milieu, a development that instigated the near thirty-year decline of music transmission, a decline that, within a generation, undermined the confidence of some singers and the stability of the local practice of communal music making. Capturing the timbre of the contemporary musical milieu in musical, social, and cultural terms, Bailiúchán Bhairbre is a remarkable achievement for an untrained local independent operator and a vital historical document.

There is another element of Bairbre's recording practice that contributes to its historical significance. In addition to the accuracy of the representation she presents, there is her recordist methodology. This keystone element prompts the question: could this innovative and successful methodology of collecting only have manifested in a collector who was both a local and an independent operator?

IDENTITIES: LOCAL AND INDEPENDENT

As a local collector, Bairbre was conveniently resident in her field on a relatively permanent basis. She spoke the local language and was often friends with or related to those whom she recorded. Her familiarity with her contributors usually helped rather than hindered her practice. Locals responded well to her and sometimes better than they responded to professional collectors. Knowing that she was not collecting music for a broadcast or for an archive, local performers may have been less intimidated by her efforts.

Apart from the convenience of residency, Bairbre was also, and more significantly, documenting a world of music from the inside. The generally democratic, pluralistic, and open-minded aesthetic of her native musical milieu forged her aesthetic principles of collecting and her style of music collecting. For Bairbre, a good musical performance—whatever its context, style, content, origin, language, or instrumentation—constituted a contribution to local musical life and, as such, deserved to be respected, valued, and cherished. Her chief motive—to connect with the people around her through music—was also a profoundly local concern. As a local, Bairbre was more emotionally invested in the practice she recorded than any visitor could be. Her emotional concern is a significant element: it establishes the sincerity of her efforts and represents the foundation upon which her recordist methodology was built.[116]

Bairbre's identity as an independent collector was equally vital to her style of music collecting. As an independent operator, she was free of the constraints imposed on professional collectors and had more choices open to her. The amount of time or money she spent on collecting was not regulated or controlled by a higher authority or by an employer. Her selection of material and of recording arena was not prescribed or regulated by an agenda of preservation, publication, or broadcasting. Consequently, Bairbre differs from professional and visiting collectors because she had the time, inclination, freedom, and the means that were necessary for her to indulge in her style of music collecting and to develop her recordist methodology, luxuries that remained beyond the reach of many professionals and visitors.

Being an independent collector also had a negative effect on Bairbre's recording practice. Along with neglecting to detail the contents of a recording, there are also some potentially surprising omissions. There are a number of performers whom Bairbre did not record, notable performers whom she might have recorded. They include Petairín a' Bheagach Ó Maoláin, Peter Peaits Ó Fátharta, Céitín Sheáinín Aindí Uí Fhátharta, and Maidhlín Mhaidhcilín Seoighe, all of whom were recorded just a few years earlier by Sidney Robertson Cowell.[117] Bairbre and her tape recorder appear never to have been present on occasions when these singers performed.[118] As the current collection of tapes does not constitute the full complement of her recordings, the missing tapes awaiting discovery may possibly feature some of the singers named above.

Nevertheless, Bailiúchán Bhairbre reveals that the negative aspects of being a local or an independent collector or both are outnumbered by the positive. In the end, we observe that being a local and independent were essential agents in the creation of the conditions in which Bairbre's recordist methodology emerged. The successes of her winning combination of methodologies for collecting music suggest that local and independent music collections deserve greater attention. Bairbre's achievement makes a strong case for such collections and in particular for her recordist methodology. This conclusion has repercussions for the canon of music in Aran and, indeed, for the canon of Irish traditional music more generally, both of which are dominated by representations created by professionals who were more often than not visitors to the places where they collected music.

QUESTIONS OF REPRESENTATION AND SELF-AWARENESS

Among the music collectors and commentators who have documented the music of Aran, Bairbre's perspective is rare. As a local and independent collector with a specific motive—a strong desire to connect with people through music making—she focused more on being a recordist than a collector. From her perspective, being a collector enabled her to document the products of music making around her, but being a recordist enabled her to enter the process of music making, through which effort she might achieve her ultimate goal. Together, her two methodologies highlight the contrast between the role of the collector and the role of the recordist and reveal the work of a collector to be comparatively confined. Bailiúchán Bhairbre demonstrates that perspective is of vital importance to representation and should always be taken into consideration when dealing with historical sources including music collections.

Through its extraordinary variety, Bailiúchán Bhairbre also provides contextualizations of the music it documents and of other collections. Its radical, unorthodox, and varied contribution to the representation of music in Aran contrasts greatly with the rest of the canon, much of which has focused solely on local performances of traditional music that occur out of their usual contexts. By showing the variability of the contemporary practice of traditional music making and performance, including different musics, styles of performance, and venues, it records in sound the repertoire, styles, and venues that were ignored, avoided, and neglected by other collectors. The contrast between Bairbre's oeuvre and that of her contemporaries and antecedents highlights the importance of considering what motivated collectors and the conditions under which they acted so that we might better understand the reasons for their successes and their shortcomings. Such contextualization is essential if we are to equip ourselves properly for the task of assembling a history—in this case, of music in Aran. The implications for other histories of Irish traditional music, of music in Ireland, of Aran and, indeed, of Ireland, are significant.

When Bairbre Quinn bought her tape recorder in the late 1950s, she could not have been aware of the legacy she would eventually create nor that her curiosity about sound technology would make such a mark. It is difficult to assess how aware Bairbre was of the significance of her practice, to determine whether she realized that she was recording a musical tradition that was gradually incurring major changes in repertoire, style, and the location, circumstances, and

manner of its performance and transmission. At the very least, she was sufficiently aware of the history of local music and of its currency in contemporary
life to recognize its value and to preserve it. Whatever degree of self-awareness
informed her practice, her agency is commendable. As a young woman who
lived and worked in rural areas all her life and who continued to record—albeit
less frequently—as she reared four children, she showed remarkable ingenuity,
resourcefulness, and skill in creating Bailiúchán Bhairbre.

Conclusion

Founded on a belief in the importance of history, which has the potential to serve people in their everyday lives, and motivated to respond to a need that was identified during the fieldwork that contributed to this work—a need to restore to Aran some of the context of its musical traditions and the representation thereof—this book offers readers new opportunities to encounter accounts of music in Aran, to "craft and recraft" the memory of music in Aran from the historical material presented herein, and to restore to the music of Aran some of its historical context.[1] It is a response that complements the current efforts of islanders to bolster their own musical practices. As such, it represents a contribution to traditional music in Aran and to the people of Aran who most value that practice.

The accounts presented here feature in individual studies of four historical collections of the music of Aran, collections that span nearly 120 years from 1857 to the 1970s. These studies contextualize each collection in order to test the integrity of its representation and so ensure the validity and efficacy of its contribution to the history of music in Aran. In so doing, this book also presents a historiography of that music, a music that has been marginalized in the Aran canon and in the canon of Irish traditional music. It offers some explanations for this marginalization, all of which focus on the agency of the authors of the representations of music in Aran or lack thereof. It reiterates the importance of contextualizing such representations if we are to succeed in our efforts to attain richer understandings of historical actualities.

The four collections discussed represent the fruits of the labors of people who were specifically interested in documenting the music of Aran during the

period in question, a purpose that contributes all the more to the integrity of
their representations. Historical poverty, relative isolation, and population
decline were significant determining factors in the development of the musical
traditions of Aran. These factors created the conditions for the formation of
an instrumental music tradition that is, in terms of instrumentation and repertoire, comparatively confined and, correspondingly, a song tradition that has
dominated the local practice of communal music making. The four collections
demonstrate how the local repertoire of sean-nós song has changed over the
decades and how, in that time, it has been consistently dominated by songs
that are mostly from the larger, more densely populated, neighboring area of
Conamara and County Mayo, where the dialect of Irish is closer to that found
in Aran than the Munster dialect of neighboring County Clare. The four collections depict the relative stability of the local practice of communal music
making in the one hundred years or more leading up to the 1960s, when the
traditional performance milieu began to be replaced by the modern performance milieu, a change that had a major impact on that practice. Furthermore,
each of the collections gives its own sense of the timbre of contemporary local
music making, with varying degrees of success.

     Only one of the collectors discussed here personally submitted a representa-
tion of the music of Aran to what Filene calls "public memory."[2] That effort—
Sidney Robertson Cowell's *Songs of Aran*—had, as discussed in chapter 3, a limited impact.[3] Despite their interest and considerable efforts, within their own
lifetimes the other four collectors did not attain the opportunity or—as suggested in the case of Séamus Ennis—exhibit the impetus to see how the
"memory work" they did on the music of Aran might contribute to the public
memory of that music.[4] They created material from which memory might
be crafted, but most of them did not disseminate or "advance" the memory of
music in Aran as did Filene's "cultural brokers" of America, "people like John
and Alan Lomax and Sam Charters, or, in Waters's case, Dixon, Lippman, Mess-
inger, and Winter—folklorists, collectors, writers, promoters, and producers who
advanced visions of America's musical past."[5] Dissemination emerges as a vital
component of representation, one that enables and increases its efficacy. In
spite of the efforts of five worthy chroniclers, the music of Aran remained for
a long time below the radar, failing to make much of an impact beyond its
own shores. The four collections have not had the opportunity to challenge the
marginalization of the music of Aran within narratives of Irish traditional

music. Until now, that is. This book, which is another but different example of memory work, affords to the four collections an opportunity to make an impact. It takes up where each of the collectors left off and advances a representation they might have appreciated.

Apart from enabling readers to access historical material on the music of Aran, most of which has never been published, the four collections discussed here also give valuable insight into the phenomenon of music collecting. Witnessing the strength of the theme of loss in each of the collections, this book observes that loss is a trope of music collecting everywhere, a ghost that haunts collectors and their collaborators alike and spurs them on in the practice of documenting music. It also charts how that sense of loss has manifested itself in different ways in different eras, through the romantic nationalism of the nineteenth century to the modernism of the twentieth century. It provides evidence of how antiquarianism, colonialism, linguistics, folkloristics, and commercialism have impacted on the music that is collected and disseminated and on the performers who share their music with collectors. It also demonstrates how developments in technology—specifically the growth in portable sound-recording machines—enabled the modernization and democratization of music collecting. In addition, this book identifies people's personalities—those of the collector(s) and their collaborators—as key elements of the work of music collecting. Each of the four collections gives some indication of how individual personalities can mold representation. The collector's identity as a local or as a visitor emerges as a vitally important factor in the practice of collecting music, one that raises questions about the precise nature and purpose of music collecting.

Finally, the story told here highlights the possibility of there being other ways of documenting music, ways that have the potential to challenge received wisdoms about music collecting and to lead us to unexpected revelations about music. This potential is realized in the example of Bairbre Quinn and her form of memory work, which stands out of the canon of music collecting in Aran as a remarkable achievement. As seen in chapter 4, Bairbre compares with other collectors because she, too, engaged in collecting and preserving music; but she differs from them because of her recordist methodology in which preservation was a secondary concern and in which she focused on the process of music making instead of on its products—songs and tunes. Collectors generate documents or recordings—objects that can be moved or dispatched—that enable people to overcome distances of time and space so that they might connect with the music they seek. Most of the objects or recordings Bairbre created were, however, by-products of her primary and intrinsically localized pursuit: to abolish all distances of time and space between herself and the people around her and their music by keeping company with them and by becoming—with the help of her recording machine—a performer within the local musical milieu. In the end, although Bairbre the recordist did not set out to manufacture memory or to produce the material from which memory might be crafted, the collection she produced presents an extraordinarily panoramic view of contemporary music making in Aran, one that is not to be found in the deliberate memory works of collectors. The success Bairbre achieved with her recordist method-ology makes a strong case for alternative methodologies of music collecting. It urges us to contextualize music collections as fully as possible so that we might better understand their significance and assess their true value. It also encourages us to consider local collections, not simply because they are local and ought to be considered in the interests of fairness and cultural equity but also because we might learn something new and unexpected from them. Unorthodox though they might be, they have the potential to be wonderfully revealing.

Appendix 1

Analysis of Petrie and O'Curry 1857 Aran Manuscripts

The provision of an edition of the Petrie and O'Curry Aran manuscripts is beyond the scope of this book. The purpose of this appendix is, rather, to take the initial step of rendering the available information on the collection more accessible. As such, this appendix includes lists of the airs and songs Petrie and O'Curry are known to have respectively transcribed in Aran, citing Deasy's (D) identifying numbers and O'Curry's page numbers and sometimes including Petrie's or Stanford's identifying numbers for ease of reference. It also shares individual analyses of most of the tunes and song airs the pair collected there. Where possible, directly after a given title, I add to each analysis the common title of a melody or song. A number of Petrie's Aran airs have yet to reveal any additional information beyond their titles, the names of the contributors, or the dates of those contributions (despite the efforts of previous editors who offered notes on potential multiforms and variants), so these partially identified airs are simply listed without detailed analysis. For want of space, the information on comparable airs and words included here is not comprehensive nor is it intended to be; it simply refers to commonly available sources. For the same reason, I have also declined to provide a close analysis of the song texts. Their unedited inclusion here is intended simply to provide wider access to them. Transcriptions of Petrie's airs are likewise absent for want of space. As they have been reprinted several times, they are already reasonably accessible.

The style of Petrie's Aran airs is generally idiomatic of Irish traditional music. For instance, the second and third phrases of the air "Donnell O'Daly" (D.724) correspond to the same phrases in the well-known song "Bríd Óg Ní Mháille"; and much of the air D.866, which Petrie calls "There is a long house at the top of the village," compares with one of the airs that can be sung to "Sagart na Cúile Báine" as performed by Maidhlín Mhaidhcilín Seoighe of Cill Éinne, Árainn, for Sidney Robertson Cowell in June 1955.[1] However, some of the airs, in particular "Far, far, down in the south of Luidach" (D.678), strike me as particularly singular and seem quite different to the airs of today's sean-nós songs. The air "Táimse i mo Chodladh" (D.560) is an interesting exception. This Munster song is not typically sung in Aran today. How it came to be in Aran in 1857 is a mystery. With so little work done on O'Curry's song collecting, and with no known contemporaneous song texts from Aran with which one might make a comparison, it is impossible to comment on the style of his Aran texts. The repertoire and language presented in his transcriptions are, however, like Petrie's airs, idiomatic of Irish traditional song.

Petrie did not satisfactorily catalog his airs.[2] Subsequent editions of his airs have thus focused on eliminating "duplicates and close variants," which hinders searches for specific transcriptions from particular localities.[3] Cooper found Stanford's edition "in most ways is identical with the manuscripts held by the National Library of Ireland," but Donal O'Sullivan criticizes it: "The transcriptions are accurate, but Petrie's invaluable notes were not reprinted and there is a complete absence of systematic arrangement. Many of the Gaelic titles are wrongly deciphered, and the book is a mine to be worked rather than a finished product of scholarship."[4] In truth, none of the editions of Petrie's collection are without fault, but for those seeking specific settings of tunes, Deasy's edition is the most useful because of her attempts to catalog the airs. Indeed, Tom Munnelly called for Deasy's work to be published.[5]

THE TUNES AND SONG AIRS

Airs from Árainn, 1857, George Petrie MSS

Number	Contributor	Title (as given by Deasy)
D.210	Mary O'Donoghue	Rossaveel
D.317	Mary O'Donoghue	?
D.328	Lord Rossmore	Uaimh Rí—The King's Cave [set in Arran 1841]
D.329	Pat O'Malley	A boat song [Title Unknown]
D.428	Pat Folan	The Good Ship Planet
D.507	Peter Mullin	[The Enchanted Valley]
D.534	Mary O'Donoghue	We'll Drink to the Health of Keenan

D.560	?	Tá mé i mo chodladh is ná dúisigh mé
D.569	Mary O'Flaherty	?
D.649	Mary O'Malley	Sweet Innismore [sung in Connemara]
D.678	Mary O'Donoghue	Far, far, down in the south of Luidach
D.700	Mary O'Donoghue	Alas that I'm not a freechaun on the mountainside
D.702	Mary O'Donoghue	O'Coghlan has a glen
D.724	Mary O'Flaherty	Donnell O'Daly
D.739	Mary O'Malley	Is cailín beag óg mé
D.751	?	[Sweet Innismore]
D.784	Mary O'Malley	Arranmore tune [Billy Byrne of Ballymanus]
D.816	John Dubhany	Tommy Regan
D.822	Mrs. John Dillane [Mary O'Flaherty]	As I strayed out on a foggy morning in Harvest
D.824	[Mary O'Malley]	The Enchanted Valley
D.866	Pat Mullin	There is a long house at the top of the village
D.880	P. Mullin	When I go down to the foot of Croagh Patrick
D.955	Mary O'Malley	[She moved through the fair]
D.1009	Mary O'Malley and James Gill	I will raise my sail black mistfully in the morning
D.1042	Mary O'Malley	Pretty Mary Bilry
D.1157	John Dubhana	I was once sailing by the head
D.1182	P. Mullin	O girl of the golden tresses
D.1266	Mary O'Donoghue	A woman and twenty of them
D.1300	Peter Cooke	If I'm alive in Ireland
D.1305	Peter Cooke	?
D.1306	Pat Mullen	'Tis long ago you promised to steal away with me
D.1317	James Gill	[Gaily we went and gaily we came]
D.1331	James Gill	Arranmore tune [Title unknown]
D.1358	Patrick Mullin	Alas that I'm not a little starling bird

Source: Marion Deasy, "New Edition of Airs and Dance Tunes from the Music Manuscripts of George Petrie, LL.D., and a Survey of His Work as a Collector of Irish Folk Music," 2 vols. (PhD diss., University College Dublin, 1982).

D.210 **Rossaveel**

SINGER: Mary O'Donoghue

Petrie identified the hornpipe "Rossaveel" as "an old version of the Flowers of Edinboro." It was also a song.

AIR: "Flowers of Edinburgh" (Miles Krassen, ed., *O'Neill's Music of Ireland* [New York: Oak Publications, 1976], 208).

D.328 **Uaimh Rí—The King's Cave**

COLLECTOR: Lord Rossmore.

The red herring of Petrie's Aran collection is the air "Uaimh Rí," "set in 1841" by his friend, the gentleman piper Lord Rossmore, whom Jimmy O'Brien Moran identifies as Colonel Henry Westenra.[6] No autograph music manuscripts of Lord Rossmore's transcriptions survive. His music lives on only in Petrie's hand. O'Brien Moran observes: "Whether Rossmore gave Petrie the tunes in manuscript form or whether Petrie transcribed the music from Rossmore's playing is difficult to ascertain although the former is more likely."[7] "Uaimh Rí—The King's Cave" (D.328) is subtitled "Arran Boat Song," leading Stokes and Stanford to count it as one of the Aran airs. Though the identification with the Aran Islands is, in all probability, an inaccuracy, in deference to Stokes and Stanford I include it in the present assessment. Lord Rossmore, who was from County Monaghan, was fond of boats and he owned a yacht, but there is no record of him having visited any of the "Arrans" of the British Isles—"Arran-More" or Árainn in County Galway, Arranmore or Árainn Mhór in County Donegal, and Arainn or the Isle of Arran in Scotland. Interestingly, there is a King's Cave at Drumadoon on the Isle of Arran. It is one of many caves throughout Scotland and on Rathlin Island off the coast of County Antrim, in which King Robert the Bruce I (1274–1329) is said to have spent three months in hiding before being inspired to emerge by a spider's persistent efforts to spin a web. So, could "Uaimh Rí—The King's Cave" be Scottish in origin? The modal quality of the tune and the intervallic leaps of fifths in the second part make it sound more Scottish than Irish. The single instance of a Scotch snap (a semiquaver followed by a dotted quaver) in bar 2 could be

another indicator of the tune's likely Scottish origin. Most
convincing of all is the similarity between the opening of this air
and the refrain of a waulking song dating from 1768 or 1786 and
attributed to Annie Campbell of the Isle of Harris in the Outer
Hebrides, "Ailein Duinn O Hì Shiùbhlainn Leat," as sung in 1960
by Captain Donald Joseph MacKinnon of Barra.[8] However, as
Petrie was not the sole author of his collection, Deasy warns that
care must be taken with the questionable rhythmic values of some
of the melodies in his collection.[9]

D.428   The Good Ship Planet
SINGER: Pat Folan
The title of this ambiguous tune suggests an English sea shanty or
    ballad, but whether or not such a song was then extant in Aran,
    it is unlikely that Petrie and O'Curry would have notated one.
    The first half of this tune compares with the air accompanying
    the song "Maidin Fhómhair" that was transcribed by Eibhlín
    Bean Mhic Choisdealbha from Katie McGath of Liskeevey, Tuam,
    Co. Galway.[10] This coincidence suggests that Petrie gave the title
    "The Good Ship Planet" to the wrong air and that D.428
    accompanies O'Curry's version of "Maidin Fhómhair"
    (Universitaetsbibliothek Leipzig [hereafter UBL], NL 291/634,
    124). However, O'Curry's text has already been successfully
    matched with another of Petrie's airs, the title of which is a direct
    translation of the opening line of O'Curry's text. Therefore, despite
    its partial similarity with Bean Mhic Choisdealbha's air, and
    despite the feasibility of combining it with O'Curry's text, we can
    assume that Petrie's D.428 was not intended to accompany
    O'Curry's "Maidin Fhómhair."
AIR: "The Good Ship Planet" (Francis O'Neill, ed., James O'Neill,
    arr., *Music of Ireland* [Chicago: Lyon & Healy, 1903], 76); O'Neill's
    version, or multiform, is virtually the same except that it is
    transposed and the trill mark is placed on a different note in the
    same bar.[11]
RECORDINGS: "A Rosebud in June" (Magpie Lane, *Jack-in-the-
    Green*, Beautiful Jo Records, BEJOCD-22, 1998).

D.507

SINGER: Peter Mullin

DATE: September 8, 1857

Petrie suggests the air is a multiform of another he collected in Aran,
   D.824 "The Enchanted Valley." As a result, Deasy suggests the title
   of D.507 might also be "The Enchanted Valley." The opening and
   closing phrases of D.507, the form of which is ABBA, compare with
   the corresponding phrases of the well-known Scottish song "Both
   Sides of the Tweed," the form of which is AABA.

VARIANT: See also D.824, as suggested by Petrie.

AIR: It may represent an early minor-key version of the air
   accompanying a song that was performed for Séamus Ennis in 1945
   by Tomás "Tyrell" Ó Briain (1890–1962) of Cill Éinne, Árainn—
   "Truagh sin mise Lá'l Pádhraic" (National Folklore Collection
   [hereafter NFC] MM 021.010).

D.534   **We'll Drink the Health of Keenan/"An Ciníneach"**

SINGER: Mary O'Donoghue

Deasy observes correctly that this tune is, as Richard Henebry stated,
   a "hornpipe."[12]

WORDS: "An Ciníneach" by Antaine Ó Raiftearaí, NFC 607: 567;
   NFC 695: 229–30; NFC 1236: 312–13; Dubhglas de hÍde, ed.,
   Abhráin agus Dánta an Reachtabhraigh (1933; repr., Baile Átha
   Cliath: Oifig Dhíolta Foilseachán Rialtais, 1974), 210; Ciarán Ó
   Coigligh, ed., *Raiftearaí: Amhráin agus Dánta* (Baile Átha Cliath:
   An Clóchomhar Tta., 1987), 204.

D.560   **Tá mé i mo chodladh is ná dúisigh mé/"Táimse im' Chodladh"**

AIR: Matt Cranitch, ed., *The Irish Fiddle Book: The Art of Traditional
   Fiddle-Playing* (1996; repr., Cork: Ossian Publications in
   association with Mercier Press, 2001.

WORDS: Fionán Mac Coluim, ed., *Bolg an tSoláthair: Cnuasach Sean-
   Rochan* (1904; repr., Dublin: Connradh na Gaedhilge, 1919).

AIR AND WORDS: "Táimse i mo Chodladh," An t-Athair Pádraig
   Breathnach, ed., *Ceól ár sínsear III* (1913; repr., Baile Átha Cliath:
   Muinntir Bhrúin agus Nualláin, 1923), 31–32; Séamus de

Chlanndiolúin and Maighréad Ní Annagáin, eds., *Londubh an Chairn* (London: Oxford University Press, 1927).

RECORDINGS: "Táimse im' chodladh," Seán Ó Sé and Ceoltóirí Chualann, *Táimse im' chodladh*, 3 vols. (Dublin: Gael Linn, 1968).

D.649   Sweet Innismore [sung in Connemara]

SINGER: Mary O'Malley

Petrie indicates this song was "sung in Connemara."

VARIANT: See also D.751, as suggested by Deasy.

AIR: The third and fourth lines of the air compare with the same lines in the air that Patsy Dan Mac Ruairí (1944–2018) of Tory Island, Co. Donegal, sang to the song "Éirigh Suas a Stóirín." A multiform of this air, D.751—given the title "Sweet Innismore" by Deasy—also compares with the air of Patsy Dan's song. See also the air of the song composed by Pádraig Fallon, "The Lovely Lady of Loughrea," as sung by Garry McMahon (1937–2008) (*Comhaltas Champions on Tour*, Comhaltas Ceoltóirí Éireann, CL11, 1975) and by Séamus Mac Mathúna.

D.700   Alas that I'm not a freechaun on the mountainside/"Séamas Ó Murchú"

SINGER: Mary O'Donoghue

AIR: The title of this air is a direct translation of the opening line of a verse from the lament for Séamas Ó Murchú or Séamus Mac Murchaidh, who is said to have been born ca. 1720 and was hanged in Armagh between 1750 and 1760.[13] The extent to which this song traveled—throughout the northeast and as far as Galway, Mayo, and Donegal—suggests it was "a very popular song which had deep resonance and was sung at wakes and at other social occasions."[14] It was sung to at least three different airs. This fourth air sits well enough with the lyrics; the rhythmic and major-sounding melody does not necessarily preclude it from serving as a vehicle for such a tragic tale. Even if Petrie attributed the wrong title to the wrong air, the title alone is so distinctive—the word "freechaun" representing "fraochán," meaning "bilberry"—and the song so well traveled that it is likely that "Séamas Ó Murchú" was sung in Aran in 1857.

WORDS: "Séamas Ó Murchú," Micheál Ó Tiománaidhe, *Amhráin
Ghaeilge an Iarthair*, ed. William Mahon (1906; repr., Indreabhán:
Cló Iar-Chonnacht, 1990), 81–83; Seosamh Mac Grianna, *Pádraic
Ó Conaire agus aistí eile* (Baile Átha Cliath: Oifig Díolta
Foilseacháin Rialtais, 1936), 157–61, 249–52; Peter Kennedy, ed.,
Folksongs of Britain and Ireland (New York: Oak Publications,
1975), 106–7; Colm Ó Baoill, *Amhráin Chúige Uladh* (Baile Átha
Cliath: Gilbert Dalton, 1977), 61–64; Pádraigín Ní Uallacháin, *A
Hidden Ulster: People, Songs and Traditions of Oriel* (Dublin: Four
Courts Press, 2003), 241–46.

D.702   O'Coghlan has a glen/"Gleanntaí Mhac Cochláin"
SINGER: Mary O'Donoghue
WORDS: "Gleanntaí Mhac Cochláin," NFC 688: 349–55; NFC 1280:
321–32; NFC 1280: 521–52; Fr. Tomás Ó Ceallaigh, ed., *Ceol na
nOileán* (1931; repr., Indreabhán: Cló Iar-Chonnacht, 1993), 78;
Ríonach uí Ógáin, ed., *Faoi Rothaí na Gréine: Amhráin as
Conamara a bhailigh Máirtín Ó Cadhain* (Baile Átha Cliath:
Coiscéim, 1999), 206–8.

D.724   Donnell O'Daly/"Dónal Ó Dálaigh"
SINGER: Mary O'Flaherty
AIR: See second and third phrases of the air to "Bríd Óg Ní Mháille"
(Micheál Ó hEidhin, *Cas Amhrán* [1975; repr., Indreabhán: Cló Iar-
Chonnacht, 1990], 60).
WORDS: "Dónal Ó Dálaigh," NFC 1280: 102–4; NFC 1280: 592–93,
NFC 236: 131–32, NFC 271: 107–8; uí Ógáin, *Faoi Rothaí na Gréine*,
63–64.

D.751
VARIANT: See also D.649, as suggested by Deasy.
AIR: Compares with the air that Patsy Dan Mac Ruairí of Tory
Island, Co. Donegal, sang to the song "Éirigh Suas a Stóirín." A
multiform of D.649, prompting Deasy to give it the title "Sweet
Innismore."

D.816 **Tommy Regan/"Tomás Bán Mac Aogáin"**
SINGER: John Dubhana
WORDS: Mícheál Ó Máille and Tomás Ó Máille, eds., *Amhráin
Chlainne Gael* (1905; repr., Indreabhán: Cló Iar-Chonnacht, 1995),
40–41; Darach Ó Catháin, *Traditional Irish Unaccompanied Singing*
(Gael Linn CEFCD040, 1975).

D.824 **The Enchanted Valley**
SINGER: [Mary O'Flaherty, Arran-More, September 9, 1857]
VARIANT: See also D.507, as suggested by Petrie.
AIR: Source, P.1553 an earlier setting. P.1552 from "Mary O'Flaherty,
alias Delane, Arran-More, Sept. 10 1857," titled "Oh Fair John My
Love," is a close variant. This air is dissimilar to the air of the same
name that appears in volume 3 of *The Roche Collection of
Traditional Irish Music* (Francis Roche, *The Roche Collection of
Traditional Irish Music*, vols.1–3 [1927; repr., Cork: Ossian
Publications, 1982], 19), and also in O'Neill's *Music of Ireland* (1).

D.866 **There is a long house at the top of the village**
SINGER: Pat Mullin
AIR: See "Sagart na Cúile Báine," as performed by Maidhlín
Mhaidhcilín Seoighe of Cill Éinne, Árainn (Cowell, *Songs of Aran*,
1957).
WORDS: See O'Curry, UBL, NL 291/634, 126, "Tá teach fada i mbarr
an bhaile 'na ccómhnaidheann sí—mo mhian."

D.880 **When I go down to the foot of Croagh Patrick/"Muirisc"**
SINGER: Pat Mullen
AIR: See Donal O'Sullivan, ed., "The Bunting Collection of Irish
Folk Music and Songs," *Journal of the Irish Folk Song Society* 28–29,
part 6 (1939): 67–69; Deirdre Ní Chonghaile, "Ní neart go cur le
chéile: Lámhscríbhínní ceoil a chruthaigh Petrie agus Ó Comhraí
in Árainn in 1857," in *Léachtaí Cholm Cille XL: Foinn agus Focail*, ed.
Ruairí Ó hUiginn (Maigh Nuad: An Sagart, 2010), 102, 108.
Mícheál Ó Gallchobhair likened the song air he heard in Iorrus,
Co. Mayo, to that sung to Thomas Davis's song "The Grave of

Wolfe Tone."[15] I have retrieved two different airs to Davis's song: a multiform of "An Lacha Bacach," or "Johnny Jump Up," and a multiform of "An Droiminn Donn Dílis" that was arranged by J. J. Johnson in the early twentieth century.[16] The latter of these two airs compares with that attributed to "Muirisc" in Séamus Ennis's 1943 transcription of a wax cylinder recording Séamus Ó Duilearga made in Chicago in 1939 when visiting Ó Gallchobhair's relatives (NFC CC 029). Of the two tunes provided by Bunting via O'Sullivan, the minor-key tune that was sung to the words of "Muiris na gCuan" by Redmond Stanton in Westport, Co. Mayo, in 1802 is comparable with the major-key "An Droiminn Donn Dílis" (O'Sullivan, "Bunting Collection," 67; Aloys Fleischmann, *Sources of Irish Traditional Music ca. 1600–1855: An Annotated Catalogue of Prints and Manuscripts, 1583–1855*, 2 vols. [New York: Garland, 1998], 905#4976).

WORDS: Royal Irish Academy (hereafter RIA), 23 H 32, 26; Ó Máille and Ó Máille, *Amhráin Chlainne Gael*, 146; Tomás Ó Máille, *Mícheál Mac Suibhne agus Filidh an tSéibhe* (Baile Atha Cliath: Foilseacháin an Rialtais, 1934), 64–65; O'Sullivan, "Bunting Collection," 67–69; Mícheál Ó Gallchobhair, "Amhráin ó Iorrus," *Béaloideas* 10, nos. 1–2 (1940): 236; Sheila Mulloy, "Murrisk and Ballyhaunis Compared," *Cathair na Mart: Journal of the Westport Historical Society* 13 (1993): 78; Ruairí Ó hUiginn, ed., *Léachtaí Cholm Cille XL: Foinn agus Focail* (Maigh Nuad: An Sagart, 2010), 102, 108.

D.1157 I was once sailing by the head/"An Coisdealach Mór"
SINGER: John Dubhana
AIR: NFC MM 018.053.
WORDS: NFC 1280: 726–27; NFC 77: 312–13; NFC 1282: 358–59.

D.1182 Oh girl of the golden tresses
SINGER: P. Mullin
AIR: A reel or hornpipe. See "Madam If You Please" (Capt. Francis O'Neill, ed., James O'Neill, arr., *The Dance Music of Ireland (1001 Gems)* [Chicago: Lyon & Healy], 1907, 161).

D.1266 A woman and twenty of them/"Sail Óg Rua"
  SINGER: Mary O'Donoghue
  AIR AND WORDS: Mhic Choisdealbha, *Amhráin Mhuighe Seóla*, 30–
    31; Seán Óg Ó Baoill and Mánus Ó Baoill, *Ceolta Gael* (Corcaigh:
    Cló Mercier, 1975), 83; see Ó Baoill and Ó Baoill, *Ceolta Gael*, 76–77.
  RECORDINGS: Ó Catháin, *Unaccompanied Singing*; see Eilís Ní
    Shúilleabháin, *Cois Abhann na Séad: Amhráin ó Mhúscraí* (Cló Iar-
    Chonnacht, CICD132, 1997).

D.1305
  SINGER: Peter Cooke
  Appears to be the second half of an untitled set dance.
  AIR: See "Johnny Allen's Reel" (O'Neill, *Dance Music*, 135).

D.1358 Alas that I'm not a little starling bird/"Éinín Troideóige"
  SINGER: Patrick Mullen
  DATE: September 10, 1857
  WORDS: Enrí Ó Muirgheasa, ed., *Dhá Chéad de Cheoltaibh Uladh*
    (Baile Átha Cliath: Oifig an tSoláthair, 1934), 115–16; Tomás Ó
    Máille, *Mícheál Mac Suibhne*, 116.

THE SONG TEXTS

Songs from Árainn, 1857, Eugene O'Curry MSS, UBL, NL 291/634

Page	Singer	Opening Line
123	Patt Mullen	Dá mbeinn gan bheith a ngrádh leat, do gheóbhain stáidbhean is muinntir shaor
124	Mrs. John Dillane	Maidin chiúin cheómhar is mé ag imtheacht 'san bhfóghmhar
125	John Duvane	A Sheáain Bháin mo ghrádh thú nó a cumain leat do mhargadh
126	Patt Mullen	Tá teach fada i mbárr an bhaile 'na ccómhnaidheann sí—mo mhian;
127	Peter Mullin	Chaith mé maidin earraigh ag siúbhal na ccladaidhe seo leam féin,
128	Mary O'Malley	Ni ar thullán cíbe, do bios mo mhiansa

129	Mary Donoghue	Is fada síos i ttir Ui Luígheach, atá rún mo chroidhe, céad fóraor géar,
130	James Gill	Má bhímse beo in Eirinn, ní thréicfidh mé imirt ná ól,
131	Mary O'Malley	Tógfaidh mé mo sheólta, go dúbhcheodhúch ar maidin
132	Mary O'Malley	Is cailín beag óg mé a's maighdean go fóil mé

The ten songs in the Stokes notebooks in Leipzig are all love songs and, as such, might be a subcollection of the love songs Petrie and O'Curry collected in Aran, specially transcribed for a member of the Stokes family, possibly Margaret; "For Miss Stokes" appears on one of the pages (UBL, NL 291/634, 126), which is also dated October 20, 1857, by Eugene O'Curry. I matched six of O'Curry's songs with Petrie's accompanying airs. I am certain of the first three matches and almost certain of the last three. All but the fourth and sixth titles were translated almost directly for their accompanying air titles. The instances of inconsistent identification noted throughout this study of the song texts warn against any attempt to match songs and airs on the basis of titles alone, such as Pádraig de Brún suggested with the O'Curry manuscripts 13 and 14 at University College Dublin: "Is léir chomh maith go bhfuil anso againn na focail a gabhadh lena lán de na foinn atá i gcló leo féin sa Complete Petrie collection [Charles Villiers Stanford, ed., *The Complete Collection of Irish Music as Noted by George Petrie, L.L.D., R.H.A. (1789–1866), Edited, from the Original Manuscripts by Charles Villiers Stanford* (London: The Irish Literary Society of London, Boosey, 1902–5)]. Gan an ceol a bhac agus gan dul thar theidil na bhfonn ansúd, is féidir dúinn bheith cinnte den méid seo dhíobh, pé scéal é" (It is clear too that we have here the words that were taken with a lot of the tunes that are already in print by themselves in the Complete Petrie collection. Ignoring the music and without going beyond the tunes therein, we can be sure of this number of them anyway).[17] My experience supports taking the melodies into account when attempting to match song words and airs.

The oral song tradition of the islands has assimilated many songs from the mainland, and over time, dynamic variation has led to new configurations of verses from disparate sources. Those whom I consulted about the song texts—including Treasa Ní Mhiolláin, Ciarán Ó Con Cheanainn, Dáibhí Ó Cróinín, Jimmy O'Brien Moran, Gearóid Denvir, Gearóid Ó hAllmhuráin,

Brian Ó Dálaigh, Tríona Ní Shíocháin, Bairbre Ní Fhloinn, Ciarán Ó Fátharta, Meaití Jó Shéamuis Ó Fátharta, Lillis Ó Laoire, Peadar Ó Ceannabháin, and Liam Mac Con Iomaire—compared O'Curry's transcriptions of songs to the songs they knew and concluded that his texts could be jumbled versions of, among others, Connacht songs, including "An Abhainn Mhór," "Cuaichín Ghleann Néifinn," "Éireoidh Mé Amáireach," "Tógfaidh mé mo sheolta," and "Caoineadh Liam Uí Raghallaigh."

My presentation of the song texts observes the following pattern: remarks preceding transcriptions constitute objective observations on the manuscripts themselves and the identifying information they provide; O'Curry's penciled glosses and amendments to his transcriptions are inserted at intervals throughout the texts or appear directly after each text, depending on their complexity or significance; and notes following transcriptions represent my analysis of each song.

D.739   Is cailín beag óg mé

SINGER: Mary O'Malley

P.1546, S.1137, D.739   Universitaetsbibliothek Leipzig (UBL), NL 291/634, 132

FIGURE 10. Petrie D739 with O'Curry, UBL, NL 291/634, 132, "Is cailín beag óg mé."

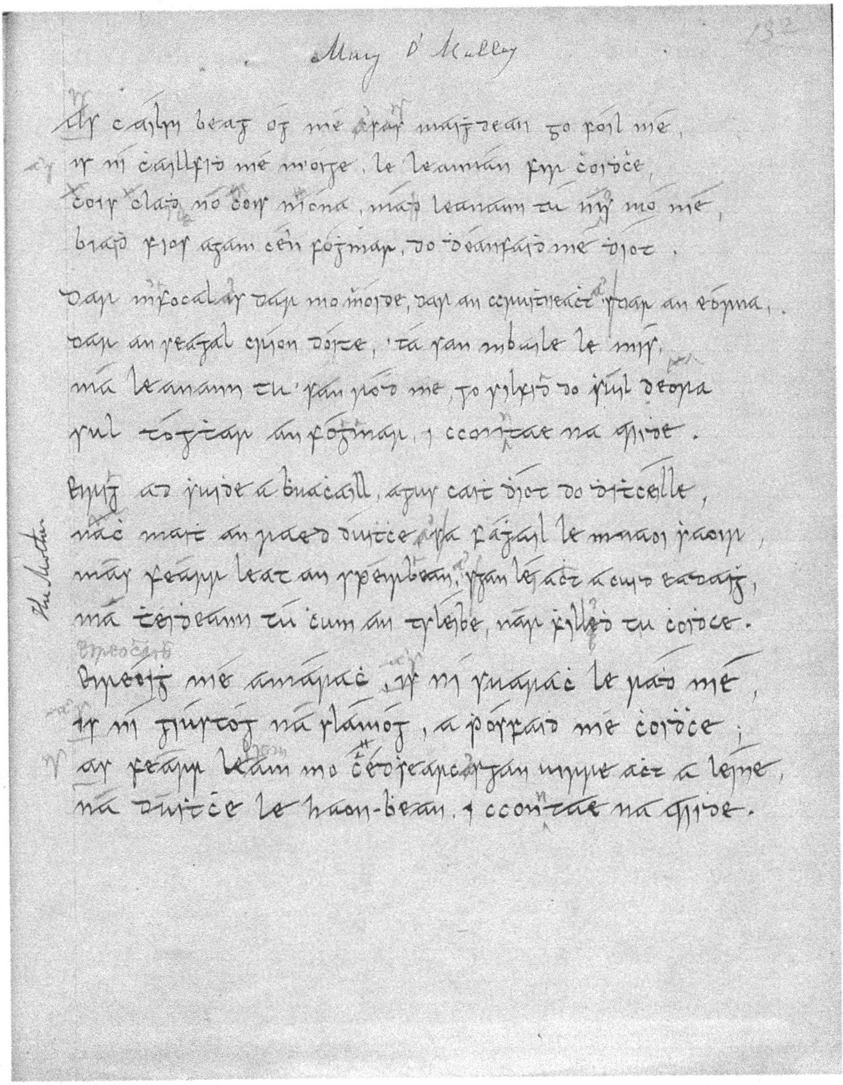

FIGURE 11. O'Curry, UBL, NL 291/634, 132, "As cailín beag óg mé a's maighdean go fóil mé."

WORDS: O'Curry, UBL, NL 291/634, 132.
SINGER: Mary O'Malley

Is

As cailín beag óg mé a's is maighdean go fóil mé,

A's Is ní chaillfidh mé m'oige, le leannán fir choidhche,

Cois claidhe nó cois móna, má leanann tú níos mó mé,

Biaidh fios agam cé'n fóghmhar, do dhéanfaidh mé dhíot.

Dar m'fhocal a's dár mo mhóide, dar an ccruithneacht a's dar an eórna,

Dar an seagal críon dóite, 'tá san mbaile le mís,

Má leanann tú 'san ród mé, go silfidh do shúil deóra

Sul tógthar an fóghmhar, i cconntae na Midhe.

["The Mother" written in the left margin beside this next verse]

Eirigh ad shuidhe a bhuachaill, agus caith dhíot do dhithchéille,

Nach maith an raed dúithche a's a fághail le mnaoi shaoir,

Más feárr leat an spéirbhean, 's gan léi acht a cuid eadaigh,

Má théidheann tú chun an tsléibhe, nár fhill'dh tu choidhce.

Eireochaibh   a's

Eireóigh mé amárach a's ní suarach le rádh mé,

A's Is ní giúrtóg ná slámóg, a phósfaidh mé choidhche;

Is As feár leam mo chédshearc a's gan uirre acht a léine,

Ná dúithche le haon-bhean i cconntae na Midhe.

O'CURRY GLOSSES AND AMENDMENTS
Line 15: leam, "liom"

D.1009 I will raise my sail black, mistfully in the morning

SINGER: Mary O'Malley and James Gill, Arran-more, September 8, 1857

The Dublin version of the text "Tógfaidh mé mo sheólta go dubhcheodhúch ar maidin" (RIA, 12 N 5, 178) differs slightly from the version that was uncovered in Leipzig (UBL, NL 291/634, 131).

I will raise my sail black, mistfully in the morning   From Mary O'Malley and James Gill, Arran-more
                                                                              8ᵗʰ September 1857

Tóg-faidh mé— mo sheól - ta, go dúbh-cheo - dhúch ar— maidin Ar—

cuaird go mo mhí - le stói - rín— a's go deó deó— ní— chasfad; Mar do

gheall mé— go— bpóg- fainn a— rós - bhéil - ín— meala, A's— ní

léir dham na— bóith - re, atáid na deo - ra— dom— dhalladh.

P.1565, S.377, D.1009   Universitaetsbibliothek Leipzig (UBL), NL 291/634, 131
                                                              Mary O'Malley, Arann More

FIGURE 12. Petrie D1009 with O'Curry, UBL, NL 291/634, 131, "Tógfaidh mé mo sheolta."

WORDS: O'Curry, UBL, NL 291/634, 131.
SINGER: Mary O'Malley, Arann More

Tógfaidh mé mo sheólta, go dúbhcheodhúch ar maidin
Ar cuaird go mo mhíle stóirín, a's go deó deó ní chasfad;
Mar do gheall mé go bpógfainn a rós-bhéilín meala,
A's ní léir dham na bóithre, atáid na deora dom dhalladh.

A bhuachaillín is gile, míne, ná'n síoda agus na'n sneachta,
An ttabharfá-sa cuaird míosa, gach oidhche chum mo leapthan;
    [penciled "?"]
Do thabharfainnsi mian do chroidhe, dá mbadh mhian leat a ghlacadh,
Dá ttógfhá suas an bíobla, ná déanfá mo mhalairt.

Do thógfainnsi suas an bíobla a's ní dhéanfainn do mhalairt,
Mar 'mbeith iomadh na ndaoineadh ar gach taoibh ag cur eadrainn;
Maseadh an fortún atá a ndán dúinn níl fághail ar dhul tairis,
Bí romham ag an crosbhóthar a's biam pósta ag teacht abhaile.

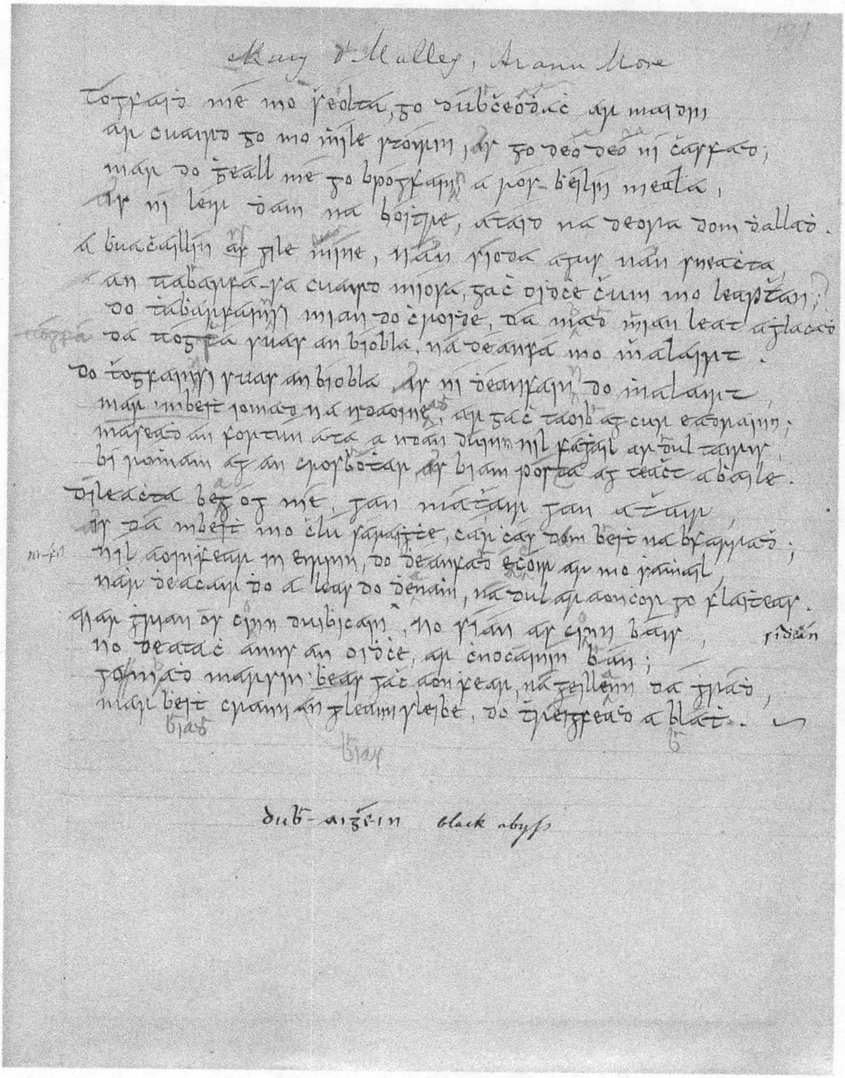

Díleachta beag óg mé, gan máthair gan athair,
A's dá mbeith mo chlú sásaighthe, cá'r chás dam bheith na bhfarradh;
Níl aoinfhear in Eirinn, do dhéanfadh éaccóir ar mo shamhail,
Ná'r dheacair dho a leas do dhéanamh, ná dul ar aon chor go Flaitheas.

Mar ghrian ós cionn duibhicain, no sían as cionn báis,
No deatach anns an oidhche ar chnocáinín bhán;
Go mbadh mar sin bheas gach aon fhear, ná geilleann dá ghrádh,
Mar bheith crann an gleann sleibhe, do thréigfeadh a bhláth.

O'CURRY GLOSSES AND AMENDMENTS
Line 8: ttógfhá, "ttógfá"
Line 15: Níl, "Ni-fhíl"
Line 17: duibhicain, "dubh-aigéin" meaning "black abyss"
Line 17: sían, "sidheán"
Line 19: bheas, "bhias"
Line 20: bheith, "bhiadh"

D.678 **Far, far, down in the south of Luidach**
SINGER: Mary O'Donoghue

Far, far, down in the south of Luidach

Mary Donohoe, Arran-More
13th September 1857

As fa - da___ síos i ttir Uí Lúigheach, atá rún___ mo___ chroidhe, céad

fór - aor___ géar, A ngeall_ ar an scáin - se do thái - nig don tír seo, do

bhreóidh_ mo___chroidhe a's do bhás-aigh mé; Is ea dúbhairt_ a muinn-tir

ó nach___bhfuiginn í, dá ttéidh sí a' ceill ná___ caoin - finn déar, Acht

ta___ fhios ag Ío - sa ná raibh mé___ faoi dhóibh

a's a Dhi - a dhí - lis cá fáth dhóibh é.

P.1529, S.335, D.678   Universitaetsbibliothek Leipzig (UBL), NL 291/634, 129
                                                                Mary Donoghue

FIGURE 14. Petrie D678 with O'Curry, NL 291/634, 129, "Is fada síos i dtír Uí
Lúigheach."

WORDS: O'Curry, UBL, NL 291/634, 129.
SINGER: Mary Donoghue

Is ttuaith ó
As fada síos i *ttir Uí* Lúigheach, atá rún mo chroidhe, céad fóraor géar,
A ngeall ar an scáinse do tháinig don tír seo, do bhreóidh mo chroidhe a's
    do bhásaigh mé;
Iseadh dúbhairt a muinntir ó nach bhfuiginn í, dá ttéidh sí a' ceill ná
    caoinfinn déar,

Acht tá a fhios ag Iosa ná raibh mé faoi dhóibh a's a Dhia dhílis cá fáth
   dhóibh é.

Níl bealach ná slighe ar bith riamh dár shíleas, do mheallfadh í nár fhéach
   mé léi,
D'fhonn síneadh síos léi do ló nó d'oidhche, mo láimh faoi na ceann a's mé
   ag pógadh a béil;
Acht an uair do shaoil mé gur leam a hinntinn a's páirt ná scaoilfeadh sí lem
   go héag,
Ba hí an chluain mhuimhneach do mheall a smaointe, do bhreoidh mo
   chroidhese go bráth dhá héis.

Mí agus lá ní bidh acht geárr, ar bhruach na trágha agus mé liom féin
Mo chroidhe ann mo lár, do shíor dá chrádhadh, sas fada ó ghrádh mo
   chaointe mé;
A righ na ngrás, ó chidhir mo chás, scaoil a ttráth mo cheasnail cléibh,
Go ttigidh an bás ar mo chinn gan spás, a's mo chaoineadh ar chlár tré mo
   chonntráil lé.

O'CURRY GLOSSES AND AMENDMENTS
Line 1: céad, "100" meaning "a hundred"; "géar" meaning "bitter"
Line 3: ttéidh, "tteidheadh"
Line 7: leam, "liom"; lem, "liom"
Line 8: an chluain mhuimhneach, "whisper" or "trick" or "wile"
Line 10: dhá chrádhadh, "being tormented"
Line 10: sar, "a's as"
Line 12: chinn, "chionn"

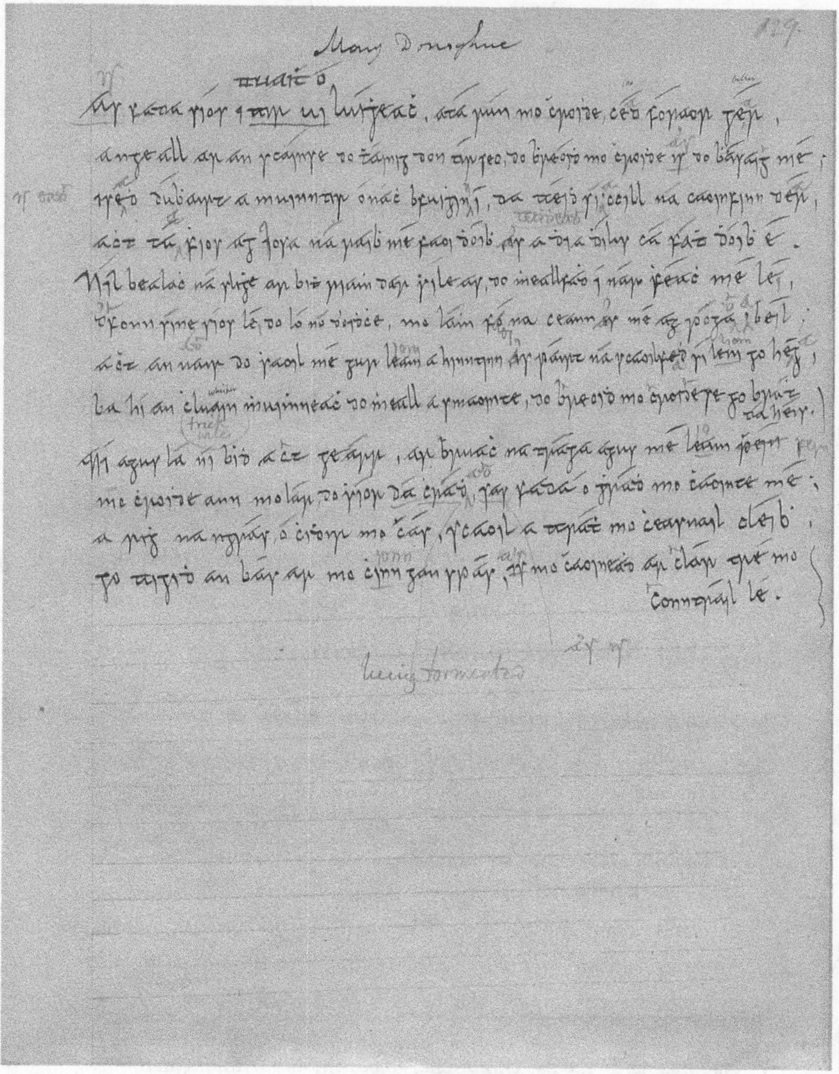

129

FIGURE 15. O'Curry, UBL, NL 291/634, 129, "As fada síos i ttir Ui Lúigheach."

D.1317   [Má Bhímse Beo in Éirinn]

SINGER: James Gill

[Gaily we went and gaily we came]   Set from James Gill
                                                                      Arran-More

P.123, S.278, D.1317   Universitaetsbibliothek Leipzig (UBL), NL 291/634, 130
                                                                                  James Gill

FIGURE 16. Petrie D1317 with O'Curry, UBL, NL 291/634, 130, "Má bhímse beo in Éirinn."

WORDS: O'Curry, UBL, NL 291/634, 130.

Má bhímse beo in Eirinn, ní thréigfidh mé imirt ná ól,
A's má bhímse beo in Eirinn, ní thréigfidh mé comhluadar spóirt;
Má bhímse beo in Eirinn, pléasgfaidh mé an jug ar an mbórd,
Seo do shláinte, mo chéad searc, ní féidir nach liomsa do phóg.

Mo chreach mhaidne, a stóirín, gan mo bhóithrín tar dorus do thighe,
Ór leat do chaith mé mo bhróga, ó thúis m'óige go deireadh mo shaoghail;
Ag dul tríd an Ard mór dham, dar leam do bhí an drúcht ina luighe,
Is mo stóirín faoi dhó thú, slán beo leat go bhfillidh mé arís.

Ná'r fhaghaidh mé bás choidhche, go ccaithidh mé dhíom an mí-ágh,
Go mbeidh ba agam 's caoire a's mo mhian do chailín deas mná;
'Tá bean anns an tír, tá do shíor ag cur eadrainn gach lá,
A's ná'r fhaghaidh bás choidhche gan fáth caointe agus mise
    ag mo ghrádh.

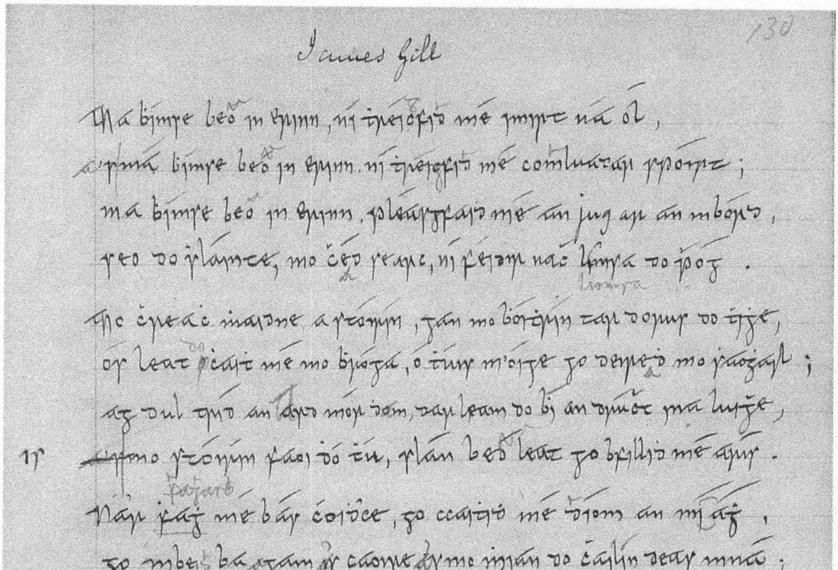

James Hill

130

1r

Thomas

Figure 17. O'Curry, UBL, NL 291/634, 130, "Má bhímse beo in Éirinn."

A Thomáis, a mhíle stór, ná cuir speois i ttalamh ná a' spréidh,
Acht do shluasad a's do ládhaigh, a's go bráth ní céim síos duit é;
Do raghainnse do'n Spáinn leat, mar 'tá tú breágh soineanta réidh,
A's d'ólfainn deoch as mhug bán leat a's tá grádh agam ar lorg do bhéil.

NOTES: Verse 1 recalls "An Abhainn Mhór" (Proinnsias Ní
   Dhorchaí, *Clár Amhrán an Achréidh* [Baile Átha Cliath: An
   Clóchomhar, 1974], 24–25). Verses 3 and 4 recall "Amhrán Rinn
   Mhaoile" (Liam Mac Con Iomaire, *Seosamh Ó hÉanaí: Nár fhágha
   mé bás choíche* [Indreabhán: Cló Iar-Chonnacht, 2007], 487–88).

D.822 **As I strayed out on a foggy morning in Harvest**

Two copies of the song "Maidin chiúin cheomhar" appear in the O'Curry manuscripts in the National University of Ireland, Maynooth ("Maidin chiúin cheoidh dár éirigh san bhfoghmhar," C 52 [a] f. 23*m*; C 113 [h] 4v. 5). However, the first of these appears to have been transcribed in 1855, and the second appears to have been transcribed from the well-known Galway piper, Paddy Conneely (ca. 1800–1851); so neither transcription relates to Aran.

As I strayed out on a foggy morning in Harvest

Mai - din__ chiú-in cheó- mhar__ Is mé ag imth- eacht_ 'san__ bhfógh- mhar, Do__ bhí mé__ du - brón- ach__ Is mo mhai-de ann mo láimh; Ag__ cuimh- neamh ar an móin - in__ A__ mbíodh mo__ mhian agus mo mhúir - ín Atá ag fear_ ei - le__ pós - da__ Is ó a Dhia nach e an feall.

P.1690, S.664, D.822

Universitaetsbibliothek Leipzig (UBL), NL 291/634, 124
Mrs John Dillane, Arann More

FIGURE 18. Petrie D822 with O'Curry, UBL, NL 291/634, 124, "Maidin Chiúin Cheómhar."

WORDS: O'Curry, UBL, NL 291/634, 124.

SINGER: Mrs. John Dillane, Arann More [Mary O'Flaherty]

	Maidin chiúin cheómhar
A's	Is mé ag imtheacht 'san bhfóghmhar,
	Do bhí mé dubrónach
A's	Is mo mhaide ann mo láimh;
	Ag cuimhneamh ar an móinin
	A mbíodh mo mhian agus mo mhúirín
	Atá ag fear eile pósda
A's	Is ó a Dhia nach e an feall.

Ar maidin gheal Domhnaigh
'S mé ag taisdiol an bhóthair,
Do chonnairc mé faoi sheol ~~cúchum~~ í—
A's   Is í ag góbhail ann mo shlíghe,
Do dhearc mé ar a bróga,
A's   Is do chuir mé fuil tsróna,
A's   Is d'iarr mise póigín,
Ar stóirín mo chroidhe.

      nidh
Cá bhfuil ní ar bith is breághtha
'Ná an ghrian ós cionn gáirdín,
Nó an cocán geal álainn,
Ag fás ar an ccraoibh;
Is mar sin atá mo ghrádhsa,
Le na finne is le na háille,
~~e, e,~~ b   Uch 's a chom chailce bhláthmhar,
Is   As leat do chaill mé mo chiall.

O'CURRY GLOSSES AND AMENDMENTS
Line 3: dubrónach, "dubbrónach"
Line 22: "This *ln* in modern Irish is pronounced = *ll*; this should be
    written *áilne*, being from *álainn* beautiful."
Line 23: "These words are in the vocative and as they are not written
    a chuim chailce bhládhmhair = o fair blooming waist, make a
    compound adjective = o fair-waisted blooming one, and must be
    joined together."

NOTES: "Maidin Fhómhair," Mhic Choisdealbha, *Amhráin Mhuighe
    Seóla*, 36–37. Some of these lines occur also in "Dónal Ó Dála"
    (Ríonach Ní Fhlathartaigh, *Clár Amhrán Bhaile na hInse* [Baile
    Átha Cliath: An Clóchomhar, 1976], 37–38#50).

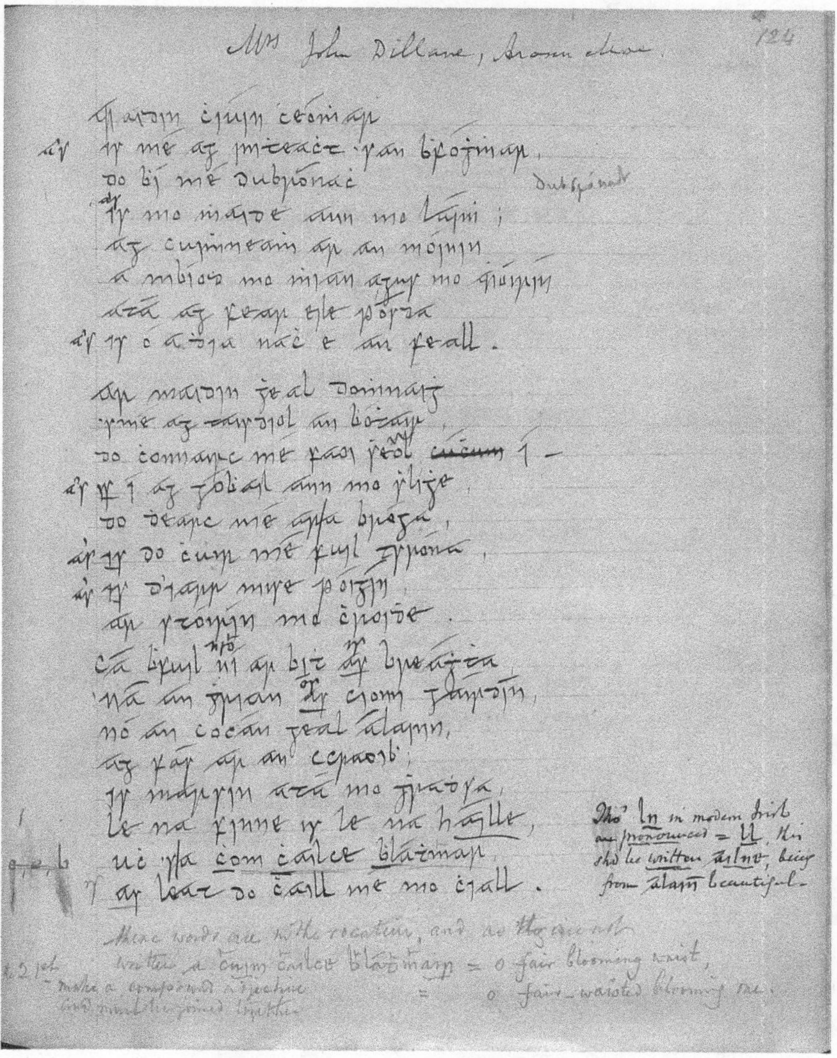

FIGURE 19. O'Curry, UBL, NL 291/634, 124, "Maidin chiúin cheómhar."

D.1306 **'Tis long ago you promised to steal away with me/"An Gabha Ceartan"**

The title of Petrie's air to the sixth song, "Is fada a gheall tú éalú liom—'Tis long ago you promised to steal away with me" (D.1036)—corresponds with the first line of the third verse of O'Curry's transcription of the accompanying words, which is "As fada o gheall tú élódh leam" (O'Curry UBL, NL 291/634, 123). Petrie's transcription would usually be identified by the first line of the first verse, which is "Dá mbeinn gan bheith a ngrádh leat."

Is fada a gheall tú éalú liom - 'Tis long ago you promised to steal away with me - very ancient.

P.634, D.1036   Universitaetsbibliothek Leipzig (UBL), NL 291/634, 123
                                                                                   Patt Mullen

FIGURE 20. Petrie D1036 with O'Curry, UBL, NL 291/634, 123, "An Gabha Ceartan."

WORDS: "Dá mbeinn gan bheith a ngrádh leat," UBL, NL 291/634, 123
SINGER: Patt Mullen

	Dá mbeinn gan bheith a ngrádh leat,	
	Do gheóbhain stáidbhean is muinntir shaor,	a's
A's	Buaibh is caoire bána	
Agus	'gus páirce le na ceur chum féir;	
fada	Codladh fada samhradh	samhraidh
	Agus greann a bheith dhá dhénamh lé;	dhéanamh léi
	Acht go mfheárr leam siúbhal na ngleannta,	liom
	Ag ól leamhnachta le grádh mo chléibh.	

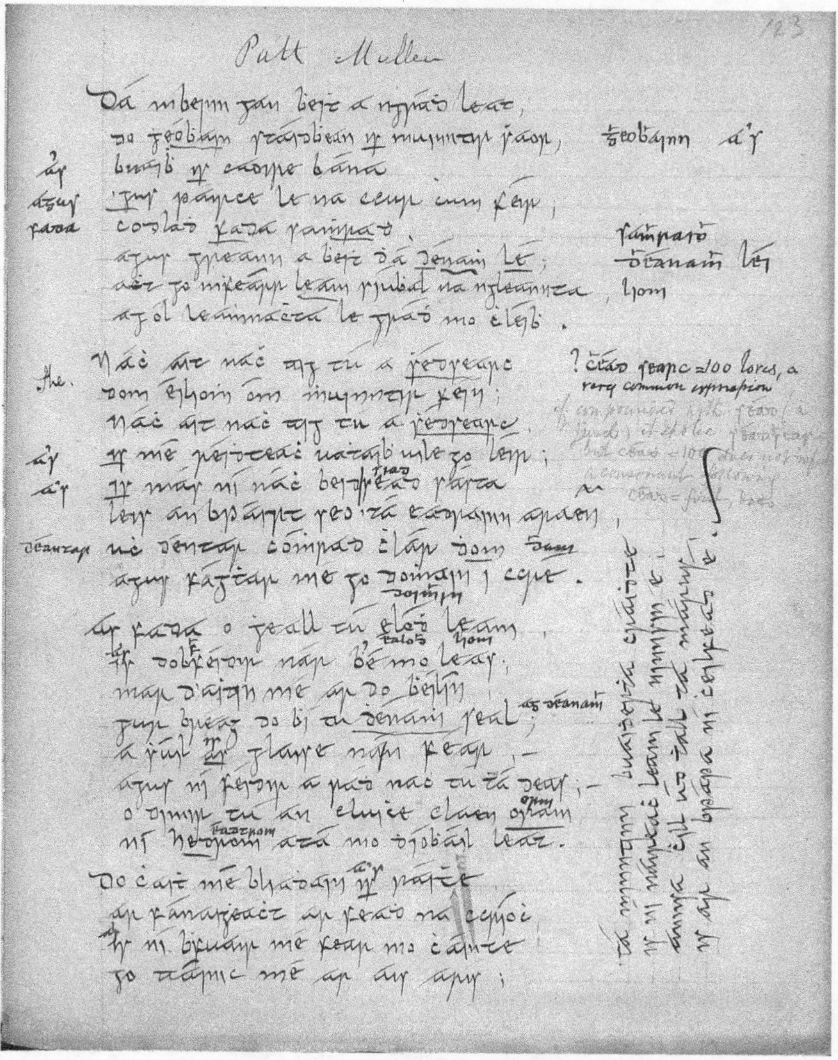

FIGURE 21. O'Curry, UBL, NL 291/634, 123, "Dá mbeinn gan bheith a ngrádh leat."

["She" written in the left margin beside this next verse]

          Nách ait nach ttig tú a shédsearc

          Dom éilioin óm mhuinntir féin;

          Nách ait nach ttig tu a shédsearc

A's   Is mé réidhteach uathaibh uile go léir;

A's   Is más ní nách beid sead sásta   siad

          Leis an bpáirt seo 'tá eadrainn araen,

déantar Uch déntar cómhradh chlár dhom   dham

          Agus fágthar mé go domhain i ccré.   doimhin

          As fada o gheall tú élódh leam,

A's   Is dobfféidir nár bh'é mo leas.

          Mar d'aithin mé ar do bhéilín,

          gur bréag do bhí tú dhénamh seal;

          A shúil is glaise ná 'n féar—

          Agus ní féidir a rádh nach tú tá deas;

          O dimir tú an cluiche claen oram   orm

          Ní héadtrom atá mo dhíobháil leat.

          Do chaith mé bliadhain a's ráithche

          Ar fánaigheacht ar feadh na ccríoch,

          A's ní bhfuair mé fear mo cháinte

          Go ttáinic mé ar ais arís;

          Tá minntinn buaidhertha cráidhte

          Is ní náireach leam le ninnsin é;

          Annsa chill úd thall tá márus

          Is ar an bpápa ní cheilfead é.

O'CURRY GLOSSES AND AMENDMENTS

Line 2: gheóbhain, "gheobhainn"

Line 9: shédsearc, "? chéad searc = 100 loves, a very common
    expression"

"if compounded with *séad* (a jewel) it spoke[?] *séad-shearc*, but *céad* =
    100 does not inflect[?]

a consonant following *céad* = first, does."

Line 17: élódh leam, "éalódh liom"
Line 20: dhénamh, "ag déanamh"

NOTES: For the air, see "An Gabha Ceartan," Mhic Choisdealbha, *Amhráin Mhuighe Seóla*, 137–39. For recordings of "An Gabha Ceartan," see Ó Catháin, *Unaccompanied Singing*; Tom Pháidín Tom [Ó Coistealbha], *Tom Pháidín Tom* (Dublin: Comhaltas Ceoltóirí Éireann, 1978).

⁊

Below, I suggest possible matches between the remaining four song texts and the remaining twenty-eight airs. I am unwilling to reunite these texts and airs in print until the rest of the manuscripts come to light, whereupon one might confirm or correct my suggested matches. The possible matches are listed here in order of success; all bar one are the love songs of young men.

Possible matches for remaining texts and airs

O'Curry Song Titles	O'Curry MS	Petrie MS
A Sheáain Bháin mo ghrádh thú	125	D.1157
Tá teach fada i mbarr an bhaile 'na ccómhnaidheann sí—mo mhian	126	D.866
Chaith mé maidin earraigh ag siúbhal na ccladhaidhe seo leam féin	127	D.507
Ni ar thullán cibe, do bios mo mhiansa	128	D.1042

O'Curry, UBL, NL 291/634, 125
SINGER: John Duvane, Conemara Boatman

A Sheáain Bháin mo ghrádh thú
Nó an cuimhin leat do mhargadh
Nó an cuimhin leat an oidhche úd
Do bhíomar ag tigh Rathbhartaigh,
Do dhá láimh am thímcheall,
A's   Is do chroidhe-se gan gangaid ann,
Is céd-gráidh lem chroidhe thú,
A mhúirnín dílis a's mé sgartha leat.

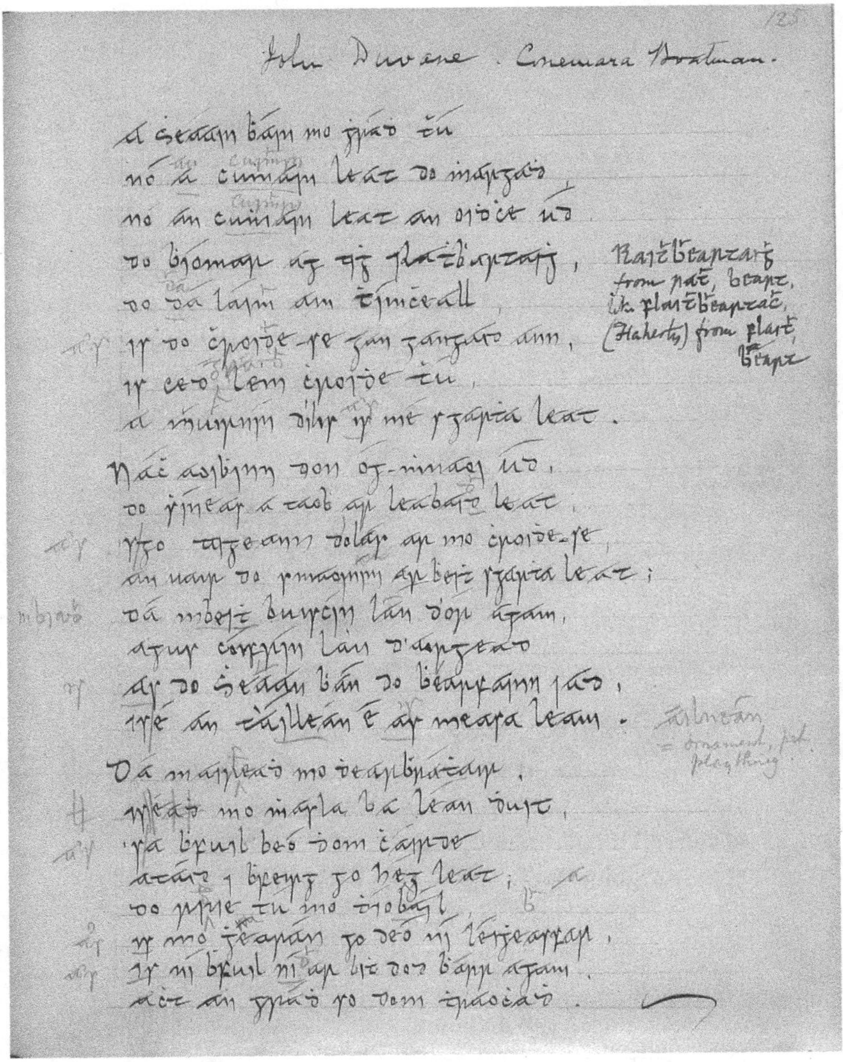

John Duane. Conemara Boatman.

FIGURE 22. O'Curry, UBL, NL 291/634, 125, "A Sheáain Bháin mo ghrádh thú."

Nách aoibhinn don óg-mhnaoi úd,
Do shíneas a taobh ar leabaidh leat;
A's   Is go ttigeann dólás ar mo chroidhe-se,
An uair do smaoiním ar bheith sgartha leat;
Dá mbeith buiscín lán d'ór agam,
Agus cóifrín lán d'airgead
Is   As do Sheáán bhán do bhéarfainn iad,
Is é an t'áilleán é is measa leam.

Dá mairfeadh mo dhearbhráthair,
Is é mo mhasla ba léan dhuit,
A's   'S a bhfuil beó dhom cháirde
Atáid i bhfeirg go héag leat;
Do righne tú mo dhíobháil,
A's   Is mo ghearán go deó ní léigheasfar,
A's   Is ní bhfuil nídh ar bidh dod bhárr agam,
Acht an grádh so dom thraochadh.

O'CURRY GLOSSES AND AMENDMENTS

Line 4: Rathbhartaigh, "*Raithbheartaigh* from *rath, beart,* like
   Flaithbheartach (Flaherty) from *flaith, beart.*"
Line 13: mbeith, "mbiadh"
Line 16: an t'áilleán, "*áilneán* = ornament, pet, plaything."

NOTES: Verses 1 and 3 occur in "Ceaitín 'n Chúil Chraobhaigh" (Ní
   Fhlathartaigh, *Clár Amhrán,* 94#138).

UBL, NL 291/634, 126

The phrase in parentheses—"(The Revenge)"—may refer to the
   subject matter of the song and potentially represents a given title.
SINGER: Patt Mullen

Tá teach fada i mbárr an bhaile,
'Na ccómhnaidheann sí—mo mhian;
A caol-chom cailce, a gruadh ar lasadh,
A's   Is a héadan mar an ael;

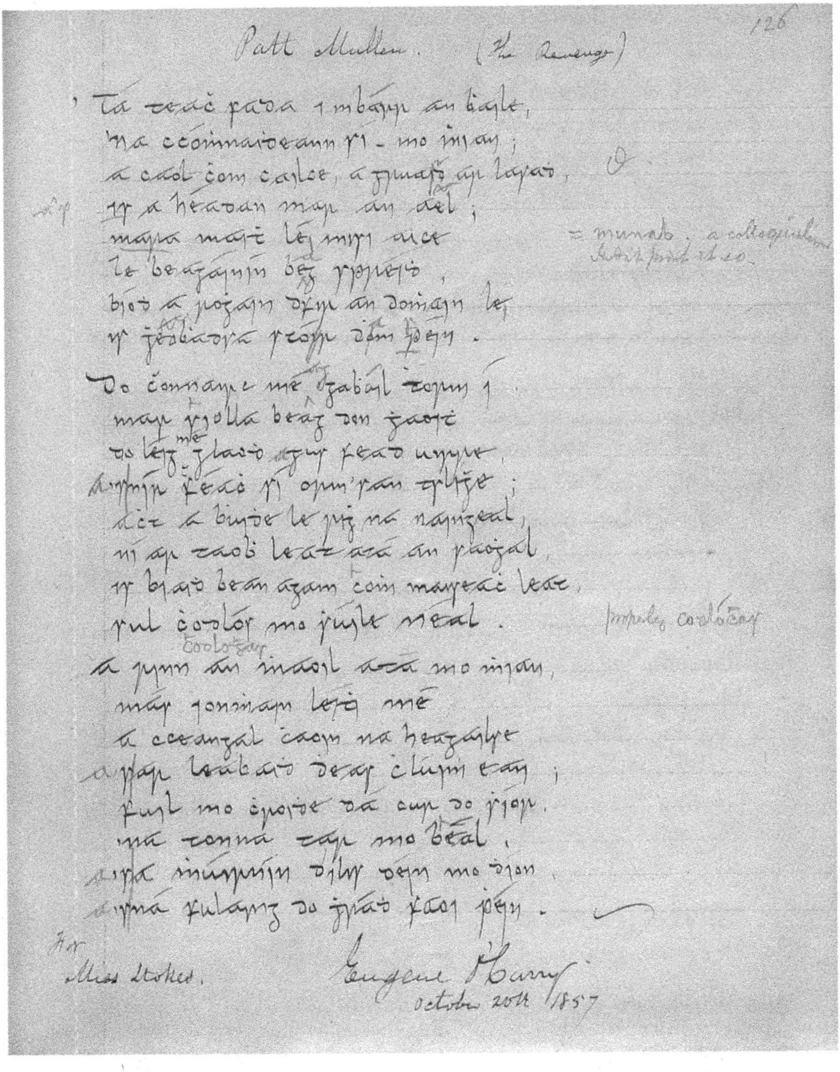

FIGURE 23. O'Curry, UBL, NL 291/634, 126, "Tá teach fada i mbarr an bhaile 'na ccómhnaidheann sí—mo mhian."

Mara maith léi misi aice
Le beagáinín beag spréidh,
Bíodh a roghain dfir an domhain lei
Is gheobhadhsa stór dham féin.

Do chonnairc mé ag gabháil tharm í
Mar shiolla beag don ghaoith
Do léig mé glaodh agus fead uirre,
A's nír fhéach sí orm 'san tslighe;
Acht a bhindhe le righ na naingeal,
Ní ar taobh leat atá an saoghal,
Is biaidh bean agam chomh maiseach leat,
Sul chodlós mo shúile néal.

A rinn an mhaoil atá mo mhian,
Más ionmhain léithi mé
A cceangal chaoin na heagailse,
A's ar leabaidh dheas chlúimh ean;
Fuil mo chroidhe dá cur do shíor,
'na tonna tar mo bhéal,
A's a mhúirnín dílis déin mo dhíon,
A's ná fulaing do ghrádh faoi phéin.

For Miss Stokes
Eugene O'Curry
October 20th 1857

O'CURRY GLOSSES AND AMENDMENTS
Line 5: mara, "= *munab*. A colloquialism"
I won't print it so."
Line 16: chodlós, "chodloghas," "Properly *codlóchas*"

NOTES: Verse 1 occurs in "Cúan Chaotharainn" (Ní Fhlathartaigh,
Clár Amhrán, 35#46).

UBL, NL 291/634, 127
SINGER: Peter Mullin

Chaith mé maidin earraigh ag siúbhal na ccladaidhe seo leam féin,
Shuidh mé síos cois cairrge, go ccodlódh mo shúile néal
Cé chasfaidhe orm act an ainnir, ba dheise a's ba bhreághta méin,
A's a stóirín ná bíodh fearg ort, a's ná géillsi do lucht na mbréag.

As truagh gan mise an Arainn, a ccontae an chláir nó a mbaile áth cliath,
Nó an áit éigin cois fairrge, am chómhnaidhe le stór mo chroidhe;
Uch! níl long ná bád dá seolann, nach tógann sí suas mo chroidhe,
A's a stóirín fan ag baile agam, nó is gairid buan mo shaoghal.

Faraoir géar 'nuair rugadh mé, nar cailleadh mé arís go hóg,
A's 's mór mór an faithcheas leam gur pheacaigh mé go mór;
'Tá súil re Dia as re Muire agam, nár righne mé aon choir fós,
Acht a liacht cailín dealb dheas, tug taithneamh do mo ghnaoi a's mo ghlór.

Tréigfidh mise an t-Earrach so, 'gus rachfaidh mé le fán
Rachfaidh mé tar fairrge, a's ní fhillfidh mé arís go bráth,
Mana bhfágh mé sgéal a's teachtaireacht, chum casadh, ó mo mhíle stór,
Uch! biadh mé ag triall abhaile ansin, a's mo loingín faoi na brataibh seóil.

O'CURRY GLOSSES AND AMENDMENTS
Line 2: ccodlódh, "ccodloghadh"
Line 13: fán, "fághan?"
Line 15: bhfágh, "bhfaghaidh or bhfighidh"; "cased[?]"

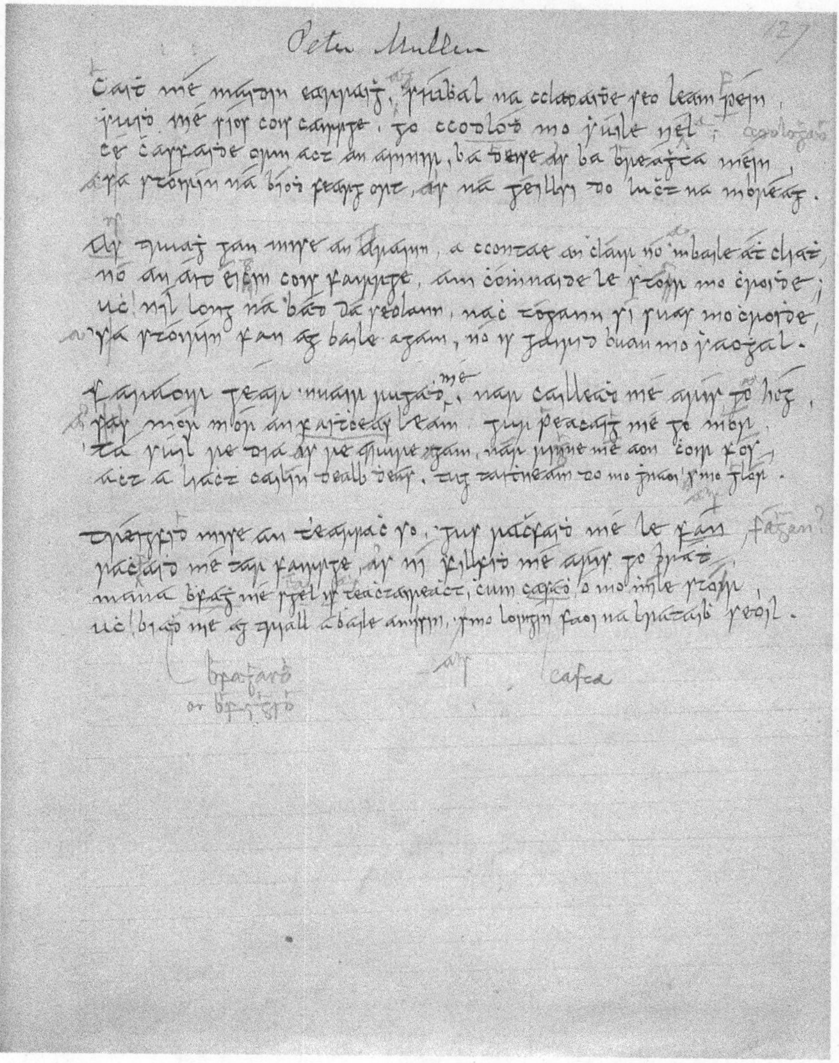

FIGURE 24. O'Curry, UBL, NL 291/634, 127, "Chaith mé maidin earraigh ag siúbhal na ccladhaidhe seo leam féin."

UBL, NL 291/634, 128
SINGER: Mary O'Malley

Ni ar thullán cíbe, do bios mo mhiansa,
Acht ar taltaidh mine 'mbionn an féar ag fás,
Bionn an chnuas ar chraoibh ann, an aghaidh gach míosa,
Bionn cruithneact mhaol ann, is coirce bán;
Bid buaibh bidh laoigh ann, bidh bric ba milte ann.
Bionn an eala chaoin ann, ar thuinn ag snámh;
Dá mbeidh an bheach tighe ann, 'bheith a harus díonta,
Is do bheith mil dá thurn, ag mo mhuirnín bán.

Nách docht an gníomh dhuit, a mhaiseach mhíonla,
Gan teacht am dhion, is mé angar don bhás;
O radais m'inntinn i ngalar chlaoite
Na leig fo líg mé, le searc dod ghrádh;
Ge iomdha caoin-bhean, ar feadh na tíre,
Ná tabharfadh earadh, ar fhear dom cháil,
Níl áit am chroidhese, do bean 's an tsaogal,
Acht bláth na ccaor, sí mo mhuirnin bán.

O'CURRY GLOSSES AND AMENDMENTS
Line 15: bean, "mhnaoi"

NOTES: Verse 1 compares with "Mullach Mór" (Ní Fhlathartaigh,
    Clár Amhrán, 99#145; see Mhic Choisdealbha, *Amhráin Mhuighe
    Seóla*, 4–6).

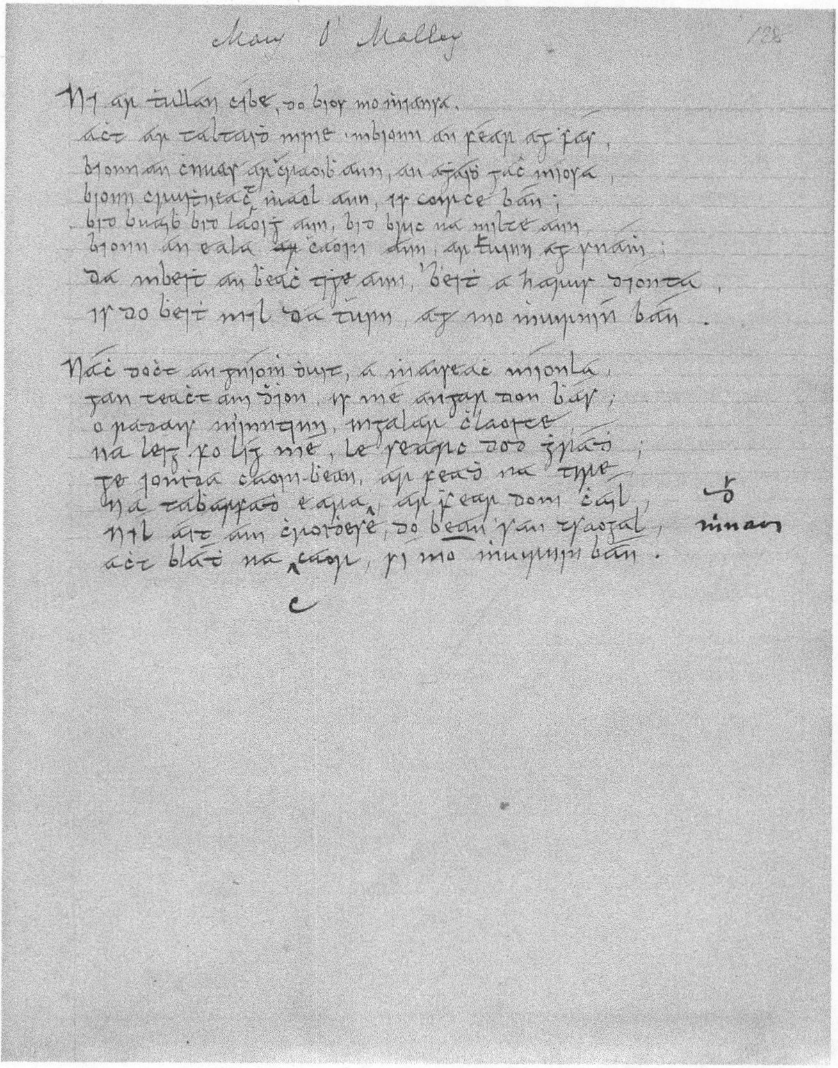

Appendix 2

Chronology: Séamus Ennis in Aran, 1945–1946

Friday, June 29–Sunday, July 1, 1945: Visits Aran for first time; hears Máire Ní Dhioráin (1922–2007) at a pattern-day céilí that is marred by controversy in which Ennis intervenes; return to Conamara delayed by storm.

Sunday, July 15–Monday, July 16, 1945: Meets Matt Neainín Ó Maoláin (1912–69); transcribes a song from Máire Ní Dhioráin; sails back to Carna with Pat Cheoinín.

Wednesday, August, 22, 1945: Arrives in Aran specifically to collect music there.

Thursday, August 23, 1945: In Eoghanacht, calls to Ó Maoláin household in search of Matt Neainín. Matt is out and will not sing for Ennis because the family are in mourning after the recent death of Matt's mother.

Friday, August 24, 1945: Calls to the Ó Maoláin household again to see Matt Neainín; Matt recommends the singers Peait Bheartla Mac Donnchadha (1871–1962) and Seán Mhurchadha de Bhailís (ca. 1877–1964). Ennis moves on to Creig an Chéirín in search of Peait Bheartla. Peait is out fishing, so Ennis talks with Peait's wife Nóra Pheaits Sheáin Ní Chonghaola (1894–1960s).

Saturday, August 25, 1945: Writes letters, updates field diary, swims, visits, and enjoys the fine weather.

Sunday, August 26, 1945: Attends céilí in Cill Rónáin, where he sings songs.

Monday, August 27, 1945: In Creig an Chéirín, he misses Peait Bheartla Mac Donnchadha again; transcribes songs from his wife, Nóra; visits Neidín Sheáin Neide Ó Tuathail (1922–93) and family.

Tuesday, August 28, 1945: Meets Tyrell for the first time; transcribes songs from him, from his sister Máire Uí Dhioráin (ca. 1896–1967), and from her daughter Máire Ní Dhioráin.

Wednesday, August 29, 1945: Goes to Inis Meáin with Cecil Galbally; collects a song from Peadar Beag Ó Meachair.

Thursday, August 30, 1945: Sails to Carna; meets Cóilín mhac Choilm Ó Flaitheartaigh (ca. 1899–1969) of Cill Éinne.

Friday, August 31, 1945: Returns to Aran; as vessel is becalmed, he helps row the boat ashore.

Saturday, September 1–Monday, September 3, 1945: In Cill Éinne, Ennis collects songs from Tyrell.

Tuesday, September 4, 1945: In Sruthán, Ennis collects songs from Seán Mhurchadha de Bhailís.

Wednesday, September 5, 1945: Ennis departs Aran for Clare via Carna and Galway.

Wednesday, October 24, 1945: In IFC headquarters, Dublin, during Oireachtas na Gaeilge Ennis records Máire Ní Dhioráin.

Saturday, June 29, 1946: With Birgitta Johansson, Ennis sails to Aran to attend pattern day events; meets Máire Ní Dhioráin, apparently by chance, who then gives Johansson a tour; Ennis visits Tyrell in Cill Éinne; attends céilí that night.

Sunday, June 30, 1946: Goes to Sruthán to collect songs from Seán Mhurchadha de Bhailís, but he is not in the mood for singing; cannot collect from Tyrell because he is away in Inis Meáin.

Monday, July 1, 1946: Ennis meets Tyrell, no time for song collecting; Ennis and Johansson depart Aran.

Appendix 3

Repertoire of Tomás "Tyrell" Ó Briain, Árainn, August–September 1945

Along with transcribing fourteen texts and seven melodies, Ennis also listed the following songs from Tyrell's repertoire: "Aithrí an Táilliúra," "A Sheáin a Mhic Mo Chomharsa," "An Boc Bán," "Peigí Mistéal," "Eochaill," and probably "An Casaideach Bán" (represented by the illegible "Thug mé an ruaig") and "An Páistín Fionn" (see the consecutive phrases "Nach tusa mo rúin" and "Mo chuidiú go buan") (NFC 1282: 384). It is difficult to determine whether he wrote "15" or "16" when he listed the number of songs he transcribed from Tyrell (NFC 1282: 355). The number fifteen could mean that he counted the two songs that appeared in Tyrell's performance of "Bhfuil sé n-a lá?," which included a verse from "Na Gamhna Geala."

Song Title	Text or Melody NFC	Notes
Creathnach Cheann Bóirne	1282: 355–56	See "Amhrán na Creathnaí": Ciarán Ó Con Cheanainn, *Clár Amhrán Mhaigh Cuilinn* (Baile Átha Cliath: Comhairle Bhéaloideas Éireann, 2011), 253–55#300; NFC 127: 701–5; NFC 786: 371–72; NFC 801: 188–90.
Amhrán Páirc an Teampuill	1282: 357–58	Ennis had already transcribed the air to "Amhrán Pháirc an Teampaill" from Seosamh Ó hÉanaí (1918–84) of An Aird Thoir, Carna. In 1955 Sidney Robertson Cowell recorded this song from Tyrell's brother, Pádraigín Ó Briain, in Tí Fitz, Cill

Song Title	Text or Melody NFC	Notes
		Éinne (Reel 4, Sidney Robertson Cowell Collection, Ralph Rinzler Archives, The Smithsonian Center for Folklife and Cultural Heritage; BBC 22403).
Bhí mise lá i gCínn Mhara tháll	1282: 358–59	See "An Coisdealach Mór": Colm Ó Caodháin's air: NFC MM 018.053. The air to Tyrell's version of "An Coisdealach Mór" is essentially the same as the version Petrie and O'Curry transcribed from John Dubhana in 1857 (D.1157); this could indicate that Tyrell's version is a survival from the local mid-nineteenth-century song repertoire.
Truagh Sin Mise Lá 'il Pádraic	1282: 360–61; MM 021.010	See "Lá Fhéile Pádraig": NFC 794: 330–32; NFC 851: 471–73; Ó Con Cheanainn, *Clár Amhrán*, 32–33#40. Ennis believed its air was a version of the air to the song "Men of the West" (NFC 1282: 361).
Faríor gear ná'r cailliú mé 'n lá baistiú mé go h-óg	1282: 362	See "Taimín Bán Mhic Choisdealbha": Mhic Choisdealbha, *Amhráin Mhuighe Seóla*, 64–65; Ó Ceallaigh, *Ceol na nOileán*, 95; Tomás Ó Concheanainn, *Nua-Dhuanaire Cuid III* (1978; repr., Baile Átha Cliath: Institiúid Ardléinn Bhaile Átha Cliath, 1981), 35; NFC 824: 151–52; NFC 1722: 168–69. The first and final verses of the song compare with the third and second verses, respectively, of one of the song texts O'Curry transcribed from Peter Mullin in 1857, "Chaith mé maidin earraigh ag siúbhal na ccladhaidhe seo leam féin," the second verse of which compares with a verse from the song "Taimín Bán Ó Riagáin" (NFC 378: 32–34), a song that appears to be a version of "Tomás Bán Mac Aogáin" (Ó Máille and Ó Máille, eds., *Amhráin Chlainne Gael*, 40–41; NFC 90: 433–35; UBL, NL 291/634, 127). So, like Peter Mullin's song,

Song Title	Text or Melody NFC	Notes
		Tyrell's song could be a version of "Taimín Bán Ó Riagáin" or "Tomás Bán Mac Aogáin." It appears that there is no direct connection between Peter Mullin's song and Tyrell's rendition because Tyrell learned it in his youth from a man named Páraicín from Tuairín, Conamara (NFC 1282: 362).
Rí Rá Ragairne an Óil	1282: 363; MM 021.004	"'Men of the West' mar fonn" ["Men of the West" as air]
Na Gamhna Geala/ Bhfuil sé n-a lá?	1282: 364–65; MM 021.005	Contains only one verse of the first song: "Ba é ba dheise a chuala mé féin le fada ó sheanfhear" [It was the nicest I myself heard for a long time from an old man] (Ríonach uí Ógáin, ed., *"Mise an fear ceoil": Séamus Ennis—Dialann Taistil 1942–1946* [Indreabhán: Cló Iar-Chonnacht, 2007], 278).
An Bás	1282: 366–67	Had no air. See "Amhrán an Bháis": Ó Con Cheanainn, *Clár Amhrán*, 367–69#439.
An Sean Duine Dóighte	1282: 367–69; MM 021.006	
Sean-bhád is í fliuch	1282: 369; MM 021.007	See "An tIascaire": NFC S1A: 113.
An Caiptín Máille	1282: 370–71; MM 021.009	
Bád Sheáin Uí Niadha	1282: 372–73	
An Seanduine Cam	1282: 375–77	
Beairtlín Domhnaill	1282: 377–78; MM 021.008	

Appendix 4

Additional Material Ennis Documented in Aran in 1945

Date	Singer	Recording Location	Song Title	Text or Melody NFC
July 15, 1945	Máire Ní Dhioráin (1922–2007)	Cill Éinne	Peigí Mistéal	1297: 27*
August 27, 1945	Nóra Pheaits Sheáin Ní Chonghaola (1894–1960s)	Creig an Chéirín	Nóra Ní Chrochúir Bháin	1282: 351–3
August 27, 1945	Nóra Pheaits Sheáin Ní Chonghaola (1894–1960s)	Creig an Chéirín	Bríghdín Phádraic	1282: 354
August– September 1945	Máire Ní Dhioráin (1922–2007)	Cill Éinne	Cúirt Bhaile Nua	MM 021.001
August– September 1945	Máire Ní Dhioráin (1922–2007)	Cill Éinne	Siúil, Siúil agus Siúil a ghrá	MM 021.002
August– September 1945	Ní Dhioráin (1922–2007)	Cill Éinne	Nach Tusa Mo Rún [An Páistín Fionn]	MM 021.003
August– September 1945	Máire Ní Dhioráin (1922–2007)	Cill Éinne	An Sagart Ó Domhnaill	1282: 374
August– September 1945	Máire Uí Dhireáin (1896–1967)	Cill Éinne	Cúirt Bhaile Nua	1282: 379–81
August– September 1945	Máire Uí Dhireáin (1896–1967)	Cill Éinne	Siúl a Ghrá	1282: 382–84

Date	Singer	Recording Location	Song Title	Text or Melody NFC
September 2, 1945	Cóilín mhac Choilm Ó Flaitheartaigh (ca. 1899–1969)	Cill Éinne	Buachaillín deas óg mé	1282: 385–86
August 29, 1945	Peadar Beag Ó Meachair	Inis Meáin	Órán a' Churrachaín	1282: 386–87
September 4, 1945	Seán Mhurchadha de Bhailís (c. 1877–1964)	Sruthán	Máire Ní Thaidhg Óig	1282: 388; MM 021.011
September 4, 1945	Seán Mhurchadha de Bhailís (c. 1877–1964)	Sruthán	Bhí bean uasal geal gia luadh liom	1282: 389–90
October 24, 1945	Máire Ní Dhioráin (1922–2007)	IFC, Dublin	Is Tusa Mo Rún	CT0260
October 24, 1945	Máire Ní Dhioráin (1922–2007)	IFC, Dublin	Siúl a Rúin	CT0260
October 24, 1945	Máire Ní Dhioráin (1922–2007)	IFC, Dublin	B'ait liom bean a d'imreodh cleas [Peigí Mistéal]	CT0260
October 24, 1945	Máire Ní Dhioráin (1922–2007)	IFC, Dublin	Cúirt Bhaile Nua	CT0260

* Mentioned in diary; song transcription is missing.

Notes

INTRODUCTION

1. James O'Brien Moran, *Take Me Tender . . . : Music for the Uilleann Pipes, Collected before the Famine* (J. O'Brien Moran, PPPCD051, 2013). See also Breandán Ó Madagáin, "Functions of Irish Song in the Nineteenth Century," *Béaloideas* 53 (1985): 169.

2. Cited in Rev. Timothy Lee, "Eugene O'Curry," *Journal of the Limerick Field Club* 2, no. 6 (1903): 184–85. The eldest of O'Curry's eleven children was born in 1829.

3. Brian Ó Dálaigh, "Eoghan Ó Comhraí and the Local Perspective," *North Munster Antiquarian Journal* 44 (2004): 2.

4. Eilís Ní Dheá, "Ár n-oidhreacht Lámhscríbhinní ó Dhún Átha thiar agus ón gceantar máguaird," in *Eoghan Ó Comhraí: Saol agus Saothar*, ed. Pádraig Ó Fiannachta (An Daingean: An Sagart, 1995), 31.

5. Pádraig Ó Fiannachta, ed., *An Barántas* (Magh Nuad: An Sagart, 1978), 108. All translations are mine unless otherwise indicated.

6. Sarah Atkinson, "Eugene O'Curry," *Irish Monthly* 2 (1874): 193–94; Breandán Ó Madagáin, "Ceol a chanadh Eoghan Mór Ó Comhraí," *Béaloideas* 51 (1983): 71–86; Ó Dálaigh, "Ó Comhraí," 2–4. For more on Eoghan Mór Ó Comhraí, see Pádraig Ó Fiannachta, ed., *Eoghan Ó Comhraí Saol agus Saothar: Ómós do Eoghan Ó Comhraí* (Daingean Uí Chúis, Co. Kerry: An Sagart, 1995); Breandán Ó Madagáin, "Eugene O'Curry 1794–1862: Pioneer of Irish Scholarship," in *Clare: History and Society: Interdisciplinary Essays on the History of an Irish County*, ed. Matthew Lynch and Patrick Nugent (Dublin: Geography Publications, 2009); Diarmuid Breathnach and Máire Ní Mhurchú, *Beathaisnéis, 1782–1881* (Baile Átha Cliath: An Clóchomhar, 1999), 88. This last volume is part of the series *Beathaisnéis*, which now forms the basis of a free online resource, www.ainm.ie, that features new biographies not available in the books.

7. The library of Peadar Ó Conaill, a close friend of Eoghan Mór Ó Comhraí, similarly contained manuscripts and up to fifty books that have since been cataloged (Eilís Ní Dheá, "Peadar Ó Conaill, scoláire agus scríobhaí [1755–1826]," in *County Clare Studies*,

ed. Ciarán Ó Murchadha [Ennis: Clare Archaeological and Historical Society, 2000], 142; Ó Madagáin, "Pioneer," 427). See also Máire Ní Shúilleabháin, *Amhráin Thomáis Rua* (Maigh Nuad: An Sagart, 1985), 20–24. On teaching his sons Irish, see Ó Dálaigh, "Ó Comhraí," 3–4. See also Lesa Ní Mhunghaile, "Bilingualism, Print Culture in Irish and the Public Sphere, 1700–c. 1830," in *Irish and English: Essays on the Irish Linguistic and Cultural Frontier, 1600–1900*, ed. James Kelly and Ciarán Mac Murchaidh (Dublin: Four Courts Press, 2012), 228; Diarmaid Ó Catháin, "O'Curry (Curry, Ó Comhraí), Eugene (Eoghan)," in *Dictionary of Irish Biography*, ed. James McGuire and James Quinn (Cambridge: Cambridge University Press, 2009).

8. See Atkinson, "Eugene O'Curry," 193–94; Ó Madagáin, "Pioneer," 444.

9. Ó Dálaigh, "Ó Comhraí," 3–4.

10. P. J. Keenan 1856, cited in Gearóid Ó Tuathaigh, *I mBéal an Bháis: The Great Famine and the Language Shift in Nineteenth-Century Ireland* (Hamden, CT: Quinnipiac University, 2015), 41.

11. Atkinson, "Eugene O'Curry," 194.

12. Nessa Ní Shéaghdha, *Collectors of Irish Manuscripts: Motives and Methods* (Dublin: Dublin Institute for Advanced Studies, 1985), 21–23.

13. Meidhbhín Ní Úrdail, "Seachadadh agus Seachadóirí Téacsaí san Ochtú agus sa Naoú Céad Déag," *Studia Hibernica* 32 (2002–3): 75–98; Ó Madagáin, "Functions."

14. Peter McQuillan, *Native and Natural: Aspects of the Concepts of "Right" and "Freedom" in Irish* (Cork: Cork University Press, in association with Field Day, 2004), 182.

15. Ó Dálaigh, "Ó Comhraí," 11.

16. Pádraig Ó Macháin, *Riobard Bheldon: Amhráin agus Dánta* (Dublin: Poddle, 1995), 137–44; Nicholas Carolan, "An tUrramach James Goodman (1828–96) Fear Eaglasta, Ceoltóir, agus Bailitheoir Ceoil," in *Léachtaí Cholm Cille XL: Foinn agus Focail*, ed. Ruairí Ó hUiginn (Maigh Nuad: An Sagart, 2010), 7–19. See Meidhbhín Ní Úrdail, *The Scribe in Eighteenth- and Nineteenth-Century Ireland: Motivations and Milieu* (Münster: Nodus Publikationen, 2000); Stiofán Ó Cadhla, "Seanchas na Fiosrachta agus Léann an Dúchais," in *Léann an Dúchais: Aistí in Ómós do Ghearóid Ó Crualaoich*, ed. Stiofán Ó Cadhla and Diarmuid Ó Giolláin (Cork: Cork University Press, 2012), 79–96.

17. Thomas Forrest Kelly, *Capturing Music: The Story of Notation* (New York: W. W. Norton, 2015), 16.

18. Jonathan Sterne, *The Audible Past: Cultural Origins of Sound Reproduction* (Durham, NC: Duke University Press, 2003), 289–311.

19. Tríona Ní Shíocháin, *Singing Ideas: Performance, Politics and Oral Poetry*, Dance and Performance Studies 12 (New York: Berghahn Books, 2018); Lillis Ó Laoire, *On a Rock in the Middle of the Ocean: Songs and Singers in Tory Island* (Indreabhán: Cló Iar-Chonnacht, in association with the Scarecrow Press, 2007).

20. Henry Glassie, *Passing the Time in Ballymenone: Folklore and History of an Ulster Community* (Dublin: O'Brien Press, 1982), 37; Ó Laoire, *On a Rock*, 125, 183–84, 188–89,

197; Stephanie Conn, "Fitting between Present and Past: Memory and Social Interaction in Cape Breton Gaelic Singing," *Ethnomusicology Forum* 21, no. 3 (December 2012): 364.

21. Lillis Ó Laoire, Sean Williams, and V. S. Blankenhorn, "Seosamh Ó hÉanaí agus Cearbhall Ó Dálaigh: Cleasa an Chrosáin san Oileán Úr," *New Hibernia Review* 15, no. 2 (Summer 2011): 80–101.

22. Ní Shíocháin, *Singing Ideas*, 21.

23. Guy Beiner, *Remembering the Year of the French: Irish Folk History and Social Memory* (Madison: University of Wisconsin Press, 2007); Conn, "Fitting."

24. Guy Beiner, "Troubles with Remembering; or, The Seven Sins of Memory Studies," *Dublin Review of Books* 94 (2017); Paul Ricoeur, *Memory, History, Forgetting* (Chicago: Chicago University Press, 2004); Elizabeth Tonkin, *Narrating Our Pasts: The Social Construction of Oral History* (Cambridge: Cambridge University Press, 1992).

25. See Daithí Ó hÓgáin, ed., *Binneas Thar Meon: Cnuasach d'amhráin agus de cheolta a dhein Liam de Noraidh in oirthear Mumhan. Iml. 1* (Baile Átha Cliath: Comhairle Bhéaloideas Éireann, 1994), 5.

26. Ó Laoire, Williams, and Blankenhorn, "Cleasa an Chrosáin."

27. Mary Daly and David Dickson, eds., *The Origins of Popular Literacy in Ireland: Language Change and Educational Development 1700–1920* (Dublin: Department of Modern History, Trinity College Dublin and Department of Modern Irish History, University College Dublin, 1990); Niall Ó Ciosáin, *Print and Popular Culture in Ireland, 1750–1850* (1997; repr., Dublin: Lilliput Press, 2010); Deirdre Nic Mhathúna, "A Journey from Manuscript to Print—The Transmission of an Elegy by Piaras Feiritéar," in *Irish and English: Essays on the Irish Linguistic and Cultural Frontier, 1600–1900*, ed. James Kelly and Ciarán Mac Murchaidh (Dublin: Four Courts Press, 2012), 243–66; Nicholas Wolf, *An Irish-Speaking Island: State, Religion, Community, and the Linguistic Landscape in Ireland, 1770–1870* (Madison: University of Wisconsin Press, 2014); Ní Mhunghaile, "Bilingualism"; Beiner, *Year of the French*.

28. Sterne, *Audible Past*, 4; Marina Warner, *Phantasmagoria* (Oxford: Oxford University Press, 2006), 78; Stephen Wade, *The Beautiful Music All around Us: Field Recordings and the American Experience* (Urbana: University of Illinois Press, 2012).

29. Aindrias Mac Craith to Richard McElligott, July 3, 1787, cited in Máire Comer Bruen and Dáithí Ó hÓgáin, *An Mangaire Súgach: Beatha agus Saothar* (Baile Átha Cliath: Coiscéim, 1996), 244.

30. Cited in Kelly, *Capturing Music*, 38. O'Curry observed an Irish connection with Notker's work: "It is worth remarking, that one of the oldest musical monuments of this period, the *Liber Ymnorum Notkeri*, noted in *Neumes*, was illuminated, if not entirely written, by an Irish hand" (Eugene O'Curry, *On the Manners and Customs of the Ancient Irish: A Series of Lectures*, edited by William Kirby Sullivan [London: Williams and Norgate, 1873], 1.dlxix).

31. Sterne, *Audible Past*; Susan M. Pearce, *On Collecting: An Investigation into Collecting in the European Tradition* (London: Routledge, 1995).

32. Asa Briggs, "Foreword," in *Collecting Printed Ephemera*, Maurice Rickards (Oxford: Phaidon-Christie's, 1988), 9; Walter Benjamin, "Unpacking My Library: A Talk about Book Collecting," in *Illuminations*, ed. Hannah Arendt (New York: Schocken Books, 1968), 59–67; Jacques Attali, *Noise: The Political Economy of Music* (1977; repr., Minneapolis: University of Minnesota Press, 1985), 17, 104; Ó Cadhla, "Seanchas na Fiosrachta."

33. Diana Taylor, *The Archive and the Repertoire: Performing Cultural Memory in the Americas* (Durham, NC: Duke University Press, 2003), 19. See Ní Úrdail, *Scribe*.

34. Taylor, *Archive*, 19.

35. Ibid., 20.

36. Ibid., 21.

37. Conn, "Fitting," 365.

38. Conn, "Fitting"; Stephanie Conn, "Private Tape Collections and Socio-musical Transmission in Mid-Century Cape Breton: The Gaelic Song Tapes of Peter MacLean," *International Journal of Traditional Arts* 1, no. 1 (2017): 1–22.

39. Stiofán Ó Cadhla, *An tSlat Féithleoige: Ealaíona an Dúchais 1800–2000* (Indreabhán: Cló Iar-Chonnacht, 2011), 213.

40. Taylor, *Archive*, 19.

41. Lillis Ó Laoire, "Ceol agus Amhránaíocht," in *Sealbhú an Traidisiúin*, ed. Niamh Ní Shiadhail, Meidhbhín Ní Úrdail, and Ríonach uí Ógáin (Baile Átha Cliath: Comhairle Bhéaloideas Éireann, 2013), 81.

42. D. K. Wilgus, *Anglo-American Folksong Scholarship since 1898* (New Brunswick, NJ: Rutgers University Press, 1959); Scott B. Spencer, ed., *The Ballad Collectors of North America: How Gathering Folksongs Transformed Academic Thought and American Identity* (Lanham, MD: Scarecrow, 2012).

43. John F. Szwed, *Alan Lomax: The Man Who Recorded the World* (New York: Viking, 2011).

44. Spencer, *Ballad Collectors*, 2; Alan Jabbour, "A Participant-Documentarian in the American Instrumental Folk Music Revival," in *The Oxford Handbook of Music Revival*, ed. Caroline Bithell and Juniper Hill (New York: Oxford University Press, 2014), 130–31. "Music collecting" should probably be replaced by "music documenting," which is a less prescriptive term that allows for a variety of motives and a variety of methodologies of documenting music. This book stops short of performing that particular amendment and defers to the colloquial "music collecting."

45. See Sterne, *Audible Past*, 218–25.

46. See Carolyn Landau and Janet Topp Fargion, "We're All Archivists Now: Towards a More Equitable Ethnomusicology," *Ethnomusicology Forum* 21, no. 2 (August 2012): 125–40.

47. Fintan Vallely observes: "Non-printed documents which contain traditional Irish music have been researched at various levels. All however merit ongoing attention

as both interpretive technologies and analytical perspectives develop and change" (*The Companion to Irish Traditional Music* [Cork: Cork University Press, 2011], 426).

48. Taylor, *Archive*.

49. In the last few decades, there have been a number of accounts of what Breandán Breathnach first termed "the great collectors" (*Folk Music and Dances of Ireland* [1971; repr., Dublin: Mercier Press, 1977], 103), accounts that have forged from this appellation a narrative of fortunate preservation: "Our debt is rather to the great systematic collectors who, like the Roman runners of Lucretius, handed on the torch [of life] from one to the other" (Donal O'Sullivan, *Irish Folk Music, Song and Dance* [*Ceol, Amhránaíocht agus Rince na hÉireann*] [1952; repr., Cork: Published for the Cultural Relations Committee of Ireland by the Mercier Press, 1974], 10). Jimmy O'Brien Moran defines the criterion for this appellation as "those who compiled substantial collections of folk *melodies* [my emphasis]" ("Irish Folk Music Collectors of the Early Nineteenth Century: Pioneer Musicologists," in *Music in Nineteenth-Century Ireland*, ed. Michael Murphy and Jan Smaczny, Irish Musical Studies 9 [Dublin: Four Courts Press, 2007], 94–95), a definition that prompted Nicholas Carolan to state that "collections of Irish *music* [my emphasis] were, as far as we know, not even made in manuscript until the eighteenth century" (*"The Most Celebrated Irish Tunes": The Publishing of Irish Music in the Eighteenth Century*, Ó Riada Memorial Lecture 5 [Cork: Irish Traditional Music Society, University College Cork, 1990], 1). That definition is too confining a criterion for the present discussion of "music collectors," which considers collectors of both melody and/or lyrics, of music and/or song, the noteworthy collections they created, and their myriad motives, only one of which was preservation. See also John Moulden, "song collectors," in *The Companion to Irish Traditional Music*, 2nd ed., ed. Fintan Vallely (Cork: Cork University Press, 2011), 658; Tom Munnelly, "song collectors," in *The Companion to Irish Traditional Music*, 2nd ed., ed. Fintan Vallely (Cork: Cork University Press, 2011), 658.

50. For *Na Bailitheoirí Ceoil*, see review by Peter Browne, *The Arts Show*, RTÉ Radio One, March 16, 2009. For the fortieth Léachtaí Cholm Cille conference, see Ruairí Ó hUiginn, ed., *Léachtaí Cholm Cille XL: Foinn agus Focail* (Maigh Nuad: An Sagart, 2010).

51. See Nicholas Carolan, "'Desire and Duty': The Collecting of Irish Traditional Music" (Breandán Breathnach Memorial Lecture, Willie Clancy Summer School, Miltown Malbay, Co. Clare, July 4, 2009), and "American Women Collectors in 1950s Ireland" (lecture, Inishowen International Folk Song and Ballad Seminar, Ballyliffin, Co. Donegal, March 18, 2011).

52. Recent examples include Mícheál Briody on the Irish Folklore Commission, Proinsias Ó Drisceoil on Seán Ó Dálaigh and Áine Ní Fhoghlú, Ríonach uí Ógáin on Séamus Ennis, David Cooper on George Petrie, Lillis Ó Laoire on Tory Island, Breda McKinney on Inishowen, Pádraigín Ní Uallacháin's *A Hidden Ulster*, and Tim Collins on Sliabh Aughty.

53. Carolan, *Most Celebrated*, 7–8.

54. Joep Leerssen, *Mere Irish and Fíor-Ghael: Studies in the Idea of Irish Nationality, Its Development and Literary Expression prior to the Nineteenth Century* (Cork: Cork University Press, 1996), 367.

55. Ibid., 363.

56. Lesa Ní Mhunghaile, *Ré órga na nGael: Joseph Cooper Walker (1761–1810)* (Indreabhán: An Clóchomhar, 2013).

57. Carolan, *Most Celebrated*, 14.

58. See Breathnach and Ní Mhurchú, *Beathaisnéis, 1782–1881*, 103–5; Leerssen, *Mere Irish*, 365–66; Diarmuid Ó Giolláin, *Locating Irish Folklore—Tradition, Modernity, Identity* (Cork: Cork University Press, 2000), 95.

59. Cited in Lesa Ní Mhunghaile, "'To Open Treasures So Long Locked Up': Aidhmeanna agus cur chuige Charlotte Brooke ina saothar *Reliques of Irish Poetry* (1789)," in *Léachtaí Cholm Cille XL: Foinn agus Focail*, ed. Ruairí Ó hUiginn (Maigh Nuad: An Sagart, 2010), 47.

60. Leerssen, *Mere Irish*, 361–63.

61. Colette Moloney, "Bunting, Edward," in *The Companion to Irish Traditional Music*, ed. Fintan Vallely (Cork: Cork University Press, 1999), 46. For Séamas Mhac Óda, see Máire Uí Bhaoill, "Séamas Mhac Óda, fear ildánach—píobaire, múinteoir Gaeilge, bailitheoir ceoil agus amhrán" (paper presented at Comhdháil na Gaeilge, National University of Ireland, Galway, October 17, 2009).

62. Carolan, *Most Celebrated*, 2.

63. Ó Cadhla, *An tSlat Féithleoige*, 45–47; Ó Dálaigh, "Ó Comhraí," 4; William Mahon, "Scríobhaithe Lámhscríbhinní Gaeilge i nGaillimh 1700–1900," in *Galway: History and Society*, ed. Gerard Moran (Dublin: Geography Publications, 1996), 623–50; Pádraig de Brún, "'Gan Teannta Buird Ná Binse': Scríobhnaithe na Gaeilge, c. 1650–1850," *Comhar* 31, no. 11 (November 1972): 15–20.

64. Standish Hayes O'Grady, *Transactions of the Ossianic Society for the year 1855*, III (Dublin, 1855), 29, cited in Vincent Morley, *Ó Chéitinn go Raiftearaí: Mar a cumadh stair na hÉireann* (Baile Átha Cliath: Coiscéim, 2011), 20, and in Ó Madagáin, "Pioneer," 426. On the wider tradition of Gaelic learning, see Niall Ó Ciosáin, *Print*, 2.

65. Brian Ó Cuív, "Ireland's Manuscript Heritage," *Éire-Ireland* 19, no. 1 (Spring 1984): 104; Breandán Ó Conchúir, *Scríobhaithe Chorcaí, 1700–1850* (Baile Átha Cliath: An Clóchomhar Tta., 1982); Proinsias Ó Drisceoil, *Seán Ó Dálaigh: Éigse agus Iomarbhá* (Cork: Cork University Press, 2007); Ciarán Dawson, *Peadar Ó Gealacáin: Scríobhaí* (Baile Átha Cliath: An Clóchomhar Tta., 1992); Ní Úrdail, *Scribe*.

66. On appending the names of airs, see Úna Nic Éinrí and Pádraig Ó Cearbhaill, *Canfar an Dán: Uilleam English agus a Chairde* (An Daingean: An Sagart, 2003), 164. On contemporary printed ballad sheets, see John Moulden, "The Printed Ballad in Ireland: A Guide to the Popular Printing of Songs in Ireland, 1760–1920" (PhD diss., National University of Ireland Galway, 2006).

67. Breandán Ó Buachalla, *I mBéal Feirste Cois Cuain* (1968; repr., Baile Átha Cliath: An Clóchomhar Tta., 1978); Roger Blaney, *Presbyterians and the Irish Language* (Belfast: Ultach Trust; Ulster Historical Foundation, 1996); Charlotte Milligan Fox, *Annals of the Irish Harpers* (London: Smith, Elder, 1911), 158–59; Rev. George Hill, *An Historical Account of the Macdonnells of Antrim: Including Notices of Some Other Septs, Irish and Scottish* (Belfast: Archer & Sons, 1873).

68. Ó Madagáin, "Ceol a chanadh"; Ó Madagáin, "Functions"; Ní Úrdail, *Scribe*; Ní Úrdail, "Seachadadh agus Seachadóirí"; de Brún, "Scríobhnaithe."

69. Leerssen, *Mere Irish*, 14.

70. Ibid., 321.

71. Ó Giolláin, *Locating*, 24.

72. Carolan, *Most Celebrated*, 7.

73. Ó Giolláin, *Locating*, 27.

74. Ibid., 24.

75. Cited in Helen F. Mulvey, *Thomas Davis and Ireland: A Biographical Study* (Washington, DC: Catholic University of America Press, 2003), 116.

76. Cited in Ó Giolláin, *Locating*, 24.

77. Jimmy O'Brien Moran describes some of the "legacy of the Irish folk music collectors of the early nineteenth century," especially Bunting's contribution to the harp tradition, but he does not question the impact of their collections beyond their ability to give some "insight into the performance style and repertoire before the Famine" or their contribution to the traditional repertoire ("Pioneer Musicologists," 113). He does not question the legacy of their influence beyond the musical tradition itself. The TG4 series *Na Bailitheoirí Ceoil*, written by Seán Corcoran, examined the work of music collectors but only a little of their impact: for example, Thomas Moore's use of Bunting's airs was highlighted briefly but only in the context of pirate publications (February 4, 2009). Likewise, in his wide-ranging survey of Irish traditional music collections, Nicholas Carolan spoke of their impact only in relation to the preservation of music (Seán Corcoran, *Na Bailitheoirí Ceoil* [Stirling Productions for TG4, 2009]).

78. Barra Boydell, "Constructs of Nationality: The Literary and Visual Politics of Irish Music in the Nineteenth Century," in *Music in Nineteenth-Century Ireland*, ed. Michael Murphy and Jan Smaczny, Irish Musical Studies 9 (Dublin: Four Courts Press, 2007), 72.

79. Barra Boydell, "Harp, Symbolism," in *The Companion to Irish Traditional Music*, ed. Fintan Vallely (Cork: Cork University Press, 1999), 181–82.

80. Glen Comiskey, "Thomas Moore," in *The Companion to Irish Traditional Music*, ed. Fintan Vallely (Cork: Cork University Press, 1999), 248; Glen Comiskey and Sara Lanier, "Thomas Moore," in *The Companion to Irish Traditional Music*, 2nd. ed., ed. Fintan Vallely (Cork: Cork University Press, 2011), 464–46.

81. Douglas Hyde, "Irish Language Movement," *Manchester Guardian Commercial*, May 10, 1923, cited in Breandán Ó Conaire, "Introduction" [1986], in *Language, Lore and*

Lyrics: Essays and Lectures, by Douglas Hyde, ed. Breandán Ó Conaire (Blackrock, Co. Dublin: Irish Academic Press, 1986), 27.

82. Breandán Ó Conaire, "Introduction" [1955], in *Songs of Connacht: Songs of O'Carolan, Songs Praising Women, Drinking Songs*, nos. 1–3, by Douglas Hyde, ed. Breandán Ó Conaire (Blackrock, Co. Dublin: Irish Academic Press, 1985), 14.

83. Ó Conaire, *Songs of Connacht*, 14–15.

84. See Diarmuid Breathnach and Máire Ní Mhurchú, *Beathaisnéis a Ceathair, 1882–1982* (Baile Átha Cliath: An Clóchomhar, 1994), 28.

85. Cited in Ó Giolláin, *Locating*, 109.

86. John P. Frayne, ed., *Uncollected Prose* [by W. B. Yeats], vol. 1 (London: Macmillan, 1970), 255. See Cathal Ó hÁinle, "'Abhráin Grádh Chúige Connacht': Saothar Ceannródaíochta?," *Studia Hibernica* 28 (1994): 117–43.

87. Declan Kiberd, *Inventing Ireland* (1995; repr., London: Vintage, 1996), 180.

88. Yeats cited in Ó Conaire, *Songs of Connacht*, 13.

89. Deirdre Ní Chonghaile, "'Listening to This Rude and Beautiful Poetry': John Millington Synge as Song Collector in the Aran Islands," *Irish University Review* 46, no. 2 (2016): 243–59.

90. John Millington Synge, *The Aran Islands* (1907; repr., London: Penguin Twentieth-Century Classics, 1992), 65.

91. Frayne, *Uncollected Prose*, 255.

92. Richard Fallis, *The Irish Renaissance: An Introduction to Anglo-Irish Literature* (Dublin: Gill and Macmillan, 1977), 32. On Hyde, see Declan Kiberd, *Irish Classics* (Cambridge, MA: Harvard University Press, 2001), 302–24.

93. Boydell, "Constructs of Nationality," 73.

94. Ibid.

95. Tim Robinson, *Stones of Aran: Pilgrimage* (1986; repr., London: Penguin Books, 1990), 148.

96. See Yann Arthus-Bertrand, *The Earth from the Air* (1999; repr., London: Thames & Hudson, 2002), 100–101.

97. See Séamas Ó Direáin, *A Survey of Spoken Irish in the Aran Islands, Co. Galway* (James J. Duran, 2014), https://aranirish.nuigalway.ie.

98. Anne Korff, J. W. O'Connell, and John Waddell, eds., *The Book of Aran* (Kinvara, Co. Galway: Tír Eolas, 1994), 9.

99. Tim Robinson, "Faithful for Life unto Aran" [Review of *An Aran Keening*, by Andrew McNeillie], *The Irish Times—Weekend*, March 10, 2001.

100. Breandán Ó hEithir and Ruairí Ó hEithir, eds., *An Aran Reader* (Dublin: Lilliput Press, 1991), 237–38.

101. Robinson, "Faithful."

102. Ó hEithir and Ó hEithir, *Aran Reader*, 237. The notion of Aran being "a place apart" is common to islands; Ó Laoire writes that Tory, for instance, "has always been regarded as a place apart, both by its own inhabitants and by others" (*On a Rock*, 9). See

also Godfrey Baldacchino, ed., *Island Songs: A Global Repertoire* (Lanham, MD: Scare-crow, 2011).

103. Ó hEithir and Ó hEithir, *Aran Reader*, 3.

104. This phenomenon occurs in nonisland settings too. See Lillis Ó Laoire, "The Gaelic Undertow: Seán Ó hEochaidh's Field Trip to the Bluestacks in 1947," in *This Landscape's Fierce Embrace: The Poetry of Francis Harvey*, ed. Donna L. Potts (New-castle: Cambridge Scholars' Press, 2013), 73–89.

105. Patrick F. Sheeran, "Aran, Paris and the Fin-de-Siècle," in *The Book of Aran*, ed. Anne Korff, J. W. O'Connell, and John Waddell (Kinvara, Co. Galway: Tír Eolas, 1994), 302.

106. Pat Mullen, *Man of Aran* (New York: E. P. Dutton, 1935); Liam Ó Flaithearta, *Dúil* (1953; repr., Baile Átha Cliath: Caoimhín Ó Marcaigh, 1983); Máirtín Ó Direáin, *Ó Mórna agus Dánta Eile* (Baile Átha Cliath: Cló Morainn, 1957); Isobel Ní Riain, *Carraig & Cathair Ó Direáin* (Baile Átha Cliath: Cois Life, 2002); Mairéad Conneely, *Between Two Shores/Idir Dhá Chladach: Writing the Aran Islands, 1890–1980* (Oxford: Peter Lang, 2011); Breandán Ó hEithir, "Pé oideachas a fuaireadar, b'iod oideachas a chuireadar orthú féin . . . ," *Comhar* (Márta 2018): 38–41.

107. Korff, O'Connell, and Waddell, *Book of Aran*, 12–13, 10.

108. Robinson, "Faithful."

109. As a diversion, John Millington Synge collected some music in Aran in 1901 (Ní Chonghaile, "Synge as Song Collector"); Maud Karpeles collected music while on holiday in Aran in 1937 (Karpeles Manuscript Collection, MK/1/4/5349–5352, Ralph Vaughan Williams Library, Cecil Sharp House, London). As color, see Mary Banim, *Here and There through Ireland*, part II (Dublin: Freeman's Journal Printers, 1892), 146–47; Synge, *Aran Islands*, 30–32, 93, 118–29; Thomas H. Mason, *The Islands of Ireland* (Dublin: Mercier Press, 1936), 73–77; Elizabeth Rivers, *Stranger in Aran* (Dublin: Cuala Press, 1946), 38–44, 70; Liam O'Flaherty, *Thy Neighbour's Wife* (1923; repr., Dublin: Wolfhound, 1992), 223–30; W. R. Rodgers, *The Bare Stones of Aran* (BBC Third Pro-gramme, May 30, 1950, British Library Sound Archive (hereafter BLSA) T11524R2); Pád-raig Ó Raghallaigh, *Gaeltacht na nOileán* (Radio Éireann, August 27, 1956, RTÉ Sound Archive Tape 186); Andrew McNeillie, *An Aran Keening* (Dublin: Lilliput Press, 2001), 201–4. As an aid to learning Irish, see Fr. Eoghan Ó Gramhnaigh, "Ára na Naomh," *Irisleab-har na Gaeilge* 3, nos. 31–32, and 4, nos. 35–36 (1889–1890): 101–3, 126–28, 45–48, 53–55; Fr. Eoghan Ó Gramhnaigh, *Tuam News/Western Advertiser* February 14, May 2 and 30, June 6, 20 and 27, 1890; Holger Pedersen papers, The Royal Library, Copenhagen, NKS 2718 folio; Ole Munch-Pedersen, ed., *Scéalta Mháirtín Neile: Bailiúchán Scéalta ó Árainn* (Baile Átha Cliath: Comhairle Bhéaloideas Éireann, 1994). As a propaganda tool, see Ó Gramhnaigh, "Ára na Naomh"; Fr. Eoghan Ó Gramhnaigh, "Gleanings from the Islands," *Tuam News/Western Advertiser*, February 14, May 2 and 30, June 6, 20, and 27, 1890.

110. See Deirdre Ní Chonghaile, "'Listening for Landfall': How Silence and Fear Marginalized the Music of the Aran Islands," *Études Irlandaises* 39, no. 1 (2014): 41–55.

111. In a chapter of his 1969 book *Inis Beag: Isle of Ireland*, titled "The Supernatural and the Esthetic," the American anthropologist John C. Messenger includes a short ethnography of "Music, Song and Dance" in Inis Oírr (*Inis Beag: Isle of Ireland* [New York: Holt, Rinehart and Winston, 1969], 117–20); the musical milieu also receives attention in the succeeding sections subtitled "Parties" (120–22) and "Pubs" (122–23). A condensed form of this ethnography appears in an earlier article (John C. Messenger, "Joe O'Donnell, *Seanchai* of Aran," *Journal of the Folklore Institute* 1, no. 3 [December 1964]: 201–2). The ethnography reappears as a single chapter titled "The Song Tradition of Inis Beag" in his 1989 book *Inis Beag Revisited: The Anthropologist as Observant Participator* (Salem, WI: Sheffield, 1989) (which is a reissue of his 1983 book *An Anthropologist at Play: Balladmongering in Ireland and Its Consequences for Research*) with some additional observations relevant to the subject of that book and with some rearrangement of the material (*Inis Beag Revisited*, 29–35). Messenger's ethnography is problematic. Not only do his efforts to conceal the identity of Inis Oírr cause him to avoid discussing some elements of the local musical milieu, but some of his observations of the local musical milieu betray a lack of understanding of that milieu. His work on local music is best approached with caution.

112. Ó hEithir and Ó hEithir, *Aran Reader*, 238.

113. Ibid., 235.

CHAPTER 1. THE PETRIE AND O'CURRY ARAN
MUSIC MANUSCRIPTS OF 1857

1. Martin Haverty, *The Aran Isles; or a Report of the Excursion of the Ethnological Section of the British Association from Dublin to the Western Islands of Aran in September 1857* (Dublin: Printed for the Excursionists at the University Press by M. H. Gill, 1859), 38, cited in Tim Robinson, *Stones of Aran: Labyrinth* (Dublin: Lilliput Press, 1995), 123.

2. William Frederick Wakeman, "Aran—Pagan and Christian," *Duffy's Hibernian Sixpenny Magazine* 1, nos. 5–6 (May–June 1862): 462. A sense of pioneering and sometimes perilous adventure pervades contemporary accounts of Aran (George Petrie, "The Islands of Aran" [abridged] [1822], in *An Aran Reader*, ed. Breandán Ó hEithir and Ruairí Ó hEithir [Dublin: Lilliput Press, 1991], 40–42; Samuel Lewis, "A Topographical Dictionary of Ireland" [1837], in Ó hEithir and Ó hEithir, *Aran Reader*, 18–22; Haverty, *Aran Isles*; Wakeman, *Aran*).

3. The term *insula sacra*, meaning "sacred island" or "holy island" or "sacred place," has a particular resonance in this context because Insula Sacra was also the name given to Ireland by the Greeks and the Romans. The term was appropriated by Irish scholars of the eighteenth and nineteenth centuries, including the nationalist-minded Sylvester O'Halloran, who published *Insula Sacra* in 1770 (see Joep Leerssen, *Mere Irish*, 358).

4. Banim, *Here and There*, 103–4.

5. Lady Mary Catherine Ferguson, *Sir Samuel Ferguson in the Ireland of His Day* (Edinburgh: William Blackwood & Sons, 1896), 1:338–39.

6. Ó Madagáin, "Ceol a chanadh."

7. Ó hEithir and Ó hEithir, *Aran Reader*, 13.

8. J. W. O'Connell, "The Rediscovery of the Aran Islands in the 19th Century," in *The Book of Aran*, ed. Anne Korff, J. W. O'Connell, and John Waddell (Kinvara, Co. Galway: Tír Eolas, 1994), 186.

9. John Waddell, "The Archaeology of Aran," in Korff, O'Connell and Waddell, *Book of Aran*, 77.

10. Ó Madagáin, "Pioneer," 426.

11. Ó Dálaigh, "Ó Comhraí," 1.

12. Ó Madagáin, "Pioneer," 431.

13. "Report Featuring Eugene O'Curry and George Petrie," *The Limerick Reporter and Tipperary Vindicator*, April 13, 1869, 4. Lenihan's choice of the phrase "racy of the soil" speaks as much to his own politics as "a moderate constitutional nationalist" (Liam Irwin, "Lenihan, Maurice," in *Dictionary of Irish Biography*, ed. James McGuire and James Quinn [Cambridge: Cambridge University Press, 2009]) as it does to the cultural sympathies and preferences of his friend Eugene O'Curry. The *Oxford English Dictionary* glosses the phrase as "strongly characteristic of a particular country or people" and attributes its coining to Stephen Woulfe (1787–1840). The political context of its first utterance ensured its distinctive currency thereafter, as Rosemary Richey explains: "During the debate on the municipal reform bill (he [Woulfe] was part of a committee set up in 1833 to inquire into the state of municipal corporations in Ireland), when [Robert] Peel questioned what good corporations would do for a country as poor as Ireland, Woulfe replied: 'They will go far to create and foster public opinion and make it racy of the soil' (Charles Gavan Duffy, *Young Ireland: A Fragment of Irish History, 1840–1850* [London: Cassell, Petter, Galpin, 1880], 63). The phrase was later adopted by the Young Irelanders and became the motto of *The Nation*" (Rosemary Richey, "Woulfe, Stephen," in *Dictionary of Irish Biography*, ed. James McGuire and James Quinn [Cambridge: Cambridge University Press, 2009]). Charles Gavan Duffy traced Woulfe's potential inspiration to an 1831 *Edinburgh Review* piece by Thomas Babington Macaulay: "Woulfe's friend and biographer Mr. Curran remarks that he has left no memorable saying but this motto, and in truth even this one is scarcely original. It bears too close a resemblance to a sentence in Macaulay's Essay on Boswell's [Life of] Johnson. 'We know no production of the human mind which has so much of what may be called the race, so much of the peculiar flavour of the soil from which it sprung [*sic*]'" (*Young Ireland*, 63). While Lenihan's use of "racy of the soil" here recalls the vision of the Young Irelanders, who had a "direct link" to the Society for the Preservation and Publication of the Music of Ireland (David Cooper, *The Petrie Collection of the Ancient Music of Ireland* [Cork: Cork University Press, 2002], 8), this particular instance demonstrates that the phrase obtained a more general cultural application along with a breadth of potential political interpretations.

14. Marian Deasy continues: "The desire to collect what he considered to be 'the most beautiful national melodies in the world' [George Petrie, *The Ancient Music of Ireland* (Dublin: Printed at the University Press for the Society for the Preservation and Publication of the Melodies of Ireland by M.H. Gill, 1855), vii] sprang from his love of music as a whole, and of Irish music in particular. This love for music is demonstrated by the fact that he used to walk for miles following the bands of the Militia regiments as they played. When 'Don Giovanni' was first produced in Dublin in 1816, he did not miss one of its forty performances. As a young violinist he was a member of several chamber music groups in Dublin, whose repertoire included works by Haydn, Beethoven and Mozart. In addition, Petrie himself, in a letter to his friend Charles Hanlon, mentions playing the harp and double flageolet [William Stokes, *The Life and Labours in Art and Archaeology of George Petrie* (London: Longmans, Green, 1868), 7]" ("New Edition of Airs and Dance Tunes from the Music Manuscripts of George Petrie LL.D., and a Survey of His Work as a Collector of Irish Folk Music" [2 vols., PhD diss., University College Dublin, 1982], 1.3).

15. Stokes, *Life and Labours*, 373.

16. Cooper, *Petrie Collection*, 5.

17. Ó Madagáin, "Pioneer," 432. See George Petrie, *The Ancient Music of Ireland*, vols. 1 and 2 (1855; repr., Farnborough: Gregg International, 1967 and 1978).

18. Cooper, *Petrie Collection*, 15.

19. Deasy, "Petrie," 1.5.

20. Cited in ibid., 4.

21. Deasy, "Petrie," 1.4.

22. Ó Dálaigh, "Ó Comhraí," 14.

23. This evocative metaphor was originally used around 1886 to refer specifically to the folk melodies of Ireland but one imagines that its creator would consider its use here—to describe how contemporary antiquarians viewed the state of the traditional music and songs of Ireland in the nineteenth century—to be justifiable (John Boyle O'Reilly, *The Poetry and Song of Ireland* [New York: Gay Brothers, 1887], vi).

24. David Cooper, "'Twas One of Those Dreams That by Music Are Brought': The Development of the Piano and the Preservation of Irish Traditional Music," in *Music in Nineteenth-Century Ireland*, ed. Michael Murphy and Jan Smaczny, Irish Musical Studies 9 (Dublin: Four Courts Press, 2007), 93.

25. Ibid., 92.

26. Ibid.

27. Ibid., 74.

28. O'Connell, "Rediscovery," 184.

29. Cooper, *Petrie Collection*, 12.

30. Ibid., 83.

31. Warner, *Phantasmagoria*, 78.

32. Cooper, *Petrie Collection*, 11. Petrie wrote: "I have availed myself of every opportunity in my power to obtain the purest settings of the airs, by noting them from the native singers, and more particularly, from such of them as resided, or had been reared, in the most purely Irish districts" (Cooper, *Petrie Collection*, 37).

33. Tom Munnelly, "George Petrie: Distorting the Voice of the People?," *JMI* 3, no. 2 (January/February 2003): 15.

34. See Cooper, *Petrie Collection*, 37.

35. The manifesto of the Society for the Preservation and Publication of the Melodies of Ireland states the society was interested in "all such words (whether in the Irish or English language) connected with any of them [melodies], as appear to possess any peculiar interest" (Cooper, *Petrie Collection*, 264). The society left itself under no obligation to song.

36. Cooper, *Petrie Collection*, 37, 36.

37. Petrie, *Ancient Music*, xii.

38. Stokes, *Life and Labours*, 373.

39. Munnelly, "Distorting," 15.

40. Ibid., 13.

41. Ibid., 16.

42. Ó Madagáin, "Pioneer," 431.

43. Ó Drisceoil, *Ó Dálaigh*, 228.

44. Grace J. Calder, *George Petrie and the Ancient Music of Ireland* (Dublin: Dolmen, 1968); Colin Hamilton, "George Petrie," in *The Companion to Irish Traditional Music*, ed. Fintan Vallely (Cork: Cork University Press, 1999), 294–95; Deasy, "Petrie"; Cooper, *Petrie Collection*; Corcoran, *Bailitheoirí Ceoil*; Ó Madagáin, "Pioneer."

45. Muiris Ó Rócháin, "Eugene O'Curry: The Neglected Scholar," *Dal gCais* 1 (1972): 65–67.

46. National Library of Ireland (hereafter NLI), MSS 9278–9280.

47. Manuscripts of George Petrie and his family, MS 3562–3566, Trinity College Dublin.

48. Veronica Kennedy, "The Petrie Manuscripts of Irish Folk Music" (MA thesis presented with a catalog of one-third of the manuscripts, University College Dublin, 1954).

49. Stokes, *Life and Labours*, 47.

50. See Chet Van Duzer, "From Odysseus to Robinson Crusoe: A Survey of Early Western Island Literature," *Island Studies Journal* 1, no. 1 (May 2006): 143–62; Godfrey Baldacchino, "Islands, Island Studies, Island Studies Journal," *Island Studies Journal* 1, no. 1 (May 2006): 5–6.

51. O'Connell, "Rediscovery," 184.

52. See Ní Chonghaile, "'Listening to This Rude and Beautiful Poetry,'" 251–52.

53. "As the *Vestal* left Cill Rónáin, firing a last salute, the antiquarians felt that Mr Wilde's stated objective, 'to render Aran an object of attraction, and an opposition shop

to Iona,' had been 'crowned with a glorious success'" (Robinson, *Labyrinth*, 123; see also Haverty, *Aran Isles*, 29–38).

54. Waddell, "Archaeology of Aran," 78. The respect and concern that Aran won from antiquarians was of critical and formative importance to the islands' future. Aran now has an "international reputation as a location of spectacular archaeology, geology and geomorphology," and its unique landscape and its "relative abundance of important national archaeological treasures" are of national and European significance (Stephen McCarron, ed., *Aran Islands/Oileáin Árann*, Irish Quaternary Association Field Guide 27 [Dublin: Irish Quaternary Association, 2007], 1). Its reputation is the foundation of its tourism industry, which represents, since the 1990s at least, the primary industry of Aran.

55. Ferguson, *Sir Samuel Ferguson*, 1:337.

56. Stokes, *Life and Labours*, 376–77.

57. Ibid., 317–18.

58. Deasy, "Petrie."

59. Sir Samuel Ferguson, "Clonmacnoise, Clare, and Arran," *Dublin University Magazine* 41, no. 1 (January–June 1853): 79. Ferguson continues: "Hitherto his intellectual pursuits have not added much to his worldly wealth; but as the island becomes better known, Mullen, I should hope, will be able to make an appearance more suitable to the dignity of his calling." The various names that appear in Petrie's manuscripts—Patrick Mullen, Pat Mullen, and P. Mullen—may have been three different people but they are more likely to have been one man.

60. Ferguson, *Sir Samuel Ferguson*, 1:337.

61. Haverty, *Aran Isles*, 34.

62. Ferguson, *Sir Samuel Ferguson*, 1:341–42.

63. Ibid., 338–39.

64. In volumes 1 and 3 of Petrie's collection in the National Library of Ireland, Petrie identifies twenty-eight of the airs with Aran or "Arran-More" (MSS 9278–9280). In his edition of Petrie's collection, Charles Villiers Stanford identifies an additional four airs from Aran (*The Complete Collection of Irish Music as Noted by George Petrie, L.L.D., R.H.A. (1789–1866). Edited, from the Original Manuscripts by Charles Villiers Stanford* [London: The Irish Literary Society of London, Boosey, 1902–1905]). Deasy concurs with Stanford's calculation (Deasy, "Petrie"). I have identified another two airs that are probably from Aran (see appendix 1). In 2007 Dáibhí Ó Cróinín found ten of O'Curry's transcriptions of Aran songs in the Stokes notebooks in the Universitaetsbibliothek Leipzig (Dáibhí Ó Cróinín, *Whitley Stokes [1830–1909]: The Lost Celtic Notebooks Rediscovered* [Dublin: Four Courts Press, 2011]). Ciarán Ó Con Cheanainn found two of them in the George Petrie manuscripts in the library of the RIA in Dublin. The two songs that were found in Dublin—"Tógfaidh mé mo sheólta go dubhcheodhúch ar maidin" (RIA, 12 N 5, 178) and "Do chaith mé maidin earraigh ag siúbhal na ccladaidhe seo leam féin" (RIA, 12 N 5, 179)—also occur among the ten songs that were found in Leipzig.

65. Copy of letter from Stokes to Meyer, August 30, 1889, Trinity College Dublin (TCD) MS 10085/90, cited in Seán Ó Lúing, *Kuno Meyer, 1858–1919: A Biography* (Dublin: Geography Publications, 1991), 6. In his letter, Stokes incorrectly recalled the year as 1858 and Petrie's first name as Charles and miscalculated the length of time they spent there. Stokes's copy also includes doodles featuring musical notes beside two pairs of mustached heads that are presumably singing.

66. Numbers prefixed with "p." refer to the page number in the O'Curry manuscript.

67. Fr. Tomás Ó Ceallaigh, *Ceol na nOileán*, edited by William Mahon (1931; repr., Indreabhán: Cló Iar-Chonnacht, 1993), 96.

68. See Séamas Ó Direáin, *Survey*.

69. See Aoife Ní Ghloinn, "Anailís Iardhearcach ar Stór Amhrán Róise Rua Uí Ghrianna," *Léann* 2 (2009): 19–42.

70. Deasy supplied titles from three sources: other settings in Petrie's manuscripts and published works; the manuscripts and publications of people like William Forde and Patrick Weston Joyce; and Tom Munnelly, who supplied "titles by which some tunes are known today" (Deasy, "Petrie," 1.181).

71. Cooper, *Petrie Collection*, 15.

72. Francis Hoffmann, arr., *Ancient Music of Ireland from the Petrie Collection* (Dublin: Pigott, 1877).

73. RIA, 12 N 5, 178.

74. Deasy, "Petrie," 1.180–81, 180.

75. Ibid., 181.

76. Breandán Breathnach, "Petrie and the Music of Clare," *Dal gCais* 2 (1975): 70.

77. Ibid.; Deasy, "Petrie," 1.180.

Chapter 2. Séamus Ennis and *Amhráin as Árainn*

1. Mná Fiontracha, *Árainn Cosáin an tSaoil*, 89#87 (number before hashtag denotes page number and number after hashtag denotes given house number) (Árainn: Bailiúchán Béaloideas Árann, 2003); National Folklore Collection (hereafter NFC) 1297: 60–62. Throughout this chapter, I cite Ennis's original documentation and share my own translations. A published edition and translation—both by Ríonach uí Ógáin— are available: *"Mise an fear ceoil": Séamus Ennis—Dialann Taistil, 1942–1946* (Indreabhán: Cló Iar-Chonnacht, 2007); and *Going to the Well for Water: The Séamus Ennis Field Diary, 1942–1946* (Cork: Cork University Press, 2009).

2. Owned by Stanley Scofield, the *Alice Webster* was a wooden trawler that took lobsters caught in Conamara, Clare, and Aran to England (NFC 1297: 60); see Brendan O'Donnell, *Galway—A Maritime Tradition: Ships, Boats and People* (Galway: Brendan O'Donnell, 2001), 19–20, 39.

3. The other known records are a sound recording created in Árainn by W. R. Rodgers in November 1949 (British Library Sound Archive [hereafter BLSA] 9CL0011095 [BBC 15829]; RTÉ Radio 100/68; Public Record Office of Northern Ireland [hereafter

PRONI] D2833/D/4/7); and a sound recording created in Tí Fitz in Cill Éinne, Árainn, in August 1959 as part of the linguistics research of the Dublin Institute of Advanced Studies (DIASGLÓRGA34). Locals, including his niece Máire Ní Dhioráin, also transcribed songs from Tyrell (NFC S1A: 103–6; Coláiste Naomh Éinne local folklore collection [this private collection is not yet cataloged]).

4. NFC S1A: 103–6; NFC 512: 54–57; NFC 633: 424–26. NFC references beginning with S (including S1A) represent the Schools' Collection, which is available online at www.duchas.ie. See the copybook from Cill Éinne National School, https://www .duchas.ie/en/cbes/4606380. For "Amhrán an Dole," see Éamon Ó Ciosáin, "Amhráin na nDaoine agus an tAthrú Saoil: 'Lomarbhá faoin Dole' agus amhráin Antaine agus Thomáis Uí Bhriain," in *Léachtaí Cholm Cille XIX Litríocht na Gaeltachta*, ed. Pádraig Ó Fiannachta (Maigh Nuad: An Sagart, 1989), 223–38.

5. Liam Nolan, *Here and Now* (RTÉ, March 12, 1971, Sound Archive AA5382); Éamon de Buitléar, *Miles and Miles of Music* (RTÉ, 1974); Peter Browne and Julian Vignoles, *The Séamus Ennis Story* (RTÉ Radio 1, March 20, 1988, RTÉ Archive AA4014); Marian Richardson, *The Giant at My Shoulder*, Liam Óg O'Flynn talking about Séamus Ennis (RTÉ Radio 1, May 7, 1999).

6. Ríonach uí Ógáin, "Fear Ceoil Ghlinsce: Colm Ó Caodháin," in *Galway: History and Society: Interdisciplinary Essays on the History of an Irish County*, ed. Gerard Moran (Dublin: Geography Publications, 1996), 703–48; Ríonach uí Ógáin, "Colm Ó Caodháin and Séamas Ennis: A Conamara Singer and his Collector," *Béaloideas* 64–65 (1996–1997): 279–338.

7. uí Ógáin, "Fear Ceoil Ghlinsce," 716–17.

8. See Gearóid Ó Tuathaigh, "The State and the Irish Language: An Historical Perspective," in *A New View of the Irish Language*, ed. Caoilfhionn Nic Pháidín and Seán Ó Cearnaigh (Dublin: Cois Life, 2008), 26–42.

9. Mícheál Briody, *The Irish Folklore Commission 1935–1970: History, Ideology, Methodology*, 2nd ed. (Helsinki: Finnish Literature Society, 2008), 19–20.

10. Ibid., 59.

11. Ibid., 521.

12. Ibid., 271.

13. His son Éimear Ó Broin (1927–2013) became an orchestral conductor. See Richard Pine, *Music and Broadcasting in Ireland since 1926* (Dublin: Four Courts Press, 2005), 97–212. For León Ó Broin's attitude, see Mícheál Briody, "'Publish or Perish': The Vicissitudes of the Irish Folklore Institute," *Ulster Folklife* 51 (2005).

14. Briody, *Commission*, 46–47.

15. Ibid., 56.

16. Ibid.

17. Valerie A. Austin, "The Céilí and the Public Dance Halls Act, 1935," *Éire-Ireland* 28, no. 3 (Fall 1993): 7.

18. Ibid.

19. Contemporary sean-nós compositions such as the songs "Amhrán Chill Déar" and "Amhrán Shéamuis" by the Ó Donncha brothers Vail Bheairtle (1898–1981) and Maidhcil Bheairtle (ca. 1902–79) of Cora na gCapall, Cill Chiaráin, represented contributions to a tradition of sean-nós song and were, therefore, acceptable to the IFC (Ríonach uí Ógáin, "A Job with No Clock: Séamus Ennis and the Irish Folklore Commission," *JMI* 6, no. 1 [January/February 2006]: 13).

20. Nolan, *Here and Now.*

21. Cited in T. K. Whitaker, "James Hamilton Delargy, 1890–1980," *Folk Life* 20 (1981–82): 101. One of the earliest song collectors in Norway, Magnus Brostrup Landstad, used the burning house analogy in the foreword to his 1853 collection of Norwegian folk songs, *Norske Folkeviser* (Christiania: Christian Tønsbergs Forlag); Angun Sønnesyn Olsen observes: "[Landstad] compared the collecting of folk songs to the rescuing of an old inherited jewellery/family treasure from a house on fire ('at redde et gammelt Familie-smykke ud af det brændende Huus' [1853, iv])" (email message to author, May 3, 2009).

22. Briody, *Commission,* 58.

23. Ibid., 59.

24. Ibid., 79.

25. Ibid., 274.

26. Ibid., 68.

27. Ibid., 274, n. 158.

28. Bo Almqvist, "The Folklore Commission: Achievement and Legacy," *Béaloideas* 45–47 (1979): 9–10.

29. Among those IFC collectors who documented music were Ciarán Bairéad (1905–76), Proinnsias de Búrca (1904–96), Seán Ó hEochaidh (1913–2002), Michael J. Murphy (1913–96), and Seán Ó Súilleabháin (1903–96).

30. See Proinnsias Ní Dhorchaí, *Clár Amhrán an Achréidh* (Baile Átha Cliath: An Clóchomhar, 1974); Ríonach Ní Fhlathartaigh, *Clár Amhrán Bhaile na hInse* (Baile Átha Cliath: An Clóchomhar, 1976); Ciarán Ó Con Cheanainn, *Clár Amhrán Mhaigh Cuilinn* (Baile Átha Cliath: Comhairle Bhéaloideas Éireann, 2011).

31. Briody, *Commission,* 280.

32. Ibid., 279.

33. Ibid., 279–80.

34. Concerning the district of Cois Fharraige, Ciarán Ó Con Cheanainn writes: "Is mór an trua, áfach, nach raibh bailitheoirí amhrán níos gníomhaí sa gceantar. Dá mbeadh, is mó i bhfad d'amhráin agus de leaganacha d'amhráin a bheadh ar fáil inniu. Is léir ó na lámhscríbhinní [in NFC] gur ar thóir seanchais nó ar thóir na scéalaíochta a bhí na bailitheoirí agus go minic, is mar aguisín ar deireadh a fhaightear na hamhráin" (It is a great pity, however, that song collectors were not more active in the district. If they had been, a far greater number of songs and of versions of songs would be available today. It is clear from the manuscripts that the collectors [of the IFC who visited Cois Fharraige] were looking for folklore or storytelling and songs are often found as an

appendix at the end) (*Clár Amhrán*, xv). Ó Con Cheanainn concludes: "Is léir ón méid amhrán atá sa cheantar seo, i mBaile na hInse agus ar an Achréidh go bhfuil flúirse ábhair fós le clárú as ceantair eile sul bhféadfar léiriú cuimhsitheach a thabhairt ar na hamhráin traidisiúnta sa Ghaeilge" (It is clear from the number of songs that are extant in this district, in Baile na hInse and in An Achréidh that there is an abundance of material from other districts yet to be catalogued before a comprehensive illustration of traditional songs in Irish can be given) (*Clár Amhrán*, xv–xvi).

35. Almqvist, "Achievement and Legacy," 13.

36. On the IFC, see Ó Giolláin, *Locating*; Briody, *Commission*. On the symbolism of sean-nós singing, see Lillis Ó Laoire, "'Up Scraitheachaí!' Aitheantas áitiúil agus náisiúnta ag comórtais an tsean-nóis ag an Oireachtas," in *Aimsir Óg Cuid a Dó: Critic, Béaloideas, Teanga*, ed. Mícheál Ó Cearúil (Baile Átha Cliath: Coiscéim, 2000), 69–70.

37. Angela Bourke, "Séamus Ennis in Co. Clare: Collecting Music in the 1940s," *Dal gCais* 8 (1986): 53.

38. The period in which the IFC operated lasted from 1935 until 1970 (Briody, *Commission*). In the last fifty years or so since the IFC became the National Folklore Collection at University College Dublin, Tom Munnelly (1944–2007) created and bequeathed to the archive the largest collection of English song in Ireland, but strictly speaking, he was not employed by the IFC; he did not join University College Dublin (UCD) until later in the 1970s (Nicholas Carolan, "Introduction," in *Dear Far-Voiced Veteran: Essays in Honour of Tom Munnelly*, ed. Anne Clune [Miltown Malbay, Co. Clare: Old Kilfarboy Society, 2007], iii–iv).

39. Briody, *Commission*, 521, 486.

40. As an "icon," see Ríonach uí Ógáin, "Ennis, Séamus (Séamus Mac Aonghusa)," in *The Companion to Irish Traditional Music*, ed. Fintan Vallely (Cork: Cork University Press, 1999), 118. For Ennis's understandings and narratives, see Daithí Kearney, "(Re) locating Irish Traditional Music: Urbanising Rural Traditions," *Chimera* 22 (2007): 181–96; Daithí Kearney, "Silently Seeing Music: The Role of the Developing Landscape of Memory in the Narratives of Irish Traditional Music" (paper presented at the International Council for Traditional Music Symposium, Waterford Institute of Technology, 2007); Daithí Kearney, "The Present and the Past in Fieldwork Experience: Understanding the Process of the Region in Irish Traditional Music" (paper presented at the Society of Musicology in Ireland Postgraduate Conference, University College Dublin, January 19, 2008). For recordings, see *The Bonny Bunch of Roses* (Tradition TLP 1013, 1959; Ossian OSS 59, 1988; TCD 1023, 1996); *The Ace and Deuce of Piping* (Collector JEI 1506, 1960); *Séamus Ennis—Ceol, Scéalta agus Amhráin* (Gael Linn CEF 009, 1961; CEFCD009, 2006); *The Drones and the Chanters* [compilation] (Claddagh CC 11, 1971); *The Pure Drop Volume 1* (Tara 1002, 1973); *The Wandering Minstrel* (Topic 12TS250, 1974; Ossian OSSCD 12, 1989; Green Linnet GLCD 3078, 1993); *Feidlim Toon Ri's Castle* (Claddagh CC19, 1977); *Forty Years of Irish Piping* (Free Reed Records FRR001, 1977; Green Linnet GLCD 1000, 2000); *The Fox Chase* (Tara 1009, 1978); *The Best of Irish*

Piping [compilation of previous Tara releases] (Tara TACD 1002–9, 1995); *The Return to Fingal* (RTÉ CD 199, 1997); and *Two Centuries of Celtic Music* (Legacy CD 499, 2001).

41. uí Ógáin, *Companion*, 118.

42. Breandán Breathnach, "Séamus Ennis: A Tribute to the Man and His Music," *Musical Traditions* 1, no. 108 (1983), https://www.mustrad.org.uk/articles/ennis.htm.

43. Ibid.; Christopher Smith, "Why Séamus? Séamus Ennis, Traditional Music, and Irish Cultural History," *JMI* 2, no. 6 (September/October 2002): 5.

44. Breathnach, "Tribute."

45. Ríonach uí Ógáin, ed., *"Mise an fear ceoil,"* 32; see Tony MacMahon, "The Master," *Journal of Music* 1, no. 6 (February/March 2010): 46–51.

46. Browne and Vignoles, *Séamus Ennis Story.*

47. Ibid.

48. Cited in Breathnach and Ní Mhurchú, *Beathaisnéis a Cúig, 1882–1982* (Baile Átha Cliath: An Clóchomhar, 1997), 58.

49. Éamon de Buitléar, "Miles and Miles," 6.

50. uí Ógáin, "A Job with No Clock," 11. Regarding the civil service opportunity, Ennis told Peter Browne that he had sat an exam for entering but "missed out on a post by only one or two places" (email message to author, June 4, 2020). See also Breathnach, "Tribute"; Smith, "Why Séamus?," 7.

51. Breathnach and Ní Mhurchú, *Beathaisnéis a Cúig,* 59.

52. Samples of this sheet music are available on the ITMA website, accessed December 1, 2020, https://www.itma.ie/digital-library/text/claisceadal-colm-o-lochlainn.

53. Cited in Mícheál Ó hAlmhain, "As I Roved Out: Seamus Ennis Talks to Micheal O hAlmhain about Collections," *Treoir* 5, no. 6 (1973): 26.

54. Cited in Breathnach and Ní Mhurchú, *Beathaisnéis a Cúig,* 59.

55. Briody, *Commission,* 279.

56. Briody observes that Delargy was disinclined to recruit women as field collectors. When Prof. Otto Anderson suggested a female colleague of his go to Ireland to collect music for the IFC in 1938, Delargy demurred: "You see our old country-people are so conservative that they would give songs more readily to a man than to a woman. Personally, I think that the Finnish lady seems to be excellent, and she knows English well and has wide experience. But I do not suppose that she could work a gramophone recording apparatus. Meier's people certainly can" (Briody, *Commission,* 273). Briody also observes that, at the time, "antipathy towards women in Irish society, particularly in rural society, affected the number of women the Commission collected from as well the amount and the nature of the material collected from them" (*Commission,* 58).

57. Briody, *Commission,* 279.

58. uí Ógáin, "A Job with No Clock," 11–12.

59. de Buitléar, "Miles and Miles," 6.

60. uí Ógáin, *"Mise an fear ceoil,"* 29; uí Ógáin, "Ennis, Séamus," 119.

61. Ibid., 118.

62. Browne and Vignoles, *Séamus Ennis Story*. Ennis's daughter Catherine observed that he was particularly "wonderful with children" (Browne and Vignoles, *Séamus Ennis Story*).

63. Ibid.

64. Breandán Breathnach, "Tribute."

65. Browne and Vignoles, *Séamus Ennis Story*.

66. Breathnach and Ní Mhurchú, *Beathaisnéis a Cúig*, 60; MacMahon, "The Master."

67. uí Ógáin, *"Mise an fear ceoil,"* 28.

68. See Almqvist, "Achievement and Legacy," 13.

69. Ennis spent his longest continuous spell of collecting for the IFC—around eighteen weeks—in the Western Isles of Scotland from mid-November 1946 to the end of March 1947 (Ríonach uí Ógáin, "Thar Farraige Anonn—Séamus Mac Aonghusa in Albain 1946–1947," in *Dear Far-Voiced Veteran: Essays in Honour of Tom Munnelly*, ed. Anne Clune [Miltown Malbay, Co. Clare: Old Kilfarboy Society, 2007], 370). Nonetheless, he spent the bulk of his collecting time in Ireland between 1942 and 1947, spending a total of sixty-two weeks collecting in Co. Galway—two of which he spent collecting in Aran—and twenty-six weeks in Co. Donegal. He also spent around twenty-six days collecting in Mayo, from August 10 to September 4, 1944. Between September and November 1945, he spent around twenty-seven days collecting in Clare. He spent "a few weeks each" in Cork and Kerry (uí Ógáin, "A Job with No Clock," 12). He made two collecting trips to Tory Island in October 1944 and May 1946 that amounted to almost twenty days. Finally, he spent a week in October 1942 collecting in Cavan; and he spent around eight days in November 1945 collecting in Limerick.

70. uí Ógáin, *"Mise an fear ceoil,"* 18; see also Almqvist, "Achievement and Legacy," 12.

71. NFC 1297: 86.

72. uí Ógáin, *"Mise an fear ceoil,"* 279.

73. de Buitléar, "Miles and Miles," 6. Uí Ógáin casts some doubt on the accuracy of this often-quoted figure of 212 but, in the same breath, stresses the magnitude of Colm Ó Caodháin's repertoire ("Fear Ceoil Ghlinsce," 748).

74. Briody, *Commission*, 82; Robert Flaherty, *Oidhche Sheanchais* (Gaumont-British Picture Corporation Ltd., 1934). On Seáinín Tom Ó Dioráin, see Tomás Ó hÍde, *Seáinín Tom Sheáin: From Árainn to the Silver Screen* (Dublin: Four Courts Press, in association with Comhairle Bhéaloideas Éireann, 2019).

75. The earliest publications of Aran folklore date from the turn of the twentieth century (Fr. Eoghan Ó Gramhnaigh, "Gleanings from the Islands," *Tuam News/Western Advertiser*, February 14, May 2 and 30, June 6, 20, and 27, 1890; Pádraig Mac Piarais, "Cuairt ar Árainn na Naomh," *Fáinne an Lae*, Samhain 12, 1898; Synge, *Aran Islands*); two more contemporaneous collections waited nearly a century to be published (Ole Munch-Pedersen, ed., *Scéalta Mháirtín Neile*; Dietrich (Hg.) Schüller, *Tondokumente aus dem Phonogrammarchiv der Österreichischen Akademie der Wissenschaften. Gesamtausgabe der historischen Bestände, 1899–1950*, Series 5/2, The Collections of Rudolf Trebitsch: Celtic Recordings 1907–9 [Österreichische Akademie der Wissenschaften,

2003]). It is unclear whether Delargy was aware that General Richard Mulcahy had recorded Seáinín Tom Ó Dioráin in 1926 (Dónal Ó Flannagáin, *Ó Thrá Anoir* [Cathair na Mart, Co. Mayo: Foilsiúcháin Náisiúnta Teo., 1985], 116). Delargy collected folktales from another local storyteller, Darach Ó Direáin, in 1932, and he may have encouraged Robin Flower to do the same in 1933 (Marion Ní Mhaoláin, *Scéalta béaloidis ó Árainn: bailiúchán 'Bhláithín'/Uí Dhireáin*, paper presented at Scoil Gheimhridh Chumann Merriman, Galway, January 30, 2010). Delargy was responsible for the publication of two of Seáinín Tom Ó Dioráin's stories, which appeared on a 1934 commercial gramophone release titled *Oídhche Sheanchais* (Parlophone E4075; see Brian Ó Catháin, "*Oidhche Sheanchais* le Robert J. Flaherty: An Chéad Scannán Gaeilge Dá nDearnadh," in *Bliainiris 4*, ed. Liam Mac Cóil and Ruairí Ó hUiginn, 151–235 [Ráth Chairn, Co. Meath: Carbad, 2004]). He appears to have encouraged Aran poet Máirtín Ó Direáin to collect material when he was home on holidays in October 1937 (NFC 494: 276–88); Ó Direáin had earlier published three items in the newspapers *An Stoc* (1931; 1936) and *Ar Aghaidh* (1937) and intended publishing more (Ailbhe Nic Giolla Chomhaill, "'An Páiste i dTír na nIontas,'" *Comhar* [Márta 2018]: 31). A proposal from the Irish Folklore Institute to publish material collected by Inis Meáin schoolteacher Úna Nic Fhualáin (1871–1929) failed to proceed (Briody, "Vicissitudes," 31, n. 41). As only two items from her collection appear to have been published—in 1903 and posthumously in 1936—her efforts remained little known; they were potentially too short lived to figure in a narrative of the collecting of folkloric material in Aran (Úna [Shéamuis] Nic Fhualáin, "An Hero/Bád Ned Bháin," *An Claidheamh Soluis*, Lúnasa 1, 1903, 2; Mícheál Langton [Fr. Benedict O.C.D.], "Paidir as Connacht: Caoineadh na Páise," *The Irish Press*, April 9, 1936, 4).

76. uí Ógáin, "A Job with No Clock," 12.

77. Mná Fiontracha, *Cosáin an tSaoil*, 25#14, 21#36.

78. Ibid., 41#10.

79. By then, Ennis believed he had collected the entirety of Ó Caodháin's repertoire (uí Ógáin, "Mise an fear ceoil," 264).

80. Browne and Vignoles, *Séamus Ennis Story*.

81. uí Ógáin, "Mise an fear ceoil," 202.

82. Irish Traditional Music Archive (hereafter ITMA) Ref#763-RTÉ-RR=CD-R 235.

83. NFC 1282: 351–53, 382–84.

84. For "Tá an Oíche Seo Dorcha," see "Ag Dul Chun Aifrinn," Ó Con Cheanainn, *Clár Amhrán*, 91–93#102 (number before hashtag denotes page number and number after hashtag denotes given song index number).

85. Information courtesy of ITMA, September 15, 2010.

86. uí Ógáin, "Mise an fear ceoil," 73, n. 13; NFC 1281: 376–77.

87. NFC 1282: 360, 382–84.

88. uí Ógáin, "A Job with No Clock," 12.

89. Browne and Vignoles, *Séamus Ennis Story*.

90. Briody, *Commission*, 278.

91. See uí Ógáin, "Mise an fear ceoil," 30.

92. Ibid.

93. NFC 1297: 74; uí Ógáin, *"Mise an fear ceoil,"* 276.

94. uí Ógáin, *"Mise an fear ceoil,"* 274.

95. uí Ógáin, "A Job with No Clock," 14.

96. Diarmuid Breathnach and Máire Ní Mhurchú, "Máire Mac Neill (1904–1987)," http://www.ainm.ie/Bio.aspx?ID=1583; Petairín a' Bheagach Ó Maoláin, interview by the author, January 4, 2001.

97. NFC 1134: 13–14.

98. NFC 1297: 51; uí Ógáin, *"Mise an fear ceoil,"* 270.

99. uí Ógáin, "A Job with No Clock," 12.

100. Mná Fiontracha, *Cosáin an tSaoil,* 25#19.

101. For "Bhí bean uasal seal ghá luadh liom," see NFC 1282: 389–90. For "Máire Ní Thaidhg Óig," see ibid., 388; NFC MM 021.011.

102. NFC 1297: 83; MM 021.011.

103. uí Ógáin, *"Mise an fear ceoil,"* 334.

104. NFC 1297: 27.

105. The scribes and contributors to this copybook are inconsistently identified, so it is difficult to calculate exactly how many of the songs were transcribed by Máire or contributed by Tyrell (NFC S1A: 103–15).

106. NFC S1A: 103–6, 103, 109, 112–13.

107. uí Ógáin, *Going to the Well for Water,* 289–90.

108. NFC 1282: 364–65; NFC MM 021.005.

109. NFC 1282: 364.

110. uí Ógáin, *"Mise an fear ceoil,"* 333.

111. NFC 1297: 95.

112. Competitors in the women's singing competition of Oireachtas na Gaeilge 1945 included Máire Ní Cheocháin, Cúil Aodha, who won first prize; Treasa Ní Mhaoilchiaráin, Ruisín na Maithniach, Carna, who won second prize; Siobhán Ní Shéaghdha, Baile an Fheirtéaraigh; Bairbre Uí Chualáin, Lochán Beag; Cáit Bean Uí Thuama, Baile Bhuirne; and Bhéra Ní Mhuireadaigh, An Cheathrú Rua. Máire Ní Dhioráin may have been one of the four other women who competed in this competition, which was judged by Sorcha Ní Ghuairim and Donncha (Dinny Pháidí Duncaí) Ó Baoighill; Máire and Dinny were among the party that spent the evening of Wednesday, October 24, 1945, in Sorcha's house (NFC 1296: 373). Having consulted with two of the competitors from that era, it is difficult to confirm or deny this suggestion. Máire Ní Cheocháin (1924–2019) could not recall whether Máire Ní Dhioráin attended or competed in the competition in 1945 and Cití Ní Ghallchóir of Dobhar Láir, Gaoth Dobhair, whom Máire Ní Dhioráin recalled meeting at James Delargy's house on Thursday, October 25, 1945 (uí Ógáin, *"Mise an fear ceoil,"* 423), could not confirm or deny her attendance at An tOireachtas that year nor could she recall meeting Máire. As Cití confirmed that she competed every year she attended An tOireachtas, we can assume she

was among the four unnamed competitors. I am grateful to Róisín Nic Dhonncha for her assistance with this query.

113. Liam Mac Con Iomaire, *Conamara—An Tír Aineoil/The Unknown Country* (Indreabhán: Cló Iar-Chonnacht, 1997), 109–25.

114. NFC 1296: 374.

115. Briody, *Commission*, 275–76.

116. NFC 1282: 382–84.

117. Ibid., 379–81.

118. Ibid., 374.

119. NFC MM 021.005; NFC MM 021.011.

120. Browne and Vignoles, *Séamus Ennis Story*.

121. Helen Gubbins, "Shortwaves, Acetates and Journeywork: Irish Traditional Music on Early Irish Radio 1926–1961" (master's thesis, University College Cork, 2009); see Peter Browne, *The Rolling Wave: In Memoriam Ciarán Mac Mathúna* (RTÉ Radio 1, December 13, 2009).

122. Christopher Smith, "Why Séamus?," 7.

123. Acknowledging the ability of radio to privilege, disseminate, and canonize music, Richard Pine observes that RÉ and RTÉ turned certain elements of Irish traditional music into "icons of authenticity" and others into "serious points of contention" (*Music and Broadcasting*, 316). Citing Peter Carr's television series *Bringing It All Back Home* (1991), Pine recounts how "the visits of Ciarán MacMathúna to the USA in 1962 and 1966, to record programmes for his radio series 'A Job of Journeywork,' acted as a catalyst in bringing to Irish listeners a strand that was, at least, unfamiliar."

124. See Peter Browne, *Tuning the Radio—The Connection between Radio and Broadcasting and Traditional Music*, Ó Riada Memorial Lecture 18 (Cork: Irish Traditional Music Society, University College Cork, 2007), 5.

125. Robin Roberts, "Recording in Ireland with Alan Lomax" [1997], in *Ireland*, The Historic Series: World Library of Folk and Primitive Music, vol. 2 (The Alan Lomax Collection) (1955; reissue, Rounder Records CD1742, 1998).

126. uí Ógáin, "Mac Aonghusa in Albain," 369; see Browne and Vignoles, *Séamus Ennis Story*.

127. Gubbins, "Shortwaves."

128. Browne and Vignoles, *Séamus Ennis Story*.

129. uí Ógáin, A Job with No Clock," 12; Ríonach uí Ógáin, "Is í an fhilíocht anam an cheoil: Sorcha Ní Ghuairim, Amhránaí Roisín na Mainiach," in *Bliainiris* 2, ed. Liam Mac Cóil and Ruairí Ó hUiginn (Ráth Chairn, Co. Meath: Carbad, 2002), 100; see Browne and Vignoles, *Séamus Ennis Story*; see John Bowman, *Bowman: Sunday Morning: 8.30*, RTÉ Radio 1, September 6, 2009.

130. Nicholas Carolan, "Introduction" [1998], in *Ireland*, The Historic Series: World Library of Folk and Primitive Music, vol. 2 (The Alan Lomax Collection), Rounder Records CD1742, 1998.

131. Alan Lomax, ed., *Ireland,* The Historic Series: World Library of Folk and Primitive Music, vol. 2 (The Alan Lomax Collection), (1955; reissue, Rounder Records CD1742, 1998).

132. Roberts, "Recording in Ireland."

133. Christopher Smith, "Why Séamus?," 6.

134. Kearney, "Urbanising," 187–88. The narratives of Irish traditional music that emerged during this period were also affected by the question of costs to RÉ. Richard Pine observes how musicians who lived at a distance from the broadcasting studios in Dublin were marginalized because the "low fees and travelling expenses" offered by RÉ in the 1930s and 1940s "operated in favour of Dublin-based bands and soloists": "Whatever the 'political' situation prevailing within RÉ at the time, there was definitely a problem insofar as the regulations (imposed on RÉ by the civil service) were unhelpful to long-distance travellers" (*Music and Broadcasting,* 321). Even after the introduction of the MRU in 1947, which went some way toward counteracting the marginalization of rural and isolated musics by RÉ up until then, the issue did not go away; in 1949, it was "being seriously argued in the Dáil."

135. Gearóid Ó hAllmhuráin, "Frank Custy of Toonagh," *Treoir* 7, no. 2 (June 1975): 18; Browne and Vignoles, *Séamus Ennis Story*; Mac Con Iomaire, *Tír Aineoil*; Fred McCormick, Review of *Amhráin ar an Sean Nós* and *Róise na nAmhrán: Songs of a Donegal Woman,* in *Musical Traditions* (1997), accessed February 2, 2010, http://www.mustrad.org.uk/reviews/sean_nos.htm; Ó Laoire, "Up Scraitheachaí!"; Tom Munnelly, "After the Fianna: Reality and Perceptions of Traditional Irish Singing," *JMI* 1, no. 2 (January/February 2001): 18–24; Máirtín Ó Fátharta [Meaití Jó Shéamuis], "Amhránaíocht ar an sean-nós i gConamara Theas" (lecture, Cork Singers' Club Festival: To Tell It in Song and in Story, An Spailpín Fánach, Cork, March 10, 2002); Angela Bourke, "Singing at the Centre of a Life," *JMI* 8, no. 3 (May/June 2008): 30; Browne, *In Memoriam Ciarán Mac Mathúna*; Ciaran Carson, "The Thing Itself," *JMI* 9, no. 1 (January/February 2009): 32–35; John O'Donnell, *In the Blood—Kilfenora Céilí Band* (Stray Dog Films for RTÉ, April 7, 2009); Daithí Kearney, "Towards a Regional Understanding of Irish Traditional Music" (PhD diss., University College Cork, 2010).

CHAPTER 3. SIDNEY ROBERTSON COWELL AND *SONGS OF ARAN*

1. Sidney Robertson Cowell, "Henry Cowell and Ireland" (memorandum, Sidney Robertson Cowell Ireland Collections, Archive of Folk Culture, American Folklife Center, Library of Congress, Washington, DC [hereafter LC], 1977), 7.

2. LT-10 7180 Ireland. Aran Isles. Folk songs. Performer: Michael Dillane. Original in: LJ-7 2; LT-10 7184 Ireland. Aran Isles. Keening (traditional singing). Original in: LJ-12 1812. Henry Cowell Collection, 1923–1986, Rodgers and Hammerstein Archives of Recorded Sound, The New York Public Library for the Performing Arts.

3. Sidney Robertson Cowell, Tape B.31, 21, JPB 00–03, Henry Cowell Papers, Music Division, The New York Public Library for the Performing Arts (hereafter NYPL), Box 87, Folder 34.

4. Sidney Robertson Cowell, undated reminiscences titled "How SRC Came to Record on Aran," LC.

5. Travel diary, May 31, 1956, LC.

6. "Ireland," NYPL, Box 87, Folder 3.

7. Throughout this chapter, her first name, Sidney, is used instead of the surname Cowell to avoid confusion with her husband and because the discussion spans her professional life, during which she was known by two names—Sidney Robertson and Sidney Robertson Cowell.

8. Lists of Irish and American women collectors compiled by the author can be accessed at https://www.itma.ie/blog/sidney-robertson-cowell.

9. The earliest US release of sean-nós singing on record was Alan Lomax's 1955 compilation of his 1951 field recordings of Irish traditional music titled *Ireland*, The Columbia World Library of Folk and Primitive Music, vol. 2, which is now available on Rounder Records: *Ireland*, The Historic Series: World Library of Folk and Primitive Music, vol. 2 (The Alan Lomax Collection) (CD1742). That same year, under the surname Hamilton, Diane Guggenheim released an album of field recordings she made in Ireland titled *The Lark in the Morning*, which included performances by the sean-nós singer Seán 'ac Dhonncha (Tradition TCD1001). Sidney was apparently unaware of these releases when she wrote in a letter to Harold Spivacke on September 10, 1956: "So far as I can find out, there are no recordings of this material now in the US at all" (LC). By July 26, 1956, Sidney knew Moe Asch hoped to release his 1945 recordings of Sorcha Ní Ghuairim (Moses Asch, ed., *Sorcha Ní Ghuairim Sings Traditional Irish Songs* (Folkways 1957 FW06861); see also uí Ógáin, "Is í an fhilíocht anam an cheoil," 103–4.

10. Though her *New York Times* obituary called her an "ethnomusicologist," Sidney did not use that term to describe her own work ("Sidney Cowell, 92, Ethnomusicologist and Teacher," *New York Times*, Obituaries, March 1, 1995). She appears to have distinguished her efforts from those of ethnomusicologists based in academic institutions. In 1992 she reflected: "There was this whole world of ethnomusicologists that I tend to stay away from because it was so competitive and they were so busy with words instead of paying attention to the music from my point of view. And I was a kind of a loner apparently" (interview by Peter Goldsmith in Shady, New York, January 3, 1992, oral history tape, Sidney Robertson Cowell Ireland Collection, Ralph Rinzler Folklife Archives and Collections, Smithsonian Center for Folklife and Cultural Heritage, Washington, DC [hereafter RR]). In 1989 she offered a potential alternative title: "I have been asked to explain how I became a *field collector of folksong* [my emphasis], and what my background was for the work" (untitled reminiscences beginning "I have been asked to explain how I became a field collector of folksong . . . ," dated September 21, 1989, LC). The descriptor "ethnographer" is commonly used by scholars to signify the extraordinary detail and fluidity of her writing.

11. Sidney states that Charles Hawkins already had a son by a previous marriage (Goldsmith interview, RR; Peter Stone, "Sidney and Henry Cowell," essay for the

Association for Cultural Equity, New York [2009], accessed November 22, 2020, http://
www.culturalequity.org/alan-lomax/friends/cowell).

12. Catherine Hiebert Kerst, "A 'Government Song Lady' in Pursuit of Folksong:
Sidney Robertson Cowell's Field Documentation in the Resettlement Administration"
(paper, American Folklore Society, Quebec City, Québec, October 18, 2007).

13. Peter Stone maintains Robertson was a medical student ("Sidney and Henry
Cowell").

14. Kerst, "Government Song Lady."

15. Stone, "Sidney and Henry Cowell."

16. Kerst, "Government Song Lady."

17. Stone, "Sidney and Henry Cowell."

18. Cited in Kerst, "Government Song Lady."

19. Shannon L. Green, "Controversy and Conflict in the Henry Street Settlement
Music School, 1927–1935," *Women and Music* 8 (2004): 73; David C. Paul, "From American Ethnographer to Cold War Icon: Charles Ives through the Eyes of Henry and Sidney Cowell," *Journal of the American Musicological Society* 59, no. 2 (Summer 2006):
423–24.

20. Cited in Kerst, "Government Song Lady."

21. Green, "Controversy," 81.

22. Ibid., 74.

23. Richard A. Reuss, "Folk Music and Social Conscience: The Musical Odyssey of
Charles Seeger," *Western Folklore* 38, no. 4 (October 1979): 221–38.

24. For his staff of fieldworkers, see Charles Seeger, *Reminiscences of an American
Musicologist*, interview by Adelaide G. Tusler and Ann M. Briegleb, conducted under
the auspices of the Oral History Program, University of California, Los Angeles (1972),
the Internet Archive, http://www.archive.org/stream/reminiscencesofaooseeg/remi
niscencesofaooseeg_djvu.txt (accessed August 6, 2009); Allan Kozinn, "Herbert Haufrecht, 88, Pianist, Composer, Folklorist and Editor," *New York Times*, July 3, 1998, A19;
Gerald Thomas, "In Memoriam: Herbert Halpert, 1911–2000," *Journal of Folklore
Research* 38, nos. 1–2 (January 2001): 173–74. For using music to ease tension and cultivate a sense of community, see Charles Seeger, *Reminiscences*, 250.

25. Reuss, "Folk Music and Social Conscience," 235.

26. Benjamin Filene, *Romancing the Folk: Public Memory and American Roots Music*
(Chapel Hill: University of North Carolina Press, 2000), 164; for quote, see Neil V.
Rosenberg, "Family Values Seeger Style: A Seeger Family Tribute at the Library of Con-
gress," *Folklife Center News* 29, nos. 1–2 (Winter–Spring 2007): 11.

27. Goldsmith interview, RR.

28. Kerst, "Government Song Lady."

29. Green, "Controversy."

30. Paul, "From American Ethnographer," 424.

31. Kerst, "Government Song Lady."

32. Filene, *Romancing the Folk*, 142.

33. On Sidney's recordings in the Midwest, see James P. Leary, "Canons and Cannonballs," in *Polkabilly: How the Goose Island Ramblers Redefined American Folk Music* (New York: Oxford University Press, 2006), 170; and James P. Leary, "The Mid-West: A Surprising Vitality" (unpublished paper, n.d.). For quote, see Kerst, "Government Song Lady."

34. Sidney Robertson Cowell, "The Recording of Folk Music in California," *California Folklore Quarterly* 1, no. 1 (January 1942): 22–23; Kerst, "Government Song Lady."

35. Kerst, "Ethnographic Experience."

36. Sidney Robertson Cowell to Henry Cowell, July 21, 1956, NYPL, Box 6, Folder 11.

37. Kerst, "Government Song Lady."

38. Ibid.

39. Nicole Saylor, "Folk Music of Wisconsin, 1937," webpage highlighting the ethnographic fieldwork of Sidney Robertson Cowell (1903–1995) in Wisconsin, Mills Music Library's Helene Stratman-Thomas project, Center for the Study of Upper Midwestern Cultures, University of Wisconsin–Madison (2004), http://digital.library.wisc.edu/17 11.dl/WiscFolkSong.

40. Cited in Kerst, "Government Song Lady."

41. Goldsmith interview, RR.

42. Ibid.

43. Kerst, "Government Song Lady."

44. Brett Topping, "The Sidney Robertson Cowell Collection," *Folklife Center News* 3, no. 3 (July 1980): 4.

45. Cited in Kerst, "Government Song Lady." Sidney drove because John A. Lomax did not drive (Stone, "Sidney and Henry Cowell").

46. Kerst, "Government Song Lady"; Saylor, "Folk Music of Wisconsin, 1937"; James P. Leary, "Woodsmen, Shanty Boys, Bawdy Songs, and Folklorists in America's Upper Midwest," *The Folklore Historian* 24 (2007): 41–63.

47. Cited in Kerst, "Government Song Lady."

48. Kerst, "Government Song Lady."

49. Roger D. Abrahams, "Mr. Lomax Meets Professor Kittredge," *Journal of Folklore Research* 37, nos. 2–3 (May 2000): 99–18; Filene, *Romancing the Folk*.

50. Filene, *Romancing the Folk*, 12–13.

51. Cited in Filene, *Romancing the Folk*, 16.

52. Cited in Kerst, "Government Song Lady."

53. Kerst, "Government Song Lady."

54. James P. Leary, "Fieldwork Forgotten, or Alan Lomax Goes North," *Midwestern Folklore* 27, no. 2 (2001): 17–18. For quotes, see Peter Garland, "Henry Cowell: Giving Us Permission," *Other Minds* (2006), accessed September 8, 2009, http://otherminds .org/shtml/Garlandoncowell.shtml.

55. Benjamin Filene, "'Our Singing Country': John and Alan Lomax, Leadbelly, and the Construction of an American Past," *American Quarterly* 43, no. 4 (December 1991): 602–24.

56. Goldsmith interview, RR. See also Stith Thompson, "John Avery Lomax (1867–1948)," *Journal of American Folklore* 61, no. 241 (July–September 1948): 305–6; Filene, "Our Singing Country"; Jerrold Hirsch, "Modernity, Nostalgia, and Southern Folklore Studies: The Case of John Lomax," *Journal of American Folklore* 105, no. 416 (Spring 1992): 183–207; Abrahams, "Lomax Meets Professor Kittredge," 99–118.

57. For Ford, see Sidney Robertson Cowell, "Wolf River Songs," in *Wolf River Songs* (Monograph Series of the Ethnic Folkways Library FE4001, 1956), 1–14. For Dusenberry, see Charles Seeger, *Reminiscences*. For children, see Sidney Robertson Cowell, "Songs of Aran: Gaelic Singing from the West of Ireland," in *Songs of Aran* (Ethnic Folkways Library Album No. FM4002, 1957), 1–11.

58. James P. Leary, *Folksongs of Another America: Field Recordings from the Upper Midwest, 1937–1946* (Madison: University of Wisconsin Press, 2015).

59. Cowell, "Wolf River Songs"; Sidney Robertson Cowell, ed., *Songs from Cape Breton Island* (Ethnic Folkways Library FE4450, 1955).

60. Cowell, "Wolf River Songs," 2.

61. Cited in Kerst, "Government Song Lady."

62. Goldsmith interview, RR.

63. Ibid.

64. Kerst, "Government Song Lady."

65. Catherine Hiebert Kerst, "Outsinging the Gas Tank: Sidney Robertson Cowell and the California Folk Music Project," *Folklife Center News* 20, no. 1 (Winter 1998): 6–12.

66. Kerst, "Government Song Lady"; Topping, "Cowell Collection," 5.

67. Catherine Hiebert Kerst, ed., "Cataloging Folk Music: A Letter from Sidney Robertson Cowell," *Folklife Center News* (Fall 1989): 10.

68. Kerst, "Government Song Lady"; Sheryl Kaskowitz, "Delight in What It Is to Be an American: Sidney Robertson on the Road, 1935 to 1937" (lecture, John W. Kluge Center, Library of Congress, November 3, 2016, https://www.loc.gov/item/webcast -7736/).

69. Cited in Kerst, "Cataloging Folk Music," 11.

70. Notes by Brett Topping on her telephone discussion with Sidney, August 1, 1980, 1, LC.

71. Sidney Robertson Cowell to Henry Cowell, "Afton, VA Saturday," NYPL, Box 201 Folder 9. See Catherine Hiebert Kerst, "Sidney Robertson Cowell and the WPA California Folk Music Project, 1938–40" (lecture, Library of Congress, May 9, 2017, https://www.loc.gov/item/webcast-7963).

72. Topping, "Cowell Collection," 5.

73. George Boziwick, "Henry Cowell at the New York Public Library: A Whole World of Music," *Notes: Quarterly Journal of the Music Library Association* 57, no. 1 (September 2000): 57.

74. Topping, "Cowell Collection," 5.

75. Stone, "Sidney and Henry Cowell."

76. Topping, "Cowell Collection," 4.

77. Leary, "Woodsmen," 57.

78. Jim Leary, email message to author, July 31, 2009.

79. Alan Jabbour, email message to author, February 2, 2009.

80. "Sidney Cowell, 92, Ethnomusicologist and Teacher." *New York Times*, Obituaries, March 1, 1995.

81. Stone, "Sidney and Henry Cowell."

82. On conflict with peers and superiors, see Sheryl Kaskowitz, "Government Song Women: The Forgotten Folk Collectors of the New Deal," *Humanities: The Magazine of the National Endowment for the Humanities* 41, no. 2 (Spring 2020): 30–58. On her Folkways projects and digital collection, see Catherine Hiebert Kerst, "The Ethnographic Experience: Sidney Robertson Cowell in Northern California," in *California Gold: Northern California Folk Music from the Thirties Collected by Sidney Robertson Cowell*, digital collection, American Folklife Center, Library of Congress, 1997, https://www .loc.gov/collections/sidney-robertson-cowell-northern-california-folk-music/articles -and-essays/the-ethnographic-experience-sidney-robertson-cowell-in-northern-califor nia/. Sidney's unpublished collections survive in the American Folklife Center and the Music Division at the Library of Congress and in the Ralph Rinzler Folklife Archives and Collections at the Smithsonian Center for Folklife and Cultural Heritage in Washington, DC, in the New York Public Library for the Performing Arts, and in the University of California at Berkeley (see bibliography). For published accounts of her life, see Kaskowitz, "Delight"; Kerst, "Cataloging Folk Music"; Catherine Hiebert Kerst, "Sidney Robertson Cowell and the WPA California Folk Music Project," in *The Sonneck Society for American Music Bulletin* 20, no. 3 (Fall 1994): 5–9; Kerst, "Outsinging the Gas Tank"; Kerst, *WPA California Folk Music Project*; Leary, *Folksongs*; Deirdre Ní Chonghaile, "In Search of America: Sidney Robertson Cowell in Ireland in 1955–56," *Journal of American Folklore*, 126, no. 500 (Spring 2013): 174–200; Saylor, "Folk Music of Wisconsin, 1937"; Topping, "Cowell Collection"; Kaskowitz, "Government Song Women."

83. Cited in Kerst, "Government Song Lady."

84. Kerst, "Outsinging the Gas Tank."

85. Catherine Hiebert Kerst, email message to author, April 3, 2007; see also Sidney [Robertson] Cowell, "The Cowells and the Written Word," in *A Celebration of American Music Words and Music in Honor of Wiley Hitchcock*, ed. Richard Crawford, R. Allen Lott, and Carol J. Oja (Ann Arbor: University of Michigan Press, 1989), 79–91.

86. Mícheál Ó hAlmhain, "As I Roved Out"; Breandán Breathnach, "Tribute"; Angela Bourke, "Séamus Ennis"; Browne and Vignoles, *Séamus Ennis Story*; de Buitléar,

"Miles"; uí Ógáin, "A Conamara Singer and His Collector"; uí Ógáin, "Ennis, Séamus"; uí Ógáin, "A Job with No Clock"; uí Ógáin, *Mise an fear ceoil*; uí Ógáin, "Mac Aonghusa in Albain"; uí Ógáin, *Going to the Well for Water*; Richardson, *Giant At My Shoulder*; Dáibhí Ó Cróinín, ed., *The Songs of Elizabeth Cronin* (Dublin: Four Courts Press, 2000); Christopher Smith, "Why Séamus?"; John Bowman, *Bowman: Sunday Morning: 8.30: Ciarán Mac Mathúna and Liam Clancy*, RTÉ Radio 1, December 13, 2009; John Bowman, *Bowman: Sunday Morning: 8.30: Ciarán Mac Mathúna*, RTÉ Radio 1, December 20, 2009; John Bowman, *Bowman: Sunday Morning: 8.30: Ciarán Mac Mathúna*, RTÉ Radio 1, December 27, 2009; Peter Browne, *Rolling Wave*; Carolan, "'Desire and Duty'"; Gubbins, "Shortwaves"; Deirdre Ní Chonghaile, "Séamus Ennis, W. R. Rodgers and Sidney Robertson Cowell on the Traditional Music of the Aran Islands," in *Anáil an Bhéil Bheo: Orality and Modern Irish Culture*, ed. Nessa Cronin, Seán Crosson, and John Eastlake (Cambridge: Cambridge Scholars Publishing, 2009), 67–86.

87. Undated reminiscences titled "How SRC Came to Record on Aran," LC. The "visiting collector" may be W. R. Rodgers or David Thomson or Proinsias Ó Conluain, who together recorded material in Árainn for the BBC and Radio Éireann in November 1949.

88. Marie Slocombe, "The BBC Folk Music Collection," *Folklore and Folk Music Archivist* 7, no. 1 (1964): 3–13. See also Maud Karpeles, Autobiography, n.d. (ca. 1975), MK/7/185 Ralph Vaughan Williams Library, Cecil Sharp House, Camden Town, London.

89. Cowell, *Songs of Aran*, 7.

90. Sidney Robertson Cowell to Rae Korson, January 18, 1956, LC. The specifics of the health scare to which Sidney refers are unclear.

91. Topping, "Cowell Collection," 4; Sidney Robertson Cowell to Harold Spivacke, May 28, 1956, NYPL, Box 28 Folder 10.

92. Cowell, *Songs of Aran*, 6; Sidney Robertson Cowell to Harold Spivacke, September 10, 1956, LC.

93. Sidney Robertson Cowell to Harold Spivacke, September 10, 1956, LC.

94. Anthony McCann and Lillis Ó Laoire, "'Raising One Higher than the Other': The Hierarchy of Tradition in Representations of Gaelic and English Language Song in Ireland," in *Global Pop, Local Language*, ed. Harris M. Berger and Michael T. Carroll (Jackson: University Press of Mississippi, 2003), 244–45; Cowell, *Songs of Aran*.

95. In discussion with Séamas Ó Direáin, January 28, 2010. See Barry Cunliffe, *Facing the Ocean: the Atlantic and Its Peoples 8000 BC–AD 1500* (Oxford: Oxford University Press, 2001); Stephen Oppenheimer, *The Origins of the British—A Genetic Detective Story* (London: Constable and Robinson, 2006).

96. Cowell, *Songs of Aran*, 6.

97. Sidney Robertson Cowell, *A Proposal for the Preservation and Circulation of Material from the Oral Tradition in Ireland*, drafted in May 1956, LC.

98. In her interview with Peter Goldsmith, Sidney explained what led her to visit the Archive of Folk Song at the Library of Congress: "I had come to find out what made an American song American" (RR).

99. Filene, *Romancing the Folk*, 12–13, 27, 133–34.

100. Leary, "Fieldwork Forgotten," 16–18.

101. Cited in Kerst, "Government Song Lady."

102. Vallely, *Irish Traditional Music*, 79.

103. Briody, *Commission*.

104. Alan Lomax, "Introduction" [1951], in *Ireland*, The Historic Series: World Library of Folk and Primitive Music, vol. 2 (The Alan Lomax Collection) (Rounder Records CD1742, 1998).

105. uí Ógáin, *Mise an fear ceoil*, 20–21.

106. See Mícheál Briody, "*The Gaelic Story-Teller* and Séamus Ó Duilearga's Views on the Role and Antiquity of *Airneán*," *Béascna* 8 (2013): 1–33.

107. Cowell, *Proposal*, LC.

108. Cowell, *Songs of Aran*, 6.

109. Ibid., 6–7.

110. NFC 1282: 351; Sidney Robertson Cowell to Harold Spivacke, September 10, 1956, LC; Cowell, *Songs of Aran*, 6.

111. Sidney Robertson Cowell to Rae Korson, June–July 1956, LC.

112. Ibid. See also Lomax, "Introduction."

113. Cowell, *Proposal*, LC.

114. Undated informal letter to Harold Spivacke enclosed with a preceding formal letter to him dated July 20, 1956, LC.

115. Writing to Harold Spivacke about the IFC, Sidney explained the negative impact of an earlier tactless gesture toward the Irish Folklore Commission: "A request from Indiana that the whole Irish Archive be *sent* there for copying in toto was the occasion for considerable indignation in the quarters that I move in, and the 'tact and vocabulary' of the suggested proposal that I sent in was much admired apparently! (because I said—knowing the feeling here—that distribution of material should be done from Ireland). I think that if the letter from Indian [*sic*] had not come, some combination of your proposal and ours might have been accepted. As it is, there is considerable fear that a wholesale pirate project is intended in the USA; and of course there is really no appreciation of the difference between book publication of tunes—of which Dr. Delargy pointed out there are plenty in print for any reasonable use outside Ireland!—and the fact that only records are any use to modern musicological study" (undated informal letter enclosed with a preceding formal letter to Spivacke dated July 20, 1956, LC).

116. Undated informal letter to Harold Spivacke enclosed with a preceding formal letter to him dated July 20, 1956, LC.

117. James P. Leary, "The Discovery of Finnish American Folk Music," in "Scandinavian Folklore," special issue of *Scandinavian Studies* 73, no. 3 (2001): 475–92; Leary, "Woodsmen"; Kerst, "Government Song Lady."

118. LC; Cowell, *Songs of Aran.*

119. Field diary, August 11, 1956, LC. This extract was probably written closer to August 18.

120. Sidney Robertson Cowell, undated reminiscences titled "IRELAND," LC.

121. "It has taken me 18 years to get around to it, but I am finally beginning the language of the Garden of Eden!" (Field diary, June 12, 1955, LC).

122. Cowell, *Songs of Aran.*

123. Undated informal letter to Harold Spivacke enclosed with a preceding formal letter to him dated July 20, 1956, LC.

124. Sidney Robertson Cowell to Harold Spivacke, September 10, 1956, LC.

125. Cowell, *Songs of Aran,* 7.

126. Sidney Robertson Cowell to Henry Cowell, June 24, 1956, LC.

127. Ibid.

128. Digital versions of this catalog are available to consult at the American Folklife Center at the Library of Congress and via the Irish Traditional Music Archive website, https://www.itma.ie/blog/sidney-robertson-cowell.

129. Cited in Kerst, "Government Song Lady."

130. Cowell, *Proposal,* LC.

131. Sidney Robertson Cowell to Harold Spivacke, May 28, 1956, NYPL, Box 28 Folder 10.

132. Letter from Sidney Robertson Cowell, March 7, 1958, LC.

133. Field diary, June 11, 1955, LC.

134. Ibid.

135. Ibid., June [12], 1955, LC; FW-ASCH-RR-5255, RR. Some of the reels are labeled with the wrong date or with no date at all. The dates supplied here have been cross-referenced with the diary entries, which themselves are slightly confused because Sidney wrote the days' entries a few at a time.

136. Field diary, June 13, 1955, LC.

137. Field diary, June 17, 1955, LC.

138. Goldsmith interview, RR.

139. Cowell, "Wolf River Songs."

140. Ibid.; Field diary, June 17, 1955, LC.

141. Sidney Robertson Cowell to Harold Spivacke, received May 31, 1956, LC.

142. Notes, Reel 3, June 14, 1955, FW-ASCH-RR-5253, RR.

143. Mná Fiontracha, *Cosáin an tSaoil,* 90#99.

144. Cowell, *Songs of Aran,* 5.

145. Field diary, June 14, 1955, LC.

146. Reel 3, FW-ASCH-RR-5253, RR.

147. Notes, Reel 3, 1955, FW-ASCH-RR-5253, RR.

148. Reel 5, FW-ASCH-RR-5251; Notes, Reel 3, June 14, 1955, FW-ASCH-RR-5251, RR.

149. Field diary, June 17, 1955, LC.

150. Mná Fiontracha, *Cosáin an tSaoil*, 45#6.

151. Notes, Reel 6, June 14, 1955, FW-ASCH-RR-5248, RR.

152. Field diary, June 14, 1955, LC.

153. Ibid.

154. Field diary, August 11, 1956, LC.

155. Cowell, *Songs of Aran*, 6.

156. Ibid.

157. Mná Fiontracha, *Cosáin an tSaoil*, 25#20.

158. Field diary, June 18, 1955, LC.

159. Cowell, *Songs of Aran*, 5.

160. Notes, Reel 5, June 14, 1955, FW-ASCH-RR-5251, RR.

161. Field diary, June 14, 1955, LC; Reel 5, FW-ASCH-RR-5251, RR; notes, Reel 5, June 14, 1955, RR.

162. Sidney Robertson Cowell, notes to accompany Tape 10, recorded June 14 and 18, 1955, RR.

163. Field diary, June 18, 1955, LC; Reel 10, FW-ASCH-RR-5256, RR; in discussion with Treasa Ní Mhiolláin, October 29, 2009.

164. Notes, Reel 11, June 18, 1955, FW-ASCH-RR-5257, RR.

165. Reel 11, FW-ASCH-RR-5257, RR.

166. In discussion with Mícheál Tom Burke Ó Conghaile, September 22, 2009.

167. uí Ógáin, "Conamara Singer and His Collector."

168. Notes, Reel 3, June 14, 1955, FW-ASCH-RR-5253, RR; Cowell, *Songs of Aran*, 5.

169. Notes, Reel 3, June 14, 1955, RR.

170. See Almqvist, "Achievement and Legacy," 13.

171. Reel 16. In 1955 and 1956, Máiria taught first aid courses in the recently opened vocational school. She recalled being recorded in Aran by Sidney but remembered little about the occasion (in discussion with the author, May 3, 2009).

172. Recording log, with BBC marks in red pencil, LC.

173. Letter from Sidney Robertson Cowell, October 31, 1955, LC.

174. Sidney Robertson Cowell to Rae Korson, January 18, 1956, LC.

175. An internal BBC memo dated December 20, 1955, from Ruth Bratt to the music booking manager Margaret Penty states: "I attach a list of songs from six singers selected by Seamus Ennis as worthy of processing from recordings made by Mrs. Sidney Robertson Cowell of New York, in June 1955" (BBC Written Archives Center [hereafter WAC] NI7/24/1 Folk Music & Dialect Recording Scheme, 1952–1958).

176. Sidney Robertson Cowell, undated reminiscences titled "Chronology," LC.

177. In her undated reminiscences titled "Chronology," Sidney wrote: "As Henry fell ill in Pakistan and had to return slowly, we did not do all we had planned" (LC). In a letter dated May 28, 1956, to Harold Spivacke, she wrote: "Henry joins me there [Ireland] in August, and we go on to Turkey, Indonesia, Manila, with the last 3–5 months in Japan and (briefly) Korea. We planned the trip originally on a modest shoestring, but two weeks ago we became the somewhat stunned recipients of a large travel grant for 7 months in the Orient, 'for study of music in the Orient' from the Rockefeller Foundation" (NYPL, Box 28, Folder 10).

178. Sidney Robertson Cowell, undated reminiscences titled "Chronology," LC.

179. Ibid.; Sidney Robertson Cowell to Harold Spivacke, May 28, 1956, NYPL, Box 28, Folder 10.

180. Sidney Robertson Cowell to Harold Spivacke, May 28, 1956, NYPL, Box 28, Folder 10.

181. Sometime after August 12, Field diary, July–August 1956, LC.

182. Sidney Robertson Cowell to the Library of Congress, March 7, 1958, LC. See also author's catalog at https://www.itma.ie/blog/sidney-robertson-cowell.

183. Sidney Robertson Cowell to Harold Spivacke, September 10, 1956, LC.

184. Sidney Robertson Cowell to Harold Spivacke, May 28, 1956, NYPL, Box 28, Folder 10.

185. Sidney Robertson Cowell to Henry Cowell, June 22, 1956, LC.

186. Ian Lee suggests that Ó Raghallaigh's assistant could have been Johnny Spillane, Jimmy Mahon, Dermot Maguire, or Ned Nugent, all of whom then worked as sound engineers in RÉ (email message to author, May 6, 2009).

187. Proinsias Ó Conluain, "Cín Lae Craoltóra," in *Written on the Wind: Personal Memories of Irish Radio, 1926–76*, ed. Louis McRedmond (Dublin: RTÉ in association with Gill & Macmillan, 1976), 97; Pádraig Ó Raghallaigh, *Gaeltacht na nOileán*, Radio Éireann, August 27, 1956, RTÉ Sound Archive Tape 186.

188. Ian Lee, email message to author, March 20, 2008.

189. This program was first broadcast on August 27, 1956 (Ian Lee, email message to author, May 6, 2009).

190. There is little or no record of the missing program and the missing material. According to the notes accompanying Sidney's recordings of June 1956, it appears that Pat Pheaidí Ó hIarnáin of Cill Mhuirbhigh, Árainn, recorded "Cill Aodáin" for Pádraig Ó Raghallaigh earlier that month (Tape 2, Side B, RR). Vailín Bheairtlín Aindí Ó Maoláin (1935–2010) of Sruthán, Árainn, recalled being recorded by RÉ in Scoil Eoghanachta (in discussion with the author, September 22, 2009).

191. Prior to Ó Raghallaigh's 1956 trip to Aran, Radio Éireann producer Proinsias Ó Conluain was asked to join the BBC Third Program team that initiated a visit to Aran in November 1949, and he later made programs based on the recordings cocreated with his BBC counterparts W. R. Rodgers and David Thomson. See Ó Conluain, "Cín Lae Craoltóra."

192. Ian Lee, email message to author, April 3, 2008.

193. On hearing the recording, Joe Antaine Ó Briain of Cill Éinne guessed the singer was Martin John Thady Dillane, with whom he fished aboard MV *Ros Éinne* (interview by the author, January 30, 2009).

194. Ian Lee, *Ar Mo Thaisteal Dhom*, first broadcast November 4, 1996, RTÉ Raidió na Gaeltachta. W. R. Rodgers and Proinsias Ó Conluain also recorded Antoine Tónaí singing "Jimí Mo Mhíle Stór" in November 1949 (Public Record Office of Northern Ireland [hereafter PRONI] D2833/D/4/7).

195. After August 12, Field diary, July–August 1956, LC. Sidney mentions elsewhere that, by August 4, she had made seven trips aboard the steamer (Field diary, August 4, 1956, LC), indicating she may have brought the machine from Árainn to Galway to have it repaired on at least one occasion in July.

196. Sidney Robertson Cowell to Folkways Records, July 26, 1956, LC.

197. The only surviving recordings Sidney made of Seán 'ac Dhonncha date from August 13, 1956 (AFS 11,341B3–15, LC; FW-ASCH-RR-5249, RR).

198. Sidney Robertson Cowell to Henry Cowell, [July] 14, 1956, NYPL, Box 28, Folder 10; *Connacht Tribune*, July 14, 1956, 12.

199. Sidney Robertson Cowell to Henry Cowell, July 17, 1956, NYPL, Box 6, Folder 11.

200. Ibid., July 19, 1956.

201. Her focus on those singers who sang at the feis emerges in a field diary extract written in Carna on August 11, 1956: "I'm promised all my time to the people I heard at the Feis—of course if Mr. Green had sung at the Feis I'd have planned to visit him" (LC).

202. Sidney Robertson Cowell to Henry Cowell, July 21, 1956, NYPL, Box 6, Folder 11.

203. Sidney Robertson Cowell to Folkways Records, July 26, 1956, LC.

204. Sidney Robertson Cowell to Henry Cowell, July 19, 1956, NYPL, Box 6, Folder 11. See Diarmuid Breathnach and Máire Ní Mhurchú, *Beathaisnéis a Dó, 1882–1982* (Baile Átha Cliath: An Clóchomhar, 1990), 31; Úna Ní Fhaircheallaigh, *Smuainte ar Árainn* (Baile Átha Cliath: Conradh na Gaeilge, 1902), 46–52.

205. Sidney Robertson Cowell to Rae Korson, July [24], 1956, LC.

206. Field diary, July–August 1956, LC.

207. Ibid.

208. Ibid.

209. Sidney Robertson Cowell to Henry Cowell, July 30, 1956, LC.

210. Field diary, July–August 1956, LC.

211. Sidney Robertson Cowell, undated reminiscences titled "IRELAND," LC.

212. Sometime after August 12, field diary, July–August 1956, LC.

213. Field diary, July–August 1956, LC.

214. Sidney Robertson Cowell, undated reminiscences titled "IRELAND," LC. See Diarmuid Breathnach and Máire Ní Mhurchú, *Beathaisnéis a hAon, 1882–1982* (Baile Átha Cliath: An Clóchomhar, 1986), 52.

215. Field diary, July–August 1956, LC.

216. Field diary, August 11, 1956, LC.

217. Breathnach and Ní Mhurchú, *Beathaisnéis a Cúig*, 38–39. In the early 1970s, Breandán Ó Buachalla interviewed Joseph Davitt ("Seosamh Dáibhéid as Nua Eabhraic," rebroadcast in Ian Lee, ed., *Siúlach Scéalach*, RTÉ Raidió na Gaeltachta, January 12, 2014, https://www.rte.ie/radio/radioplayer/html5/#/rnag/20504571 (accessed 10 December 2020). See also Tomás de Bhaldraithe, "Seosamh Daibhéid—agus cuid dá chairde," *Feasta* 41, no. 10 (Deireadh Fómhair 1988): 19–23.

218. AFS 11,342, LC; FW-ASCH-RR-5243 (Tape 1), FW-ASCH-RR-5242 (Tape 2), RR.

219. Tape notes "Aran 1956 Tape 2 Side 2," FW-ASCH-RR-5242, RR.

220. Sidney Robertson Cowell to Henry Cowell, July 19, 1956, NYPL, Box 6, Folder 11.

221. August 11, Field diary, July-August 1956, LC.

222. Sidney Robertson Cowell to Harold Spivacke, July 20, 1956, LC.

223. Field diary, August 11, 1956, LC.

224. Ibid.

225. "[Bairbre Keane's] uncle is one of the famous singers of Ireland, long known to every collector." (Sidney Robertson Cowell, undated reminiscences titled "IRELAND," LC).

226. On August 11, 1956, Sidney wrote in her field diary: "A cross lady outside the door is objecting to the places Seán [Ó Gaora] has been taking "the Yank with the box" to and advocating her husband's tales and songs. . . . There's really quite a fuss going on outside, more than one indignant voice. Personal ambition is cloaked behind village patriotism, in a 'what has Ard-West got that we don't have in G?' form. I think I'd better just leave Seán and Mrs. Geary to handle 'em—the story of course is: 'If not this time why perhaps I'll be back—I'm promised all my time to the people I heard at the Feis—of course if Mr. Green had sung at the Feis I'd have planned to visit him—It's too bad!' Promises (but not exact hours or days) are taken very seriously and must never be broken—People talk very fast and snarly toned in Connemara anyway, so they may not be as cross as I think.

"Later, No, they weren't expecially [*sic*] cross, just having word firmly for me lest they be neglected. I can't go everywhere, alas, so must choose according to local reputation for large repertory, popularity, prevalence of sean-nós (*old* songs, traditional ones), and most active singing trad[ition]. in the home" (LC).

227. FW-ASCH-RR-5241, RR.

228. Sidney Robertson Cowell, undated reminiscences titled "IRELAND," LC.

229. See Uí Ógáin, "A Job with No Clock," 13; FW-ASCH-RR-5239, RR; FW-ASCH-RR-5249, RR.

230. AFS 11,341A, LC.

231. uí Ógáin, *Mise an fear ceoil,* 412; FW-ASCH-RR-5239, RR. Through a slip of the tongue on the part of Jackie Geary, who called Pádraig by the name of "Joe Keane" while he was recording an introduction to one of Barbara's performances, Sidney mistakenly documented that this recording was made in the house of Barbara's uncle "Joe Keane" when, in fact, it was made in the family home in Maíros. I am grateful to Josie Sheáin Jeaic Mac Donncha (1943–2017) for helping to correctly identify the people and the houses in which Sidney recorded in Carna (in discussion with the author, January 16, 2010).

232. Sidney Robertson Cowell, undated reminiscences titled "IRELAND," LC. Seán Ó Conghaoile's recollections contradict Sidney's: he says they did not stay overnight in Carna (in discussion, November 2009). Sidney seems here to confuse the location of Colm's house with that of his brother Pádraig's house in Maíros, which was not quite as close to the shoreline as she depicts.

233. uí Ógáin, "Conamara Singer and His Collector."

234. Connemara C, Side 1, RR.

235. Sidney Robertson Cowell to Henry Cowell, July 30, 1956, LC. Dara Beag Ó Fáthartaigh of Inis Meáin recalls that his sister Peige Dara Pheigín later made a red flannel skirt for Sidney and sent it to her in America (phone discussion with the author, March 15, 2010).

236. Field diary, July–August 1956, LC.

237. Field diary, August 4, 1956, LC.

238. Ibid.

239. I am grateful to Mairéad Conneely of Inis Meáin and MacDara Ó Conaola of Inis Oírr for helping to identify the performers (respective phone and email discussions, April 17, 2008, and May 12, 2009); and also to Dara Beag Ó Fáthartaigh (interview by the author, September 24, 2010).

240. Sidney Robertson Cowell, undated reminiscences titled "IRELAND," LC; AFS 11,342B and 11,343A, LC.

241. AFS 11,342B8-10, LC; FW-ASCH-RR-5244, RR. The Library of Congress online catalog incorrectly lists Mary Faherty's surname as Farquey.

242. Dara Beag Ó Fáthartaigh, interview.

243. Ibid.

244. Ibid.

245. In discussion with the author, September 1, 2009.

246. Dara told Sidney that he had already recorded two of his own compositions, "Amhrán an Dún Aengus" and "Dún Chonchubhair," for "the radio," but it is unclear whether he recorded them for the BBC in 1949 or 1950 or for RÉ in 1956. These earlier

recordings of Dara do not survive, and there is no record of them in the catalogs of the BBC or RTÉ.

247. AFS 11,343A8, LC. See also NFC 90: 478–80; NFC 786: 267–68; NFC CB0146.1.

248. Dara Beag Ó Fatharta [Fáthartaigh], *Cloch an Fhaoileáin* (Indreabhán: Clódóirí Lurgan, 1982), 34–35; ibid., 14–15; ibid., 11–13.

249. AFS 11,343A5, LC. See also NFC T0028; Tadhg Seoighe Collection G4, James Hardiman Library, National University Ireland Galway (hereafter NUIG); Norbert Sheerin, *Renmore and Its Environs: An Historical Perspective* (Galway: Renmore Residents' Association, 2000), 110–11.

250. Dara Beag Ó Fáthartaigh suspected this may have been performed by Peigí Teaimín (interview). It could also have been Peigí Sheáin Pheaidí Ní Mheachair.

251. Breandán Ó Madagáin, *Caointe agus Seancheolta Eile/Keening and Other Old Irish Musics* (Indreabhán: Cló Iar-Chonnacht, 2005), 81.

252. Ibid.

253. Keening was performed more recently by Treasa Ní Cheannabháin in Robert Quinn's film adaptation of Máirtín Ó Cadhain's masterpiece, *Cré na Cille* (Rosg for TG4 and BCI, 2007). That same year, Lillis Ó Laoire wrote: "I am able to report that the practice of keening has not completely disappeared in Tory" (*On a Rock*, 273).

254. Mairéad Uí Choncheanainn (b. 1925) recalls hearing keening in Mainistir, Árainn, at a wake in the 1960s (in discussion with the author, November 26, 2009). Maggie Dainín Uí Fhlaithearta of Bun Gabhla, Árainn, recalls hearing keening at her father's funeral in 1968 (in discussion with the author, February 25, 2010).

255. I am grateful to Anna Bale of the NFC for assisting my efforts to enumerate the extant sound recordings of caoineadh.

256. RTÉ B692; see Méadhbh Nic an Airchinnigh, "Caointeoireacht na Gaeilge: Béalaireacht agus Litearthacht" (PhD diss., National University Ireland Galway, 2012), 21.

257. "Reports of the Islands and Coast Society, 1843–50" [1843], in *An Aran Reader*, ed. Breandán Ó hEithir and Ruairí Ó hEithir (Dublin: Lilliput Press, 1991), 23–24; Ó Gramhnaigh, "Ára na Naomh," 54; Alfred Cort Haddon and Charles R. Browne, "The Ethnography of the Aran Islands, County Galway," *Proceedings of the Royal Irish Academy* 37–39 (1891–93): 812; Ní Fhaircheallaigh, *Smuainte ar Árainn*, 53; John Millington Synge, "The Last Fortress of the Celt," *The Gael* (April 1901): 109–12; Synge, *Aran Islands*, 30–32, 88, and 112–14; Henry Cecil Watson, *Inis Meáin Images: Ten Days in August 1912* (Dublin: Wolfhound Press, 1999), 42.

258. Sidney Robertson Cowell to Harold Spivacke, received May 31, 1956, LC.

259. Cowell, *Songs of Aran*, 11. Brett Topping gives the following description of the Molokans and their liturgical music: "The Molokans, a breakaway sect from the Russian Orthodox Church, believe that the entire congregation should participate in the church service, conducted in Russian. Their singing uses psalm texts and other biblical passages. As with 'lining-out' hymns in Anglo-American and Afro-American

traditions, Molokan songs are intoned by a precentor, after which the congregation joins in" ("Cowell Collection," 5).

260. Field diary, June 17, 1955, LC; FW-ASCH-RR-5256, RR; BLSA 9CL0028665 (BBC 22405).

261. Notes, Reel 10, June 17, 1955, FW-ASCH-RR-5256, RR.

262. Field diary, August 4, 1956, LC.

263. LT-10 7184 Ireland, Aran Isles, Keening (traditional singing). Performer: Maggie Dirrane. Original in: LJ-12 1812. Henry Cowell Collection, Rodgers and Hammerstein Archives of Recorded Sound, New York Public Library for the Performing Arts.

264. Reel 10, FW-ASCH-RR-5256–05, RR; NFC C0714; Reel 14, FW-ASCH-RR-5259, RR; NFC C0.

265. Information courtesy of Mícheál Tom Burke Ó Conghaile, September 2007.

266. "Bhuel bhí daoine roimpi sin a bhí fiú, deir siad, níos fearr aríst ná í ag caoineadh, glór níos binne acu" [Well there were people before her who were even, they said, better again at keening than her, they had a sweeter voice] (interview with Pádraig Ó hEithir by Proinsias Ó Conluain, first broadcast March 3, 1972, RTÉ Sound Archive BB2124). John Beag Johnny Ó Dioráin named two other women who keened: he praised Máire Chite Uí Fhlaitheartaigh of Eoghanacht (Mná Fiontracha, *Cosáin an tSaoil*, 21#18) in particular; and Neain Chitín Uí Fhlaithbheartaigh of Bun Gabhla (Mná Fiontracha, *Cosáin an tSaoil*, 9#2) (interview by Áine Pheaits Bheachlaín Uí Fhlaithearta, February 22, 2002, Bailiúchán Béaloideas Árann, minidisc 45).

267. Mullen, *Man of Aran*, 71–78, 131–32.

268. BLSA 9CL0002370 (BBC 15834); RTÉ Radio 100/68; NFC CT0467; PRONI D2833/D/4/7.

269. Cowell, *Songs of Aran*, 5–6.

270. Ibid., 6.

271. Field diary, June 17, 1955, LC.

272. Field diary, August 4, 1956, LC.

273. Cowell, *Songs of Aran*, 11.

274. Field diary, August 4, 1956, LC.

275. The text continues: "(My failure to depart as I had intended led to various attempts to persuade me out of what was assumed to be a superstitious fear of travelling on a boat that had just carried a corpse. On the next trip of the *Dún Aengus*, a vacationing priest was due to travel home from the Big Island, and several people kindly brought me word of this so I might feel reassured about the trip.)" (Field diary, August 4, 1956, LC).

276. Sidney Robertson Cowell to Henry Cowell, July 30, 1956, LC.

277. Field diary, August 4, 1956, LC.

278. It is unclear whether it was Sidney or Frances Flaherty who took this photograph. Flaherty permitted Sidney to use some of her images of Aran for the album (Cowell, *Songs of Aran*, 7).

279. Cowell, *Songs of Aran*, 2.

280. Mullen, *Man of Aran*.

281. Cowell, *Songs of Aran*, 6.

282. Recording log 5, LC. Ennis's comments do not appear to be in his own handwriting.

283. Recording log 2, LC.

284. Field diary, June 17, 1955, LC.

285. Bailiúchán Bhairbre (hereafter BB), Tape 1A; Deirdre Ní Chonghaile, minidisc 14.

286. *Songs of Aran*, Folkways 1957 (FM4002).

287. Sidney Robertson Cowell to Folkways, July 26, 1956, LC. See Veronica Kennedy, *Dandy, Dandy; Ailiú Aonaigh* (78rpm record, Gael Linn, 1950s); Kennedy, "Petrie Manuscripts"; Veronica Ní Chinnéide, "The Sources of Moore's Melodies," *The Journal of the Royal Society of Antiquaries of Ireland* 89, part II (1959): 109–34; Veronica Kennedy, "Thomas Moore and the Irish tradition," *The Thomas Davis Lectures*, Series 22, Irish Traditional Music, Radio Éireann, January 24, 1960; Sr. Veronica Ní Chinnéide, *Salm Caintic Cruit* (Baile Átha Cliath: Iníonacha na Carthanachta, 1992); Sr. Veronica Ní Chinnéide, *Salm Caintic Cruit II* (Baile Átha Cliath: Iníonacha na Carthanachta, 2003).

288. Field diary, June 17, 1955, LC. Here she refers to the "Galway Bay" written by Dr. Arthur Colahan (1884–1952) in 1927, not the "Galway Bay" composed by Francis Fahy (1854–1935) sometime between 1887 and 1935, probably around 1910 (Caoilte Breatnach, email message to author, December 3, 2009). See Various, "The Ould Plaid Shawl Songs of Francis Fahy," Francis A. Fahy Society, FAF01, 2001.

289. Cowell, *Songs of Aran*, 6.

290. Ibid., 8, 5.

291. Sidney writes: "You might be interested in listening to Sean Dirrane and the family of Sean Colm McDonogh in Carna, Connemara, to hear (if you have n't heard it before) the decorate [*sic*] musical style that lies behind our oldest singers in the South" (letter to Harold Spivacke, September 10, 1956, LC).

292. Cowell, *Songs of Aran*, 6.

293. Field diary, August 11, 1956, LC.

294. Máirtín Ó Fátharta [Meaití Jó Shéamuis], "Amhránaíocht."

295. Ciarán Mac Mathúna might be cited here as an exception among professional collectors, as John Bowman observes: "'Good, bad or indifferent.' Ciarán Mac Mathúna recorded all comers on the basis that a man who was playing a tune he had learned from his grandfather might well be leaving us the only version of that tune, or a local variant, or establishing that the tune, perhaps thought to have been only played in Munster, was now to be found in the north of the country too. All recordings had value, and even if you couldn't always exhaustively evaluate them now, to capture them on sound

was better than the alternative—silence, loss" (John Bowman, *Ciarán Mac Mathúna*, December 20, 2009).

296. See lists of Irish and American women collectors compiled by the author, available at Irish Traditional Music Archive, June 2021, https://www.itma.ie/blog/sidney -robertson-cowell.

Chapter 4. Bairbre Quinn and Bailiúchán Bhairbre

1. Just a few days earlier, Sidney had bought from Bairbre gifts to present to her contributors. In a field diary extract dated Thursday, June 16, she wrote: "Maggie [Dirrane] asked [me] for ninepence of peppermints but Barbara had only barley sugar drops" (LC). In another diary extract dated Friday, June 17, Sidney wrote that she bought a bottle of whiskey from Bairbre (LC). The whiskey was intended to encourage John Beag Johnny Ó Dioráin and Pádraig Mhurchadha de Bhailís to sing for Sidney's tape recorder.

Throughout this chapter, her first name, Bairbre, is used instead of the surname Quinn because the discussion spans her collecting career during which she was known by two names—Bairbre Ní Chonghaile and Bairbre Quinn. To her family she was known as Barbara, but as the first public presentation of her collection occurred through Irish on RTÉ Raidió na Gaeltachta, I have maintained the use of Bairbre in all print discussions to ensure a consistent discoverability.

2. Bailiúchán Bhairbre is the name I have given to the collection of tapes created by Bairbre Quinn. *Bailiúchán Bhairbre* is the radio series that Máirtín Jaimsie Ó Flaithbheartaigh and the author created for RTÉ Raidió na Gaeltachta in 2006.

3. Tape 6 may have been recorded in 1968 or sometime thereafter when Bairbre's relatives, the Gill family, moved to Cill Mhuirbhigh; Ronan Gill reckoned the tape was recorded earlier in Dublin (in discussion with the author, January 21, 2008).

4. Hugh Cheape comments in relation to the work of the Scottish scholar and collector John Lorne Campbell: "With [John 'Coddy' Macpherson], and other Barra notables such as Neil Sinclair, the Sgoilear Ruadh, and Annie and Calum Johnston, [John Lorne Campbell] began to explore this unusual world of the Hebrides, then still, as in his own words, 'like the old Highlands of the early 19th century.' Here Campbell became the pioneer of the modern collection and preservation of Gaelic song and story. He worked outside the conventional institutional framework of the universities, which arguably has given his work a freshness of approach in the study of Gaelic literature and history" (Hugh Cheape, "Obituary: John Lorne Campbell," *London Independent*, May 2, 1996).

5. For Conamara, see Micheál Ó Conghaile, *Croch Suas É!* (1986; repr., Indreabhán: Cló Iar-Chonnacht, 2003, 233). In the same period in County Clare, the population fell from 112,334 in 1901 to 77,176 in 1956 to 75,008 in 1971 (http://www.clarelibrary .ie/eolas/coclare/history/faqs/18212006.htm). See Gearóid Ó hAllmhuráin, *Flowing

Tides: History and Memory in an Irish Soundscape (New York: Oxford University Press, 2016).

6. Mná Fiontracha, ed., *Ár nOileán Tuile 's Trá* (Árainn: Bailiúchán Béaloideas Árann, 2004), 16.

7. The competition between both forms of entertainment in the home—house visiting and television—is represented graphically on Tape 32 where a television can be heard in the background as Nóirín Mhary Johnny Phádraig of Ros Muc sings "Tá na Páipéir dá Saighneáil."

8. Deirdre Ní Chonghaile, "An Teach Ósta: Tinteán an Cheoil Thraidisiúnta?," in *Bliainiris 7*, ed. Liam Mac Cóil and Ruairí Ó hUiginn (Ráth Chairn, Co. Meath: Carbad, 2007), 72–84.

9. Stiophán Ó Conghaile, interview by the author, September 15, 2006.

10. The hotel Teach Furbo was then run by Des Kelly, who was a founding member of the Capitol Showband. It is now called the Connemara Coast Hotel.

11. 1901 census record for house 22, Kilmurvey, Inishmore, Co. Galway (http://cen sus.nationalarchives.ie/pages/1901/Galway/Inishmore/Kilmurvy/1376193/); 1911 census record for house 18, Kilmurvey, Inishmore, Co. Galway (http://census.national archives.ie/pages/1911/Galway/Inishmore/Kilmurvy/456165/), National Archives of Ireland.

12. Robert Flaherty, *Man of Aran* (Gainsborough Pictures, 1934).

13. Mná Fiontracha, *Cosáin an tSaoil*, 31#19.

14. Maura Conneely, "Nótaí Nana—An Islandwoman's Life" (unpublished reminiscences, 1986).

15. Máirtín Ó Conghaile, in discussion with the author, April 21, 2008.

16. BB, Tape 1; Máirtín Ó Conghaile, in discussion with the author, January 22, 2008.

17. Bairbre's brother Stiophán explains how they learned English: "Ní raibh sé againn ag dul ag an scoil, ach d'fhoghlaim muinn ó na cuairteoirí é." (We did not have it going to school, but we learned it from the visitors) (Ó Conghaile, interview).

18. Conneely, "Nótaí Nana"; information courtesy of Máirtín Ó Conghaile and Mary Conneely. See Brendan Behan, *The Confessions of an Irish Rebel* (London: Hutchinson, 1965), 249.

19. Ó Conghaile, interview.

20. Ibid.

21. He is referring to the handball alley in Cill Mhuirbhigh.

22. Pierre Travassac, *Les Îles Aran Scènes et paysages d'Irlande* (Paris: Imprimerie Centrale de Paris, 1960), 72–73.

23. Translation by Olof Gill.

24. Conneely, "Nótaí Nana."

25. BB, Tapes 1 and 38.

26. Cóilín Ó Ceallaigh, in conversation with the author, March 3, 2010.

27. Bairbre's name appears in the roll book of September 1961. Bríd or Bridie Ní Fhátharta was school principal; her father, Pádraig Bhile Ó Fátharta from Cor na Rón, was police sergeant for a time in Árainn.

28. Deirdre Ní Chonghaile (presenter) and Máirtín Jaimsie Ó Flaithbheartaigh (producer), *Bailiúchán Bhairbre*, Episode 1, November 26, 2006, RTÉ Raidió na Gaeltachta (hereafter RnaG).

29. Ibid.

30. BB, Tape 19.

31. Bairbre Tónaí Ní Fhlatharta was a member of the prize-winning choir Cór Árann na Naomh that was victorious at Feis Chonnacht in 1904 (Antoine Powell, *Oileáin Árann Stair na n-oileán anuas go dtí 1922* (Dublin: Wolfhound, 1984), 89. Nell Quinn (1913–2009) recalled that she used to sing "Lay Him Away on the Hillside."

32. Paddy Quinn, interview by the author, September 21, 2006.

33. Máirtín Jaimsie Ó Flaithbheartaigh, phone discussion with the author, September 21, 2010.

34. Information courtesy of Mary Conneely, March 2008.

35. Ó Conghaile, interview.

36. BB, Tape 26. It was recorded sometime in the early 1970s.

37. "Bhí sí an-ghéimiúil, caithfidh mé [a rá], bhíodh gáire ar a béal i gcónaí" (Ní Chonghaile and Ó Flaithbheartaigh, *Bailiúchán Bhairbre*, Episode 1, November 26, 2006, RnaG).

38. BB, Tape 32.

39. Ó Conghaile, interview.

40. Glassie, *Passing the Time*, 36–37, 141.

41. BB, Tape 24. Patsy also made recordings in Árainn to bring with him on his return to Africa. The fate of his tapes—which were in storage in Bacita, Nigeria—is unknown (letter to the author, September 14, 2007). See Pádraig O'Toole, *Aran to Africa: An Irishman's Unique Odyssey* (Nuascéalta, 2013).

42. Tape 22 consists of recordings of music from the radio and, perhaps, the television, and Paddy playing the accordion. Side A of Tape 23 contains recordings of Bairbre's children Mary and Teresa singing. Side B is blank. Side A of Tape 36 contains a Christmas letter to American relatives recorded in Aran. Side B is blank.

43. BB, Tape 6.

44. BB, Tape 26; Tape 36. I was unable to establish who recorded Tape 36 because I had difficulties in listening to it. I have yet to determine the exact speed at which it was recorded.

45. Séamas Ó Direáin's linguistic study of the Aran Islands provides the basis for this methodology (*Survey*).

46. Mná Fiontracha, *Cosáin an tSaoil*, 31#19, 31#44, 21#19, 25#16. An Cuan is a small house by the beach at Cill Mhuirbhigh. From May 1969, Bairbre's sister Mary opened a "nightclub" therein on summer nights at 11 p.m., Monday to Saturday, to sell tea, soup,

and sandwiches after the pubs had closed. Some revelers secretly brought their own alcohol and often the music that had begun in Tí Chreig up the hill would continue in An Cuan. It was closed on Sunday nights because revelers were more likely to attend the céilí in the hall in Cill Rónáin.

47. Mná Fiontracha, *Cosáin an tSaoil*, 31#8, 41#13. Stiophán Ó Conghaile suggested Bairbre might have recorded in these places (Ó Conghaile, interview).

48. Mná Fiontracha, *Cosáin an tSaoil*, 65#11, 66#68, 70#129, 71#171, 87#27.

49. Johnny Mháirtín Learaí Mac Donnchadha, discussion with the author, Ní Chonghaile and Ó Flaithbheartaigh, *Bailiúchán Bhairbre*, Episode 1, November 26, 2006, RnaG.

50. See Peter Browne, *Tuning the Radio*, 6–7. John Bowman observes: "In fact, Ciarán Mac Mathúna was one of the major cultural figures of twentieth-century Ireland. He did nothing less than turn back the tide in his own field of provincialism, and when it comes to provincialism, we [the Irish] can be world-beaters, believing that London or New York or Paris or California is where it's at, and not noticing or celebrating what we already have. Ciarán noticed, celebrated, showcased and gave a platform to Irish traditional music which has transformed popular music in Ireland and beyond" (John Bowman, *Bowman: Sunday Morning: 8.30: Ciarán Mac Mathúna* [RTÉ Radio 1, December 20, 2009]). Mac Mathúna himself recognized that he was a chronicler of Irish traditional music: "Radio Éireann, later RTÉ, gave me the opportunity to explore the hidden Ireland of traditional music, song, poetry, dance and story and to share this heritage with our listeners and, later, viewers, all over the country. We were recycling heritage that was out there before us" (Peter Browne, *The Rolling Wave: In Memoriam Ciarán Mac Mathúna* [RTÉ Radio 1, December 13, 2009]).

51. Glassie, *Passing the Time*, 141. Glassie's theory is based on the following interpretation of life in Ballymenone: "The social unit is not the individual, it is the group formed by common problems and collective action. So individuals have the means to endure. If they fall, others will lift them. If they begin a dangerous fight, others will stop them. They have talent and knowledge, wit and courage, even if they do not have them in their lone selves. And if they do, they are not shot into isolation. The community is compounded of diverse excellence.

"A community conceived as a series of individuals and aspiring to equality must eliminate aristocracy in the name of democracy. The community conceived in egalitarian oneness exploits aristocracy for its own well-being. Its stories celebrate exceptional individuals: courageous characters and witty stars, saints, outlaws, heroes. "Artistic performance is the aristocratic enactment of communal will. It comes from, leads to—and is in itself—engaged union" (147).

52. Glassie, *Passing the Time*, 141.

53. Grace Toland recalls that the same purpose inspired her parents to make recordings in their pub in Clonmany, Inishowen, Co. Donegal. They bought a tape recorder in the 1960s with the purpose of enabling customers to pass the time by recording various

singers for fun. There was no thought of conservation. Instead, as was sometimes the case for Bairbre's recordings, the intention was to give people an opportunity to hear the recorded sound of their own performances and those of their friends and neighbors. At the time, Toland observes, performers in many rural, marginalized areas, including Aran and Inishowen, were rarely heard on the radio, so the tape recorder provided a welcome opportunity to experience the recorded sound of local singers (in discussion with the author, June 30, 2008).

In the 1930s the Ó Flannagáin family had a copy of Seáinín Tom Ó Dioráin's Parlophone record, *Oidhche Sheanchais,* which they played on a gramophone (Dónal Ó Flannagáin, *Ó Thrá Anoir,* 216). In 1950 some islanders in Inis Oírr overcame challenges in receiving a BBC Third Program transmission to hear the live broadcast of *The Bare Stones of Aran* (BLSA T11524R2), produced by W. R. Rodgers (M. J. Gillan letter to W. R. Rodgers, June 7, 1950, PRONI D2833/C/2/13/9). In 1956 islanders heard Pádraig Ó Raghallaigh's recordings from Aran on the Radio Éireann series *Gaeltacht na nOileán* (Ó Conluain, "Cín Lae Craoltóra, 97; Ó Raghallaigh, *Gaeltacht na nOileán*).

54. Glassie, *Passing the Time,* 469.

55. The word "recordist" is frequently used as an alternative to "collector." Here, its meaning is more specific.

56. Filene, *Romancing the Folk,* 131.

57. BB, Tapes 1, 10, and 30.

58. As a recordist: BB, Tapes 3–5, 7, 9–15, 17, 19–21, 23, 27, 29, 31–34, 37–41, and 43–44. As a collector: BB, Tapes 3, 18–20, 29–30, 32, 40, and 42.

59. Glassie, *Passing the Time,* 37.

60. Ó Conghaile, interview.

61. Ibid., 102, 472.

62. See Lillis Ó Laoire, "Ceathrar banamhránaithe i ndialanna Sheáin Uí Eochaidh," in *Binneas an tSiansa: Aistí in onóir do Ríonach uí Ógáin,* ed. Kelly Fitzgerald, Bairbre Ní Fhloinn, Meidhbhín Ní Úrdail, and Anne O'Connor (Baile Átha Cliath: Comhairle Bhéaloideas Éireann and Four Courts Press, 2019), 160–77.

63. Ó Laoire, *On a Rock,* xiv.

64. Ibid., 258.

65. Ibid.

66. Glassie, *Passing the Time,* 37.

67. This recording has been dated according to the rest of the material on the tape. A database of recordings created at the Scoileanna Éigse agus Seanchais of Conamara and Árainn, recordings that are now held by National University Ireland Galway, reveals that Matt twice submitted "Oileán Glas Árann na Naomh" to the competition for newly composed ballads: his 1962 performance was recorded by Prof. Liam Ó Buachalla in An Cnoc, Indreabhán (RG08A; CD012/B); and his 1967 performance was recorded by Patsy Nic Fhlannchadha, also in An Cnoc, Indreabhán (RG05B; CD007/O).

68. BB, Tapes 3, 18, 19, 20, 29, 30, 32, 40, and 42.

69. Fionnuala: BB, Tape 29; Mary Folan: BB, Tape 3; and the young woman: BB, Tape 20.

70. John Beag Johnny Ó Dioráin: BB, Tape 1 (see also Treasa Ní Mhiolláin, *Lán Mara* [Cló Iar-Chonnacht CICD208, 2019]); Matt Neainín Ó Maoláin: BB, Tape 19; Cóilín Mhicilín Ó hIarnáin: BB, Tape 18. See extract from *Bailiúchán Bhairbre* on the compilation CD *ICTM Ireland Fieldwork*, Track 8 (Various, *ICTM Ireland Fieldwork*, ed. Desi Wilkinson [ICTM Ireland, 2013]).

71. BB, Tape 14; Tape 9.

72. BB, Tape 9.

73. BB, Tape 34; Tapes 4 and 5; Tape 42; Tapes 37 and 43; Tape 19.

74. BB, Tapes 2, 14, and 42; Tapes 17, 19, and 20; Tape 41; Tape 30; Tapes 30 and 41; Tape 6; Tape 10. The recordings that sound distorted (because the recording machine battery was dying) appear to have been made by Bairbre's husband, Paddy, and not by Bairbre (BB, Tapes 21, 39, and 40).

75. BB, Tape 32; Tapes 7, 34, and 43; Tape 34.

76. BB, Tape 17.

77. BB, Tape 18.

78. BB, Tape 32. Fr. Connolly or Stiofán Ó Conghaile (1893–1965) was a Redemptorist priest who is still known throughout Conamara as "sagart an phoitín" (the poteen priest) because of his vociferous opposition to illicit liquor. Séamus Ennis attended one of his mission masses on November 14, 1943, in Carna: "Cainteoir breá é ach ní maith leis na daoine é, de réir mar chluinimse, mar gheall ar an gcaint mhaslaíoch a bhíonn aige ón altóir leo. Tá neart cloiste agam faoi le cúpla lá" (He is a good speaker but the people dislike him, as I hear, because of his derisive talk from the altar to them. I have heard lots about him these past few days) (uí Ógáin, *"Mise an fear ceoil,"* 113–14). See Diarmuid Breathnach and Máire Ní Mhurchú, "Ó Conghaile, Stiofán (1893–1965)," *Ainm.ie*, https://www.ainm.ie/Bio.aspx?ID=1186.

79. BB, Tape 21.

80. BB, Tape 9.

81. BB, Tapes 1, 2, 4, 6, 8, 9, 10, 14, 18, 20, 30, 32, 33, 39, 41, 43, and 44.

82. Bairbre's recording of Nóra Pheaits Sheáin Mhic Dhonnchadha née Ní Chonghaola (1894–1960s) of Creig an Chéirín talking and singing three songs in the guesthouse may represent one other such recording (BB, Tape 7). Nóra had probably come to collect her pension at the post office that day (in conversation with Máirtín Jaimsie Ó Flaithbheartaigh, October 2006).

83. Ó Conghaile, interview.

84. BB, Tape 30.

85. By 1911 Fr. Luke Donnellan had recorded at least two Aran islanders on wax cylinders: Maria Gorham in Cill Rónáin and Mrs. Flaherty of Baile an Chaisleáin, Inis Oírr (Luke Donnellan, "The Coulin," *Journal of the County Louth Archaeological Society* 3, no. 1 [December 1912]: 11–15; Luke Donnellan, "Eibhlin a Rúin," *Journal of the County*

Louth Archaeological Society 2, no. 4 [November 1911]: 417–25). In 1926 Seáinín Tom Ó Dioráin appears to have been recorded by Gen. Richard Mulcahy in Sruthán, Árainn (Ó Flannagáin, *Ó Thrá Anoir*, 116–17). He also recorded for Parlophone Records in London in January 1934. Later that year, Maggie Dirrane and Micilín Dillane were recorded in New York by Henry Cowell and Charles Seeger. The BBC and Radio Éireann brought the first disc-cutting equipment to Aran in November 1949. Sidney Robertson Cowell appears to be the first person to bring a magnetic reel-to-reel tape recorder to the islands in 1955 and 1956. Expanding this question to include sound film, two early examples include Fox Movietone News, which filmed sean-nós singing and dancing in Eoghanacht in May 1929, and Norris Davidson, who collaborated with local poets Tomás and Antaine Ó Briain to film *Damhsa Árann* in Cill Éinne in the summer of 1934.

86. Ó Conghaile, interview.

87. Confirming which of Bairbre's recordings were made surreptitiously is fraught with difficulty. As there is no written indication identifying them, the author relied on anecdotal evidence from people who recalled that surreptitious recording had occurred and on aural interpretation of the recordings themselves.

88. Anthony Seeger, "The Role of Sound Archives in Ethnomusicology Today," *Ethnomusicology* 30, no. 2 (Spring–Summer 1986): 271.

89. Paddy recalled how Maidhcilín Gill listened to his own performance of "Danny Boy" in the American Bar, and praised the voice on tape, not realizing it was his own (Quinn, interview).

90. See Ní Chonghaile and Ó Flaithbheartaigh, *Bailiúchán Bhairbre*; Deirdre Ní Chonghaile, "Broadcasting *Bailiúchán Bhairbre*: Researching and Representing Record-ings via Radio," in *Ancestral Imprints: Histories of Irish Traditional Music and Dance*, ed. Thérèse Smith (Cork: Cork University Press, 2012), 118–27.

91. Ibid.

92. BB, Tapes 25 and 29; Quinn, interview.

93. BB, Tape 16.

94. BB, Tape 39.

95. "Oh it was a small miracle at that time" (Quinn, interview).

96. On one occasion, Tom Beatty jokingly referred to the microphone and the machine as the telephone. Signing off from his audio greetings to friends in America, he said: "This is Tom Beatty leaving the phone!" (BB, Tape 5).

97. BB, Tapes 5, 13, and 15.

98. BB, Tape 26.

99. Information courtesy of Sarah Dan Uí Fhlaithearta and Patsy Ó Tuathail.

100. The practice of recording audio letters was probably widespread. Tom Biuso gives evidence of their occurrence in the Blasket Islands: "Inquiries of the local natives who were former inhabitants of the Blaskets assured me that written correspondence with relatives in Springfield had always been maintained, and that until recently, when

magnetic tape began to be used, there was a constant flow of written communication between all of West Kerry and the Springfield Area" (Tom Biuso, "Tom Biuso," *An Caomhnóir* 29 [2008]: 13).

101. BB, Tape 1; Tape 4; Tapes 9 and 14; Tapes 18 and 19; Tape 10; Tape 20; Tape 30; Tape 32.

102. BB, Tape 33; Tape 33; Tape 2; Tape 30; Tape 33.

103. BB, Tape 6; Tape 9; Tape 8.

104. BB, Tape 2; Tape 3.

105. BB, Tape 4; Tape 9; Tape 3; Tape 17; Tape 29. Stiophán Ó Conghaile was one of the islanders who attended dances at the Hanger Ballroom (Ó Conghaile, interview). See BB, Tape 28.

106. BB, Tapes 7, 9, 12, 15, 17, 19, 29, 35, 38, and 44; information on Halla Rónáin courtesy of Máire Uí Chonghaile.

107. BB, Tapes 7, 23, 27, 29, and 38.

108. BB, Tape 7; Tape 18; Tape 12; Tape 9; Tape 25; Tape 28.

109. BB, Tape 2.

110. uí Ógáin, *"Mise an fear ceoil,"* 15.

111. Johnny Joyce, interview by the author, September 2, 2001. In recent years, Johnny has taken to learning songs including "Tomás Bán Mac Aogáin" and "Púcán Mhicil Pháidín." "Caithfidh mé a rá, tá an-suim go deo agam anois iontu ach, coinneoidh mé orm. An fhad a bheidh's mé in ann iad a fhoghlaim, beidh mé á bhfoghlaim. Tá mé ag foghlaim cúpla ceann faoi láthair anois . . ." (I must say, I am now exceedingly interested in them but, I will continue. For as long as I can learn them, I will be learning them. I am learning a few at the moment now . . .).

112. BB, Tapes 11, 33, 34, and 39.

113. Irish music had the power to make island emigrants and their descendants long to be in Aran. Bailiúchán Bhairbre poignantly represents the harsh reality of their homesickness in audio letters and in recordings of parties, which were intended to bring some of the atmosphere back to their adopted homes. Sometimes the recordings bear witness to their regret, resentment, and resignation. At a party held in his sister Nell Quinn's house in honor of his departure, Jack Folan recorded some greetings and some commentary on the raucous scene of music and dance before him; he spoke of his imminent return to his emigrant life in Boston: "I'm sorry to be going back, but I have to—I have no choice" (BB, Tape 5).

114. Ó Conghaile, interview.

115. Treasa Ní Mhiolláin, "An Sean Nós," in *Ár nOileán Tuile 's Trá*, ed. Mná Fiontracha (Árainn: Bailiúchán Béaloideas Árann, 2004), 25.

116. See Kay Anderson and Susan J. Smith, "Editorial: Emotional Geographies," *Transactions of the Institute of British Geographers*, n.s. 26, no. 1 (2001): 7–10.

117. The absence of a recording by Maggie Dirrane in Bailiúchán Bhairbre is probably due to Maggie omitting herself from Bairbre's localized recording project. The

performances Maggie contributed to the recording machines of Henry Cowell and Sidney Robertson Cowell were exceptional. In Aran, she was inclined to present other singers, better singers to her mind—her son John Beag Johnny and Pádraig Mhurchadha, for instance—as possible candidates for recording.

118. Seán Ó Conghaoile, in discussion with the author, September 21, 2010.

CONCLUSION

1. Filene, *Romancing the Folk,* 7; Glassie, *Passing the Time,* 33.
2. Filene, *Romancing the Folk.*
3. Cowell, *Songs of Aran.*
4. Filene, *Romancing the Folk,* 131.
5. Ibid.

APPENDIX 1. ANALYSIS OF PETRIE AND O'CURRY 1857 ARAN MANUSCRIPTS

1. Micheál Ó hEidhin, *Cas Amhrán* (1975; repr., Indreabhán: Cló-Iar Chonnacht, 1990), 60; Sidney Robertson Cowell, ed., *Songs of Aran* (Ethnic Folkways Library FE4002, 1957).

2. David Cooper, *The Petrie Collection of the Ancient Music of Ireland* (Cork: Cork University Press, 2002), 17.

3. Marian Deasy, "New Edition of Airs and Dance Tunes from the Music Manuscripts of George Petrie LL.D., and a Survey of His Work as a Collector of Irish Folk Music" (PhD diss., University College Dublin, 1982), 1.ii.

4. Cooper, *Petrie Collection,* 23; Donal O'Sullivan, *Irish Folk Music, Song and Dance* [*Ceol, Amhránaíocht agus Rince na hÉireann*] (1952; repr., Cork: Published for the Cultural Relations Committee of Ireland by the Mercier Press, 1974), 19.

5. Tom Munnelly, "George Petrie: Distorting the Voice of the People?," *JMI* 3, no. 2 (January/February 2003), 17.

6. James O'Brien Moran, "Paddy Conneely—The Galway Piper: The Legacy of a Pre-Famine Folk Musician" (PhD diss., University of Limerick, 2006), 120.

7. Ibid., 119.

8. "Ailein Duinn O Hì Shiùbhlainn Leat" sung by Captain Donald Joseph MacKinnon, recorded in 1960 by Dr. John MacInnes (1930–2019). Original Track ID: SA1960.225.A2; Track ID: 75575, Tobar an Dualchais/Kist o' Riches, School of Scottish Studies, University of Edinburgh, accessed July 9, 2020, http://tobarandualchais.co.uk/en/fullrecord/75575. See also "Morrison, Allan, c. 1730–1768 (Ailean Donn | sea captain | Crosbost | Isle of Lewis)," Carmichael-Watson Collection, Edinburgh University Library Special Collections Repository, https://archives.collections.ed.ac.uk/agents/people/3543; notes on "Ailein Duinn, o hó hì, shiùbhlainn leat," John Lorne Campbell, ed. and trans., *Hebridean Folksong: A Collection of Waulking Songs by Donald MacCormick* (Oxford: Clarendon, 1969), 161–62.

9. Deasy, "Petrie," 1.180.

10. Eibhlín Bean Mhic Choisdealbha, ed., *Amhráin Mhuighe Seóla: Traditional Folksongs from Galway and Mayo* (1923; repr., Indreabhán: Cló Iar-Chonnacht, 1990), 6.

11. In the context of this book, which regularly compares multiforms of melodies and songs, the term "version" is problematic because it infers that there is an Ur-form to which all "versions" might be traced. The term "multiform" avoids the inference and is, therefore, more accurate. Throughout this work, however, in deference to the local lexicon—in which the less specific Irish term *leagan* is consistently translated as "version"—I usually decline the scholarly "multiform" and choose instead the more colloquial "version."

12. Richard Henebry, *A Handbook of Irish Music* (Dublin and Cork: Cork University Press; Educational Co. of Ireland; Longmans, Green and Co. Ltd., 1928), 102, cited in Deasy, "Petrie," 2.416.

13. Pádraigín Ní Uallacháin, *A Hidden Ulster: People, Songs and Traditions of Oriel* (Dublin: Four Courts Press, 2003), 244.

14. Ibid., 246.

15. Mícheál Ó Gallchobhair, "Amhráin ó Iorrus," *Béaloideas* 10, nos. 1–2 (1940): 236.

16. Frank Harte and Donal Lunny, *Frank Harte: 1798—The First Year of Liberty* (Hummingbird HBCD 0014, 1998).

17. Pádraig de Brún, "Amhráin a thiomsaigh Eoghan Ó Comhraí," *Ceol* 4, no. 4 (1981): 117.

Bibliography

PRIMARY SOURCES

Ireland

Aran Islands
    Bailiúchán Bhairbre, Árainn
    Bailiúchán Béaloideas Árann, Mná Fiontracha, Fearann an Choirce, Árainn
    Conneely, Maura. "Nótaí Nana—An Islandwoman's Life." Unpublished reminiscences, 1986.
    Leabhar na gCuairteoirí: Teach Uí Chonghaoile, Cill Mhuirbhigh, Árainn, ca. 1933–86
    Local folklore collection, Coláiste Naomh Éinne, Cill Rónáin, Árainn
    Teach an tSagairt, Cill Rónáin, Árainn
        Leabhair Póstaí (1872–)
        Leabhar Pósanna (1905–)
        Leabhar Básanna (1920–)
Dublin Institute of Advanced Studies
Irish Traditional Music Archive (ITMA)
Maynooth University: Russell Library
    Eugene O'Curry manuscripts
National Archives of Ireland
National Library of Ireland (NLI)
    George Petrie Music manuscripts, MS 9,278–MS 9,280, 3 vols. of Irish tunes, with an index of titles
National University of Ireland, Galway: James Hardiman Library, Special Collections (NUIG)
    Scoileanna Éigse agus Seanchais of Conamara and Árainn, recordings
    Tadhg Seoighe Collection G4
Royal Irish Academy (RIA)
    George Petrie manuscripts RIA 12 N 5, 178–79

Trinity College Dublin: Berkeley Library; Manuscripts and Archives Research Library,
The Old Library, Special Collections
  John Millington Synge Collection, MS 4328–4429
  Manuscripts of George Petrie and his family, MS 3562–3566
University College Dublin: The Library, Special Collections
  Eugene O'Curry manuscripts
University College Dublin, Delargy Center for Irish Folklore and the National Folklore
Collection (NFC)
  Bailiúchán na Scol, 1937–38
  Séamus Ennis, *Amhráin as Árainn*, 1945

United Kingdom

Belfast
  Public Record Office of Northern Ireland (PRONI): W. R. Rodgers Collection,
  PRONI D2833
Edinburgh
  University of Edinburgh: Carmichael-Watson Collection Coll-97, University Library
  University of Edinburgh: Tobar an Dualchais/Kist o' Riches, School of Scottish
  Studies
London
  Ralph Vaughan Williams Library, Cecil Sharp House: Maud Karpeles Manuscript
  Collection, MK/1/4/5349–5352
  British Library: British Library Sound Archive (BLSA)
Caversham, Reading
  BBC Written Archives Center, WAC NI7 Folk Music & Dialect Recording Scheme

Europe

Copenhagen, Denmark
  Holger Pedersen papers, Royal Library, Copenhagen, NKS 2718 folio
Leipzig, Germany
  Universitaetsbibliothek Leipzig (Bibliotheca Albertina) (UBL): O'Curry, Eugene,
  song manuscripts among the Stokes Family notebooks, NL 291/634, 123–32

United States

Bloomington, Indiana
  Indiana University, Archives of Traditional Music: John C. Messenger Ireland
  recordings, Galway, Donegal, Mayo and Clare Counties, 1959–64. ATL6072
  EC3964–ATL6077 EC3992; ATL6079 EC3996–3997.
New York City
  New York Public Library: Lady Augusta Gregory Collection
  New York Public Library for the Performing Arts (NYPL)

Henry Cowell Collection, LT-10 7180 and LT-10 7184, Rodgers and Hammerstein
  Archives of Recorded Sound
Henry Cowell Papers, JPB 00–03, Music Division
Washington, DC
  Library of Congress (LC)
    Alan Lomax Collections, American Folklife Center AFC 2004/004
    Sidney Robertson Cowell Irish Sound Recording Collection, American Folklife
      Center AFC 1959/004
    Sidney Robertson Cowell Collection, Music Division ML31.C78
  Ralph Rinzler Folklife Archives and Collections, The Smithsonian Center for Folk-
  life and Cultural Heritage
    Folkways Collection
    Sidney Robertson Cowell Collection

JOURNALS AND NEWSPAPERS

American Quarterly (1949–)
An Caomhnóir (1989–)
An Claidheamh Soluis (Dublin, 1899–1917)
An Gaodhal / The Gael (1881–1904)
An linn bhuí: Iris Ghaeltacht na nDéise (1997–)
An Stoc (1917–31)
Ar Aghaidh (Galway, 1931–70)
Béaloideas (Dublin, 1927–)
Béascna (2002–)
Bliainiris (1999–)
British Journal of Ethnomusicology / Ethnomusicology Forum (1992–)
California Folklore Quarterly / Western Folklore (1942–)
Cathair na Mart: Journal of the Westport Historical Society (1981–)
Ceol: A Journal of Irish Music (Dublin, 1963–86)
Chimera (Cork: Department of Geography, UCC, 1986–)
Comhar (Dublin, 1938–)
Connacht Tribune (1909–)
Dal gCais (1972–93)
Dublin Review of Books (2007–)
Dublin University Magazine (1833–82)
Dúchas 's Dóchas—Iris na nDaltaí, Coláiste Naomh Eoin (Inis Meáin, 2002–)
Duffy's Hibernian Sixpenny Magazine (1862–64)
Éire-Ireland (1966–)
Ethnomusicology (1953–)
Fáinne an Lae (Dublin, 1898–1900, 1918–19, 1922)
Feasta (Dublin, 1948–)
Foinse (An Cheathrú Rua 1996–)

Folklife Center News (1978–)

Folklore and Folk Music Archivist (1958–1968)

The Folklore Historian (1984–)

Gwerin: A Half-Yearly Journal of Folk Life / Folk Life: Journal of Ethnological Studies (1956–)

Humanities: The Magazine of the National Endowment for the Humanities (1969–)

International Journal of Traditional Arts (2017–)

The Irish Monthly (1873–1954)

Irish Press (1931–95)

The Irish Times (1859–)

Irisleabhar na Gaedhilge (Dublin, 1882–1909)

Island Studies Journal (2006–)

Journal of American Folklore (1888–)

Journal of Folklore Research (1983–)

The Journal of Music—originally *The Journal of Music in Ireland [JMI]* (Bray & An Spidéal 2000–); https://journalofmusic.com/

Journal of the American Musicological Society (1948–)

Journal of the County Louth Archaeological Society (1904–69)

Journal of the Folklore Institute (1964–82)

Journal of the Limerick Field Club (1897–1908)

The Journal of the Royal Society of Antiquaries of Ireland (1849–)

Lá (Belfast, 1984–2008)

Léachtaí Cholm Cille (Maynooth, 1970–)

Léann (2007–)

Lessons from the Edge: North Atlantic Islands Programme Distribution Newsletter (Institute of Island Studies, University of Prince Edward Island, Canada, 1994–96)

Limerick Reporter and Tipperary Vindicator (1839–96)

The Independent (London Independent) (1986–)

Midwestern Folklore (1987–)

Musical Traditions; edited by Rod Stradling (1997–); https://www.mustrad.org.uk/

New Hibernia Review (1997–)

New York Times (1851–)

North Munster Antiquarian Journal (1936–)

Notes: Quarterly Journal of the Music Library Association (1934–)

Saol na nOileán: Irisleabhar Chomhdháil Oileáin na hÉireann; published by Comharchumann Chomhdháil Oileáin na hÉireann Teo (Inis Oírr, 1994–)

Scandinavian Studies (1941–)

Shima: The International Journal of Research into Island Cultures (Sydney, Australia, 2007–)

The Sonneck Society for American Music Bulletin (1975–)

Studia Hibernica (1961–)

Transactions of the Institute of British Geographers (1965–)

Treoir (1968–)

Tuam News/Western Advertiser (Tuam, Co. Galway, 1871–1904)

Ulster Folklife (1955–2015)

Women and Music (1997–)

BOOKS AND ARTICLES

Abrahams, Roger D. "Mr. Lomax Meets Professor Kittredge." *Journal of Folklore Research* 37, nos. 2–3 (May 2000): 99–118.

Almqvist, Bo. "The Folklore Commission: Achievement and Legacy." *Béaloideas* 45–47 (1979): 6–26.

Anderson, Kay, and Susan J. Smith. "Editorial: Emotional Geographies." *Transactions of the Institute of British Geographers*, n.s. 26, no. 1 (2001): 7–10.

Arthus-Bertrand, Yann. *The Earth from the Air.* 1999. Reprint, London: Thames & Hudson, 2002.

Atkinson, Sarah. "Eugene O'Curry." *Irish Monthly* 2 (1874): 191–210.

Attali, Jacques. *Noise: The Political Economy of Music.* Theory and History of Literature 16. Translated by Brian Massumi. 1977. Reprint, Minneapolis: University of Minnesota Press, 1985.

Austin, Valerie A. "The Céilí and the Public Dance Halls Act, 1935." *Éire-Ireland* 28, no. 3 (Fall 1993): 7–16.

Baldacchino, Godfrey. "Islands, Island Studies, Island Studies Journal." *Island Studies Journal* 1, no. 1 (May 2006): 3–18.

Baldacchino, Godfrey, ed. *Island Songs: A Global Repertoire.* Lanham, MD: Scarecrow, 2011.

Banim, Mary. *Here and There through Ireland: Part II.* Reprinted from two volumes of the *Weekly Freeman.* Dublin: Freeman's Journal Printers, 1892.

Behan, Brendan. *The Confessions of an Irish Rebel.* London: Hutchinson, 1965.

Beiner, Guy. *Remembering the Year of the French: Irish Folk History and Social Memory.* Madison: University of Wisconsin Press, 2007.

Beiner, Guy. "Troubles with Remembering; or, The Seven Sins of Memory Studies." *Dublin Review of Books* 94 (2017).

Benjamin, Walter. "Unpacking My Library: A Talk About Book Collecting." In *Illuminations,* edited by Hannah Arendt, 59–67. Translated by Harry Zohn. New York: Schocken Books, 1968.

Biuso, Tom. "Tom Biuso." *An Caomhnóir* 29 (2008): 13.

Blaney, Roger. *Presbyterians and the Irish Language.* Belfast: Ultach Trust; Ulster Historical Foundation, 1996.

Bourke, Angela. "Séamus Ennis in Co. Clare: Collecting Music in the 1940s." *Dal gCais* 8 (1986): 53–56.

Bourke, Angela. "Singing at the Centre of a Life." *JMI* 8, no. 3 (May/June 2008): 28–31.

Boydell, Barra. "Constructs of Nationality: The Literary and Visual Politics of Irish Music in the Nineteenth Century." In *Music in Nineteenth-Century Ireland,* edited by

Michael Murphy and Jan Smaczny, 52–73. Irish Musical Studies 9. Dublin: Four Courts Press, 2007.

Boydell, Barra. "Harp, Symbolism." In *The Companion to Irish Traditional Music*, edited by Fintan Vallely, 181–82. Cork: Cork University Press, 1999.

Boziwick, George. "Henry Cowell at the New York Public Library: A Whole World of Music." *Notes: Quarterly Journal of the Music Library Association* 57, no. 1 (September 2000): 46–58.

Breathnach, An t-Athair Pádraig, ed. *Ceól ár sínsear III*. 1913. Reprint, Baile Átha Cliath: Muinntir Bhrúin agus Nualláin, 1923.

Breathnach, Breandán. *Folk Music and Dances of Ireland*. 1971. Reprint, Dublin: Mercier Press, 1977.

Breathnach, Breandán. "Petrie and the Music of Clare." *Dal gCais* 2 (1975): 63–71.

Breathnach, Breandán. "Séamus Ennis: A Tribute to the Man and His Music." *Musical Traditions* 1, MT108 (1983). Accessed December 11, 2020. https://www.mustrad.org .uk/articles/ennis.htm.

Breathnach, Diarmuid, and Máire Ní Mhurchú. *Beathaisnéis, 1782–1881*. Baile Átha Cliath: An Clóchomhar, 1999.

Breathnach, Diarmuid, and Máire Ní Mhurchú. *Beathaisnéis a hAon, 1882–1982*. Baile Átha Cliath: An Clóchomhar, 1986.

Breathnach, Diarmuid, and Máire Ní Mhurchú. *Beathaisnéis a Dó, 1882–1982*. Baile Átha Cliath: An Clóchomhar, 1990.

Breathnach, Diarmuid, and Máire Ní Mhurchú. *Beathaisnéis a Ceathair, 1882–1982*. Baile Átha Cliath: An Clóchomhar, 1994.

Breathnach, Diarmuid, and Máire Ní Mhurchú. *Beathaisnéis a Cúig, 1882–1982*. Baile Átha Cliath: An Clóchomhar, 1997.

Breathnach, Diarmuid, and Máire Ní Mhurchú. "Máire Mac Neill (1904–1987)." *Ainm. ie*. Accessed December 11, 2020. https://www.ainm.ie/Bio.aspx?ID=1583.

Breathnach, Diarmuid, and Máire Ní Mhurchú. "Ó Conghaile, Stiofán (1893–1965)." *Ainm.ie*. Accessed December 11, 2020. https://www.ainm.ie/Bio.aspx?ID=1186.

Briggs, Asa. "Foreword." In *Collecting Printed Ephemera*, Maurice Rickards, 9. Oxford: Phaidon-Christie's, 1988.

Briody, Mícheál. "*The Gaelic Story-Teller* and Séamus Ó Duilearga's Views on the Role and Antiquity of *Airneán*." *Béascna* 8 (2013): 1–33.

Briody, Mícheál. *The Irish Folklore Commission, 1935–1970: History, Ideology, Methodology*. 2nd ed. Helsinki: Finnish Literature Society, 2008.

Briody, Mícheál. "'Publish or Perish': The Vicissitudes of the Irish Folklore Institute." *Ulster Folklife* 51 (2005): 10–33.

Browne, Peter. *Tuning the Radio—The Connection between Radio and Broadcasting and Traditional Music*. Ó Riada Memorial Lecture 18. Cork: Irish Traditional Music Society, University College Cork, 2007.

Bruen, Máire Comer, and Dáithí Ó hÓgáin. *An Mangaire Súgach: Beatha agus Saothar.* Baile Átha Cliath: Coiscéim, 1996.

Calder, Grace J. *George Petrie and the Ancient Music of Ireland.* Dublin: Dolmen Press, 1968.

Campbell, John Lorne, ed. and trans. *Hebridean Folksong: A Collection of Waulking Songs by Donald MacCormick.* Tunes transcribed by Francis Collinson. Oxford: Clarendon, 1969.

Carolan, Nicholas. "American Women Collectors in 1950s Ireland." Lecture presented at the Inishowen International Folk Song & Ballad Seminar, Ballyliffin, Co. Donegal, March 18, 2011.

Carolan, Nicholas. "An tUrramach James Goodman (1828–96) Fear Eaglasta, Ceoltóir, agus Bailitheoir Ceoil." In *Léachtaí Cholm Cille XL: Foinn agus Focail,* edited by Ruairí Ó hUiginn, 7–19. Maigh Nuad: An Sagart, 2010.

Carolan, Nicholas. "'Desire and Duty': The Collecting of Irish Traditional Music." Breandán Breathnach Memorial Lecture presented at the Willie Clancy Summer School, Miltown Malbay, Co. Clare, July 4, 2009.

Carolan, Nicholas. "Introduction." In *Dear Far-Voiced Veteran: Essays in Honour of Tom Munnelly,* edited by Anne Clune, i–viii. Miltown Malbay, Co. Clare: Old Kilfarboy Society, 2007.

Carolan, Nicholas. "Introduction." In *Ireland.* The Historic Series: World Library of Folk and Primitive Music. Vol. 2 (The Alan Lomax Collection). Rounder Records CD1742, 1998.

Carolan, Nicholas. *"The Most Celebrated Irish Tunes": The Publishing of Irish Music in the Eighteenth Century.* Ó Riada Memorial Lecture 5. Cork: Irish Traditional Music Society, University College Cork, 1990.

Carson, Ciaran. "The Thing Itself." *JMI* 9, no. 1 (January/February 2009): 32–35.

Cheape, Hugh. "Obituary: John Lorne Campbell." *London Independent,* May 2, 1996.

Collins, Tim. "From Sliabh Aughty to Ellis Island: The East Clare/Southeast Galway Music Diaspora and Their Influence on Irish-American Music Culture." Paper presented at the American Conference for Irish Studies, CUNY Graduate Center, New York, April 21, 2007.

Collins, Tim. "Music Mountain: Space, Place and Irish Traditional Music Practices in Sliabh Aughty." PhD diss., National University of Ireland Galway, 2013.

Collins, Tim. "Terpsichore's Votaries and Fashions: Exploring Identity, Place and Memory in the Traditional Dancing of East Clare and Southeast Galway." Lecture presented at the Willie Clancy Summer School, Miltown Malbay, Co. Clare, July 6, 2009.

Collins, Tim. "'Tis Like They Never Left: Locating 'Home' in the Music of Sliabh Aughty's Diaspora." *Journal of the Society for American Music* 4, no. 4 (2010): 491–507.

Collins, Tim, Gesche Kindermann, Conor Newman, and Nessa Cronin, eds. *Landscape Values: Place and Praxis.* Center for Landscape Studies, National University of Ireland

Galway, 2016, https://www.uniscape.eu/wp-content/uploads/2017/06/Landscape-Values-Place-and-Praxis-2016-06-Internet-Version.pdf.

Comiskey, Glen. "Thomas Moore." In *The Companion to Irish Traditional Music*, edited by Fintan Vallely, 247–48. Cork: Cork University Press, 1999.

Comiskey, Glen, and Sara Lanier. "Thomas Moore." In *The Companion to Irish Traditional Music*, edited by Fintan Vallely, 464–66. Cork: Cork University Press, 2011.

Conn, Stephanie. "Fitting between Present and Past: Memory and Social Interaction in Cape Breton Gaelic Singing." *Ethnomusicology Forum* 21, no. 3 (December 2012): 354–73.

Conn, Stephanie. "Private Tape Collections and Socio-Musical Transmission in Mid-Century Cape Breton: The Gaelic Song Tapes of Peter MacLean." *International Journal of Traditional Arts* 1, no. 1 (2017): 1–22.

Conneely, Mairéad. *Between Two Shores / Idir Dhá Chladach: Writing the Aran Islands, 1890–1980*. Reimagining Ireland 32. Oxford: Peter Lang, 2011.

Cooper, David, ed. "George Petrie." In *The New Grove Dictionary of Music and Musicians*, edited by Stanley Sadie, 509. London: Macmillan, 2001.

Cooper, David. *The Petrie Collection of the Ancient Music of Ireland*. Cork: Cork University Press, 2002.

Cooper, David. *The Petrie Collection of the Ancient Music of Ireland*. Online Archive, University of Leeds, 2005. Accessed September 7, 2009. http://www.leeds.ac.uk/music/research/petrie/home.htm.

Cooper, David. "'Twas One of Those Dreams That by Music Are Brought': The Development of the Piano and the Preservation of Irish Traditional Music." In *Music in Nineteenth-Century Ireland*, edited by Michael Murphy and Jan Smaczny, 74–113. Irish Musical Studies 9. Dublin: Four Courts Press, 2007.

Cowell, Sidney [Robertson]. "The Cowells and the Written Word." In *A Celebration of American Music: Words and Music in Honor of Wiley Hitchcock*, edited by Richard Crawford, R. Allen Lott, and Carol J. Oja, 79–91. Ann Arbor: University of Michigan Press, 1989.

Cowell, Sidney Robertson. "Henry Cowell and Ireland." Memorandum, Sidney Robertson Cowell Ireland Collections, Archive of Folk Culture, American Folklife Center, AFC 1959/004, Library of Congress, 1977.

Cowell, Sidney Robertson. "The Recording of Folk Music in California." *California Folklore Quarterly* 1, no. 1 (January 1942): 7–23.

Cowell, Sidney Robertson. "Songs from Cape Breton Island." In *Songs from Cape Breton Island*, 1–8. Ethnic Folkways Library FE4450, 1955.

Cowell, Sidney Robertson. "Songs of Aran Gaelic Singing from the West of Ireland." In *Songs of Aran*, 1–11. Ethnic Folkways Library FM4002, 1957.

Cowell, Sidney Robertson. "Wolf River Songs." In *Wolf River Songs*, 1–14. Monograph Series of the Ethnic Folkways Library FE4001, 1956.

Cranitch, Matt, ed. *The Irish Fiddle Book: The Art of Traditional Fiddle-Playing.* 1996. Reprint, Cork: Ossian Publications in association with Mercier Press, 2001.

Cunliffe, Barry. *Facing the Ocean: The Atlantic and Its Peoples, 8000 BC–AD 1500.* Oxford: Oxford University Press, 2001.

Daly, Mary E., and David Dickson, eds. *The Origins of Popular Literacy in Ireland: Language Change and Educational Development, 1700–1920.* Dublin: Department of Modern History, Trinity College Dublin, and Department of Modern Irish History, University College Dublin, 1990.

Dawson, Ciarán. *Peadar Ó Gealacáin: Scríobhaí.* Baile Átha Cliath: An Clóchomhar Tta., 1992.

Deasy, Marian. "New Edition of Airs and Dance Tunes from the Music Manuscripts of George Petrie LL.D., and a Survey of His Work as a Collector of Irish Folk Music." 2 vols. PhD diss., University College Dublin, 1982.

de Bhaldraithe, Tomás. "Seosamh Daibhéid—agus cuid dá chairde." *Feasta* 41, no. 10 (Deireadh Fómhair 1988): 19–23.

de Brún, Pádraig. "Amhráin a thiomsaigh Eoghan Ó Comhraí." *Ceol* 4, no. 4 (1981): 115–26.

de Brún, Pádraig. "'Gan Teannta Buird Ná Binse': Scríobhnaithe na Gaeilge, c. 1650–1850." *Comhar* 31, no. 11 (November 1972): 15–20.

de Buitléar, Éamon. "Miles and Miles of Music: Séamus Ennis (1919–1982)." In *The RTÉ Book,* 6–7. Dublin: Town House, in association with RTÉ, 1989.

de Chlanndiolúin, Séamus, and Maighréad Ní Annagáin, eds. *Londubh an Chairn.* 3 vols. London: Oxford University Press, 1927.

de hÍde, Dubhglas, ed. *Abhráin agus Dánta an Reachtabhraigh.* 1933. Reprint, Baile Átha Cliath: Oifig Dhíolta Foilseachán Rialtais, 1974.

Donnellan, Luke. "The Coulin." *Journal of the County Louth Archaeological Society* 3, no. 1 (December 1912), 11–15.

Donnellan, Luke. "Eibhlin a Rúin." *Journal of the County Louth Archaeological Society* 2, no. 4 (November 1911), 417–25.

Duffy, Charles Gavan. *Young Ireland: A Fragment of Irish History, 1840–1850.* London: Cassell, Petter, Galpin, 1880.

Fallis, Richard. *The Irish Renaissance: An Introduction to Anglo-Irish Literature.* Dublin: Gill and Macmillan, 1977.

Ferguson, Lady Mary Catherine. *Sir Samuel Ferguson in the Ireland of His Day.* 2 vols. Edinburgh: William Blackwood & Sons, 1896.

Ferguson, Sir Samuel. "Clonmacnoise, Clare, and Arran." *The Dublin University Magazine* 41, nos. 241–44 (January–April 1853): 79–95, 492–505.

Filene, Benjamin. "'Our Singing Country': John and Alan Lomax, Leadbelly, and the Construction of an American Past." *American Quarterly* 43, no. 4 (December 1991): 602–24.

Filene, Benjamin. *Romancing the Folk: Public Memory and American Roots Music*. Chapel Hill: University of North Carolina Press, 2000.

Fleischmann, Aloys. *Sources of Irish Traditional Music c. 1600–1855: An Annotated Catalogue of Prints and Manuscripts, 1583–1855*. 2 vols. New York: Garland, 1998.

Frayne, John P., ed. *Uncollected Prose [by W. B. Yeats]*. Vol. 1. London: Macmillan, 1970.

Freeman, A. M. "An Irish Concert." *Journal of the Folk Song Society* 6, no. 23 (1920): xxi–xxvii.

Garland, Peter. "Henry Cowell: Giving Us Permission." *Other Minds* (2006). Accessed September 8, 2009. http://otherminds.org/shtml/Garlandoncowell.shtml.

Glassie, Henry. *Passing the Time in Ballymenone: Folklore and History of an Ulster Community*. Dublin: O'Brien, 1982.

Green, Shannon L. "Controversy and Conflict in the Henry Street Settlement Music School, 1927–1935." *Women and Music* 8 (2004): 73–85.

Gubbins, Helen. "Shortwaves, Acetates and Journeywork: Irish Traditional Music on Early Irish Radio, 1926–1961." Master's thesis, University College Cork, 2009.

Haddon, Alfred Cort, and Charles R. Browne. "The Ethnography of the Aran Islands, County Galway." *Proceedings of the Royal Irish Academy* 37–39 (1891–93): 768–829.

Hamilton, Colin. "George Petrie." In *The Companion to Irish Traditional Music*, edited by Fintan Vallely, 294–95. Cork: Cork University Press, 1999.

Haverty, Martin. *The Aran Isles; or a Report of the Excursion of the Ethnological Section of the British Association from Dublin to the Western Islands of Aran in September 1857*. Dublin: Printed for the Excursionists at the University Press by M. H. Gill, 1859.

Henebry, Richard. *A Handbook of Irish Music*. Dublin and Cork: Cork University Press; Educational Co. of Ireland; Longmans, Green and Co. Ltd., 1928.

Hill, Rev. George. *An Historical Account of the Macdonnells of Antrim: Including Notices of Some Other Septs, Irish and Scottish*. Belfast: Archer & Sons, 1873.

Hirsch, Jerrold. "Modernity, Nostalgia, and Southern Folklore Studies: The Case of John Lomax." *Journal of American Folklore* 105, no. 416 (Spring 1992): 183–207.

Hoffmann, Francis, arr. *Ancient Music of Ireland from the Petrie Collection*. Dublin: Pigott, 1877.

Irwin, Liam. "Lenihan, Maurice." In *Dictionary of Irish Biography*, edited by James McGuire and James Quinn. Cambridge: Cambridge University Press, 2009.

Jabbour, Alan. "A Participant-Documentarian in the American Instrumental Folk Music Revival." In *The Oxford Handbook of Music Revival*, edited by Caroline Bithell and Juniper Hill, 116–32. New York: Oxford University Press, 2014.

Kaskowitz, Sheryl. "Delight in What It Is to Be an American: Sidney Robertson on the Road, 1935 to 1937." Lecture presented at the John W. Kluge Center, Library of Congress, November 3, 2016. Accessed September 5, 2019. https://youtu.be/zRN JMxnTH_0.

Kaskowitz, Sheryl. "Government Song Women: The Forgotten Folk Collectors of the New Deal." *Humanities: The Magazine of the National Endowment for the Humanities* 41, no. 2 (Spring 2020): 30–58.

Kearney, Daithí. "The Present and the Past in Fieldwork Experience: Understanding the Process of the Region in Irish Traditional Music." Paper presented at the Society of Musicology in Ireland Postgraduate Conference, University College Dublin, January 19, 2008.

Kearney, Daithí. "(Re)locating Irish Traditional Music: Urbanising Rural Traditions." *Chimera* 22 (2007): 181–96.

Kearney, Daithí. "Silently Seeing Music: The Role of the Developing Landscape of Memory in the Narratives of Irish Traditional Music." Paper presented at the International Council for Traditional Music Symposium, Waterford Institute of Technology, 2007.

Kearney, Daithí. "Towards a Regional Understanding of Irish Traditional Music." PhD diss., Schools of Music and Geography, University College Cork, 2010.

Kelly, Thomas Forrest. *Capturing Music: The Story of Notation.* New York: W. W. Norton, 2015.

Kennedy, Peter, ed. *Folksongs of Britain and Ireland.* New York: Oak Publications, 1975.

Kennedy, Veronica. "The Petrie Manuscripts of Irish Folk Music." MA diss. presented with a catalog of one-third of the manuscripts, University College Dublin, 1954.

Kennedy, Veronica. *See also* Ní Chinnéide, Veronica.

Kerst, Catherine Hiebert, ed. "Cataloging Folk Music: A Letter from Sidney Robertson Cowell." *Folklife Center News* (Fall 1989): 10–11.

Kerst, Catherine Hiebert. "The Ethnographic Experience: Sidney Robertson Cowell in Northern California." *California Gold: Northern California Folk Music from the Thirties Collected by Sidney Robertson Cowell,* digital collection, American Folklife Center, Library of Congress, 1997. https://www.loc.gov/collections/sidney-robert son-cowell-northern-california-folk-music/articles-and-essays/the-ethnographic -experience-sidney-robertson-cowell-in-northern-california/.

Kerst, Catherine Hiebert. "A 'Government Song Lady' in Pursuit of Folksong: Sidney Robertson's New Deal Field Documentation for the Resettlement Administration." Paper presented at the American Folklore Society meeting, Quebec City, Quebec, October 18, 2007.

Kerst, Catherine Hiebert. "Outsinging the Gas Tank: Sidney Robertson Cowell and the California Folk Music Project." *Folklife Center News* 20, no. 1 (Winter 1998): 6–12.

Kerst, Catherine Hiebert. "Sidney Robertson Cowell and the WPA California Folk Music Project." *The Sonneck Society for American Music Bulletin* 20, no. 3 (Fall 1994): 5–9.

Kerst, Catherine Hiebert. "Sidney Robertson Cowell and the WPA California Folk Music Project, 1938–40." Lecture presented at the Library of Congress, May 9, 2017. Accessed October 25, 2019. https://www.loc.gov/item/webcast-7963.

Kiberd, Declan. *Inventing Ireland.* 1995. Reprint, London: Vintage, 1996.

Kiberd, Declan. *Irish Classics.* Cambridge, MA: Harvard University Press, 2001.

Korff, Anne, J. W. O'Connell, and John Waddell, eds. _The Book of Aran_. Kinvara, Co. Galway: Tír Eolas, 1994.

Kozinn, Allan. "Herbert Haufrecht, 88, Pianist, Composer, Folklorist and Editor." _New York Times_, July 3, 1998.

Krassen, Miles, ed. _O'Neill's Music of Ireland_. New York: Oak Publications, 1976.

Landau, Carolyn, and Janet Topp Fargion. "We're All Archivists Now: Towards a More Equitable Ethnomusicology." _Ethnomusicology Forum_ 21, no. 2 (August 2012): 125–40.

Landstad, Magnus Brostrup. _Norske Folkeviser_. Christiania: Christian Tønsbergs Forlag, 1853.

Langton, Mícheál (Fr. Benedict O.C.D.). "Paidir as Connacht: Caoineadh na Páise." _Irish Press_, April 9, 1936, 4.

Leary, James P. "Canons and Cannonballs." In _Polkabilly: How the Goose Island Ramblers Redefined American Folk Music_, 161–84. New York: Oxford University Press, 2006.

Leary, James P. "The Discovery of Finnish American Folk Music." In "Scandinavian Folklore," special issue of _Scandinavian Studies_, 73, no. 3 (2001): 475–92.

Leary, James P. "Fieldwork Forgotten, or Alan Lomax Goes North." _Midwestern Folklore_ 27, no. 2 (2001): 5–20.

Leary, James P. "The Mid-West: A Surprising Vitality." Unpublished paper, n.d.

Leary, James P. "Woodsmen, Shanty Boys, Bawdy Songs, and Folklorists in America's Upper Midwest." _The Folklore Historian_ 24 (2007): 41–63.

Lee, Rev. Timothy. "Eugene O'Curry." _Journal of the Limerick Field Club_ 1, no. 1 (1897): 26–31; 1, no. 3 (1899): 1–11; 2, no. 6 (1903): 177–89.

Leerssen, Joep. _Mere Irish and Fíor-Ghael: Studies in the Idea of Irish Nationality, Its Development and Literary Expression prior to the Nineteenth Century_. Critical Editions: Field Day Monographs 3. Cork: Cork University Press, 1996.

Lenihan, Maurice. "Report Featuring Eugene O'Curry and George Petrie." _Limerick Reporter and Tipperary Vindicator_, April 13, 1869.

Lewis, Samuel. "A Topographical Dictionary of Ireland." 1837. In _An Aran Reader_, edited by Breandán Ó hEithir and Ruairí Ó hEithir, 18–22. Dublin: Lilliput Press, 1991.

Lomax, Alan. "Introduction" [1951]. In _Ireland_. World Library of Folk and Primitive Music, vol. 2 (The Alan Lomax Collection). Rounder Records CD1742, 1998.

Mac Coluim, Fionán ("Finghin na Leamhna"), ed. _Bolg an tSoláthair: Cnuasach Sean-Rochan_. 1904. Reprint, Dublin: Connradh na Gaedhilge, 1919.

Mac Con Iomaire, Liam. _Conamara—An Tír Aineoil/The Unknown Country_. Photographs by Bob Quinn. Indreabhán: Cló Iar-Chonnacht, 1997.

Mac Con Iomaire, Liam. _Seosamh Ó hÉanaí: Nár fhágha mé bás choíche_. Indreabhán: Cló Iar-Chonnacht, 2007.

Mac Grianna, Seosamh. _Pádraic Ó Conaire agus aistí eile_. Baile Átha Cliath: Oifig Díolta Foilseacháin Rialtais, 1936.

MacMahon, Tony. "The Master." *Journal of Music* 1, no. 6 (February/March 2010): 46–51.

Mac Piarais, Pádraig. "Cuairt ar Árainn na Naomh." *Fáinne an Lae*, Samhain 12, 1898.

Mahon, William. "Scríobhaithe Lámhscríbhinní Gaeilge i nGaillimh, 1700–1900." In *Galway: History and Society*, edited by Gerard Moran, 623–50. Dublin: Geography Publications, 1996.

Mason, Thomas H. *The Islands of Ireland*. Dublin: Mercier Press, 1936.

McCann, Anthony, and Lillis Ó Laoire. "'Raising One Higher than the Other': The Hierarchy of Tradition in Representations of Gaelic and English Language Song in Ireland." In *Global Pop, Local Language*, edited by Harris M. Berger and Michael T. Carroll, 233–65. Jackson: University Press of Mississippi, 2003.

McCarron, Stephen, ed. *Aran Islands/Oileáin Árann*. Irish Quaternary Association Field Guide 27. Dublin: Irish Quaternary Association, 2007.

McCormick, Fred. Review of *Amhráin ar an Sean Nós* and *Róise na nAmhrán: Songs of a Donegal Woman*. In *Musical Traditions* (1997). Accessed February 2, 2010. http://www.mustrad.org.uk/reviews/sean_nos.htm.

McKinney, Breda. "Song of Eoghan: An Introduction to the Tradition of Singing in Inishowen, Co. Donegal." Master's thesis, University College Cork, 2003.

McKinney, Breda. "The Tradition of Singing in Families and Communities in Inishowen, Co. Donegal." In *It's Us They're Talkin' About: Proceedings from the McGlinchey Summer School 2004*, Issue No. 7, edited by Marius Ó hEarcáin, 22–27. Clonmany, Co. Donegal: The McGlinchey Summer School, 2005.

McNeillie, Andrew. *An Aran Keening*. Dublin: Lilliput Press, 2001.

McQuillan, Peter. *Native and Natural: Aspects of the Concepts of "Right" and "Freedom" in Irish*. Cork: Cork University Press, in association with Field Day, 2004.

Messenger, John C. *An Anthropologist at Play: Balladmongering in Ireland and Its Consequences for Research*. Lanham, MD: University Press of America, 1983.

Messenger, John C. *Inis Beag: Isle of Ireland*. New York: Holt, Rinehart and Winston, 1969.

Messenger, John C. *Inis Beag Revisited: The Anthropologist as Observant Participator* [reissue of *An Anthropologist at Play: Balladmongering in Ireland and Its Consequences for Research*]. Salem, WI: Sheffield, 1989.

Messenger, John C. "Joe O'Donnell, *Seanchai* of Aran." *Journal of the Folklore Institute* 1, no. 3 (December 1964): 197–213.

Mhic Choisdealbha, Eibhlín Bean, ed. *Amhráin Mhuighe Seóla: Traditional Folksongs from Galway and Mayo*. 1923. Reprint, Indreabhán: Cló Iar-Chonnacht, 1990. Originally published in London and Dublin in volume 16 of the *Journal of the Irish Folk Song Society* (1919).

Milligan Fox, Charlotte. *Annals of the Irish Harpers*. London: Smith, Elder & Co., 1911.

Mná Fiontracha. *Árainn Cosáin an tSaoil*. Árainn: Bailiúchán Béaloideas Árann, 2003.

Mná Fiontracha, ed. *Ár nOileán Tuile 's Trá*. Árainn: Bailiúchán Béaloideas Árann, 2004.

Moloney, Colette. "Bunting, Edward." In *The Companion to Irish Traditional Music*, edited by Fintan Vallely, 46–47. Cork: Cork University Press, 1999.

Morley, Vincent. *Ó Chéitinn go Raiftearaí: Mar a cumadh stair na hÉireann.* Baile Átha Cliath: Coiscéim, 2011.

Moulden, John. "The Printed Ballad in Ireland: A Guide to the Popular Printing of Songs in Ireland, 1760–1920." PhD diss., National University of Ireland Galway, 2006.

Moulden, John. "Song Collectors." In *The Companion to Irish Traditional Music*, 2nd ed., edited by Fintan Vallely, 658. Cork: Cork University Press, 2011.

Mullen, Pat. *Man of Aran.* New York: E. P. Dutton, 1935.

Mulloy, Sheila. "Murrisk and Ballyhaunis Compared." *Cathair na Mart: Journal of the Westport Historical Society* 13 (1993): 78–81.

Mulvey, Helen F. *Thomas Davis and Ireland: A Biographical Study.* Washington, DC: Catholic University of America Press, 2003.

Munch-Pedersen, Ole, ed. *Scéalta Mháirtín Neile: Bailiúchán Scéalta ó Árainn.* Baile Átha Cliath: Comhairle Bhéaloideas Éireann, 1994.

Munnelly, Tom. "After the Fianna: Reality and Perceptions of Traditional Irish Singing." *JMI* 1, no. 2 (January/February 2001): 18–24.

Munnelly, Tom. "George Petrie: Distorting the Voice of the People?" *JMI* 3, no. 2 (January/February 2003): 13–17.

Munnelly, Tom. "Song Collectors." In *The Companion to Irish Traditional Music*, 2nd ed., edited by Fintan Vallely, 658. Cork: Cork University Press, 2011.

Nic an Airchinnigh, Méadhbh. "Caointeoireacht na Gaeilge: Béalaireacht agus Liteartacht." PhD diss., National University of Ireland Galway, 2012.

Nic Éinrí, Úna, and Pádraig Ó Cearbhaill. *Canfar an Dán: Uilleam English agus a Chairde.* An Daingean: An Sagart, 2003.

Nic Fhualáin, Úna [Shéamuis]. "An Hero/Bád Ned Bháin." *An Claidheamh Soluis*, Lúnasa 1, 1903, 2.

Nic Giolla Chomhaill, Ailbhe. "'An Páiste i dTír na nIontas.'" *Comhar* (Márta 2018): 28–31.

Ní Chinnéide, Sr. Veronica. *Salm Caintic Cruit.* Baile Átha Cliath: Iníonacha na Carthanachta, 1992.

Ní Chinnéide, Sr. Veronica. *Salm Caintic Cruit II.* Baile Átha Cliath: Iníonacha na Carthanachta, 2003.

Ní Chinnéide, Veronica. "The Sources of Moore's Melodies." *The Journal of the Royal Society of Antiquaries of Ireland* 89, part II (1959): 109–134.

Ní Chinnéide, Veronica. *See also* Kennedy, Veronica.

Ní Chonghaile, Deirdre. "An Teach Ósta: Tinteán an Cheoil Thraidisiúnta?" In *Bliainiris* 7, edited by Liam Mac Cóil and Ruairí Ó hUiginn, 72–84. Ráth Chairn, Co. Meath: Carbad, 2007.

Ní Chonghaile, Deirdre. "Broadcasting *Bailiúchán Bhairbre*: Researching and Representing Recordings via Radio." In *Ancestral Imprints: Histories of Irish Traditional Music and Dance*, edited by Thérèse Smith, 118–27. Cork: Cork University Press, 2012.

Ní Chonghaile, Deirdre. *Catalog of the Sidney Robertson Cowell Ireland Recordings, 1955–6*. Digital catalogs in .csv and SKOS formats, Irish Traditional Music Archive, June 2021. https://www.itma.ie/blog/sidney-robertson-cowell.

Ní Chonghaile, Deirdre. "'In Search of America': Sidney Robertson Cowell in Ireland in 1955–1956." *Journal of American Folklore* 126, no. 500 (Spring 2013): 174–200.

Ní Chonghaile, Deirdre. "'Listening for Landfall': How Silence and Fear Marginalized the Music of the Aran Islands." *Études Irlandaises* 39, no. 1 (2014): 41–55.

Ní Chonghaile, Deirdre. "'Listening to This Rude and Beautiful Poetry': John Millington Synge as Song Collector in the Aran Islands." *Irish University Review* 46, no. 2 (2016): 243–59.

Ní Chonghaile, Deirdre. "Ní neart go cur le chéile: Lámhscríbhinní ceoil a chruthaigh Petrie agus Ó Comhraí in Árainn in 1857." In *Léachtaí Cholm Cille XL: Foinn agus Focail*, edited by Ruairí Ó hUiginn, 86–108. Maigh Nuad: An Sagart, 2010.

Ní Chonghaile, Deirdre. "Séamus Ennis, W. R. Rodgers and Sidney Robertson Cowell on the Traditional Music of the Aran Islands." In *Anáil an Bhéil Bheo: Orality and Modern Irish Culture*, edited by Nessa Cronin, Seán Crosson, and John Eastlake, 67–86. Cambridge: Cambridge Scholars, 2009.

Nic Mhathúna, Deirdre. "A Journey from Manuscript to Print—the Transmission of an Elegy by Piaras Feiritéar." In *Irish and English: Essays on the Irish Linguistic and Cultural Frontier, 1600–1900*, edited by James Kelly and Ciarán Mac Murchaidh, 243–66. Dublin: Four Courts Press, 2012.

Ní Dheá, Eilís. "Ár n-oidhreacht Lámhscríbhinní ó Dhún Átha thiar agus ón gceantar máguaird." In *Eoghan Ó Comhraí Saol agus Saothar: Ómós do Eoghan Ó Comhraí*, edited by Pádraig Ó Fiannachta, 31–42. An Daingean: An Sagart, 1995.

Ní Dheá, Eilís. "Peadar Ó Conaill, scoláire agus scríobhaí (1755–1826)." In *County Clare Studies*, edited by Ciarán Ó Murchadha, 137–49. Ennis: Clare Archaeological and Historical Society, 2000.

Ní Dhorchaí, Proinnsias. *Clár Amhrán an Achréidh*. Baile Átha Cliath: An Clóchomhar, 1974.

Ní Fhaircheallaigh, Úna. *Smuainte ar Árainn*. Baile Átha Cliath: Conradh na Gaeilge, 1902.

Ní Fhlathartaigh, Ríonach. *Clár Amhrán Bhaile na hInse*. Baile Átha Cliath: An Clóchomhar, 1976.

Ní Fhlathartaigh, Ríonach. *See also* uí Ógáin, Ríonach.

Ní Ghloinn, Aoife. "Anailís Iardhearcach ar Stór Amhrán Róise Rua Uí Ghrianna." *Léann* 2 (2009): 19–42.

Ní Mhaoláin, Marion. "Scéalta béaloidis ó Árainn: Bailiúchán 'Bhláithín'/Uí Dhireáin." Paper presented at Scoil Gheimhridh Chumann Merriman, Galway, January 30, 2010.

Ní Mhiolláin, Treasa. "An Sean Nós." In *Ár nOileán Tuile 's Trá*, edited by Mná Fiontracha, 19–25. Árainn: Bailiúchán Béaloideas Árann, 2004.

Ní Mhunghaile, Lesa. "Bilingualism, Print Culture in Irish and the Public Sphere, 1700–c. 1830." In *Irish and English: Essays on the Irish Linguistic and Cultural Frontier, 1600–1900*, edited by James Kelly and Ciarán Mac Murchaidh, 218–42. Dublin: Four Courts Press, 2012.

Ní Mhunghaile, Lesa. *Ré órga na nGael: Joseph Cooper Walker (1761–1810)*. Indreabhán: An Clóchomhar, 2013.

Ní Mhunghaile, Lesa. "'To Open Treasures So Long Locked Up': Aidhmeanna agus cur chuige Charlotte Brooke ina saothar *Reliques of Irish Poetry* (1789)." In *Léachtaí Cholm Cille XL: Foinn agus Focail*, edited by Ruairí Ó hUiginn, 47–62. Maigh Nuad: An Sagart, 2010.

Ní Riain, Isobel. *Carraig & Cathair Ó Direáin*. Baile Átha Cliath: Cois Life, 2002.

Ní Shéaghdha, Nessa. *Collectors of Irish Manuscripts: Motives and Methods*. Richard Irvine Best Lecture 1984. Dublin: Dublin Institute for Advanced Studies, 1985.

Ní Shíocháin, Tríona. *Singing Ideas: Performance, Politics and Oral Poetry*. Dance and Performance Studies 12. New York: Berghahn Books, 2018.

Ní Shúilleabháin, Máire. *Amhráin Thomáis Rua*. Maigh Nuad: An Sagart, 1985.

Ní Uallacháin, Pádraigín. *A Hidden Ulster: People, Songs and Traditions of Oriel*. Dublin: Four Courts Press, 2003.

Ní Úrdail, Meidhbhín. *The Scribe in Eighteenth- and Nineteenth-Century Ireland: Motivations and Milieu*. Münster: Nodus Publikationen, 2000.

Ní Úrdail, Meidhbhín. "Seachadadh agus Seachadóirí Téacsaí san Ochtú agus sa Naoú Céad Déag." *Studia Hibernica* 32 (2002–3): 75–98.

Ó Baoill, Colm. *Amhráin Chúige Uladh*. Baile Átha Cliath: Gilbert Dalton, 1977.

Ó Baoill, Seán Óg, and Mánus Ó Baoill. *Ceolta Gael*. Corcaigh: Cló Mercier, 1975.

O'Brien Moran, James. "Irish Folk Music Collectors of the Early Nineteenth Century: Pioneer Musicologists." In *Music in Nineteenth-Century Ireland*, edited by Michael Murphy and Jan Smaczny, 94–113. Irish Musical Studies 9. Dublin: Four Courts Press, 2007.

O'Brien Moran, James. "Paddy Conneely—The Galway Piper: The Legacy of a Pre-Famine Folk Musician." PhD diss., University of Limerick, 2006.

Ó Buachalla, Breandán. *I mBéal Feirste Cois Cuain*. 1968. Reprint, Baile Átha Cliath: An Clóchomhar Tta., 1978.

Ó Cadhla, Stiofán. *An tSlat Féithleoige: Ealaíona an Dúchais, 1800–2000*. Indreabhán: Cló Iar-Chonnacht, 2011.

Ó Cadhla, Stiofán. "Seanchas na Fiosrachta agus Léann an Dúchais." In *Léann an Dúchais: Aistí in Ómós do Ghearóid Ó Crualaoich*, edited by Stiofán Ó Cadhla and Diarmuid Ó Giolláin, 79–96. Cork: Cork University Press, 2012.

Ó Catháin, Brian. "*Oidhche Sheanchais* le Robert J. Flaherty: An Chéad Scannán Gaeilge Dá nDearnadh." In *Bliainiris 4*, edited by Liam Mac Cóil and Ruairí Ó hUiginn, 151–235. Ráth Chairn, Co. Meath: Carbad, 2004.

Ó Catháin, Diarmaid. "O'Curry (Curry, Ó Comhraí), Eugene (Eoghan)." In *Dictionary of Irish Biography*, edited by James McGuire and James Quinn. Cambridge: Cambridge University Press, 2009.

Ó Ceallaigh, Fr. Tomás. *Ceol na nOileán.* Edited by William Mahon. 1931. Reprint, Indreabhán: Cló Iar-Chonnacht, 1993.

Ó Ciosáin, Éamon. "Amhráin na nDaoine agus an tAthrú Saoil: 'Lomarbhá faoin Dole' agus amhráin Antaine agus Thomáis Uí Bhriain." In *Léachtaí Cholm Cille XIX Litríocht na Gaeltachta,* ed. Pádraig Ó Fiannachta, 223–38. Maigh Nuad: An Sagart, 1989.

Ó Ciosáin, Éamon. "Amhráin na nDaoine agus an tAthrú Saoil: 'Lomarbhá faoin Dole' agus amhráin Antaine agus Thomáis Uí Bhriain." In *Léachtaí Cholm Cille XIX Litríocht na Gaeltachta,* ed. Pádraig Ó Fiannachta, 223–38. Maigh Nuad: An Sagart, 1989.

Ó Ciosáin, Niall. *Print and Popular Culture in Ireland, 1750–1850.* 1997. Reprint, Dublin: Lilliput Press, 2010.

Ó Coigligh, Ciarán, ed. *Raiftearaí: Amhráin agus Dánta.* Baile Átha Cliath: An Clóchomhar Tta., 1987.

Ó Conaire, Breandán. "Introduction." In *Language, Lore and Lyrics: Essays and Lectures,* Douglas Hyde, 11–53. Edited by Breandán Ó Conaire. Blackrock, Co. Dublin: Irish Academic Press, 1986.

Ó Conaire, Breandán. "Introduction." 1955. In *Songs of Connacht: Songs of O'Carolan, Songs Praising Women, Drinking Songs,* nos. 1–3, Douglas Hyde, 7–19. Edited by Breandán Ó Conaire. Blackrock, Co. Dublin: Irish Academic Press, 1985.

Ó Con Cheanainn, Ciarán. *Clár Amhrán Mhaigh Cuilinn.* Baile Átha Cliath: Comhairle Bhéaloideas Éireann, 2011.

Ó Concheanainn, Tomás. *Nua-Dhuanaire Cuid III.* 1978. Reprint, Baile Átha Cliath: Institiúid Ardléinn Bhaile Átha Cliath, 1981.

Ó Conchúir, Breandán. *Scríobhaithe Chorcaí, 1700–1850.* Baile Átha Cliath: An Clóchomhar Tta., 1982.

Ó Conghaile, Micheál. *Croch Suas É!* 1986. Reprint, Indreabhán: Cló Iar-Chonnacht, 2003.

Ó Conluain, Proinsias. "Cín Lae Craoltóra." In *Written on the Wind: Personal Memories of Irish Radio, 1926–76,* edited by Louis McRedmond, 87–106. Dublin: RTÉ in association with Gill & Macmillan, 1976.

O'Connell, J. W. "The Rediscovery of the Aran Islands in the 19th Century." In *The Book of Aran,* edited by Anne Korff, J. W. O'Connell, and John Waddell, 183–93. Kinvara, Co. Galway: Tír Eolas, 1994.

Ó Cróinín, Dáibhí, ed. *The Songs of Elizabeth Cronin.* Dublin: Four Courts Press, 2000.

Ó Cróinín, Dáibhí. *Whitley Stokes (1830–1909): The Lost Celtic Notebooks Rediscovered.* Dublin: Four Courts Press, 2011.

Ó Cuív, Brian. "Ireland's Manuscript Heritage." *Éire-Ireland* 19, no. 1 (Spring 1984): 87–110.

O'Curry, Eugene. *On the Manners and Customs of the Ancient Irish: A Series of Lectures.* Vol. 1. Edited by William Kirby Sullivan. London: Williams and Norgate, 1873.

Ó Dálaigh, Brian. "Eoghan Ó Comhraí and the Local Perspective." *North Munster Antiquarian Journal* 44 (2004): 1–14.

Ó Direáin, Máirtín. *Ó Mórna agus Dánta Eile.* Baile Átha Cliath: Cló Morainn, 1957.

Ó Direáin, Séamas. *A Survey of Spoken Irish in the Aran Islands, Co. Galway.* 2014. https://aranirish.nuigalway.ie.

O'Donnell, Brendan. *Galway—A Maritime Tradition: Ships, Boats and People.* Galway: Brendan O'Donnell, 2001.

Ó Drisceoil, Proinsias. "Áine Ní Fhoghlú (1880–1932) mar bhailitheoir amhrán sna Déise." Paper presented at Comhdháil ar Litríocht agus Cultúr na Gaeilge, Scoil na Gaeilge, Ollscoil na hÉireann, Gaillimh, October 18, 2008.

Ó Drisceoil, Proinsias. *Seán Ó Dálaigh: Éigse agus Iomarbhá.* Cork: Cork University Press, 2007.

Ó Fatharta, Dara Beag. *Cloch an Fhaoileáin.* Edited by M. F. Ó Conchúir. Indreabhán: Clódóirí Lurgan, 1982.

Ó Fátharta, Máirtín [Meaití Jó Shéamuis]. "Amhránaíocht ar an sean-nós i gConamara Theas." Lecture presented at the Cork Singers' Club Festival: To Tell It in Song and in Story, An Spailpín Fánach, Cork, March 10, 2002.

Ó Fiannachta, Pádraig, ed. *An Barántas.* Magh Nuad: An Sagart, 1978.

Ó Fiannachta, Pádraig, ed. *Eoghan Ó Comhraí Saol agus Saothar: Ómós do Eoghan Ó Comhraí.* Daingean Uí Chúis, Co. Kerry: An Sagart, 1995.

Ó Fiannachta, Pádraig, ed. *Léachtaí Cholm Cille XIX Litríocht na Gaeltachta.* Maigh Nuad: An Sagart, 1989.

O'Flaherty, Liam. *Thy Neighbour's Wife.* 1923. Reprint, Dublin: Wolfhound, 1992.

O'Flaherty, Liam. *See also* Ó Flaithearta, Liam.

Ó Flaithearta, Liam. *Dúil.* 1953. Reprint, Baile Átha Cliath: Caoimhín Ó Marcaigh, 1983.

Ó Flaithearta, Liam. *See also* O'Flaherty, Liam.

Ó Flannagáin, Dónal. *Ó Thrá Anoir.* Cathair na Mart, Co. Mayo: Foilseacháin Náisiúnta Teo., 1985.

Ó Flannagáin, Seosamh. "Tiachóg Sgéalta ó Árainn." *Béaloideas* 4 (1933–1934): 228–53.

O'Flynn, John. "National Identity and Music in Transition: Issues of Authenticity in a Global Setting." In *Music, National Identity and the Politics of Location: Between the Local and the Global,* edited by Ian Biddle and Vanessa Knights, 19–38. Aldershot, UK: Ashgate, 2007.

O'Flynn, John. "Vocal Authority? Perceptions of Singing Style and Singer Personality among Irish-Based Audiences." Paper presented at the IASPM World Conference, Rome, July 18–23, 2005.

Ó Fotharta, Dónall. *Siamsa a' Gheimhri Cois Teallaí in Iar-Chonnachta.* Baile Átha Cliath: Faoi Chóartha na dTrí gCoinneal, 1892.

Ó Gallchobhair, Mícheál. "Amhráin ó Iorrus." *Béaloideas* 10, nos. 1–2 (1941): 210–84; *Corrigenda* 13 (1943): 292–94.

Ó Giolláin, Diarmuid. *Locating Irish Folklore—Tradition, Modernity, Identity.* Cork: Cork University Press, 2000.

Ó Gramhnaigh, Fr. Eoghan. "Ára na Naomh." *Irisleabhar na Gaeilge* 3, nos. 31–32; 4, nos. 35–36 (1889–1890): 101–3; 126–28; 45–48; 53–55.

Ó Gramhnaigh, Fr. Eoghan. "Gleanings from the Islands." *Tuam News/Western Advertiser,* February 14, May 2 and 30, June 6, 20, and 27, 1890.

Ó hÁinle, Cathal. "'Abhráin Grádh Chúige Connacht': Saothar Ceannródaíochta?" *Studia Hibernica* 28 (1994): 117–43.

Ó hAllmhuráin, Gearóid. *Flowing Tides: History and Memory in an Irish Soundscape.* New York: Oxford University Press, 2016.

Ó hAllmhuráin, Gearóid. "Frank Custy of Toonagh." *Treoir* 7, no. 2 (June 1975): 18–20.

Ó hAlmhain, Mícheál. "As I Roved Out: Seamus Ennis talks to Micheal O hAlmhain about Collections." *Treoir* 5, no. 6 (1973): 26–27.

Ó hEidhin, Micheál. *Cas Amhrán.* 1975. Reprint, Indreabhán: Cló-Iar Chonnacht, 1990.

Ó hEithir, Breandán. "Pé oideachas a fuaireadar, b'iod oideachas a chuireadar orthu féin . . ." *Comhar* (Márta 2018): 38–41.

Ó hEithir, Breandán, and Ruairí Ó hEithir, eds. *An Aran Reader.* Dublin: Lilliput Press, 1991.

Ó hÍde, Tomás. *Seáinín Tom Sheáin: From Árainn to the Silver Screen.* Dublin: Four Courts Press, in association with Comhairle Bhéaloideas Éireann, 2019.

Ó hÓgáin, Daithí, ed. *Binneas Thar Meon: Cnuasach d'amhráin agus de cheolta a dhein Liam de Noraidh in oirthear Mumhan. Iml. 1.* In association with Marion Deasy and Ríonach Uí Ógáin. Baile Átha Cliath: Comhairle Bhéaloideas Éireann, 1994.

Ó hUiginn, Ruairí, ed. *Léachtaí Cholm Cille XL: Foinn agus Focail.* Maigh Nuad: An Sagart, 2010.

Ó Laoire, Lillis. *Ar Chreag i Lár na Farraige: Amhráin agus Amhránaithe i dToraigh.* Indreabhán: Cló Iar-Chonnacht, 2002.

Ó Laoire, Lillis. "Ceathrar banamhránaithe i ndialanna Sheáin Uí Eochaidh." In *Binneas an tSiansa: Aistí in onóir do Ríonach uí Ógáin,* edited by Kelly Fitzgerald, Bairbre Ní Fhloinn, Meidhbhín Ní Úrdail, and Anne O'Connor, 160–77. Baile Átha Cliath: Comhairle Bhéaloideas Éireann and Four Courts Press, 2019.

Ó Laoire, Lillis. "Ceol agus Amhránaíocht." In *Sealbhú an Traidisiúin,* edited by Niamh Ní Shiadhail, Meidhbhín Ní Úrdail, and Ríonach uí Ógáin, 81–96. Baile Átha Cliath: Comhairle Bhéaloideas Éireann, 2013.

Ó Laoire, Lillis. "The Gaelic Undertow: Seán Ó hEochaidh's Field Trip to the Bluestacks in 1947." In *This Landscape's Fierce Embrace: The Poetry of Francis Harvey,* edited by Donna L. Potts, 73–89. Newcastle: Cambridge Scholars, 2013.

Ó Laoire, Lillis. *On a Rock in the Middle of the Ocean: Songs and Singers in Tory Island.* First published in the United States in 2005 as *Europea: Ethnomusicologies and Modernities,* No. 4, by Scarecrow Press. Indreabhán: Cló Iar-Chonnacht, in association with the Scarecrow Press, 2007.

Ó Laoire, Lillis. ""Up Scraitheachaí!" Aitheantas áitiúil agus náisiúnta ag comórtais an tsean-nóis ag an Oireachtas." In *Aimsir Óg Cuid a Dó: Critic, Béaloideas, Teanga,* edited by Mícheál Ó Cearúil, 66–78. Baile Átha Cliath: Coiscéim, 2000.

Ó Laoire, Lillis, Sean Williams, and V. S. Blankenhorn. "Seosamh Ó hÉanaí agus Cearbhall Ó Dálaigh: Cleasa an Chrosáin san Oileán Úr." *New Hibernia Review* 15, no. 2 (Summer 2011): 80–101.

Ó Lúing, Seán. *Kuno Meyer, 1858–1919: A Biography.* Dublin: Geography Publications, 1991.

Ó Macháin, Pádraig. *Riobard Bheldon: Amhráin agus Dánta.* Dublin: Poddle, 1995.

Ó Madagáin, Breandán. *Caointe agus Seancheolta Eile/Keening and Other Old Irish Musics.* Indreabhán: Cló Iar-Chonnacht, 2005.

Ó Madagáin, Breandán. "Ceol a chanadh Eoghan Mór Ó Comhraí." *Béaloideas* 51 (1983): 71–86.

Ó Madagáin, Breandán. "Eugene O'Curry, 1794–1862, Pioneer of Irish Scholarship." In *Clare: History and Society: Interdisciplinary Essays on the History of an Irish County,* edited by Matthew Lynch and Patrick Nugent, 425–48. Dublin: Geography Publications, 2009.

Ó Madagáin, Breandán. "Functions of Irish Song in the Nineteenth Century." *Béaloideas* 53 (1985): 130–216.

Ó Máille, Mícheál, and Tomás Ó Máille, eds. *Amhráin Chlainne Gael.* Edited by William Mahon. 1905. Reprint, Indreabhán: Cló Iar-Chonnacht, 1995.

Ó Máille, Tomás. *Mícheál Mac Suibhne agus Filidh an tSéibhe.* Baile Atha Cliath: Foilseacháin an Rialtais, 1934.

Ó Muirgheasa, Enrí, ed. *Dhá Chéad de Cheoltaibh Uladh.* Baile Átha Cliath: Oifig an tSoláthair, 1934.

O'Neill, Capt. Francis, ed., and James O'Neill, arr. *The Dance Music of Ireland (1001 Gems).* Chicago: Lyon & Healy, 1907.

O'Neill, Capt. Francis ed., and James O'Neill, arr. *Music of Ireland.* Chicago: Lyon & Healy, 1903.

Oppenheimer, Stephen. *The Origins of the British—A Genetic Detective Story.* London: Constable and Robinson, 2006.

O'Reilly, John Boyle. *The Poetry and Song of Ireland.* New York: Gay Brothers, 1887.

Ó Rócháin, Muiris. "Eugene O'Curry: The Neglected Scholar." *Dal gCais* 1 (1972): 65–67.

O'Sullivan, Donal, ed. "The Bunting Collection of Irish Folk Music and Songs." *Journal of the Irish Folk Song Society* 28–29, part 6 (1939): 1–106.

O'Sullivan, Donal. *Irish Folk Music, Song and Dance [Ceol, Amhránaíocht agus Rince na hÉireann].* 1952. Reprint, Cork: Published for the Cultural Relations Committee of Ireland by the Mercier Press, 1974.

Ó Tiománaidhe, Micheál. *Amhráin Ghaeilge an Iarthair.* Edited by William Mahon. 1906. Reprint, Indreabhán: Cló Iar-Chonnacht, 1990.

O'Toole, Pádraig [Patsy Bhid Bhile]. *Aran to Africa: An Irishman's Unique Odyssey.* n.p.: Nuascéalta, 2013.

Ó Tuathaigh, Gearóid. *I mBéal an Bháis: The Great Famine and the Language Shift in Nineteenth-Century Ireland.* Hamden, CT: Quinnipiac University, 2015.

Ó Tuathaigh, Gearóid. "The State and the Irish Language: An Historical Perspective." In *A New View of the Irish Language,* edited by Caoilfhionn Nic Pháidín and Seán Ó Cearnaigh, 26–42. Dublin: Cois Life, 2008.

Paul, David C. "From American Ethnographer to Cold War Icon: Charles Ives through the Eyes of Henry and Sidney Cowell." *Journal of the American Musicological Society* 59, no. 2 (Summer 2006): 399–457.

Pearce, Susan M. *On Collecting: An Investigation into Collecting in the European Tradition.* Collecting Cultures Series. London: Routledge, 1995.

Petrie, George. *The Ancient Music of Ireland.* Vols. 1 and 2. 1855. Reprint, Farnborough: Gregg International, 1967 and 1978.

Petrie, George. "The Islands of Aran" [abridged] (1822). In *An Aran Reader*, edited by Breandán Ó hEithir and Ruairí Ó hEithir, 40–42. Dublin: Lilliput Press, 1991.

Pine, Richard. *Music and Broadcasting in Ireland since 1926.* Dublin: Four Courts Press, 2005.

Powell, Antoine. *Oileáin Árann Stair na n-oileán anuas go dtí 1922.* Dublin: Wolfhound, 1984.

Power, Patrick. *Aran of the Saints: A Brief Introduction to the Island's Antiquities.* Dublin: 1926.

"Reports of the Islands and Coast Society, 1843–50." In *An Aran Reader*, edited by Breandán Ó hEithir and Ruairí Ó hEithir, 23–28. Dublin: Lilliput Press, 1991.

Reuss, Richard A. "Folk Music and Social Conscience: The Musical Odyssey of Charles Seeger." *Western Folklore* 38, no. 4 (October 1979): 221–38.

Richey, Rosemary. "Woulfe, Stephen." In *Dictionary of Irish Biography*, edited by James McGuire and James Quinn. Cambridge: Cambridge University Press, 2009.

Ricoeur, Paul. *Memory, History, Forgetting.* Translated by Kathleen Blamey and David Pellauer. Chicago: Chicago University Press, 2004.

Rivers, Elizabeth. *Stranger in Aran.* Dublin: Cuala Press, 1946. Reprinted 1971 by photo-lithography in the Republic of Ireland for the Irish University Press, Shannon—T. M. MacGlinchey, Publisher. Robert Hogg, Printer.

Roberts, Robin. "Recording in Ireland with Alan Lomax" [1997]. In *Ireland*, World Library of Folk and Primitive Music, vol. 2 (The Alan Lomax Collection). Rounder Records CD1742, 1998.

Robinson, Tim. "Faithful for Life unto Aran." Review of *An Aran Keening*, by Andrew McNeillie. *Irish Times—Weekend*, March 10, 2001.

Robinson, Tim. *Stones of Aran: Labyrinth.* Dublin: Lilliput Press, 1995.

Robinson, Tim. *Stones of Aran: Pilgrimage.* 1986. Reprint, London: Penguin Books, 1990.

Roche, Francis. *The Roche Collection of Traditional Irish Music.* Vols. 1–3. 1927. Reprint, Cork: Ossian Publications, 1982.

Rosenberg, Neil V. "Family Values Seeger Style: A Seeger Family Tribute at the Library of Congress." *Folklife Center News* 29, nos. 1–2 (Winter–Spring 2007): 3–11.

Saorstát Éireann. *Acht Um Hallaí Rinnce Puiblí 1935.* Baile Átha Cliath: Saorstát Éireann, 1935.

Saorstát Éireann. *Oidhche Sheanchais: Sean-Scéal a innsigheann Seáinín Tom Sheáin as Árainn.* Baile Átha Cliath: ar n-a scríobhadh síos do Roinn an Oideachais, 1934.

Saylor, Nicole. "Folk Music of Wisconsin, 1937." Website featuring a page highlighting the ethnographic fieldwork of Sidney Robertson Cowell (1903–95) in Wisconsin. Mills Music Library's Helene Stratman-Thomas Project, Center for the Study of Upper Midwestern Cultures, University of Wisconsin–Madison (2004). http://csumc.wisc.edu/src/collector.htm.

Seeger, Anthony. "The Role of Sound Archives in Ethnomusicology Today." *Ethnomusicology* 30, no. 2 (Spring–Summer 1986): 261–76.

Seeger, Charles. *Reminiscences of an American Musicologist.* Interview with Adelaide G. Tusler and Ann M. Briegleb, conducted under the auspices of the Oral History Program, University of California, Los Angeles (1972), Internet Archive. http://www.archive.org/stream/reminiscencesofaooseeg/reminiscencesofaooseeg_djvu.txt.

Seeger, Nancy. "Sidney Robertson Cowell Collection Finding Aid." Washington, DC: Music Division, Library of Congress, 2010, http://hdl.loc.gov/loc.music/eadmus.mu010010.

Sheeran, Patrick F. "Aran, Paris and the Fin-de-siècle." In *The Book of Aran*, edited by Anne Korff, J. W. O'Connell, and John Waddell, 299–305. Kinvara, Co. Galway: Tír Eolas, 1994.

Sheerin, Norbert. *Renmore and Its Environs: An Historical Perspective.* Galway: Renmore Residents' Association, 2000.

"Sidney Cowell, 92, Ethnomusicologist and Teacher." *New York Times*, March 1, 1995.

Slocombe, Marie. "The BBC Folk Music Collection." *Folklore and Folk Music Archivist* 7, no. 1 (1964): 3–13.

Smith, Christopher. "Why Séamus? Séamus Ennis, Traditional Music, and Irish Cultural History." *JMI* 2, no. 6 (September/October 2002): 5–9.

Somerville, Edith Oenone, and Martin Ross [Violet Martin]. "An Outpost of Ireland." In *Some Irish Yesterdays*, 3–32. London: Longmans, Green, 1906.

Spencer, Scott B., ed. *The Ballad Collectors of North America: How Gathering Folksongs Transformed Academic Thought and American Identity.* Lanham, MD: Scarecrow, 2012.

Stanford, Charles Villiers, ed. *The Complete Collection of Irish Music as Noted by George Petrie, L.L.D., R.H.A. (1789–1866). Edited, from the Original Manuscripts by Charles Villiers Stanford.* London: The Irish Literary Society of London, Boosey, 1902–1905.

Sterne, Jonathan. *The Audible Past: Cultural Origins of Sound Reproduction.* Durham, NC: Duke University Press, 2003.

Stokes, William. *The Life and Labours in Art and Archaeology of George Petrie.* London: Longmans, Green, 1868.

Stone, Peter. "Sidney and Henry Cowell." Association for Cultural Equity, New York (2009). http://www.culturalequity.org/alan-lomax/friends/cowell.

Synge, John Millington. *The Aran Islands.* Introduction essay and notes by Tim Robinson. 1907. Reprint, London: Penguin Twentieth-Century Classics, 1992.

Synge, John Millington. "The Last Fortress of the Celt." *The Gael* (April 1901): 109–12.

Szwed, John F. *Alan Lomax: The Man Who Recorded the World.* New York: Viking, 2011.

Taylor, Diana. *The Archive and the Repertoire: Performing Cultural Memory in the Americas*. Durham, NC: Duke University Press, 2003.

Thomas, Gerald. "In Memoriam: Herbert Halpert, 1911–2000." *Journal of Folklore Research* 38, nos. 1–2 (January 2001): 171–74.

Thompson, Stith. "John Avery Lomax (1867–1948)." *Journal of American Folklore* 61, no. 241 (July–September 1948): 305–6.

Tonkin, Elizabeth. *Narrating Our Pasts: The Social Construction of Oral History*. Cambridge Studies in Oral and Literate Culture, no. 22. Cambridge: Cambridge University Press, 1992.

Topping, Brett. "The Sidney Robertson Cowell Collection." *Folklife Center News* 3, no. 3 (July 1980): 4–5, 8.

Travassac, Pierre. *Les Îles Aran Scènes et paysages d'Irlande*. Paris: Imprimerie Centrale de Paris, 1960.

Uí Bhaoill, Máire. "Séamas Mhac Óda, fear ildánach—píobaire, múinteoir Gaeilge, bailitheoir ceoil agus amhrán." Paper presented at Comhdháil na Gaeilge, National University of Ireland, Galway, October 17, 2009.

uí Ógáin, Ríonach. "Colm Ó Caodháin and Séamas Ennis: A Conamara Singer and His Collector." *Béaloideas* 64–65 (1996–1997): 279–338.

uí Ógáin, Ríonach. "Ennis, Séamus (Séamus Mac Aonghusa)." In *The Companion to Irish Traditional Music*, ed. Fintan Vallely, 118–19. Cork: Cork University Press, 1999.

uí Ógáin, Ríonach. "Ethnomusicology and the World of Séamus Ennis." *Béaloideas* 85 (2017): 195–217.

uí Ógáin, Ríonach, ed. *Faoi Rothaí na Gréine: Amhráin as Conamara a bhailigh Máirtín Ó Cadhain*. Buneagarthóireacht: Seosamh Ó Cadhain. Baile Átha Cliath: Coiscéim, 1999.

uí Ógáin, Ríonach. "Fear Ceoil Ghlinsce: Colm Ó Caodháin." In *Galway: History and Society: Interdisciplinary Essays on the History of an Irish County*, ed. Gerard Moran, 703–48. Associate editor, Raymond Gillespie. Dublin: Geography Publications, 1996.

uí Ógáin, Ríonach, ed. *Going to the Well for Water: The Séamus Ennis Field Diary, 1942–1946*. Cork: Cork University Press, 2009.

uí Ógáin, Ríonach. "Is í an fhilíocht anam an cheoil: Sorcha Ní Ghuairim, Amhránaí Roisín na Mainiach." In *Bliainiris 2*, edited by Liam Mac Cóil and Ruairí Ó hUiginn, 84–107. Ráth Chairn, Co. Meath: Carbad, 2002.

uí Ógáin, Ríonach. "A Job with No Clock: Séamus Ennis and the Irish Folklore Commission." *JMI* 6, no. 1 (January/February 2006): 10–14.

uí Ógáin, Ríonach, ed. *"Mise an fear ceoil": Séamus Ennis—Dialann Taistil, 1942–1946*. Indreabhán: Cló Iar-Chonnacht, 2007.

uí Ógáin, Ríonach. "Thar Farraige Anonn—Séamus Mac Aonghusa in Albain, 1946–1947." In *Dear Far-Voiced Veteran: Essays in Honour of Tom Munnelly*, ed. Anne Clune, 361–71. Miltown Malbay, Co. Clare: Old Kilfarboy Society, 2007.

uí Ógáin, Ríonach. *See also* Ní Fhlathartaigh, Ríonach.

Vallely, Fintan, ed. *The Companion to Irish Traditional Music*. Cork: Cork University Press, 1999.

Vallely, Fintan, ed. *The Companion to Irish Traditional Music*. 2nd ed. Cork: Cork University Press, 2011.

Van Duzer, Chet. "From Odysseus to Robinson Crusoe: A Survey of Early Western Island Literature." *Island Studies Journal* 1, no. 1 (May 2006): 143–62.

Waddell, John. "The Archaeology of Aran." In *The Book of Aran*, edited by Anne Korff, J. W. O'Connell, and John Waddell, 75–135. Kinvara, Co. Galway: Tír Eolas, 1994.

Wade, Stephen. *The Beautiful Music All around Us: Field Recordings and the American Experience*. Music in American Life. Urbana: University of Illinois Press, 2012.

Wakeman, William Frederick. "Aran—Pagan and Christian." *Duffy's Hibernian Sixpenny Magazine* 1, nos. 5–6 (May–June 1862): 460–71; 567–77.

Warner, Marina. *Phantasmagoria*. Oxford: Oxford University Press, 2006.

Watson, Henry Cecil. *Inis Meáin Images: Ten Days in August, 1912*. Dublin: Wolfhound Press, 1999.

Whitaker, T. K. "James Hamilton Delargy, 1890–1980." *Folk Life* 20 (1981–82): 101–6.

Wilgus, D. K. *Anglo-American Folksong Scholarship since 1898*. New Brunswick, NJ: Rutgers University Press, 1959.

Wolf, Nicholas. *An Irish-Speaking Island: State, Religion, Community, and the Linguistic Landscape in Ireland, 1770–1870*. Madison: University of Wisconsin Press, 2014.

COMMERCIAL RECORDINGS

Asch, Moses, ed. *Sorcha Ní Ghuairim Sings Traditional Irish Songs*. Folkways FW06861, 1957.

Browne, Peter, ed. *Tuning the Radio: Early Traditional Music Recordings from the RTÉ Libraries and Archives*. RTÉ 285CD, 2010.

Cowell, Sidney Robertson, ed. *Songs from Cape Breton Island*. Ethnic Folkways Library FE4450, 1955.

Cowell, Sidney Robertson, ed. *Songs of Aran*. Ethnic Folkways Library FE4002, 1957; Ossian OSS16, 1989.

Cowell, Sidney Robertson, ed. *Wolf River Songs*. Monograph Series of the Ethnic Folkways Library FE4001, 1956.

Ennis, Séamus. *The Ace and Deuce of Piping*. Collector JEI 1506, 1960.

Ennis, Séamus. *The Best of Irish Piping* [compilation of previous Tara releases]. Tara TACD 1002–9, 1995.

Ennis, Séamus. *The Bonny Bunch of Roses*. Tradition TLP 1013, 1959; Ossian OSS 59, 1988; TCD 1023, 1996.

Ennis, Séamus. *The Drones and the Chanters* [compilation]. Claddagh CC 11, 1971.

Ennis, Séamus. *Feidlim Toon Ri's Castle*. Claddagh CC19, 1977.

Ennis, Séamus. *Forty Years of Irish Piping*. Green Linnet 1977; GLCD1000, 2000.

Ennis, Séamus. *The Fox Chase.* Tara 1009, 1978.

Ennis, Séamus. *The Pure Drop,* volume 1. Tara 1002, 1973.

Ennis, Séamus. *The Return to Fingal.* RTÉ CD 199, 1997.

Ennis, Séamus. *Séamus Ennis—Ceol, Scéalta agus Amhráin.* Gael Linn CEF009, 1961; CEFCD009, 2006.

Ennis, Séamus. *Two Centuries of Celtic Music.* Legacy CD 499, 2001.

Ennis, Séamus. *The Wandering Minstrel.* Topic 12TS250, 1974; Ossian OSSCD 12, 1989; Green Linnet GLCD 3078, 1993.

Hamilton, Diane. *The Lark in the Morning.* Tradition TCD1001, 1955.

Harte, Frank, and Donal Lunny. *Frank Harte: 1798—The First Year of Liberty.* Hummingbird HBCD 0014, 1998.

Kennedy, Veronica. *Dandy, Dandy; Ailiú Aonaigh.* 78rpm record, Gael Linn, 1950s.

Leary, James P. *Folksongs of the Another America: Field Recordings from the Upper Midwest, 1937–1946.* Madison: University of Wisconsin Press, 2015.

Lomax, Alan, ed. *Ireland.* The Historic Series: World Library of Folk and Primitive Music. Vol. 2 (The Alan Lomax Collection). Rounder Records CD1742, 1955 (1998).

Magpie Lane. *Jack-in-the-Green.* Beautiful Jo Records, BEJOCD-22, 1998.

Ní Mhiolláin, Treasa. *Lán Mara.* Cló Iar-Chonnacht CICD208, 2019.

Ní Shúilleabháin, Eilís. *Cois Abhann na Séad: Amhráin ó Mhúsrcraí.* Cló Iar-Chonnacht, CICD132, 1997.

O'Brien Moran, James. *Take Me Tender . . . : Music for the Uilleann Pipes, Collected before the Famine.* J. O'Brien Moran, PPPCD051, 2013.

Ó Catháin, Darach. *Traditional Irish Unaccompanied Singing.* Gael Linn CEFCD040, 1975.

[Ó Coistealbha], Tom Pháidín Tom. *Tom Pháidín Tom.* Dublin: Comhaltas Ceoltóirí Éireann, 1978.

Ó Dioráin, Seáinín Tom Sheáin. *Oídhche Sheanchais.* Parlophone E4075, 1934.

Ó Sé, Seán and Ceoltóirí Chualann. *Táimse im' chodladh.* 3 vols. Dublin: Gael Linn, 1968.

Schüller, Dietrich, ed. *Tondokumente aus dem Phonogrammarchiv der Österreichischen Akademie der Wissenschaften. Gesamtausgabe der historischen Bestände 1899–1950. Series 5/2: The Collections of Rudolf Trebitsch: Celtic Recordings 1907–9.* Österreichische Akademie der Wissenschaften, 2003.

Various. *Bringing It All Back Home: Music from the BBC Series.* Produced by Donal Lunny and Brian Talbot. British Broadcasting Corporation, BBC CD844, 1991.

Various. *Comhaltas Champions on Tour.* Comhaltas Ceoltóirí Éireann CL11, 1975.

Various. *ICTM Ireland Fieldwork.* Edited by Desi Wilkinson. ICTM Ireland, 2013.

Various. *The Ould Plaid Shawl Songs of Francis Fahy.* Francis A[rthur]. Fahy Society FAF01, 2001.

RADIO

Bowman, John. *Bowman: Sunday Morning: 8.30.* RTÉ Radio 1, September 6, 2009.

Bowman, John. *Bowman: Sunday Morning: 8.30: Ciarán Mac Mathúna and Liam Clancy.* RTÉ Radio 1, December 13, 2009.

Bowman, John. *Bowman: Sunday Morning: 8.30: Ciarán Mac Mathúna.* RTÉ Radio 1, December 20, 2009.

Bowman, John. *Bowman: Sunday Morning: 8.30: Ciarán Mac Mathúna.* RTÉ Radio 1, December 27, 2009.

Browne, Peter. Review of *Na Bailitheoirí Ceoil,* by Seán Corcoran. *The Arts Show,* RTÉ Radio 1, March 16, 2009.

Browne, Peter. *The Rolling Wave: In Memoriam Ciarán Mac Mathúna.* RTÉ Radio 1, December 13, 2009.

Browne, Peter, and Julian Vignoles. *The Séamus Ennis Story.* Four-part series presented by Peter Browne. Producer: Julian Vignoles. RTÉ Radio 1, March 20, 1988, RTÉ Archive AA4014.

Kennedy, Veronica. "Thomas Moore and the Irish Tradition." *The Thomas Davis Lectures,* Series 22, Irish Traditional Music. Radio Éireann, January 24, 1960.

Lee, Ian. *Ar Mo Thaisteal Dhom.* Raidió na Gaeltachta, November 4, 1996, RTE RnaG Casla CD0181.

Lee, Ian. *Siúlach Scéalach.* RTÉ Raidió na Gaeltacht, January 12, 2014.

Lomax, Alan. *The Stone of Tory: A Ballad Opera from the West of Ireland.* BBC Home Service, May 20, 1951. Alan Lomax Collection, Manuscripts, BBC, 1951; American Folklife Center, Library of Congress, AFC 2004/004: MS 04.03.30.

Ní Chonghaile, Deirdre (presenter), and Máirtín Jaimsie Ó Flaithbheartaigh (producer). *Bailiúchán Bhairbre.* RTÉ Raidió na Gaeltachta, November 2006–February 2007.

Ní Mhaoileoin, Máirín. *Scoileanna Éigse & Seanchais.* RTÉ Raidió na Gaeltachta, Series 1, September–December 2005, Series 2, September–December 2006.

Nolan, Liam. *Here and Now.* ["Professor Séamus Delargy (Ó Duilearga) in conversation with Liam Nolan about his early childhood in Cushendall, Co. Antrim, the first folktales he heard, his love of the Irish language, which he first heard from native speakers in the Glens Antrim, and the collectors who worked for him in the Irish Folklore Commission."] RTÉ, March 12, 1971, Sound Archive AA5382.

Ó Raghallaigh, Pádraig. *Gaeltacht na nOileán.* Radio Éireann, August 27, 1956, RTÉ Sound Archive Tape 186.

Richardson, Marian. *The Giant at My Shoulder.* Liam Óg O'Flynn talking about Séamus Ennis. RTÉ Radio 1, May 7, 1999.

Rodgers, W. R. *The Bare Stones of Aran.* BBC Third Program, May 30, 1950, BLSA T11524R2; script in the possession of the author's grandmother Mairéad Uí Choncheanainn.

FILM AND TELEVISION

Carr, Peter. *Bringing It All Back Home.* Hummingbird Production for BBC Northern
Ireland in association with RTÉ, 1991.

Corcoran, Seán. *Na Bailitheoirí Ceoil.* Stirling Productions for TG4, 2009.

Davidson, Norris. *Damhsa Árann.* Zenifilms, 1934 (no copy survives).

de Buitléar, Éamon. *Miles and Miles of Music.* RTÉ, 1974.

Flaherty, Robert. *Man of Aran.* Gainsborough Pictures, 1934.

Flaherty, Robert. *Oidhche Sheanchais.* Gaumont-British Picture Corporation, 1934.

O'Donnell, John. *In the Blood—Kilfenora Céilí Band.* Stray Dog Films for RTÉ, April 7,
2009.

Quinn, Robert. *Cré na Cille.* Rosg for TG4 and BCI, 2007.

ONLINE RESOURCES

Carmichael-Watson Collection. Coll-97, University Library, University of Edinburgh.
https://www.ed.ac.uk/information-services/library-museum-gallery/crc/research
-resources/gaelic/carmichael-watson.

Census of Ireland 1901/1911 and Census Fragments and Substitutes, 1821–51. https://www
.census.nationalarchives.ie

Dúchas.ie National Folklore Collection UCD Digitization Project. https://www.duchas.ie.

Tobar an Dualchais/Kist o' Riches. School of Scottish Studies, University of Edinburgh.
http://tobarandualchais.co.uk.

INTERVIEWS

Joyce, Johnny. Interviewed by the author in the author's home, Sruthán, Árainn, September 2, 2001.

Ó Briain, Joe Antoine. Interviewed in his home by the author, Cill Éinne, Árainn,
January 30, 2009.

Ó Conghaile, Stiophán. Interviewed in his home by the author, Sruthán, Árainn, September 15, 2006.

Ó Fáthartaigh, Dara Beag. Interviewed in his home by the author, Inis Meáin, September 24, 2010.

Ó Maoláin, Peterín a' Bheagach. Interviewed in his home by the author, Bun Gabhla,
Árainn, January 4, 2001.

Quinn, Paddy. Interviewed by the author in Cill Mhuirbhigh, Árainn, September 21,
2006.

Index

"Creig Sheáin Phádraig" (song), 75, 121
Croatian music, 91–92
Croke Park, 80
Cronin, Bess, 84
"Cruacha Glasa na hÉireann" (song),
159
"Cúirt an tSrutháin Bhuí" (song), 134–35
"Cúirt Bhaile Nua" (song), 75, 81, 228–29
culture: Aran, 22–26, 42, 49, 170–72; cul-
tural assimilation, 42, 143, 145, 170, 173;
Irish traditional music and, 4–6, 11, 15,
19, 58–59, 61, 102–4, 141–42; music
collecting and, 37, 109; youth, 145, 172

Daibhéid, Seosamh [Joseph Davitt], 120,
136, 266n217
Damhsa Árann (Davidson), 55
dance, 8, 49, 60, 95–96, 122, 124, 137, 172
Davidson, Norris, 55
Davitt, Joseph. *See* Daibhéid, Seosamh
[Joseph Davitt]
Deasy, Marian, 36, 40, 48, 51–52, 183–84
de Bhailís, Baibín Mhurchadha, 163
de Bhailís, Pádraig Mhurchadha, 101,
110
de Bhailís, Seán Mhurchadha, 71, 78–79,
82, 223–24
de Blaghad, Earnán, 147
de Buitléar, Éamon, 70
Defoe, Daniel, 30
Delargy, James Hamilton [Séamus Ó
Duilearga], 59, 59–63, 60–62, 67, 70,
106, 136, 146, 192, 249n56, 250n75,
252n112, 261n115
de Noraidh, Liam, 67
depopulation, 22, 81, 139, 144, 180
de Valera, Máirín, 147
dialect, 18, 48, 58, 77, 180; of cant, 58; of
Ulster Scots, 58
Dillane, John, 185, 207–9
Dillane, Martin John Thady, 117

Dillane, Micilín, 87
Dirrane, Maggie, 78, 87–88, 101, 109–10,
121, 126–33, 135–36, 138
Dirrane, Sean. *See* Ó Dioráin, John Beag
Johnny [Sean Dirrane]
documenting music. *See* transcription
"Dónal Ó Dálaigh" (song), 48, 183–85,
190
Donegal, 70, 72–73, 77–78, 160, 186, 189–
90, 250n69, 274n53
Donnellan, Luke, 17, 67
"Donnell O'Daly" (song). *See* "Dónal
Ó Dálaigh" (song)
drama, 18
drawing, 8, 29–31
Duanaire Gaedhilge (Ní Ógáin), 107
Dubhany, John, 185, 191–92
Dublin, 3, 6, 12, 29–31, 34–36, 40–50,
55–57, 65–73, 78–82, 107, 120–24, 139–
41, 152, 161, 197, 224, 229, 242n14,
244n64, 245n3, 254n134, 271n3
the Dubliners, 170
Dublin Penny Journal, 37
dúchas, 5–6
Dun Aengus Fort, Inismore, Aran Islands
(Petrie), 37
Dún Aonghusa (fort), 37, 44, 46
"Dún Chonchubhair" (song), 125
Dusenberry, Emma, 96

"Eanach Dhúin" (song), 126
East end (of Árainn), 53, 79, 109, 152
economics, 20, 104
Ediphones, 77, 81
education, 34, 37. *See also* literacy
"Éinín Troideoige" (song), 193
electricity, 117, 144–47; batteries, 95, 112,
145, 162, 276n74
"The Enchanted Valley" (song air), 184–
85, 191
England, 103

Leitir Mealláin, 148, 152; Scoil Rónáin, 118

Scoileanna Éigse agus Seanchais, 67, 275n67

Scottish Gaelic music, 92

"Séamas Ó Murchú" (song), 48, 189–90

"Sean-bhád is í fliuch" (song), 227

seanchas, 6, 171, 247n34

sean-nós song: Cowell and, 88, 101–3, 107–8, 112–14, 119, 122, 127, 138; Irish traditional music and, 19, 180; music collecting and, 47, 51; recording, 161

"Sean South of Garryowen" (song), 161

Seeger, Anthony, 91, 166–67

Seeger, Charles, 87, 90–91, 93, 98

Seeger, Mike, 91

Seeger, Peggy, 91

Seeger, Pete, 91

"Sé Fáth Mo Bhuartha" (song), 161

Seoighe, Maidhlín Mhaidhcilín, 110–11, 114, 134, 172

Seoighe, Tadhg, 125

"Seoithín Seotho" (song), 134–35

Serbian music, 92

Sharp, Cecil, 98, 103, 138

Sheeran, Patrick, 24

"She moved through the fair" (song), 185

"The Shoals of Herring" (songs), 170

"The Shores of Amerikay" (song), 159, 170

showband music, 170–72

silence, 38, 124, 156, 159

singing, 7, 46–47, 82, 94, 101. *See also* sean-nós song

singing competitions. *See* music competitions

"Siúil a Rúin" (song), 73–74, 76, 81, 228–29

Sligo, 113

Smith, Christopher J., 55

song, 37–40; composition, 75, 80, 83, 96, 113, 121, 125, 247n19; local songs, 8, 75, 121, 125, 159, 161, 267n246. *See also* poetry

Songs from Cape Breton Island (Cowell), 98

Songs of Aran (Cowell), 87–88, 98, 100–102, 108, 110–12, 114–15, 121, 129, 133, 135, 137, 180

sound recording technology: Cowell and, 87–88, 101, 106, 115–20, 123, 129, 139–40; Ennis and, 81–82; music collecting and, 17; Quinn and, 141, 144, 151–52, 165, 168. *See also* recording

sovereignty, 15. *See also* nationalism

Spanish music, 89

Spivacke, Harold, 102, 110, 121–22

Sruthán, 70–71, 75–78, 109–12, 128, 135–38, 152, 169, 224, 229, 264n190, 276n85

"The Stack of Barley" (tune), 169

Stanford, Charles Villiers, 40, 183

Stokes, Margaret, 29, 44

Stokes, Whitley, 29, 44

Stokes, William, 29, 35, 41

"Stranger on the Shore" (Bilk), 170

"Sweet Innismore" (song air), 185, 189–90

Swift, Jonathan, 30

Swiss music, 92

Synge, John Millington, 19–20, 28, 124

"Tá an Oíche Seo Dorcha" (songs), 75

"Táimse i mo Chodladh" (song), 51, 184–85, 188

talkies, 70

Talty, Martin, 73

"Tá na Páipéir dá Saighneáil" (song), 161

tape recorders, 101, 115–16, 141, 151–52

Taylor, Diana, 8–9

technology, 144

television, 84, 144–45

Thai music, 99

"There is a long house at the top of the village" (song), 185, 191

Thierry, Augustin, 16
"Thoba Mo Leanbh" (song), 114, 135
Thomson, David, 86
Tí Chreig (pub), 152
Tí Daly (pub), 152, 165
Tí Fitz (pub), 152
time: Glassie on, 155; relationship with, 155–56
"Tiocfaidh an Samhraidh" (song), 161
Tí Pheaitín Mháirtín Bheairtlín (house), 148
Tipperary, 141, 152
Tí Sheáinín Thomáis (house), 125
"'Tis long ago you promised to steal away with me [An Gabha Ceartan]" (song), 185, 210–13
"Tógfaidh mé mo sheólta go dubhcheodhúch ar maidin" (song), 48–50, 197–200
"Tomás Bán Mac Aogáin" (song air), 191, 226–27, 278n111. *See also* "Tommy Regan" (song air)
"Tommy Regan" (song air), 185, 191
tonality, 51–52
Topping, Brett, 98
Tory Island, 77, 189–90, 235n52, 250n69
tourism, 20, 24, 144
tradition, 9, 14–16, 19–20, 37, 58–62, 68, 72, 75–76, 83, 95–96, 103–6, 114, 119–22, 126–27, 137–39, 161, 176–80, 194, 237n77
transcription: Irish traditional music and, 6–8, 14–15; music collecting and, 27, 35–36, 43, 49–52, 56, 67–68, 76–79, 119, 184
translation, 6, 18–19, 34, 48–51. *See also* language
transport, 16–17, 72, 119
Travassac, Pierre, 147–48
Trebitsch, Rudolf, 17
"Truagh Sin Mise Lá'il Pádraic" (song), 226

Tuam, Co. Galway, 119, 187
"'Twas Early, Early in the Spring" (song), 138

"Uaimh Rí—The King's Cave" (song air), 184, 186
Uí Chatháin, Maura, 147
Uí Chonaola, Peige Dara Pheigín, 124–25
Uí Dhioráin, Máirín (*née* Ní Bhriain), 53–54, 74, 80, 224, 228
Uí Dhomhnaill, Máirín Thomáis (*née* Ní Chonghaile), 124–25
Uí Fhátharta, Máire Pháidín Bheartlaí, 124–25
Uí Fhátharta, Peige Jóin, 111, 134–35
Uí Fhátharta, Céitín Sheáinín Aindí, 112–14, 134–35, 137–38
Uí Fhlaithearta, Bairbre Pheait, 78
Uí Iarnáin, Winnie Cheaite, 163
uilleann piping, 62–76, 248n40
Uí Mhaoláin, Méiní Tom, 78
Uí Mheachair, Nóra Dara Pheigín, 102, 124–25
uí Ógáin, Ríonach, 55–57, 64, 70, 77–78, 170–71, 235n52
the United States, 11–12, 17, 90–91, 105–6, 113, 180. *See also* American folk music
urban spaces, 42, 58
utopianism, 37, 42

Valiant, Margaret, 90–91
Victorianism, 30
voice, 7, 11, 19, 24, 37–40, 54, 79, 107–23, 128–35, 160–66

Waddell, John, 22, 25
Wakeman, William, 29
Walker, Joseph Cooper, 13, 104
Walsh, Sean, 120